Postcolonial African Philosophy

Postcolonial African Philosophy
A Critical Reader

Edited by
Emmanuel Chukwudi Eze
Bucknell University, Lewisburg, PA

Copyright © Blackwell Publishers Ltd, 1997
Introduction and arrangement © Emmanuel Chukwudi Eze 1997

First published 1997

2 4 6 8 10 9 7 5 3 1

Blackwell Publishers Inc.
238 Main Street
Cambridge, Massachusetts 02142
USA

Blackwell Publishers Ltd
108 Cowley Road
Oxford OX4 1JF
UK

Library of Congress Cataloging-in-Publication Data

Postcolonial African philosophy: a critical reader / edited by
Emmanuel Chukwudi Eze.
    p.   cm.
Includes bibliographical references and index.
ISBN 0-631-20339-7 (alk. paper). — ISBN 0-631-20340-0 (pbk.:
alk. paper)
    1. Philosophy, African.   2. Philosophy, Modern—20th century.
I. Eze, Emmanuel Chukwudi.
B5320.P67   1997
199'.6—dc20   96-24388
                                                           CIP

British Library Cataloguing in Publication Data

A CIP catalogue record for this book is available from the British Library.

Commissioning Editor: Steve Smith
Desk Editor: Cameron Laux
Production Controller: Lisa Eaton

Typeset in 10½ on 12 pt Ehrhardt by Ace Filmsetting, Frome, Somerset
Printed in Great Britain by Hartnolls Ltd, Bodmin, Cornwall
This book is printed on acid-free paper

Contents

Notes on Contributors

Peter Amato is the founding editor of the journal *Conference*. He edited the volume *Virtue, Order, Mind: Ancient, Modern and Postmodern Perspectives* in the SUNY-Oneonta Philosophy Series, and also contributed several essays to the forthcoming *Encyclopedia of African Philosophy and Religion*, under the editorship of V.Y. Mudimbe. He holds master's degrees in Philosophy and Anthropology, and is currently completing his doctorate in Philosophy at Fordham University.

Richard H. Bell is a Professor of Philosophy at the College of Wooster. He recently completed a sabbatical leave which he spent as a Visiting Fellow at Clare Hall, Cambridge. He has published numerous essays on Wittgenstein and on African Philosophy.

Robert Bernasconi is Moss Professor of Philosophy at the University of Memphis. He is the author of *The Question of Language in Heidegger's History of Being* and *Heidegger in Question*. He has published numerous articles on Hegel, Continental Philosophy, Social Philosophy, and the history of race thinking in philosophy.

Emmanuel Chukwudi Eze teaches Philosophy at Bucknell University. His teaching and research interests are in: Critical Social Theory, Modern European Philosophy, and African Philosophy. In addition to published essays on on Hume, Kant, and Habermas, he is the editor of *Race and the Enlightenment* (Blackwell 1996) and *Africana Philosophy: An Anthology* (1997).

Lewis Gordon teaches African American Studies and Philosophy at Purdue University. He is author of *Bad Faith and Antiblack Racism* (1995) and *Fanon and the Crises of European Man: An Essay on Philosophy and the Human Sciences* (1995), as well as editor of *Existence in Black: An Anthology of Black Existential Philosophy* (1996) and co-editor of *Frantz Fanon: A Critical Reader* (1996). He is currently completing a book of essays entitled, *Her Majesty's Other Children: Philosophical Sketches from a Neocolonial Age*.

Kwame Gyekye is Professor of Philosophy at the University of Ghana. He was a Visiting Professor of Philosophy at Temple University in the spring of 1995 and at the University of Pennsylvania in the 1995/6 academic year. His most recent work includes a revised edition of his *An Essay on African*

Philosophical Thought (1995) and *Tradition and Modernity in the African Experience* (forthcoming).

Sandra Harding is Professor of Philosophy at the University of Delaware and the University of California, Los Angeles. Her publications include: *Whose Science? Whose Knowledge?* and *The Science Question in Feminism* (1986). She is also the editor of *Feminism and Methodology: Social Science Issues*, and author of "The curious coincidence of feminine and African moralities: challenges for feminist theory" (in *Women and Moral Theory*, ed. by Eva Kittay and Diana T. Meyers, 1987).

Leonard Harris is the Director of the African American Studies Center and a Professor in the Department of Philosophy at Purdue University. He has published numerous essays, and several books, including: *Philosophy Born of Struggle: Anthology of Afro-American Philosophy from 1917* (1993); *The Philosophy of Alaine Locke: Harlem Renaissance and Beyond* (1989); and several co-edited volumes.

Bruce Janz is Associate Professor of Philosophy at Augustana University College in Camrose, Alberta, Canada. He also directs the Centre for Interdisicplinary Research in the Liberal Arts (CIRLA). His research interests, in addition to African Philosophy, are in the areas of Hermeneutics, the History of Mysticism, and Interdisciplinarity. He has published articles in *Dialogue*, *Dianoia*, and *Studies in Religion*.

Jean-Marie Makang is Assistant Professor of Philosophy at Frostburg University in Maryland. His teaching and research specializations are in Ethics, Political and Social Philosophy, and African and African-American philosophy. He has taught philosophy in Cameroon, Zaire, and Kenya, and has been a Research Associate at the African Institute for Economic and Social Development in Abidjan, Côte d'Ivoire.

D.A. Masolo is Visiting Professor of Philosophy at Antioch College and Senior Lecturer in Philosophy at the University of Nairobi. His recent publications include *African Philosophy in Search of Identity* (1994).

John Pittman teaches philosophy at John Jay College of Criminal Justice in New York City. He edited *African-American Perspectives and Philosophical Traditions*, a volume forthcoming from Routledge (and also originally published as a special issue of the *Philosophical Forum*). Pittman is also co-editor of the forthcoming *Blackwell Companion to African-American Philosophy*.

Gail Presbey is Assistant Professor of Philosophy at Marist College in Poughkeepsie, New York. Her areas of interest are Social and Political Philosophy, and Cross-Cultural Philosophy. She spent her recent sabbatical year as Visiting Scholar in several African universities. (Her essay in this volume was presented to an audience of philosophers at the University of Stellenbosch in South Africa). Presbey is also the editor of *The Philosophical Quest: A Cross-Cultural Reader* (1994), and has published numerous articles and book-chapters on Hannah Arendt, Frantz Fanon, and Ghandi.

Tsenay Serequeberhan is Alumni Chair and Associate Professor of Philosophy and African Studies at Simmons College, Boston. He is the author of *The Hermeneutics of African Philosophy* (1995) and editor of the collection, *African Philosophy: The Essential Readings* (1991). He has published numerous essays on Kant, Hegel, and Marx.

Kwasi Wiredu is Professor of Philosophy at the University of South Florida. He was until recently a Visiting Professor at Duke University. Wiredu has published numerous books and articles in African Philosophy, including *Philosophy and an African Culture* (1980).

Introduction: Philosophy and the (Post)colonial

Emmanuel Chukwudi Eze

Within the last two decades, the field of African philosophy has blossomed in North American universities and colleges. In 1995 alone, over forty textbooks and scholarly monographs in African and Africana philosophy appeared in print from leading publishing houses and academic presses. Similarly, membership in professional organizations such as the Society for African Philosophy in North America and the Society for the Study of Africana Philosophy – associations of philosophers, largely with doctorate degrees, whose teaching and research specialization are exclusively or primarily focused in African or Africana philosophy – has soared. Increasingly, the American Philosophical Association, through its Committee on Blacks in Philosophy as well as through its Committee on Philosophy and International Cooperation, has felt the growing impact of the field of African philosophy on teaching and research in the discipline as a whole. At the 1995 Eastern Division conference of the Association, for example, there were numerous panels and symposia devoted entirely to philosophical themes and questions central to African philosophy. Given this growth in interest, questions arise: (1) What distinguishes *African* philosophy from other philosophies (for instance, Asian, European, etc.)?; (2) What accounts for the strong emergence of contemporary African philosophy, as professional and intellectual practice, in North America?; and (3) What are the core questions that constitute this practice? The essays collected here seek to answer these questions, from both substantive and programmatic points of view.

1 (Post)colonial African Philosophy

From one point of view, to designate a field of philosophy as "African" is consistent with the custom of naming philosophical traditions and practices according to their cultural, ethnic, national, or merely geographic origins.[1] Thus we have "American philosophy," "Jewish philosophy," "British philosophy," "German philosophy," and "French philosophy." Following Vincent Descombes who, in his influential book *Le Même et l'autre*,[2] defines "contemporary French philosophy" as "coincident with the sum of the discourses elaborated in France and considered by the public of today as philosophical," African philosophy may be said to consist of all intellectual and discursive productions elaborated in Africa and considered "philosophical" by today's public. But this imitative definition would woefully fail to capture the historical, political, and cultural complexities – and contradictions – which animate the historical dynamic of African philosophy as an academic and professional discipline.

For example, if one focuses on the African continent, and attempts to extend the meaning of the qualifier "African" beyond the scope of its *geographical* meaning, it becomes notoriously difficult to define what kind of philosophical production is "African" or not. If the designation "African philosophy" is meant to highlight the ethnic or cultural origin of the philosophy in question, then should one not speak of African philosophies ("Akan philosophy," "Igbo philosophy," "Yoruba philosophy," "Luo philosophy," and so forth) rather than of philosophy in the singular, since Africa is made up of significantly diverse national and ethnocultural sources and traditions that constitute the philosophic originations?

Or: if one focuses on the national or ethnic point of view, is the African national or ethnic identity of a philosopher, regardless of the method or the content of his or her philosophy, necessary and/or sufficient to warrant the qualification of such philosophy as belonging to the African tradition? If this is the case, then how does one characterize the works of so many non-African nationals that have enormously influenced, enriched, and, in many cases, transformed both substantive issues and orientations in the field and practice of African philosophy? (Prominent examples are Placide Tempels, Robin Horton, and Barry Hallen.) More importantly, however, is the next question: How do we articulate the conceptual and the historical relationships between traditional African philosophies (predominantly practiced and recorded in "unwritten" traditions) and the contemporary practices of the profession which is dominated by philosophers whose technical training is quite often strictly defined by, if not limited to, the modern European philosophic traditions? Moreover, how does one understand the conceptual and historical relationship between these two dimensions of African philosophy, the "traditional" and the "modern," on the one hand, and the philosophies of the African Diaspora, especially African–American and Afro–Caribbean philosophies, on the other?

It is this bewildering multiplicity and pluralism among what is currently studied under the rubric of "African" philosophy that prompted Lucius Outlaw and others to undertake the laborious conceptual and programmatic elaboration of the notion of "African*a*" philosophy as an "umbrella-term" that would maintain a serious sense of its historical and cultural range and diversity – while encompassing the field under a non-essentialist conceptual organization. But what does the notion of "Africana" stand for? According to Outlaw:

> the range of the universality of the term "Africana," in its boundaries and "contents," coincides with the experiences and situated practices of dispersed *geographic race*: that is, not a genetically homogenous group but persons and peoples who, through shared lines of descent and ancestry, share a relatively permanent geographical site of origin and development from which descendants are dispersed, and, thereby, who share a relatively distinct gene pool that determines the relative frequencies of various physical characteristics, even in the Diaspora; and persons who share – more or less – evolved social and cultural elements of life-worlds that are, in part, traceable to those of the "ancestors." In turn, geographical, cultural, social, and natural-selection factors influence the shared gene pool and cultural practices to condition *raciation*: that is, the formation and evolution of the biological and cultural factors collectively characterizing the "race."[3]

Having thus described the meaning(s) of "Africana," the path along which Outlaw would pursue a definition of the nature and the scope of "African philosophy" is predictable: "to identify the features that make certain intellectual practices and legacies of persons who are situated in geographically and historically-socially diverse societies 'philosophy,' features characteristic of – though not necessarily *unique* to – the persons as *members of a dispersed race*."[4]

I cite Professor Outlaw at length not necessarily because his reflection here "solves" the problems that our preceding questions raise, but to highlight the miasmic nature of the issues confronting anyone who attempts to specify what boundaries define the present practices of African philosophy. Although the issue of "race" cannot be discounted, I wonder whether Outlaw's foregrounding of the notion of "geographic race" is the most pertinent or productive here. Outlaw allows that his concept of "geographic race" does not imply "a genetically homogenous group." He also explicitly insists that he will not subscribe to "biological or racial essentialism."[5] Yet, it is not clear to me that his emphasis on Africa's "distinct *gene* pool" – a gene pool that "determines the relative frequencies of various physical [biological] characteristics" – does not tie the criteria and the boundaries of African/a philosophy too closely to factors and categories of (geographic) origin, "race," and raciation. As I pointed out earlier – and Outlaw's essay shows this in places – there are individuals who neither characterize themselves as geographically or racially "African", nor are characterized by others as such, whose cultural experience and philosophical works and ideas nonetheless define in a decisive and substantive way *both* the form *and* the content of the field of African philosophy as an academic and professional discipline.

The significance of Outlaw's contribution here, I think, lies not in complete success at establishing a comprehensive sense, or comprehensive criteria according to which the boundaries of the academic and professional field may be determined, but in the very attempt to argue that such criteria and boundaries *can* be established and, in fact, are – as in every discipline, no matter how "multi-" or "interdisciplinary" – a necessity. But the multiplicity and pluralism of "African/a" philosophy within (and, for some, outside of) Outlaw's conceptual "umbrella" inevitably invites, indeed demands, that further careful attention be given to the *historical* forces that account for the emergence, development, and prospects of its constituent philosophic formations and dynamics. The works collected here, in addition to my position (which will be stated below) on how to situate them, may be fruitfully thought of as a continuation of this dialogue with Outlaw, and therefore, perhaps, complementary to his stated interests.

In order to find our way, then, I suggest that for the moment we allow ourselves to return to, and be guided by, the concept of the "(post)colonial" of the title of this volume. Admittedly, the concept of the "(post)colonial" also quickly embroils us in the question of its cousins: the "colonial" and the "precolonial," and it is a legitimate gesture to ask, in protest: Why should colonialism be accorded the status and role of a singular and dominant prism through which the nature and the boundaries of African/a philosophy ought to be thematized and articulated? This, surely, is a credible and, in some cases (for example, in the writing of *African history* as such) an appropriate objection. However, when the question concerns the professional field of African philosophy, the strength of this objection nearly evaporates, or at least is significantly attenuated. This is simply because *the single most important factor that drives the field and the contemporary practice of African/a Philosophy has to do with the brutal encounter of the African world with European modernity* – an encounter epitomized in the colonial phenomena.

2 Colonialism and the "Age of Europe"

By "colonialism" we should understand the indescribable crisis disproportionately suffered and endured by the African peoples in their tragic encounter with the European world, from the beginning of the fifteenth century through the end of the nineteenth into the first half of the twentieth. This is a period marked by the horror and violence of the transatlantic slave trade, the imperial occupation of most parts of Africa and the forced administrations of its peoples, and the resilient and enduring ideologies and practices of European cultural superiority (ethnocentrism) and "racial" supremacy (racism). In vain do we seek to limit the colonial period to the "brief" seventy years between the 1884 Berlin Conference, which partitioned and legitimized European occupation of Africa, and the early 1960s, when most African countries attained constitutional decolonization.[6]

The beginnings of colonialism need to be traced to both the sporadic and the systematic maritime commercial incursions into Africa by European fortune seekers which began in the mid-fifteenth century. These commercial interests, individual as well as institutional, were aimed at the extraction and trading of gold, ivory, and other natural resources and raw materials, but they quickly expanded into the exportation of able-bodied Africans and their children as slaves to the Americas and other parts of the world. It was the wealth and capital accumulated by European merchants and institutions (the Barclays, the Lloyds, etc.) in the Triangular Trade that financed technological innovations in arms and other sailing equipment. These, in turn, made possible subsequent large-scale military expeditions that eventually "pacified" African kingdoms. Most of these trading companies kept salaried armies, or financed, through taxes, the (European) governmental administrations of the conquered territories. Aijaz Ahmad's observation about Britain, in this regard, is accurate:

> *[C]ommercial developers and adventurers* like Cecil Rhodes in Southern Africa, Frederick Luggard in Nigeria, and Hugh Cholmondeley Delamere in Kenya, *played important roles in later British colonization* on the African continent. Although the British government initially kept a safe distance from these adventurers and their questionable aims and practices, it later adopted many of their early dreams and ambitions to justify colonial expansion . . . And the English government in most cases provided the companies with protection to ensure free trading rights. Eventually the government took the natural step of establishing administrative, colonial control over those areas in which British trading companies were involved.[7]

With respect to Africa, then, I use the term "colonialism" as a clustered concept to designate the historical realities of: (1) the European imperial incursions into Africa, which began in the late fifteenth and early sixteenth centuries, and grew into the massive transatlantic slave trade; (2) the violent conquest and occupation of the various parts of the continent by diverse European powers which took place in the late nineteenth and early twentieth centuries; and (3) the forced administration of African lands and peoples which followed this conquest, and which lasted into the years of independence in the 1950s and 1960s, and – in the case of Zimbabwe and South Africa – into the 1980s and the 1990s. Slave trade, conquest, occupation, and forced administration of peoples, in that order, were all part of an unfolding history of colonialism.

3 Philosophy, Modernity, and Colonialism

The "colonial period," in a larger sense, should then be understood to cover, roughly, what Cornel West has correctly characterized as "the Age of Europe." This, according to West, is the period "[b]etween 1492 and 1945," a period that was marked by "European breakthroughs in oceanic transportation, agricultural production, state consolidation, bureaucratization, industrialization, urbanization and *imperial dominion* [that] shaped the makings of the modern world."[8] And since the imperial and the colonial domination of Africa were, at root, constitutive elements in the historical formation of the economic, political, and cultural expressions of the Age of Europe, including the Enlightenment, it is imperative that, when we study the nature and the dynamic of European modernity, we examine the intellectual and the philosophical productions of the time in order to understand how, in too many cases, they justified imperialism and colonialism. Significant aspects of the philosophies produced by Hume, Kant, Hegel, and Marx have been shown to originate in, and to be intelligible only when understood as an organic development within, larger sociohistorical contexts of European colonialism and the ethnocentric idea: Europe is *the* model of humanity, culture, and history in itself. It is precisely this critical (re)examination of the colonial intentions organic to Western modern philosophy that animates at least one wing of contemporary African/a philosophy. It is a philosophical project aptly captured by Serequeberhan's phrase, "the critique of Eurocentrism." The first group of essays in part II of this volume are examples of such critical work.

Basil Davidson, in *Africa: History of a Continent* and in his recent *The African Genius* (as well as in his other numerous publications on African history), points out that the earliest recorded encounters between Europeans and African kingdoms at the beginning of the fifteenth century reveal remarkable accounts of relationships between equals – the exchange of diplomatic counsels was routine – and glowing European accounts of the thriving and vibrant nations of Bini, Dahomey, Ashanti, etc., whose organizational powers and influence were constantly favorably compared by the Europeans to that of the Roman Papacy.[9] However, as the plantations in the Americas developed and Afro–European trade demands shifted from raw material to human labor, there was also a shift in the European literary, artistic, and philosophical characterizations of Africans.[10] Specifically within philosophy, Africans became identified as a subhuman "race," and speculations about the "savage" and "inferior" nature of "the African" and the "the African mind" became widespread and intertextually entrenched within the *univers du discours* of the French, British, and German Enlightenment thinkers. David Hume, for example, who at one time served in the British Colonial Office, wrote in the famous footnote to his essay, "On national character":

I am apt to suspect the Negroes to be naturally inferior to the whites. There scarcely ever was a civilized nation of that complexion, nor even any individual eminent in action or speculation. No ingenious manufacturers amongst them, no arts, no sciences. On the other hand, the most rude and barbarous of the whites, such as the ancient GERMANS, the present TARTARS, have still something eminent about them . . . Such a uniform and constant difference could not happen . . . if nature had not made original distinction betwixt these breeds of men . . .[11]

What is philosophically significant here, I think, is Hume's casting of the "difference" between Europeans and Africans, "whites" and "Negroes" (*negre*, black), as a "constant" (read: permanent) and "original distinction" established by "nature." It is this form of "natural" philosophical casting of racial differences that framed the African outside of "proper" (read: European) humanity. And since, for the Enlightenment philosophers, European humanity was not only universal, but the embodiment of, and coincident with, humanity *as such*, the framing of the African as being of a different, subhuman, species therefore philosophically and anthropologically sanctioned the exploitation of Africans in barbaric ways that were not allowed for Europeans.

Such formulations of philosophical prejudices against Africa and Africans (and other non-European peoples generally) were easily circulated and recycled among modern European philosophers – with little originality. In his essay "On the varieties of the different races of man," Immanuel Kant amplified and completed the remarks he had made about "the Negro" elsewhere (*Observations On the Feeling of the Beautiful and Sublime*) with the following hierarchical chart on the different "races":

STEM GENUS: *white brunette*
First race, very blond (northern Europe)
Second race, Copper-Red (America)
Third race, Black (Senegambia)
Fourth race, Olive-Yellow (Indians)[12]

As in Hume, the assumption behind this arrangement and this order is precisely skin color: white, black, red, yellow; and the ideal skin tone is the "white" – the *white brunette* – to which others are superior or inferior as they approximate the "white." It is therefore not unfair to point to Kant's statement: "This man was black from head to toe, *a clear proof* that what he said was stupid" as clear proof that Kant ascribed to skin color (white or black) the evidence of rational (and therefore human) capacity – or the lack of it. But when he needed to justify his statement and his positions on this issue, Kant directly appealed to Hume's footnote, already cited.[13]

If the trade and practices of transatlantic slavery were carefully philosophically constructed on the alleged subhumanity of the African "race," the practice of colonialism was predicated in parallel on a metaphysical denial of the historicity of African existence. Nowhere is this line of modern European thought as evident as in Hegel's twin treatise: *Lectures on Philosophy of History* and *Lectures on the Philosophy of Right*. In the former, Hegel positions Africa *outside* of History, as the absolute, non-historical beginning of the movement of Spirit. Accordingly, Africans are depicted as incapable of rational thought or ethical conduct. They therefore have no laws, religion, and political order. Africa, in human terms, is, for Hegel, a wasteland filled with "lawlessness," "fetishism," and "cannibalism" – waiting for European soldiers and missionaries to conquer it and impose "order" and "morality."[14] For Hegel, the African *deserved* to be enslaved. Besides, slavery to Europeans, Hegel argued, benefited *the African*, as it provided him or her with moral "education"! Accordingly, colonialism was also a benefit to Africa because Europe inseminated it with its reason, ethic, culture and mores, and thereby historicized it.

Although he was already quite aware of the colonial phenomenon in the *Philosophy of History*,[15] it was not until the *Philosophy of Right* that Hegel elaborately laid out the theoretical structures that at once directly justify and explain colonialism – as the inevitable logic of the unfolding of Spirit in (European) history. Building upon the metaphysical schemes laid out in the *Logic* and in the *Philosophy of History*, Hegel, in the *Philosophy of Right*, accurately and painstakingly explains why and how the modern capitalist organization of state and economy in Europe necessarily leads to imperialism and colonialism.

For Hegel, the imperial and the colonial expansion of Europe is the necessary and *logical* outlet for resolving the problem of poverty inherent to capitalism. When the capitalist division of labor and trade that is meant to satisfy the "system of wants" of a civil society generates at the same time a class of paupers and disenfranchised segments of the population, there are, for Hegel, only two ways of resolving this contradiction. The first option is welfare, while the second is more jobs. The consequences of both options, however, violate what Hegel considered the basic tenets of the civil society. Welfare deprives the individual [the poor] of initiative and self-respect and independence, while the second – the creation of more jobs – according to Hegel, would cause overproduction of goods and services in proportion to the available market. This is how Hegel stages the scenario:

> When the masses begin to decline into poverty, (a) the burden of maintaining them at their ordinary standards of living might be directly laid on the wealthier class [higher taxes, for example], or they might receive the means of livelihood directly from other public sources of wealth . . . In either case, however, the needy would receive subsistence directly, not by means of their work, and this would violate the principle of civil society and the feeling of individual independence and self-respect . . . (b) As an alternative, they might be given subsistence

indirectly through being given work, i.e., opportunity to work. In this event the volume of production would be increased, but the evil consists precisely in an excess of production and in the lack of a proportionate number of consumers . . . It hence becomes apparent that despite an excess of wealth civil society is not rich enough, i.e., its own resources are insufficient to check excessive poverty and the creation of a penurious rabble.[16]

In order, then, to resolve the problem of the poverty of the "penurious rabble" which results from the unequal distribution of wealth inherent to modern European capitalist societies, the solution that Hegel recommends is the generation of more wealth for Europe from outside of Europe, through expansion of the market for European goods as well as through colonist and colonialist expansions. Poverty and the need for market, Hegel says,

drives it [the capitalistically "mature" European society] to push beyond its own limits and seek markets and so its necessary means of subsistence, in other lands which are either deficient in the goods it overproduced, or else generally backward in industry.[17]

Colonial and capitalist expansions are therefore a logical necessity for the realization of the obviously universal European Idea, and by labeling the non-European territories and peoples as "backward" in "industry," they become legitimate prey for colonial and colonialist activities. According to Hegel: "All great peoples . . . press onward to the sea," because

the sea *affords the means for the colonizing activity* – sporadic or systematic – to which the mature civil society is driven and by which it supplies to part of its population a return to life on the family basis in a new land and so also supplies itself with a new demand and field for its industry.[18]

In this articulation of Europe's rush for wealth and for territory in other lands, Hegel does not raise any ethical questions or moral considerations precisely because, in addition to Hume and Kant, Hegel himself had declared the African subhuman: the African lacked reason and therefore moral and ethical content. This philosophically articulated "natural" status of the African automatically precludes the possibility that the relationship between Europe and Africa, the European and the African, the colonizer and the colonized, may be governed or regulated by any sort of law or ethics. In Hegel's words (*Philosophy of Right*): "The civilized nation [Europe] is conscious that the rights of the barbarians [Africans, for example] are unequal to its own and treats their autonomy as only a formality."[19]

It is clear, then, that nowhere is the *direct* conjunction/intersection of the philosophical and the political and economic interests in the European denigration and exploitation of Africans so evident and shameless as in Hegel.

Since Africa, for Hegel, "is the Gold-land compressed within itself," the continent *and* its peoples become, all at once, a treasure island and a *terra nulla*, a virgin territory brimming with natural and human raw material passively waiting for Europe to exploit and turn it into mini-European territories.[20]

It is for good reasons then that "the critique of Eurocentrism" has become a significant, if "negative," moment in the practice of African philosophy.[21] For it is with the authorities of Hume, Kant, Hegel, and Marx behind them, and with the enduring image of "the African" as "black," "savage," "primitive," and so forth, in conjunction with clearly articulated political and economic colonial interests, that nineteenth- and twentieth-century European anthropologists descended upon Africa. And *quelle surprise!*: the Lévy-Bruhls and the Evans-Pritchards report that the "African mind" is "prelogical," "mystical," and "irrational;" or, when it is recognized as "logical" (such as by Evans-Pritchard), it is still compared and considered "inferior" to the "Western" scientific mind – as if all Westeners' minds are scientific, or as if all Africans must have the scientist's mind in order to be rationally human. These anthropological productions, often commissioned after military invasion of an African territory or after a rebellion against occupying European powers,[22] were intended to provide the European administrations and missionary-cultural workers with information about the "primitive" both to guarantee efficient administration and to provide knowledge of the "African mentality," so that, while demonizing and repressing African practices, the "superior" European values and attitudes could be effectively inculcated into the African conscience. From the trans-formations in the African economies and politics to religion and the educational institutions, the goal was to maximize European profit, secure the total domination and subjection of the colonial territory to the metropole, and reproduce Europe and European values not only in the material lives, but also in the cultural and spiritual lives and expressions of the African.[23]

4 African Philosophy as Counter-Colonial Practice

1. It is within the colonial context that we must explore the significance of a book which, more than any other, influenced, at the continental level, the development and self-understanding of twentieth-century history of African philosophy. I refer to Father Placide Tempels' *Bantu Philosophy* (1945). As stated by the author, the aim of the book is to serve the European colonialist as a handbook on indigenous African "philosophy." According to the argument of the book, the European needed to understand the African world-views and belief systems so that the missionary message and "civilizationary" projects could be implanted in the vital nodes of the structures of faith and the existential interiority of the African. Thus, colonization could succeed, and succeed in a self-sustaining manner. Tempels' work is predominantly an exposition of the

ontological systems of the Baluba, an ethnic group in Zaire, where Tempels, a Belgian missionary, worked for many years. Tempels believed that the Baluba ontology grounded and regulated the daily ethical, political, and economic existence of the African. In order to elevate the "pagan" existence of the African to "civilization," one must work through this ontological system which grounds the subjectivity of the Bantu.

But the volcanic historical significance of Tempels' work is not necessarily located in its intentions. It is located elsewhere – in the title of the book; specifically the author's explicit use of the term "philosophy" to characterize an intellectual product associated with the African. Whereas the anthropologist spoke of "savage mentality," or "primitive thought," Tempels spoke of *philosophy*; and because philosophy, to the Western mind, is the honorific term symbolizing the highest exercise of the faculty of reason, the book's title amounted to an admission of the existence of an African philosophy, the existence of African reason, and hence – following this logocentric European logic – African humanity. This notion flew in the face of the entire intellectual edifice of slavery and colonialism, which was built precisely on the negation of this possibility.

Tempels' book, then, became inadvertently fruitfully complex. The author intended it as a "handbook" for the missionary-cultural worker: a plea to the European colonialist administrator or missionary that the African's "philosophy" and culture ought to be understood and respected in order for the "civilizing" mission to succeed. But the ambiguous conjunction of "philosophy" as an implicit ontological system which underlies and sustains an African communal world-view, and the honorific notion of "philosophy" in the West as the highest rational (human) achievement was not lost on the African intelligentsia engaged in anticolonial projects. Tempels' book, for them, collapsed the ideological scaffold that had supported and sustained racism and colonialism, and the book became for these Africans a manual for cultural and political revolt.[24]

With the "discovery" of Bantu philosophy in Africa and the emergence in the United States of the Harlem Renaissance – with its philosophers and intellectuals: Alain Locke, Claude McKay, W.E.B. Dubois and others – where Africans in the Diaspora were already engaged in the critique of African colonialism and the racism of the New World, a third moment in the history of African philosophy was born: negritude.[25] As a literary, artistic, and philosophical movement originated in Paris by African and Afro-Caribbean students, negritude, through Aimé Césaire and Leopold Sedar Senghor, found in *Bantu Philosophy*, in the pluralist anthropologies of Frobenius, Herskovits, and Delafosse, and in the cultural movements of the Harlem Renaissance renewed energy and resources for a continuing struggle against European denigration and depravation of Africans, on the continent and in Europe. The idea of "African philosophy" as a field of inquiry thus has its contemporary roots in the effort of African thinkers to combat political and economic exploitations, and to examine, question, and contest identities imposed upon them by Europeans. The claims and counter-claims, justifications, and alienations that characterize such historical and conceptual protests and contestations indelibly mark the discipline of African philosophy.

2.   A major and continuing dilemma for African philosophy, then, is its attempt to understand and articulate Africa's experience of the "Age of Europe." How, it is asked, could the same European modernity and Enlightenment that promoted "precious ideals like the dignity of persons" and "democracy" also be so intimately and inextricably implicated in slavery and the colonial projects?

Confronted with this duplicity at the heart of European modernity – the subscription to the ideals of universal humanity and democracy on the one hand, and the imperial and colonial subjugation of non-European peoples and racism on the other – some critics are satisfied to attribute the contradictions, as Cornel West suggests, to an inevitable "discrepancy between sterling rhetoric and lived reality," between "glowing principles and actual practices."[26] Abiola Irele, for example, while recognizing that "many have been betrayed by . . . the Enlightenment ideals of universal reason and universal equality . . . by the difference between word and deed," recommends that we "separate" the ideal from the real, holding on to one while rejecting the other. According to Irele:

> Africans have suffered greatly from the derogatory insults of the Enlightenment.
> I believe we must separate the ideals of universal reason and equality from their
> historical implementation. We must, as it were, trust the tale and not the teller,
> for though the messenger be tainted, the message need not be.[27]

But how does one, even conceptually, nicely and neatly separate the "ideals" of European modernity, the Age of Europe, from its concreteness or "historical implementation?" Were the European philosophers' ideas about "humanity" and "freedom" pure and "sterling" and perfect, as this argument presumes – in which case it is only in the "implementation" that imperfections (racism, colonialism, etc.) arose? Is it not possible that these "imperfections" were conceptualized as integral and as constitutive of the logic of capitalist and ethnocentric and racist modernity?

Irele's exhortation that "we must separate the [European] ideals of universal reason" from the imperfect "historical implementation" operates a false dichotomy that may mislead one to believe that we can clearly separate the "ideal" from the "real" (the tale from the teller, the message from the messenger, etc.) How do we know what constitutes "ideal" except in/through the way it was and has been practiced? Furthermore, to speak of ideals or ideas as universally neutral schemes or models which we historically perfectly or imperfectly implement obscures the fact that these ideals and ideas and models are always already part and parcel of – i.e., always already infused with – historical practices and intentions out of which ideals are, in the first place, constituted as such – and judged worthy of pursuit. Ideals do not have meaning in a historical vacuum.

It is more appropriate, I think, to consider Africa's experience of the "Age of Europe" as the *cost* of Occidental modernity. This idea of "cost," introduced but left undeveloped by West, is to be understood literally, as that which had to be *sacrificed* in order to purchase, or pursue, European modernity's "order," "progress," "culture," "civilization," etc. By dialectically *negating* Africa, Europe was able to posit and represent itself and its contingent historicity as the ideal culture, the ideal humanity, and ideal history. While "reason" and "humanity" and "light" remained in Europe, "irrationality" and "savagery" and "darkness" (even in the instances when these were of European origins) were conveniently – and perhaps unconsciously – projected on to Africa, the Big, Bad, Primeval Evil, the "Dark Continent." Is it not important to ask whether or not the very condition of the possibility of European modernity as an Idea was the explicit metaphysical negation and theoretical exclusion of Africa and the African, archetypally frozen as "savage" and "primitive"?

To gain a general understanding of the historical scope of this "Africa" in the European imaginary, one has only to carefully study V.Y. Mudimbe's most recent works: *The Invention of Africa* and the sequel, *The Idea of Africa*.[28] But to appreciate its continuing depth and endurance within professional European philosophy, one could easily point to the works of those who claim to be the most radical critics of modernity, such as Martin Heidegger or the critical-reformist philosopher of European modernity, Jürgen Habermas. Consider Heidegger's very recent comments, to this effect: "Nature has its history. But then *Negroes* would also have history. Or does nature then have no history? It can enter into the past as something transitory, but not everything that fades away enters into history."[29] Or consider Habermas' willful typologies of Africa and the African world-view in his two-volume *Theory of Communicative Action*.[30] The aims and intentions, the questions and the problems, that preoccupy twentieth-century African philosophy are stalked by a singular and incisive Occidental model of man.

When Western philosophy speaks of "reason," it is not just speaking of "science" and "knowledge" and "method," and "critique," or even "thought." In and through these codes it is more fundamentally the question of the "anthropos," of the human, that is at stake, for questions of knowledge and identity, logos and anthropos, always hang together. It is within this background of *anthropos* as *logikos*, the interlacing of human understanding and the understanding of the human, that Europeans originally introduced the notion of a *difference in kind* between themselves and Africans as a way of justifying unspeakable exploitation and denigration of Africans.

5 Philosophy and the (Post)colonial

African philosophy labors under this yet-to-end exploitation and denigration of African humanity. It challenges the long-standing exclusion of Africa or, more accurately, its inclusion as the negative "other" of reason and of the Western world in the major traditions of modern Western philosophy. And because this is an ongoing task, as well as in light of many other factors not unconnected with the colonial and neocolonial nature of Africa's relationship with the West, the "post" of "postcolonial" African philosophy has to be written under erasure, or – more conveniently – in brackets. Scribing the "post" of the postcolonial under erasure or brackets serves as signal and pointer to the (in many parts of Africa) unfulfilled dreams of the independence achievements of the 1960s.

It also highlights the paradoxical – and productively "deconstructive" – nature of a self-conscious (post)colonial critical philosophical work. For, to borrow an eloquent passage from Gayatri Spivak:

> Postcoloniality – the heritage of imperialism in the rest of the globe – is a deconstructive case. As follows: Those of us from formerly colonized countries are able to communicate with each other and with the metropolis to exchange and to establish sociality and transnationality, because we have had access to the culture of imperialism. Shall we then assign to that culture, in the words of the ethical philosopher Bernard Williams, a measure of "moral luck"? I think there can be no question that the answer is "no". This impossible "no" to a structure which one critiques, yet inhabits intimately, is the deconstructive philosophical position, and the everyday here and now of "postcoloniality" is a case of it.[31]

Spivak's "impossible 'no'" confirms what I have always known from an enduring truth of the Igbo proverb: *Ọkụkọ bere na ngugu na-azọ isi, na-azọkwa ọdu*. Like this Igbo proverbial hen, on a rope minding both its head and tail, distrustful of one-dimensional vision, the "(post)colonial" in philosophy, historically, is also a place of dangerous potency, and, as critical project, it must necessarily remain a project in double-gesture.[32]

We know that the earliest Africans in America and Europe were largely forcefully brought there through slavery, and that the succeeding generation who came after the abolition of slave trade came largely to learn the ways of the West in preparation for the revolutions that would crystallize in constitutional decolonization (Kwame Nkrumah, Nnamdi Azikiwe, Senghor, etc.). Today, however, for the first time in known history, large numbers of Africans come to Europe and America to find – ironically – a place of refuge, a refuge always precarious because of racism and discriminatory immigration laws. This sad and ironic recent development results from the fact that Africa's transition from colony to nation-states has failed to translate into freedom – and, in some cases, responsibility. A commentator recently stated:

> The oppressive class configuration which colonialism epitomized, in essence, remains intact, as direct colonial presence was effectively replaced with indigenous clones. Not only did strife ensue, thanks in part to the conceited manner of colonial withdrawal, repression returned and [political] opposition was once more anathematized, often with a crudity and brutality equaling the barbarism of colonialism.[33]

With migration and instability as chronic elements in the modern history of Africa, African/a philosophy must find ways to make sense and speak of the multiplicities and the pluralisms of these historical "African" experiences.

"The African experience," however, has never really been a monolith, on the continent or abroad. From Amo to Nkrumah to Du Bois; from Equiano to Locke to Senghor; continental and Diaspora modern Africans found a "language" – largely based upon their awareness of a collective entanglement with the history of the modern West, and their objectification and "thingfication" (*Verdinglichung*) by this West – and so have also always individually and collectively struggled in multifaceted and pluralistic ways against the oppressive tendencies within European capitalist cultures, and the illegitimate colonial structures that crush African initiatives on the continent.

Contemporary African philosophy raises questions about the ambiguous and enduring legacies of modern Europe to Africa: an economy that, within the scheme of transatlantic capitalism, caters to the needs and the interests of Europe rather than of Africa, the cultural hegemony, and the racism that oppresses Africans in the Diaspora. (Post)colonial African philosophy in North America, therefore, is as much about the African continent as it is about the fate of African-descended peoples outside of the continent.[34] This volume brings together "philosophic texts ... born of" and/or sympathetically – although not uncritically – engaged in the African "struggle,"[35] in the hope of influencing not only the way we look at society, but also the way we read inherited philosophic texts.

I have grouped the contributions in five overlapping parts. Part I, "Africa and Modern Scientific Reason," deals with Africa's encounter with the *scientific/ technological reason* of the West: Kwame Gyekye's "Philosophy, culture, and technology in the postcolonial" explores the ambiguous question of the depth and the nature of the practice of "science" in postcolonial, "traditional" Africa cultures – particularly in relation to the idea of "science" as we know it from the history of the modern Western world. Sandra Harding's provocative piece, "Is modern science an ethnoscience?," raises crucial issues that are of utmost interest in light of the preceding essay. In what ways, Harding asks, is the idea of modern science (*vis-à-vis* the "ethnosciences" of Africa and other places) separable from the "religious, social, political, and economic assumptions, values, and interests" that constitute this science, even in its core universal intentions? The last essay in this section, Peter Amato's "African philosophy and modernity" questions, from a historical perspective, the range of the dichotomies – "open/closed," "rational/traditional," "modern/ premodern," etc. – which, both covertly and overtly, preframes most serious discussions of science and philosophy in Africa.

Part II, "Africa and Modern Philosophic Reason," also in three chapters, constitutes an engagement of the *philosophical reason* of the modern Western world through two readings of Kant and a reading of Hannah Arendt. Hence, Emmanuel Chukwudi Eze's "The color of reason: the idea of 'race' in Kant's anthropology" seeks to open up the question of whether or not there exist thematic and theoretical relations between Kant's cross-cultural racial anthropology on the one hand, and his critical ethics, aesthetics, and metaphysics, on the other. Tsenay Serequeberhan's "The critique of Eurocentrism and the practice of African philosophy," which also has a considerable focus on Kant, tries to show several ways in which modern European philosophy conceptualized the African existence as ahistorical and as metaphysical negativity. Finally, Gail Presbey's "Critic of Boers or Africans? Arendt's treatment of South Africa in *The Origins of Totalitarianism*" examines the highly perplexing, and perhaps "half-hearted" or unconvincing, critique of African colonialism contained in Hannah Arendt's important volume.

Part III, "Rebuilding Bridges," consists of three chapters that may be characterized as "bridge-building" reflections. They explore different and alternative modes of intercultural and interphilosophical experience between Africa and the Western world. These chapters are: Robert Bernasconi's "African philosophy's challenge to Continental philosophy"; Richard Bell's "Understanding African philosophy from a non-African point of view: an exercise in cross-cultural philosophy"; and Bruce Janz's "Alterity, dialogue, and African philosophy."

Part IV, "The Politics of the 'Postcolonial,'" consists of four contributions, two of which are both explorations and critiques of what the authors consider the apolitical (or better: *mis*political) nature of "postcolonial" Diasporic African thought. Hence Lewis Gordon's "Tragic dimensions of our neocolonial 'postcolonial' world", and Leonard Harris's "Honor, eunuchs, and the postcolonial subject." John Pittman's "Postphilosophy, politics, and 'race'" is an attempt to situate the "postcolonial" African–American thought – exemplified in Cornel West's work – against Richard Rorty's formulations of "postphilosophy" by articulating both thinkers' conceptions of philosophy around the political question of "race" in America. D.A. Masolo's "African philosophy and the postcolonial: some misleading abstractions about identity" explores the various philosophical and epistemological conflicts, i.e., the politics of the discourses within and through which Africans seek to positively constitute themselves as "postcolonial" subjects.

Finally, Part V, "Thoughts for a Postcolonial Future," composed of four chapters, addresses the postcolonial and post independence condition on the African continent. Kwasi Wiredu's "Democracy and consensus in African traditional politics: a plea for non-party polity" and Emmanuel Chukwudi Eze's "Democracy or consensus? A response to Wiredu" demonstrate how African philosophers explore and seek to recuperate vital relations between "precolonial" and "postcolonial" Africa, between "tradition and modernity" – in this case, in political practices. The type of conversation in which the two essays engage also demonstrates in an exemplary manner the vigorous critical exchanges that go on among postcolonial African thinkers. Jean-Marie Makang's "Of the good use of tradition: keeping the critical perspective in African Philosophy" elicits, from the strong African francophone philosophies of Towa and Eboussi-Boulaga, dynamic conceptions of "tradition" that allow for critical appropriation rather than blind application. Emmanuel Chukwudi Eze's "Toward a critical theory of postcolonial identities," an essay prompted by the spiraling political destabilization unfolding in Nigeria in 1995 and early 1996, is an examination of the role of "the West" in Africa's social imaginary.

Notes

1 Lucius Outlaw, in a related context, elaborates this issue in his essay: "African, African-American, and Africana philosophy," *The Philosophical Forum* (guest ed. John Pittman), vol. xxiv, nos 1–3, Fall–Spring 1992–3, pp. 63–93. Quotes are from pp. 72 and 73.

2 Translated into English by L. Scott-Fox and J.M. Harding as Vincent Descombes, *Modern French Philosophy* (Cambridge University Press, Cambridge, 1980).

3 Lucius Outlaw, "African, African-American, Africana philosophy," pp. 72–3.

4 Ibid.; emphases in original.

5 "African, African-American, Africana philosophy," p. 73. Outlaw's concept of "geographic race," by his own references, is influenced by Michael Banton and Jonathan Harwood's *The Race Concept* (Praeger, New York, 1975).

6 Ali Mazrui refers to this point of view as the "episodic" theory of African colonialism. This theory "asserts that the European [occupation] of Africa has been shallow rather than deep, transitional rather than long-lasting." As proof, the theorists argue: "It is not often realized how brief the colonial period was," and they offer, as an example, "When Jomo Kenyatta was born, Kenya was not yet a crown colony. Kenyatta lived right through the period of British rule and outlasted British rule by fifteen years." Conclusion: "If the entire period of colonialism could be compressed into the life-span of a single individual, how deep was the impact?" See: Mazrui, *The African: A Triple Heritage* (Little, Brown and Company, Boston, MA, 1986), p. 14. The position I take and my arguments are against this "theory."

7 "The politics of literary postcoloniality," *Race and Class*, vol. 36, no. 3, January–

March 1995, p. 7; my emphasis.

8 Cornel West, *Keeping Faith: Philosophy and Race in America* (Routledge, New York, 1993), p. 5; my emphasis.

9 Basil Davidson, *Africa: History of a Continent* (Macmillan, New York, 1966); *The African Genius: An Introduction to African Cultural and Social History* (Little, Brown and Co., Boston, MA, 1969).

10 See, for example, Peter Martin, *Schwarze Teufel, edle Mohren: Afrikaner in Bewußtsein und Geschichte der Deutschen* (Junius, Hamburg, 1993); Hugh Honour, *The Representation of the Black in Western Art* (Harvard University Press, Cambridge, MA, 1989); Sander Gilman, *On Blackness without Blacks* (G.K. Hall, Boston, MA, 1982); and Henry Louis Gates, "The history and theory of Afro–American literary criticism, 1773–1831: the arts, aesthetic theory and the nature of the African" (doctoral thesis, Cambridge University, 1978).

11 I am quoting from a later version of this statement which incorporated corrections Hume had made to it in response to criticisms and objections raised against the original by James Beattie (*An Essay on the Nature and Immutability of Truth in Opposition to Sophistry and Skepticism* (1770)). For a detailed discussion of the differences between the earlier and the later versions, see my Editorial notes in *Race and the Enlightenment* (forthcoming from Blackwell, Fall 1996); or my essay, "The idea of 'race' in Hume's social philosophy and its impact on eighteenth-century America," delivered at the College of William and Mary, April 6, 1995, and included in Dorothy Coleman (ed.), *Hume and Eighteenth-Century America* (forthcoming).

12 The most extensive discussion of the role that the idea of "race" plays in Kant's thought is probably my essay, "The color of reason: the idea of 'race' in Kant's anthropology." Originally published in Katherine Faull (ed.), *Anthropology and the German Enlightenment* (Bucknell and Associated University Press, London, 1994, pp. 201–41), it is partially reprinted in SAPINA, *Bulletin of Society for African Philosophy in North American*, vol. VIII, nos. 1–2, January–July 1995, pp. 53–78, and in part II of this volume.

13 According to Kant: "Mr Hume challenges anyone to cite a simple example in which a Negro has shown talents, and asserts that among the hundreds of thousands of blacks . . . not a single one was ever found who presented anything great in art or science . . . So fundamental is the difference between the two races of man, and it appears to be great in regard to mental capacities as in color." *Observations*, trans. John T. Goldthwait (University of California Press, Berkeley, CA, 1960), pp. 110–11. Kant's previous statement can be found in ibid., p. 113.

14 Within a few pages of *Philosophy of History*, Hegel has used the following terms to describe African peoples: "barbarism and savagery," "barbarous ferocity," "terrible hordes," "barbarity," "animal man," "savagery and lawlessness," "primitive," "animality," "the most terrible manifestation of human nature," "wild confusion," and "Unhistorical, Undeveloped Spirit." A first-year Bucknell student, Sean Gray, who researched this language as part of an assignment for my course, "Hegel, Modernity and the African World," had this to say: "This [Hegel's] language is argumentative in nature, attempting to shock the reader into following what he said. These words show up way before Hegel provides specific accounts of any historical African peoples. By formulating such steep language

ahead of time, the reader is psychologically set to look for the worst and so won't be shocked by whatever fantasies or exaggerations about Africa Hegel chooses to provide." (Sean Gray, "The notions of barbarism and savagery in Hegel's treatment of Africa.") Critical literature on Hegel's ideas about Africa include Serequeberhan, "The idea of colonialism in Hegel's *Philosophy of Right*," *International Philosophical Quarterly*, vol. xxix, no. 3, September 1989, pp. 302–18; and Robert Bernasconi, "Hegel at the Court of the Ashanti," forthcoming.

15 Hegel, for example, writes in this volume that "the North American states . . . were entirely *colonized* [emphasis in the original] by the Europeans." *Lectures on the Philosophy of World History*, trans. H.B. Nisbet (Cambridge University Press, Cambridge, 1993), p. 167.

16 Hegel, *Philosophy of Right*, trans. T.M. Knox, (Oxford University Press, Oxford, 1967), p. 150.

17 Hegel, *The Essential Writings*, ed. F. Weiss (Harper, New York, 1974), pp. 282–3.

18 Ibid.; my emphasis.

19 Knox trans., par. 351, p. 219.

20 As we know, subsequent major European philosophers reinscribed these Hegelian colonialist intentions on Africa into their own philosophical systems. Edward Said pointed out in *Orientalism* that, although Marx may have "turned Hegel on his head," his views on European colonization of India and Africa were no different.

21 It is, however, only a "negative" moment in a qualified sense. Positively, it is a way of deblocking African philosophical consciousness clouded over by Eurocentric and racist writings; a way of critiquing in order to reject the pernicious parts of the philosophical traditions that we ambiguously inherit from European modernity, because we recognize human and humane elements in them that may also speak cross-culturally and with less exploitation, less racism, and less ethnocentrism.

22 See the excellent volume edited by Talal Asad, *Anthropology and the Colonial Encounter* (Ithaca Press, London, 1973); see also some choice essays in Chinua Achebe, *Hopes and Impediments* (Doubleday, New York, 1988).

23 The works of V.Y. Mudimbe supremely chronicle in all details and complexity (religious, anthropological, philosophical and literary) both the methods and the astonishing success of these procedures of colonization apropos Africa. See, for example, The *Invention of Africa* (1988) and *The Idea of Africa* (1994), both published by Indiana University Press.

24 It was not until much later that African philosophers such as Aimé Césaire (*Discourse on Colonialism*, trans. J. Pinkham, Monthly Review Press, New York, 1972) and Frantz Fanon started to focus negative-critical attention explicitly and publicly on the colonialist and ideological intentions of Tempels' *Bantu Philosophy*. The more widespread immediate response was similar to that of Aléxis Kagamé and a host of others now identified in the "ethnophilosophy" schools. They revised and expanded, but continued Tempels' major methodological orientation: namely, the documentation and analysis of evidence of philosophical thought in African languages and in the unwritten traditions of various African peoples.

25 I do not intend to make Tempels, or the three "moments" I discuss here, the absolute beginning for African philosophical practice. In addition to philosophical works in the "oral" traditions (for example, the "Ifa" (or "Afa") Corpus among the

Yorubas and the Igbos of West Africa), there are bodies of written antislavery and anticolonial philosophical works that date back to the sixteenth century. On the continent, the rational hermeneutics of the Abyssinian Zera Yecob (1599–1692), for example, was concerned with the question of the nature of reason and faith in the context of the acute crisis of Abyssinian cultural and political integrity, "in confrontation with the subversive work of Jesuit missionaries and aggressive Catholicism" (Tsenay Serequeberhan, *The Hermeneutics of African Philosophy: Discourse and Horizon*, Routledge, New York, 1994, p. 18). In the Diaspora, in 1732, William Amo, a native of a little town in present Ghana, at age 27 received what is today called a doctorate degree in philosophy from the University of Wittenberg. He taught at the universities of Halle and Jena, and, in addition to extant works on epistemology and philosophical psychology, also wrote, and perhaps published, a lost work entitled *On the Freedom of Africans in Europe*. Amo returned to Ghana in 1747 and lived there as a hermit for the rest of his life (his date of death is unknown). Likewise, the autobiography of the Igbo gentleman Olaudah Equiano, although written from the point of view of his involvement in abolitionist movements in eighteenth- and nineteenth-century England, is an excellent document of the racist and colonialist social and political thinking on Africa in modern Europe. The examples of Amo and Equiano only alert us to Leonard Harris's landmark collection, *Philosophy Born of Struggle* (Kendall/Hunt, Dubuque, IA, 1983), which chronicles the enormous wide-ranging philosophical productivity in Afro-America from the beginning of the twentieth century. Today, as we know, African and African-Diasporic men and women of letters – Chinua Achebe, Wole Soyinka, Toni Morrison, Cheikh Hamidou-Kane, etc. – in addition to the efforts of those whose professional vocation is more strictly "philosophy," are producing literary resources of unsurpassed philosophical depths that powerfully articulate and chronicle our contemporary experiences. Finally, we should specifically mention the numerous successful attempts by Osabutey (1936), G. James (1954), Diop (1974), Henry Olela (1980), Onyenwuenyi (1994), Th. Obenga (1973; 1990), and Martin Bernal (1991–) to (re)write the history of the African origins of Greek and European philosophy. Regardless of the admittedly ideological functions of *some* of these works, others are needed antidotes to some of the impossible claims ahistorically made about the "Greek Miracle," and in such a way that the history of African and Semitic contributions to the development of ancient philosophy became marginalized or forgotten.

26   *Keeping Faith*, p. 6.
27   Abiola Irele, "Contemporary thought in French speaking Africa," in Albert Mosley (ed.), *African Philosophy: Selected Readings* (Prentice Hall, Englewood Cliffs, NJ, 1995), p. 296.
28   Both published by Indiana University Press, (Bloomington, IN, 1988 and 1994).
29   Heidegger went on to illustrate his assertion with the following example: "When an airplane's propeller turns, then nothing actually 'occurs.' Conversely, when the same airplane takes the Führer to Mussolini, then history occurs." We wish this plane would make a return trip for the Abachas and the Mobutus and the Idi Amins and the Bokassas – so that "history" will truly fully "occur"!
30   See especially the first chapters of volume 1, subtitled *Reason and the Rationalization of Society*, trans. Thomas McCarthy (Beacon Press, Boston, MA, 1984).

31 *Outside in the Teaching Machine* (Routledge, London, 1993), p. 60.
32 Lucius Outlaw's "African philosophy: deconstructive and reconstructive challenges," in *Sage Philosophy: Indigenous Thinkers and Modern Debate on African Philosophy* (E.J. Brill, Leiden, 1990) is an elaborate case of this; Serequeberhan's *Hermeneutics of African Philosophy* and Amilcar Cabral's *Return to the Source: Selected Speeches* (Monthly Review Press, New York, 1979) are exemplar in terms of working with colonial "tools" to dismantle the house that colonialism built – in pursuit of a (re)new(ed) sense of humanity and social order.
33 Olu Oguibe (ed.), *Sojourners: New Writings by Africans in Britain* (Africa Refugee Publishing Collective, London, 1994), pp. xiv–xv. In the last chapter in this book, "Toward a critical theory of postcolonial African identities," I attempt an example of an immanent critique of postcolonial African societies – especially of the African leaders and intellectuals, who sometimes mask internal economic exploitation and political repression with anticolonial rhetoric. This sort of auto-critique is needed now more than ever if we are to uncover the extraversions for what they are: evasion of responsibility.
34 Cornel West argues that one of the reasons why this conjunction in African and Afro-Diasporic experience may not be obvious is primarily because "decolonization in the New World for Africans is more a matter of self and mind than masses of land, and hence more subject to delusion and deception in the New World than in the Old." *Keeping Faith*, p. xiv.
35 Harris, *Philosophy Born of Struggle*, p. ix.

PART I
Africa and Modern Scientific Reason

1

Philosophy, Culture, and Technology in the Postcolonial

Kwame Gyekye

1 Prologue

The postcolonial era in Africa is the era that follows the *re*gaining of the political independence of African states from the European colonial powers. On the one hand, postcoloniality brings down the curtain on the period of dictation, forcible imposition of a variety of alien values and institutions, and the display of hubris: features or phenomena that characterized the colonial era of European subjugation and rule in Africa. On the other hand, postcoloniality represents – at least potentially – a period of autonomous self-expression on the part of the formerly colonized peoples, as well as of self-assertion, sober reflection on (and profound and sophisticated assessment of) values and goals, and the gradual weaning away from the self-flagellating aspects of colonial mentality acquired through decades of coloniality.

Let it be noted, however, that postcoloniality is not necessarily a rejection of the entire corpus of a colonial heritage, in view of the fact that there would undoubtedly be features or elements of that heritage which the formerly colonized peoples would themselves have considered worthwhile and conducive to the course of their cultural and intellectual development. The adoption by them of some features of the colonial heritage would be appropriate and would merely be an aspect of the historical phenomenon of cultural borrowing which has been a seminal factor in the growth and evolution of cultures throughout the history of humankind. The postcolonial adoption of features of the colonial heritage would in some sense be voluntary, for those features could have been rejected. Thus, postcoloniality makes possible the sorting out, selection, choice, and finally *voluntary* adoption of some ideas, values, outlooks, and institutions of an encountered culture.

Needless to say, there have been some reflections, mainly by African political leaders, on, for instance, the appropriate ideology (or ideologies) that must underpin and guide the policies and actions of postcolonial African governments. We see this in the new concepts of African personality, African socialism, and others. It behooves contemporary African philosophers to turn their reflective and analytic attention *also* to this new experience – that is, the entire postcolonial phenomenon – and to seek to clarify issues at the fundamental level. The philosopher need not be reminded that the philosophical enterprise, whatever else it is, involves a conceptual response to human problems at different epochs. Conceptual and critical attention to the complex cultural (using "culture" in a comprehensive sense that encompasses the entire life of a people) and historical problems of Africa will, in my opinion, also help in the emergence of a genuinely (modern) African philosophy.

2 Science and our Cultures

Even though the main subject of this chapter is a critical look at the career of technology in the traditional cultures of Africa, and the methods of acquiring and pursuing technology in postcolonial Africa, I consider it appropriate to preface my discussion of the subject with an elaborate attention to science in the cultural traditions of a postcolonial state, such as Ghana. This attention to science is considered appropriate in view of the fact that the lack of technological advancement, or the ossified state in which the techniques of production found themselves, in the traditional setting of Africa and, in many ways, even in colonial and postcolonial Africa, is certainly attributable to the incomprehensible inattention to the search for scientific principles by the traditional technologists. I will therefore start off with observations on how science and knowledge fared in the traditional culture of the postcolonial state.

In a previous publication I pointed out the empirical orientation of African thought, maintaining that African proverbs, for instance – a number of which bear some philosophical content – addressed or resulted from reflections on specific situations, events, or experiences in the lives of the people, and that even such a metaphysical concept as destiny (or fate) was reached inductively, experience being the basis of the reasoning that led to it.[1] Observation and experience constituted a great part of the sources of knowledge in African traditions.[2] The empirical basis of knowledge had immediate practical results in such areas as agriculture and herbal medicine: our ancestors, whose main occupation was farming, knew of the system of rotation of crops; they knew when to allow a piece of land to lie fallow for a while; they had some knowledge of the technology of food processing and preservation; and there is a great deal of evidence about their knowledge of the medicinal potencies of herbs and plants – the main source of their health care delivery system long before the introduction of Western medicine. (Even today, there are countless testimonies of people who have received cures from "traditional" healers where the application of Western therapeutics could not cope.)

It has been asserted by several scholars that African life in the traditional setting is intensely religious or spiritual. Mbiti opined that "Africans are notoriously religious, and each people has its own religious system with a set of beliefs and practices. Religion permeates into all the departments of life so fully that it is not easy or possible to isolate it."[3] According to him, "in traditional life there are no atheists."[4] Busia observed that Africa's cultural heritage "is intensely and pervasively religious,"[5] and that "in traditional African communities, it was not possible to distinguish between religious and nonreligious areas of life. All life was religious."[6] Many colonial administrators in Africa used to refer to Africans, according to Parrinder, as "this incurably religious people."[7] Yet, despite the alleged religiosity of the African cultural heritage, the empirical orientation or approach to most of their enterprises was very much to the fore. I strongly suspect that even the African knowledge of God in the traditional setting was, in the context of a non-revealed religion of traditional Africa, empirically reached.

Now, one would have thought that such a characteristically empirical epistemic outlook would naturally lead to a profound and extensive interest in science as a theory: that is, in the acquisition of theoretical knowledge of nature, beyond the practical knowledge which they seem to have had of it, and which they utilized to their benefit. But, surprisingly, there is no evidence that such an empirical orientation of thought in traditional African culture led to the creation of the scientific outlook or a deep scientific understanding of nature. It is possible, arguably, to credit people who practiced crafts and pursued such activities as food preservation, food fermentation, and herbal therapeutics with some amount of scientific knowledge; after all, the traditional technologies, one would assume, must have had some basis in science. Yet, it does not appear that their practical knowledge of crafts or forms of technologies led to any deep scientific understanding or analysis of the enterprises they were engaged in. Observations made by them may have led to interesting facts about the workings of nature; but those facts needed to be given elaborate and coherent theoretical explanations. Science requires explanations that are generalizable, facts that are disciplined by experiments, and experiments that are repeatable and verifiable elsewhere. But the inability (or is it lack of interest?) of the users of our culture to engage in sustained investigations and to provide intelligible scientific explanations or analyses of their own observations and experiences stunted the growth of science.

Science begins not only in sustained observations and investigations into natural phenomena, but also in the ascription of causal explanations or analyses to those phenomena. The notion of causality is, of course, very crucial to the pursuit of science. Our cultures appreciated the notion of causality very well. But, for a reason which must be linked to the alleged intense religiosity of the cultures, causality was generally understood in terms of spirit, of mystical power. The consequence of this was that purely scientific or empirical causal explanations, of which the users of our culture were somehow aware, were often not regarded as profound enough to offer complete satisfaction. This led them to give up, but too soon, on the search for empirical causal explanations – even of causal relations between natural phenomena or events – and to resort to supernatural causation.

Empirical causation, which asks what- and how-questions, too quickly gave way to agentive causation, which asks who- and why-questions. Agentive causation led to the postulation of spirits or mystical powers as causal agents; so that a particular metaphysic was at the basis of this sort of agentive causation. According to Mbiti, "The physical and spiritual are but two dimensions of one and the same universe. These dimensions dove-tail into each other to the extent that at times and in places one is apparently more real than, but not exclusive of, the other."[8] It is the lack of distinction between the purely material (natural) and the immaterial (supernatural, spiritual) that led to the postulation of agentive causation in all matters. For, in a conception of a hierarchy of causes, it was easy to identify the spiritual as the agent that causes changes in relations even among empirical phenomena. In view of the critical importance of causality to the development of the science of nature, a culture that was obsessed with supernaturalistic or mystical causal explanations would hardly develop the scientific attitude in the users of that culture, and would, consequently, not attain knowledge of the external world that can empirically be ascertained by others, including future generations.

Yet, the alleged intense religiosity of the African cultural heritage need not have hindered interest in science: that is, in scientific investigations both for their own sake and as sure foundations for the development of technology. Religion and science, even though they perceive reality differently, need not be incompatible. Thus it is possible for religious persons to acquire scientific knowledge and outlook. But to be able to do so most satisfactorily, one should be able to separate the two, based on the conviction that purely scientific knowledge and understanding of the external world would not detract from one's faith in an ultimate being. A culture may be a religious culture, even an intensely religious culture; but, in view of the tremendous importance of science for the progress of many other aspects of the culture, it should be able to render unto Caesar what is Caesar's and unto God what is God's ("Caesar" here referring to the pursuit of the knowledge of the natural world). The inability of our traditional cultures to separate religion from science, as well as the African conception of nature as essentially animated or spirit-filled (leading to the belief that natural objects contained mystical powers to be feared or kept at bay, or, when convenient, to be exploited for man's immediate material benefit), was the ground of the agentive causal explanations so esteemed by the users of our cultures in the traditional setting. Science, as already stated, is based on a profound understanding and exploitation of the important notion of causality: that is, on a deep appreciation of the causal interactions between natural phenomena. But where this is enmeshed with – made inextricable from – supernaturalistic molds and orientations, science, as a purely empirical pursuit, hardly makes progress.

Also, religion, even if it is pursued by a whole society or generation, is still a highly subjective cognitive activity, in that its postulates and conclusions are not immediately accessible to objective scrutiny or verification by others outside it. Science, on the contrary, is manifestly an objective, impartial enterprise whose conclusions are open to scrutiny by others at any time or place, a scrutiny that may lead to the rejection or amendment or confirmation of those conclusions. Now, the mesh in which both religion and science (or, rather, the pursuit of science) found themselves in African traditional cultures made the relevant objective approach to scientific investigations into nature well-nigh impossible. Moreover, in consequence of this mesh, what could have become scientific knowledge accessible to all others became an esoteric knowledge, a specialized knowledge, accessible only to initiates probably under an oath of secrecy administered by priests and priestesses, traditionally acknowledged as the custodians of the verities and secrets of nature. These custodians, it was, who "knew," and were often consulted on, the causes of frequent low crop yield, lack of adequate rainfall over a long period of time, the occurrence of bush fires, and so on. Knowledge-claims about the operations of nature became not only esoteric, but also, if for that reason, personal rather than exoteric and impersonal. This pre-empted the participatory nature of the search for deep and extensive knowledge of the natural world. For others would not have access to, let alone participate in, the type of knowledge that is regarded as personal and arcane.

Knowledge of the potencies of herbs and other medicinal plants was in the traditional setting probably the most secretive of all. Even if the claims made by African medicine men and women of having discovered cures for deadly diseases could be substantiated scientifically, those claims cannot be pursued for verification, since their knowledge-claims were esoteric and personal. The desire to make knowledge of the external world personal has been the characteristic attitude of our traditional healers. In the past, all such possibly credible claims to knowledge of medicinal plants just evaporated on the death of the traditional healer or priest. And science, including the science of medicine, stagnated.

I think that the personalization of the knowledge of the external world is attributable to the mode of acquiring that knowledge: that mode was simply not based on experiment. And, in the circumstance, the only way one could come by one's knowledge of, say, herbal therapeutics was most probably through mystical or magical means, a means not subject to public or objective scrutiny and analysis.

The lack of the appropriate attitude to sustained scientific probing, required for both vertical and horizontal advancement of knowledge, appears to have been a characteristic of our African cultural past. One need not ascribe this want of the appropriate scientific attitude to the lack of the capacity for science. I would like to make a distinction here: between having the intellectual capacity on the one hand, and having the proclivity or impulse to exercise that capacity on a sustained basis that would yield appreciable results on the other. The impulse for sustained scientific or intellectual probing does not appear to have been nurtured and promoted by our traditional cultures.

It appears, in fact, that the traditional cultures rather throttled the impulse towards sustained and profound inquiry, for reasons that are not fully known or intelligible. One reason, however, may be extracted from the Akan (Ghanaian) maxim, literally translated as: "if you insist on probing deeply into the eye sockets of a dead person, you see a ghost."[9] The maxim clearly loses something in translation. But what it is saying is that curiosity or deep probing may lead to dreadful consequences (the ghost is something of which most people are apprehensive). The maxim, as Laing also saw, stunts the "development of the spirit of inquiry, exploration and adventure."[10] The attitude sanctioned by the maxim would, as Laing pointed out, be "inimical to science;"[11] and not only to science, but, I might add, to all kinds of knowledge. My colleague, Opoku,[12] however, explained to me in a conversation that the intention of the maxim is to put an end to a protracted dispute which might tear a family or lineage apart: a dispute that has been settled, in other words, should not be resuscitated, for the consequences of the resuscitation would not be good for the solidarity of the family. Thus, Opoku would deny that this maxim is to be interpreted as damaging to intellectual or scientific probing. In response to Opoku's interpretation, one would like to raise the following questions: Why should further evidence not be looked for, if it would indeed help to settle the matter more satisfactorily? Why should further investigation be stopped if it would unravel fresh evidence and lead to what was not previously known? To end a dispute prematurely for the sake of family solidarity to the dissatisfaction of some members of the family certainly does violence to the pursuit of moral or legal knowledge. So, whether in the area of legal, moral, or scientific knowledge, it seems to me that the maxim places a damper on the impulse or proclivity to deep probing, to the pursuit of further knowledge.

The general attitude of the users of the African traditional cultures – expressed in oft-used statements such as "this is what the ancestors said," "this is what the ancestors did" and similar references to what are regarded as the ancestral habits or modes of thought and action – may be put down to the inexplicable reluctance, or lack of the impulse, to pursue sustained inquiries into the pristine ideas and values of the culture. It is this kind of mindset, one might add, which often makes the elderly people even in our contemporary (African) societies try to stop children with inquisitive minds from persistently asking certain kinds of question and, thus, from pursuing intellectual exploration on their own. (I do not have the space to provide evidence to show that our forefathers did not expect later generations to regard their modes of thought and action as sacrosanct and unalterable, and to think and act in the same way they did. This means that, if their descendants failed to make changes, amendments or refinements such as were required by their own times and situations, this would have to be put down to the intellectual indolence or shallowness of those descendants.)

Finally let me say this: the pursuit of science – the cultivation of rational or theoretical knowledge of the natural world – seems to presuppose an intense desire, at least initially, for knowledge for its own sake, not for the sake of some immediate practical results. It appears that our cultures had very little, if any, conception of knowledge for its own sake. They had a conception of knowledge that was practically oriented. Such an epistemic conception seems to have had a parallel in the African conception of art. For it has been said by several scholars[13] that art was conceived in the African traditional setting in functional (or teleological) terms, that the African aesthetic sense did not find the concept of "art for art's sake" hospitable. Even though I think that the purely aesthetic element of art was not lost sight of, this element does not appear to have been stressed in African art appreciation, as was the functional conception. This practical or functional conception of art, which dwarfed a conception of art for art's sake, must have infected the African conception of knowledge, resulting in a lack of interest in the acquisition of knowledge, including scientific knowledge, *for its own sake.*

It is clear from the foregoing discussion of the attitude of our indigenous African cultures to science that: (1) the cultures did not have a commitment to the advancement of the scientific knowledge of the natural world; (2) they made not the slightest attempt to investigate the scientific theories underpinning the technologies they developed, as I will point out in some detail below; (3) the disposition to pursue sustained inquiries into many areas of their life and thought does not seem to have been fostered by our African cultures; and (4) the successive generations of participants in the culture could not, consequent upon (3), augment the compendium of knowledge that they had inherited from their forefathers, but rather gleefully felt satisfied with it, making it into a hallowed or mummified basis of their own thought and action. In our contemporary world, where sustainable development, a great aspect of which is concerned with the enhancement of the material well-being of people, depends on the intelligent and efficient exploitation of the resources of nature – an exploitation that can be effected only through science and its progeny, technology – the need to acquire the cultivation of the appropriate scientific attitudes is an imperative.

Contemporary African culture will have to come to terms with the contemporary scientific attitudes and approaches to looking at things in Africa's own environment – attitudes and approaches that have been adopted in the wake of the contact with the Western cultural traditions. The governments of African nations have for decades been insisting on the cultivation of science in the schools and universities as an unavoidable basis for technological, and hence industrial, advancement. More places, incentives, and facilities are made available for those students who are interested in the pursuit of science. Yet, *mirabile dictu*, very many more students register for courses in the humanities and the social sciences than in the mathematical and natural sciences. Has the traditional culture anything to do with this lack of real or adequate or sustained interest in the natural sciences, or not?

3 Technology and our Cultures

Like science, technology – which is the application of knowledge or discovery to practical use – is also a feature or product of culture. It develops in the cultural milieu of a people, and its career or future is also determined by the characteristics of the culture. Technology is an enterprise that can be said to be common to all human cultures; it can certainly be regarded as among the earliest creations of any human society. This is because the material existence and survival of the human society depend on the ability of humankind to make at least simple tools and equipment, and to develop techniques essential for the production of basic human needs such as food, clothing, shelter, and security. The concern for such needs was naturally more immediate than the pursuit and acquisition of the systematic knowledge of nature – that is, science. Thus, in all human cultures and societies, the creation of simple forms of technology antedates science – the rational and systematic pursuit of knowledge and understanding of the natural world, of the processes of nature, based on observation and experiment. The historical and functional priority of technology over science was a phenomenon even in the cultures of Western societies, historically the home of advanced and sophisticated technology. From antiquity on, and through the Middle Ages into the modern European world, innovative technology showed no traces of the application of consciously scientific principles.[14] Science-based technology was not developed until about the middle of the nineteenth century.[15] Thus, technology was for centuries based on completely empirical knowledge.

The empirical character of African thought in general, and of its epistemology in particular, was pointed out in section 2. The pursuit of empirical knowledge – knowledge based on experience and observation, and generally oriented towards the attainment of practical results – underpinned a great deal of the intellectual enterprise of the traditional setting. (Note that philosophical knowledge was also thought to have a practical orientation.) And so, like other cultures of the world, practical knowledge and the pursuit of sheer material well-being and survival led the cultures of Africa in premodern times to develop simple technologies and techniques. Basic craftsmanship emerged: farming implements such as the cutlass, hoe, and ax were made by the blacksmith; the goldsmith produced the bracelet, necklace, and rings (including the earring): "African coppersmiths have for centuries produced wire to make bracelets and ornaments – archaeologists have found the draw-plates and other wire-making tools."[16] There were carpenters, wood-carvers, potters, and cloth-weavers, all of whom evolved techniques for achieving results. Food production, processing, and preservation techniques were developed, and so were techniques for extracting medicinal potencies from plants, herbs, and roots. A number of these technical activities in time burgeoned into industries.

There was, needless to say, a great respect and appreciation for technology because of what it could offer the people by way of its products. The need for, and the appreciation of, technology should have translated into real desire for innovation and improvement of existing technological products and techniques. There is, however, not much evidence to support the view that there were attempts to innovate technologies and refine techniques received from previous generations. There were no doubts whatsoever about the potencies of traditional medicines extracted from plants and herbs – the basis of the health care delivery system in the traditional setting and, to a very great extent, in much of rural Africa today. Yet, there were – and are – enormous problems about both the nature of the diagnosis and the appropriate or reliable dosage, problems which do not seem to have been grappled with. Diagnosis requires systematic analysis of cause and effect, an approach which would not be fully exploited in a system, like the one evolved by our cultures, which often explained the causes of illness, as it did many other natural occurrences, in agentive (i.e. supernatural, mystical) terms. Such a causal approach to coping with disease would hardly dispose a people towards the search for effective diagnostic technologies.

Traditional healers were often not short on prescriptive capabilities: they were capable in a number of cases of prescribing therapies often found to be efficacious. But their methods generated two problems: one was the preparation of the medicine to be administered to a patient; the other was the dosage – the quantity of the medicine for a specific illness. Having convinced himself of the appropriate therapeutic for a particular disease, a therapeutic which would often consist of a concoction, the next step for the herbal healer was to decide on the proportion of each herbal ingredient for the concoction. A decision then had to be taken on the appropriate and effective dosage for a particular illness. Both steps obviously required exact measurement of quantity. The failure to provide exact measurement would affect the efficacy of the concoction as well as the therapeutic effect of the dosage; in the case of the latter, there was the possibility of underdosage or overdosage. Yet the need for exact measurement does not seem to have been valued and pursued by our cultures, a cultural defect which is still taking its toll in the maintenance of machines by our mechanics today. Wiredu mentions the case of a Ghanaian mechanic who, in working on engine maintenance, would resort to the use of his sense of sight rather than of a feeler gauge in adjusting the contact breaker point in the distributor of a car.[17] The mechanic, by refusing to use a feeler gauge and such other technical aids, of course fails to achieve the required precision measurement. Since the habit or attitude of the mechanic was not peculiar to him, but is prevalent among a number of mechanics in our environment, it can be said that the development of the habit is a function of the culture. If you consider that precision measurement is basic not only for the proper maintenance of machines, but also for the quality of manufactured products of all kinds, you can appreciate the seriousness of the damage to the growth of technology caused by our cultures' failure to promote the value of precision measurement.

Even though it is true to say that, historically, technology was for centuries applied without resort to scientific principles, it must be the case that this fact slowed down the advancement of technology. It deprived technology of a necessary scientific base. The making of simple tools and equipment may not require or rest on the knowledge of scientific principles; but not so the pursuit of most other technological enterprises and methods. The preparation of medicinal concoctions by traditional African herbal healers and their prescriptive dosages must have been greatly hampered by the failure to attend to the appropriate scientific testing of the potencies of the various herbs and the amounts of each (herb or plant) required in a particular concoction. Theoretical knowledge should have been pursued to complement their practical knowledge.

Food technology, practiced in the traditional setting mainly by African women, was a vibrant activity, even though the scientific aspect of it was not attended to. According to Sefa-Dede, who has done an enormous amount of research in traditional food technology in Ghana, "The scientific principles behind the various unit operations may be the same as found in modern food technologies, but the mode of application may be different."[18] The techniques traditionally deployed in food preservation undoubtedly involve the application of principles of science – physics, chemistry, and biology – which the users of those techniques may not be aware of. The techniques of preserving food all over Africa include drying, smoking, salting, and fermenting. The drying technique is aimed at killing bacteria and other decay-causing micro-organisms, and thus preserving food intact for a long time; smoking serves as a chemical preservative; and so does salting, which draws moisture and micro-organisms from foods; fermentation of food causes considerable reduction of acidity levels and so creates conditions that prevent microbial multiplication.[19] It is thus clear that there are scientific principles underlying these methods.

Let us take the case of a woman in the central region of Ghana, whose practice of food technology is clearly supported by a knowledge of some principles of physics, chemistry, and metallurgy. The woman in question is a processor of "fante kenkey", a fermented cereal dumpling made from maize. Maize dough is fermented for two to four days. A portion of the dough is made into a slurry and cooked into a stiff paste. This is mixed with the remaining portion through a process called aflatization to produce aflata. This is wrapped in dried banana leaves and boiled for three to four hours until it is cooked. Now, this woman challenged a modern scientific research team studying traditional food technology to indicate how they could solve a very practical problem which can arise when one is boiling fante kenkey in a 44-gallon drum.[20] This was the problem:

> Imagine that you have loaded a 44-gallon barrel with uncooked fante kenkey. You set the system up on the traditional cooking stove, which uses firewood. The fire is lit and the boiling process starts. In the middle of the boiling process, you notice that the barrel has developed a leak at its bottom. The boiling water is gushing into the fire and gradually putting off the fire. What will you do to save the situation?

The possible solutions suggested by the research team were found to be impractical. One solution given by the team was to transfer the product from the leaking barrel into a new one. There are several reasons why this could not be done: the kenkey will be very hot and difficult to unpack; the process will also be time-consuming; and another barrel may not be available.

The traditional woman food technologist provided the solution: adjust the firewood in the stove to allow increased burning; then collect two or three handfuls of dry palm kernels and throw them into the fire – these will heat up and turn red hot; finally, collect coarse table salt and throw it on to the hot kernels. The salt will explode and in the process seal the leak at the bottom of the barrel. According to Sefa-Dede, the solution provided by the woman is based on the sublimation of the salt. The explosion carries particles of salt with it, which fill the opening. It is possible that there is a reaction between the sodium chloride in the salt and the iron and other cations forming the structure of the barrel.

Two questions may arise as one attempts to understand the source of knowledge of the traditional practitioners: Why were dry palm kernels used as the heat exchange medium? What is peculiar about table salt (sodium chloride) in this process? In the case under discussion, it can certainly be said that the woman had some knowledge about the thermal properties of palm kernels. (It is possible that there is traditional knowledge about the excellent heat properties of palm kernels. Traditional metal smelters, blacksmiths, and goldsmiths are known to use palm kernels for heating and melting various metals.) The woman also had knowledge of some chemistry and metallurgy. But although it is clear

that the ideas and solutions which the woman was able to come up with are
rooted in basic and applied scientific principles, she could not explain and
articulate those principles. In this, she is the same as most other traditional
technology practitioners. They must have thought that the whys and hows did
not matter: it was enough to have found practical ways to solve practical
problems of human survival.

To summarize, the users of traditional technologies were concerned about
reaping immediate practical results from their activities. The result was that
there was no real understanding of the scientific processes involved in the
technologies they found so useful. Yet, the concern for investigating and
understanding those principles would probably have generated extensive
innovative practices and the application of those principles to *other* yet-
unknown technological possibilities. It can therefore be said that the weak
scientific base of the traditional technology stunted its growth, and accounted
for the maintenance and continual practice of the same old techniques. It clearly
appears to be the case that, once some technique or equipment was known to
be working, there was no desire or enthusiasm on the part of its creators or users
to innovate and improve on its quality, to make it work better or more
efficiently, or to build other, more efficient tools. Was this sort of complacency,
or the feeling of having come to the end of one's intellectual or technological
tether, a reflection on the levels of capability that could be attained by our
cultures?

4 Approaches to Developing a Modern Technology in the Postcolonial

It can hardly be denied that technology, along with science, has historically been
among the central pillars – as well as the engines – of modernity. It is equally
undeniable that the modern world is increasingly becoming a technological
world: technology is, by all indications, going to become the distinguishing
feature of global culture in the coming decades. Africa will have to participate
significantly in the cultivation and promotion of this aspect of human culture,
if it is to benefit from it fully. But the extensive and sustained understanding
and acquisition of modern technology insistently require adequate cultivation
of science and the scientific outlook. The acquisition of a scientific and
technological outlook will in turn require a new mental orientation on the part
of the African people, a new and sustained interest in science to provide a firm
base for technology, a new intellectual attitude to the external world uncluttered
by superstition, mysticism, and other forms of irrationality; the alleged
spirituality of the African world, which in the precolonial world was allowed
in many ways to impede sustained inquiries into the world of nature, will have
to come to terms with materiality: that is, the physical world of science. This

is not to suggest by any means that a spiritual life must be abandoned; it is to suggest, rather, that, as I said earlier, Caesar's world must be clearly demarcated from God's. Knowledge of medicinal plants, for instance, *qua* scientific knowledge, must be rescued from the quagmire of mysticism and spirituality and brought to the glare of publicity, and its language must be made exoteric and accessible to many others.

The need for sustained interest in science is important for at least two reasons. The first is to provide an enduring base for a real technological take-off at a time in the history of the world when the dynamic connections between science and technology have increasingly been recognized and made the basis of equal attention to both: technology has become science based, while science has become technology directed. The second reason, a corollary of the first, is that it is the application of science to technology that will help improve traditional technologies.

Ideally, technology, as a cultural product, should rise from the culture of a people, if it is to be directly accessible to a large section of the population and if its nuances are to be fully appreciated by them. For this reason, one approach to creating modern technology in a developing country is to upgrade or improve existing traditional technologies whose developments, as I have already indicated, seem to have been stunted in the traditional setting because of its very weak science base. Let us recall the case of the woman food technologist referred to in section 3. She was able to find practical ways of solving problems that emerged in the course of utilizing some technology, by resorting to ideas and solutions which are obviously rooted in basic science, but without the benefit of the knowledge of chemistry, physics, engineering or metallurgy. As we have seen, for most traditional technology practitioners the whys and hows did not often matter, so long as some concrete results could be achieved through the use of a particular existing technology. But the why- and how-questions, of course, *do* matter – and matter a great deal. Improving traditional technologies will require not only looking for answers to such questions, but also searching for areas or activities to which the application of existing technologies (having been improved) can be extended.

Traditional technologies have certain characteristics which could – and must – be featured in the approach to modern technology in a developing country. Traditional technologies are usually simple, not highly specialized technologies: this fact makes for the involvement of large numbers of people in the application or use of the technologies, as well as in their development; but it also promotes indigenous technological awareness. The materials that are used are locally available and the processes are effective. (In the case of the woman's food technology, the materials in question – namely, palm kernels and table salt – are household items which are readily available.) Traditional technologies are developed to meet material or economic needs – to deal with specific problems of material survival. They can thus be immediately seen both as having direct connections with societal problems and as being appropriate to meeting certain basic or specific needs. If the technologies that will be created by a developing country in the modern world feature some of the characteristics of the traditional technologies, they will have greater relevance and impact on the social and economic life of the people.

The improvement of traditional technologies is contingent on at least two factors. One is the existence or availability of autonomous, indigenous technological capacities. These capacities would need to be considerably developed. The development of capacities in this connection is a matter not simply of acquiring skills or techniques but, perhaps more importantly, of understanding, and being able to apply, the relevant scientific principles. It might be assumed that the ability to acquire skills presupposes the appreciation of scientific principles; such an assumption, however, would be false. One could acquire skills without understanding the relevant underpinning scientific principles. The situation of the woman food technologist is a clear case in point. However, the lack of understanding of the relevant scientific principles will impede the improvement exercise itself.

The other factor relates to the need for change in certain cultural habits and attitudes on the part of artisans, technicians, and other practitioners of traditional technologies. Practitioners of traditional technologies will have to be weaned away from certain traditional attitudes and be prepared to learn and apply new or improved techniques and practices. Some old, traditional habits, such as the habit, referred to in section 3, of the automatic use of the senses in matters of precision measurements, will have to be abandoned; adaptation to new – and generally more effective – ways of practicing technology, such as resorting to technical aids in precision measurements, will need to be pursued. It is the cultivation of appropriate attitudes to improved – or modern – technology and the development of indigenous technological capacity that will provide the suitable cultural and intellectual receptacle for the modern technologies that may be transferred from the technologically advanced industrial countries of the world to a developing country.

Now, the transfer of technology from the technologically developed world is an outstanding approach to bringing sophisticated technology to a developing country. It could also be an important basis for developing, in time, an indigenous technological capacity and the generation of fairly advanced indigenous technologies. But all this will depend on how the whole complex matter of technology transfer is tackled. If the idea is not executed well enough, it may lead to complacency and passivity on the part of the recipients, reduce them to permanent technological dependency, and involve them in technological pursuits that may not immediately be appropriate to their objectives of social and economic development. On the other hand, an adroit approach to technology transfer by its recipients will be a sure basis for a real technological take-off for a developing country.

Transfer of technology involves taking techniques and practices developed in a technologically advanced country to a developing country. The assumption or anticipation is that the local people – that is, the technicians or technologists in the developing country – will be able to acquire the techniques transferred to them. Acquiring techniques theoretically means being able to learn, understand, analyze, and explain the whys and hows of those techniques, and thus, finally, being able to replicate and design the techniques locally. It is also anticipated that the local technologist, who is the beneficiary of the transferred technology, will be able not only to adapt the received technology to suit the needs and circumstances of the developing country, but also to build on it and, if the creative capacity is available, to use it as an inspiration to create new technologies appropriate to the development requirements and objectives of the developing country.

The assumptions and anticipations underlying the transfer of technology, of course, presuppose the existence, locally, of an autonomous technological capacity which can competently deal with – that is, disentangle – the intricacies of the transferred technology. In the event of the non-existence of an adequate indigenous technological capacity, the intentions in transferring technology will hardly be achieved. There is some kind of paradox here: autonomous, indigenous technological capacities are expected to be developed *through* dealing with transferred technologies (this is certainly the ultimate goal of technology transfer); yet, the ability to deal effectively with transferred technologies requires or presupposes the existence of indigenous technological capacities adequate for the purpose. However, the paradox can be resolved if we assume that indigenous technological capacities will exist, albeit of a minimum kind, which would, therefore, need to be nurtured, developed, and augmented to the level of sophistication required in operating a modern technology. The assumptions also presuppose that the transferred technology, developed in a specific cultural milieu different in a number of ways from that of a developing country, is easily adaptable to the social and cultural environment of the developing country. This presupposition may not be wholly true. However, despite the problems that may be said to be attendant to the transfer of technology, technology transfer is an important medium for generating a more efficient modern technology in a developing country.

Now, technology is, of course, developed within a culture; it is thus an aspect – a product – of culture. Technology transfer, then, is certainly an aspect of the whole phenomenon of cultural borrowing or appropriation which follows on the encounters between cultures. There appears, however, to be a difference between transfer of technology to a developing country and the normal appropriation by a culture of an alien cultural product. The difference arises because of the way the notion of technology transfer is conceived and executed. It can be admitted that what is anticipated in technology transfer is primarily *knowledge* of techniques, methods, and materials, all of which are relevant to matters of industrial production. But knowledge is acquired through the active participation of the recipient; it is not transferred on to a passive agent or receptacle. In the absence of adequate and extensive knowledge and understanding of the relevant scientific principles, the attitudes of the recipients of transferred technology will only be passive, not responsive in any significant way to the niceties of the new cultural products being introduced to them. In this circumstance, that which is transferred will most probably remain a thin veneer, hardly affecting their scientific or technological outlook and orientation. Machines and equipment can be transferred to passive recipients who may be able to use them for a while; but the acquisition of knowledge (or understanding) of techniques – which is what is basically involved in the proper meaning of technology – has to be prosecuted *actively*: that is, through the active exercise of the intellects of the recipients.

In an ideal situation of cultural borrowing, an element or product of the cultural tradition of one people is accepted and taken possession of by another people. The alien cultural product is not simply "transferred" to the recipients. Rather, goaded by their own appreciation of the significance of the product, they would seek it, acquire it, and appropriate it – that is, make it their own. This means that they would participate actively and purposefully in the acquisition of the product. To the extent, (1) that what is called technology transfer is, in its essentials, an aspect of the phenomenon of cultural borrowing, and (2) that the people to whom some technology is transferred are, thus, expected to understand and take possession of it through active and purposeful participation in its acquisition, "transfer of technology" is, in my view, a misnomer. For what is transferred may not be acquired, appropriated or assimilated.

For the same reasons, Ali Mazrui's biological metaphor of "technology transplant" will not do either. In Mazrui's view, "there has been a considerable amount of technology transfer to the Third World in the last thirty years – but very little technology transplant. Especially in Africa very little of what has been transferred has in fact been successfully transplanted."[21] To the extent, (1) that this biological or medical metaphor clearly involves passivity on the part of the recipient (i.e., the patient), who, thus, has no choice in actively deciding on the "quality" of the foreign body tissue to be sewn on to his own body, and (2) that there is no knowing whether the physical constitution of the recipient will accept or reject the new body tissue, the biological perception of acquiring the technological products of other cultures is very misleading. On a further ground, the biological metaphor will not do: the body on to which a foreign body tissue is to be transplanted is in a diseased condition which makes it impossible for it to react in a wholly positive manner to its new "addition" and to take advantage of it. Even if we assume, analogically, that the society that is badly in need of the technological products of other cultures is technologically or epistemically "diseased," the fact would still remain that, in the case of the human society, the members of the society would, guided by their needs, be in a position not only to decide on which technological products of foreign origin they would want to acquire, but also to participate actively and positively in the appropriation of those products.

Thus, neither technology transfer nor technology transplant is a fruitful way of perceiving – and pursuing – the acquisition of technology from other cultures; neither has been a real feature or method in the phenomenon of cultural borrowing. Our historical knowledge of how the results of cultural encounters occur seems to suggest the conviction that what is needed is not the transfer or transplant of technology, but the *appropriation* of technology – a perception or method which features the active, adroit, and purposeful initiative and participation of the recipients in the pursuit and acquisition of a technology of foreign production.

It must also be noted that, just as in cultural borrowing there are surely some principles or criteria that guide the borrowers in their selection of products from the alien (i.e., the encountered) culture, so, in the appropriation of technology some principles or criteria would need to be established to guide the choice of the products of technology created in one cultural environment for use in a different environment. Technology can transform human society in numerous ways. For this reason, the postcolonial developing country will have to consider technology rather as an instrument for the realization of *basic* human needs than as an end – as merely a way of demonstrating human power or ingenuity. The word "basic" is important here and is used advisedly: to point up the need for technology to be concerned fundamentally and essentially with such human needs as food, shelter, clothing, and health. The pursuit and satisfaction of these basic needs should guide the choice and appropriation of technology. Thus, what ought to be chosen is the technology that will be applied to industry, food and agriculture, water, health, housing, road and transportation, and other relevant activities that make ordinary life bearable. On this showing, military and space exploration technologies, for instance, may not be needed by the postcolonial state – certainly not in the early decades of its postcolonial existence. However, as that state comes to be increasingly shaped by technology, certain aspects of technology will become a specialized knowledge; it may *then* become necessary to create a leaven of experts to deal with the highly specialized aspects of those technologies.

The adaptability of technological products to local circumstances and objectives must be an important criterion in the appropriation and development of technology.

Finally, the fundamental, most cherished values of a culture will also constitute a criterion in the choice of technology. Technology, as I have said, can transform human society. This social transformation will involve changes not only in our ways and patterns of living, but also in our values. But human beings will have to decide whether the (new) values spewed out by technology are the kinds of values we need and would want to cherish. Technology emerges in, and is fashioned by, a culture; thus, right from the outset, technology is driven or directed by human purposes, values, and goals. And, if this historical relation between technology and values is maintained, what will be produced for us by technology will (have to) be consonant with those purposes, values, and goals. Technology was made by humanity, and not humanity for technology. This means that human beings and their welfare should be the center of the focus of the technological enterprise. Technology and humanism (i.e., concern for human welfare) are – and should not be – antithetical concepts; technology and industrialism should be able to coexist with the concern for the interests and welfare of the people in the technological society. So, it should be possible for the postcolonial African people to embark on the "technologicalization" of their society without losing the humanist essence of their culture. The value of concern for human well-being is a fundamental, intrinsic, and self-justifying value which should be cordoned off against any technological subversion of it.

In this connection, let me refer to the views expressed by Kenneth Kaunda in the following quote:

> I am deeply concerned that this high valuation of Man and respect for human dignity which is a legacy of our [African] tradition should not be lost in the new Africa. However "modern" and "advanced" in a Western sense the new nations of Africa may become, we are fiercely determined that this humanism will not be obscured. African society has always been Man-centred. We intend that it will remain so.[22]

I support the view that the humanist essence of African culture – an essence that is basically moral[23] – ought to be maintained and cherished in the attempt to create a postcolonial modernity in Africa. It must be realized that technology alone cannot solve all the deep-rooted social problems such as poverty, exploitation, economic inequalities, and oppression in human societies *unless* it is underpinned and guided by some basic moral values; in the absence of the strict application of those values, technology can in fact create other problems, including environmental problems. Social transformation, which is an outstanding goal of the comprehensive use of technology, cannot be achieved unless technology moves along under the aegis of basic human values.

Technology is a human value, of course. And because it is basic to the fulfillment of the material welfare of human beings, there is a tendency to privilege it over other human values. But to do so would be a mistake. The reason is that technology is obviously an instrumental value, not an intrinsic value to be pursued for its own sake. As an instrument in the whole quest for human fulfillment, its use ought to be guided by other – perhaps intrinsic and ultimate – human values, in order to realize its maximum relevance to humanity.

In considering technology's aim of fulfilling the material needs of humans, the pursuit of the humanist and social ethic of the traditional African society can be of considerable relevance because of the impact this ethic can have on the distributive patterns in respect of the economic goods that will result from the application of technology. In this way, extensive and genuine social – and, in the sequel, political – transformation of postcolonial African society can be ensured, and the maximum impact of technology on society achieved.

Notes

1 Kwame Gyekye, *An Essay on African Philosophical Thought* (Cambridge University Press, New York, 1987; revised edn, Temple University Press, Philadelphia, PA 1995), pp. 16–18 and 106–7.

2 It is instructive to note that the word for "knowledge" in Ewe, a prominent language in Ghana, is *nunya*, a word which actually means "thing observed." This clearly means that observation or experience was regarded as the source of knowledge in Ewe thought: see N.K. Dzobo, "Knowledge and truth: Ewe and Akan conceptions," in Kwasi Wiredu and Kwame Gyekye (eds.), *Person and Community: Ghanaian Philosophical Studies* (Council for Research in Values and Philosophy, Washington, DC, 1992), pp. 74ff. The empirical character of African thought generally can most probably not be doubted.

3 John S. Mbiti, *African Religions and Philosophy* (Doubleday, New York, 1970), p. 1.

4 Ibid., p. 38.

5 K.A. Busia, *Africa in Search of Democracy* (Praeger, New York, 1967), p. 1.

6 Ibid., p. 7.

7 G. Parrinder, *African Traditional Religion* (Harper and Row, New York 1962), p. 9.

8 Mbiti, *African Religions and Philosophy*, p. 74.

9 The Akan version is: *wo feefee efun n'aniwa ase a, wohu saman.*

10 E. Laing, *Science and Society in Ghana*, The J.B. Danquah Memorial Lectures (Ghana Academy of Arts and Sciences, 1990), p. 21.

11 Ibid.

12 Kofi Asare Opoku of the Institute of African Studies, University of Ghana, Legon.

13 Robert W. July, for example, says: "Art for art's sake had no place in traditional African society" and that it was "essentially functional." See his *An African Voice: The Role of the Humanities in African Independence* (Duke University Press, Durham, NC, 1987), p. 49; also Claude Wauthier, *The Literature and Thought of Modern Africa* (Heinemann, London, 1978), pp. 173–4.

14 Lynn White, *Medieval Religion and Technology: Collected Essays* (University of California Press, Berkeley, CA, 1978), p. 127.

15 Lord Todd, *Problems of the Technological Society*, The Aggrey–Fraser–Guggisberg Memorial Lectures (published for the University of Ghana by the Ghana Publishing Corporation, Accra, 1973), p. 8.

16   Arnold Pacey, *The Culture of Technology* (Blackwell, Oxford, 1983), p. 145.
17   Kwasi Wiredu, *Philosophy and an African Culture* (Cambridge University Press, Cambridge, 1980), p. 15.
18   S. Sefa-Dede, "Traditional food technology", in R. Macrae, R. Robinson and M. Sadler *Encyclopedia of Food Science, Food Technology and Nutrition* (Academy Press, New York, 1993), p. 4600.
19   Ibid. See also S. Sefa-Dede, "Harnessing food technology for development", in S. Sefa-Dede and R. Orraca-Tetteh (eds), *Harnessing Traditional Food Technology for Development* (Department of Nutrition and Food Science, University of Ghana, Legon, 1989); Esi Colecraft, "Traditional food preservation: an overview", *African Technology Forum*, vol. 6, no. 1, Feb./March, 1993, pp. 15–17.
20   The encounter was between this traditional woman food technologist and research scientists and students from the Department of Nutrition and Food Science of the University of Ghana, headed by Professor S. Sefa-Dede. The account of the encounter presented here was given to me by Sefa-Dede both orally and in writing, and I am greatly indebted to him.
21   Ali A. Mazrui, "Africa between ideology and technology: two frustrated forces of change", in Gwendolen M. Carter and Patrick O'Meara (eds.), *African Independence: The First Twenty-Five Years* (Indiana University Press, Bloomington, IN, 1985), pp. 281–2.
22   Kenneth Kaunda, *A Humanist in Africa* (Longman, London, 1966), p. 28.
23   Gyekye, *Essay on African Philosophical Thought*, pp. 143–6.

2

Is Modern Science an Ethnoscience? Rethinking Epistemological Assumptions*

Sandra Harding

1 Science as Practice and Culture vs Internalist Epistemologies

A central focus of recent work in the social and cultural studies of science and technology (SCSST, for short) has been to show how modern sciences have been constituted by their practices and cultures, not just externally enabled by them in ways that leave no marks on their cognitive cores.[1] They are local knowledge systems or, in other words, "ethnosciences." Most of these authors have insisted on abandoning claims to universality, objectivity, and rationality for modern sciences, since such claims are themselves only socially established. Or, to put the point another way, since the perception of scientific claims as universal, objective, and rational is itself locally constructed, not an internal, transcultural feature of any truly scientific process, any appeal to such notions should carry no more authority than the claims can command on other grounds.

Their epistemological (rather, they would say, anti-epistemological) position

* This chapter was developed from a theme in my paper, "Is science multicultural? Challenges, resources, opportunities, uncertainties," *Configurations*, vol. 2, no. 2; reprinted in David Theo Goldberg (ed.), *Multiculturalism: A Reader* (Blackwell, London, 1994). It was written originally for the April 1993 UCLA conference on "Located Knowledges: Intersections between Cultural, Gender and Science Studies." For helpful comments on various versions I thank Donna Haraway and the participants in the UCLA conference. The chapter also appears in Spaapen and Shinn (eds.) *Sociology Yearbook* (Kluwer, 1996).

thus coincides with a main tendency in the comparative studies of modern sciences and other cultures' ethnosciences that originated primarily in anthropology in the 1960s.[2] This ethnoscience discourse called for treating all cognitive systems on a par as belief systems, thereby refusing to recognize the usual epistemological distinctions between real knowledge and mere local belief. These studies did not deny that some belief systems were able to achieve more powerful effects than others, of course. Instead they denied only that any causes of such successes were to be found in the "internal" epistemological features of modern scientific processes – their inherent rationality, unique logic of justification, universal language, objectivity-achieving method, etc. Thus both schools of recent science studies have sought some other way than appealing to the standard epistemological notions to explain why some scientific practices "work" far from the sites of their original development and others do not. I shall refer to the rejected epistemological stance of these two schools as "internalist epistemology," since it holds that the epistemological status of scientific claims is a function of science's transcultural, internal processes – plus, of course, "the way nature is."[3]

For many science theorists, scientists, science policy analysts, and other science-observers from both the North and the South, these two kinds of science studies and the conclusions at which they arrive appear to have "gone too far." The constructivism in these approaches, their apparent leveling of the epistemological statuses of knowledge claims – especially, their abandonment of the notions of the universality, objectivity, and rationality of European sciences – all these are anathema to them for reasons located on both the "right" and the "left." However, there is yet a third set of tendencies in contemporary science studies which include a focus on science policy and, one might say, science studies policy, and which choose not to abandon the epistemological notions, in contrast to main-stream Northern SCSST and the comparative ethnosciences studies. Rather, they want to strengthen them and make them more effective at identifying patterns of historically determinate components of sciences. Adherents to such new epistemological tendencies are feminist science studies in the North, and what I shall refer to as "Southern" SCSST, ones coming from the postcolonial, single-stream histories that I shall shortly describe, including certain kinds of critique of science and technology transfer to the South in the name of "development." Southern SCSST have a central focus on developing fully modern sciences that, in contrast to the European ones currently being imported through Northern-controlled "development" policy, take root in the cultural traditions and social needs of the great majority of the peoples of the South (and, therefore, of the world), who are the most economically, politically, and socially vulnerable.[4]

One might think that this recentering of epistemological concerns would cheer up adherents of the older epistemological traditions. However, it has not and will not because the feminist and postcolonial studies to which I refer reject the internalist status of epistemology – a position that the older histories, philosophies, epistemologies, and sociologies of science will not countenance. These new epistemological tendencies fully recognize the validity of the arguments about the cultural situatedness of modern sciences; indeed, these scholars are contributors to them. However, they think that, for scientific and political reasons – and, for them, the knowledge and power that sciences generate are inseparable – their own science and science studies projects need to develop a more robust epistemological stance than the SCSST and comparative ethnoscience schools have been willing to legitimate. Thus their strategy has been to appropriate and strengthen some of the central meanings and practices of the older epistemologies, rejecting the internalist features that sustained the distorting contrast between modern European sciences and "only" ethnosciences. What they do is try to identify and explain at least some broad patterns of some social, economic, political conditions that advance the growth of knowledge and those that retard it. Thus they advocate the arguments about the cultural situatedness of modern sciences, but take them to provide good reasons to reject the internalist features of the epistemological notions, not the notions themselves.[5] Such a knowledge-project does not stand "above" any others, but neither does it stand "beneath" them.

These feminist and Southern SCSST tendencies are almost invariably "misread" by both the SCSST and comparative ethnosciences schools as simply ignorant and unappreciative of the criticisms of internalist epistemology. One reason for this "misreading" could be that the Northern SCSST and comparative ethnoscience scholars are so preoccupied with rejecting the older, still widely persuasive (even in some contemporary science studies) internalist epistemological stance that they overlook the possibilities of appropriating some of the epistemological concepts for other kinds of anti-internalist project. Their preoccupations with combatting the legacy of positivism blinds them to such new epistemological possibilities. It could be that they have not yet reflected on the political, epistemological, and scientific needs expressed in such appropriative projects – needs visible in the Southern SCSST and Northern feminist science studies with which they are largely unfamiliar. It could be that, for some, history having made illegitimate the familiar Eurocentric epistemologies, they are unwilling to countenance epistemological standards that might at some point turn out to favor the scientific cultures and practices of non-European cultures. Whatever the reasons, my task here is to try to make more attractive the possibility that there still can be desirable epistemological standards after the demise of Eurocentric, internalist ones. This essay does so by reflecting on some of the distinctive ways that European sciences appear to be local knowledge systems from the perspective of Southern SCSST, on the local character of all schools of science studies, too, and on the more robust epistemological needs that Southern SCSST generate.[6]

In pursuing and supporting this argument, I must provide an overview of a broad intellectual landscape that is not yet familiar to many readers (though it may be overly familiar to some). This situation presents me with an insurmountable problem, for the plausibility of my argument requires both extended exploration of the challenging philosophical and epistemological problems that it raises, and a report of the range and wealth of empirical examples that would fill in its outlines. Moreover, such explorations and reports must respond to the diversity of interests and discursive frameworks that readers bring to this essay. These problems are both much more than this short essay can fully resolve. The empirical examples are already available; however, they appear in writings that are dispersed in several science studies areas that mostly do not communicate with each other, and that will thus be at least in some part unfamiliar to many readers. Postcolonial, "single-stream" global science and technology histories, histories of the mutual resources exchanged between European expansion and the growth of modern sciences in Europe, "development" studies, mainstream postpositivist Anglo-American philosophies of science, feminist approaches to science and epistemology, comparative ethnoscience traditions, and the last thirty years of Northern SCSST are some of the fields in which evidence for my argument can be found. Given the space constraints here, I can only gesture toward these studies by citing examples that do not require extended development, and sketch out possible ways to deal effectively with the philosophical issues that, I argue, these literatures raise. The analysis that follows can only leave many questions in readers' minds. However, my justification for continuing this chapter in the face of such difficulties is the hope that what must be lost for lack of detail and more extended argument can be compensated by the gain of a kind of map in which diverse science studies approaches can be seen each to contribute distinctive resources to more accurate and comprehensive understandings of relations between natural knowledge and social power. It is precisely the lack of such a map, I suggest, that has left obscure important relations between histories of sciences and of cultures.

Two more caveats must be made at the outset. They both address inevitable challenges of postcolonial discourses these days.

2 Controversial Postcolonial Discursive Frameworks

First, the terms of any discussion of global science relations are and must be controversial, for who gets to name natural and social realities gets to control how they will be organized and managed. Postcolonial discourses are still young, older terms familiar to most of us carry unwanted Eurocentric meanings and referents; many different groups with partially conflicting interests are all part of such discourses.[7] We might do best to think of the term "postcolonial" as naming a discursive space where new kinds of analysis and dialogue can occur, as David Hess puts the point.[8]

Of course, the ways I, like the comparative ethnoscience and Southern

SCSST analysts, use the terms "science" and "ethnoscience" are at odds with their uses in the conventional discourses. Moreover, the inclusion of empirical knowledge traditions of other cultures under the label "science" reinstates the superiority of a European conceptual framework: the European term names the standard, I may appear to be arguing, that any desirable knowledge tradition must achieve.[9] As is always the case, the hegemonic Eurocentric discourses block easy exit from their conceptual frameworks. "Modern science" reinscribes the Eurocentric dichotomy between the dynamic, progressive sciences of the North and the static, historically unchanging traditional knowledge of other cultures. Only the North carries forward the trajectory of human history, for the cultures of the South have only static, unchanging tradition, this contrast implies. Moreover, "Western science" replicates the dualistic, "orientalist" thinking that I want to avoid, and "European science" misstates this tradition's multicultural origins and current participants.[10] There is no "solution" to such problems, since what is missing is not a set of correct terms, but a widely shared postcolonial discourse or episteme to connect them in uncontroversial ways. I shall here settle for the recently appearing (though still problematically dualistic) language of "North" and "South."

Of course, we still must ask: which of the diverse peoples living in Europe and North America get to count as Northern/Western? And is Japan Southern and Third World? (Of course, "Third World" is an artifact of the Cold War.) Moreover, the cultures of the developing world are diverse; and they are internally heterogeneous by class, gender, ethnicity, religion, politics, and other features. This important complexity is sometimes lost from view in attempts to gain a more comprehensive picture. Another reality easy to lose in all of this familiar dichotomizing language is that there are powerful "Norths" in the South and increasingly large areas of "the South" in the North. Does ignoring all these complexities not further disseminate characteristic Eurocentric and imperialist attitudes toward the West's Other? And "development" has been criticized as a term that hides the history and present practices of more than three decades of dedevelopment of the vast majority of the citizens of the South (and many in the North) in order further to benefit already advantaged Northerners and their allies in the South. Moreover, does "neocolonial" not designate better than "postcolonial" the present relationship between the West and its former colonies and other diverse kinds of dependency? Finally, how can we avoid all these problems and yet retain a clear focus on the uneven distribution of power through the global political economy within which Northern sciences and technologies play such a central role?

A second problem to solve is the following. I do not intend anything said here to support the claim that people from Southern cultures should pursue the kinds of newly universally valid ethnoscience identified below, leaving the now newly localized, but no less powerful sciences of the North for the Northerners. A long history of European preoccupation with the exotic "difference" of non-

European cultures has remained fully embedded in contemporary Eurocentric global politics. This history makes crucial the task of trying to separate my project here from those. It is indeed necessary that the current South to North flow of resources be ended. The South to North braindrain, and movement of natural resources, labor, goods, and profit, is well documented in recent development criticisms and in the postcolonial studies of European expansion from the "Voyages of Discovery" through the current policies of Northern-controlled development agencies. Changing conceptual frameworks cannot in itself bring about political change. But if the conceptual shifts to which I point are plausible and valuable for understanding the current cultures and practices of diverse empirical knowledge traditions, they will "rationalize" and thus make attractive a much more multidirectional circulation of peoples and political and cultural resources than is likely under the continued Northern expansion that is rationalized, in part, by wholesale acceptance of the internalist epistemology, and possibly, I shall argue, also by its wholesale rejection.

My procedure in what follows will be, first, to clear the ground for the ensuing analysis by identifying briefly major themes in the last three decades of Northern SCSST that show how no science could in principle be free of local social and cultural fingerprints, and then to identify several of the distinctively European elements in modern sciences that have been repeatedly noted in the Southern SCSST. The concluding sections identify some useful ways to classify why it is that local features can indeed be resources for the growth of knowledge, and reflect on the more robust epistemological needs that arise from the standpoint of the Southern SCSST.

3 Postpositivist Northern SCSST: All Sciences are Local Knowledge Systems

By the end of the 1960s, even mainstream US philosophy of science, still far from successful at shedding its positivist framework, nevertheless had come to recognize that scientific claims could not in principle provide a glassy mirror of a reality that is out there and ready made for such reflecting. Observations are inextricably theory laden. Moreover, our beliefs form a network such that none is in principle immune from revision. If scientists could come up with no more satisfying ways to bring their theories and observations into better fit with each other, then even the laws of logic could come to be reasonable candidates for revision, as W. V. O. Quine argued in pointing to the untenability of the analytic/synthetic distinction. Consequently, scientific theories are underdetermined not just by any collection of existing evidence for them, but by any possible collection of evidence.[11] Subsequently, philosophers, sociologists, ethnographers, historians, and other science theorists showed in great detail how scientific processes are not transparent; their culturally regional features contribute to and sometimes even constitute the conceptual frameworks for our descriptions and explanations of nature's order. They have clearly advanced the growth of scientific knowledge.

One consequence of these critical reflections on the Enlightenment vision is the understanding that more than one scientific theory or model can be consistent with any given set of data, and that each such theoretical representation can have more than one reasonable interpretation. More startling is the emerging understanding that this looseness or slack in scientific explanation, far from being the unmitigated defect that it appears in older philosophies of science, turns out to be a major source of the growth of scientific knowledge. It is this feature that permits scientists to "see nature" in ever new ways that advance the increased accuracy and comprehensiveness of their claims.[12]

However, most of this SCSST has focussed on the "high sciences" of the modern North – on physics, chemistry, and the more abstract areas of biology. This is an exciting and important area for SCSST's focus, since if even those sciences can be shown to be socially constituted, one hardly needs to worry about the plausibility of such arguments for sciences more generally recognized to have been shaped by their social histories – environmental sciences, population genetics, other areas of biology, and, of course, social sciences. Nevertheless, a down-side of such a focus is that these Northern SCSST authors have only rarely even glimpsed the possibility that the many competing scientific theories that their studies imply could include ones from other cultural traditions. Nor are they led to think that Northern "high science" studies have anything to learn from studies such as the Southern SCSST, of which they are largely unaware, but which do focus on such traditions.[13] Thus they leave intact the "modern science vs ethnoscience" construct, the unbalanced valuing of modern vs other scientific traditions that it legitimates, ignorance about ways in which the histories and destinies of Northern and other scientific traditions are linked, and a set of puzzling philosophical positions. So it will be worthwhile to see what can be learned by focussing on the Southern SCSST analyses of Northern science and science studies projects.

4 Southern SCSST: Modern Sciences are European Ethnosciences

Southern SCSST point out many ways in which modern science in Europe is distinctively European science, not transculturally "human" science. Of course, all of the local features marked by the Northern SCSST – those characteristic of French, or Protestant, or social Darwinist presuppositions, or of only locally used technologies and methods of research, etc. – are also distinctively European, since they are local to some European subculture. However, other features are visible only or more easily from the standpoint of people's lives in the South. This is because the "culture" of such features is or was so widely shared across diverse European subcultures that it was virtually invisible to Europeans. Taking a standpoint "outside" European culture enables the identification of aspects of the conceptual frameworks, paradigms, and epistemes of European sciences and technologies not so easily detected from "inside" European culture. We can sample a few of the striking European "ethnoscience" features that appear in such analyses.

4.1 Christian laws of nature

Let us begin with an argument by Joseph Needham, who could be regarded as one of the early contributors to Southern SCSST. He pointed out that the European conception of laws of nature drew on both Judeo-Christian religious beliefs and the increasing familiarity in early modern Europe with centralized royal authority, with royal absolutism. The idea that the universe was a "great empire, ruled by a divine Logos"[14] was never comprehensible at any time within the long and culturally varying history of Chinese science that was the object of his studies. A common thread in the diverse Chinese traditions was that nature is self-governed, a web of relationships without a weaver, in which humans intervened at their own peril.

> Universal harmony comes about not by the celestial fiat of some King of Kings, but by the spontaneous co-operation of all beings in the universe brought about by their following the internal necessities of their own natures . . . all entities at all levels behave in accordance with their position in the greater patterns (organisms) of which they are parts.[15]

Compared to Renaissance science, the Chinese conception of nature was problematic, blocking interest in discovering "precisely formulated abstract laws ordained from the beginning by a celestial lawgiver for non-human nature."

> There was no confidence that the code of Nature's laws could be unveiled and read, because there was no assurance that a divine being, even more rational than ourselves, had ever formulated such a code capable of being read.[16]

Of course, such notions of "command and duty in the 'Laws' of Nature" have disappeared from modern science, replaced by the notion of statistical regularities that describe rather than prescribe nature's order – in a sense, a return, Needham comments, to the Taoist perspective.[17] And yet other residues of the earlier conception remain in Western sciences. For example, Evelyn Fox Keller has pointed to the regressive politics of the language of "laws," and to the positive political implications of conceptualizing nature simply as ordered rather than as law-governed.

[L]aws of nature, like laws of the state, are historically imposed from above and obeyed from below ... The concept of order, wider than law and free from its coercive, hierarchical, and centralizing implications has the potential to expand our conception of science. Order is a category comprising patterns of organization that can be spontaneous, self-generated, *or* externally imposed.[18]

European sciences advanced because of the constitution of their projects through these Christian and absolute monarchical assumptions, values, and interests. However, as Needham pointed out, the very same Christian culture retarded European astronomy relative to that of the Chinese, for the latter was not burdened with the Christian notion that the heavens consisted of crystal spheres. Thus Christian values advanced modern sciences in some respects and retarded it in others.

4.2 European expansion: creating patterns of knowledge and ignorance

One of the several main concerns of Southern SCSST is to chart the mutually powerful effects that European expansion had on the advance of modern science in Europe, and vice versa. As one historian of French colonial science in the Caribbean puts the point:

The rise of modern science and the colonial expansion of Europe after 1492 constitute two fundamental and characteristic features of modern world history. The story [of the relation between these two features] is a dual one. One of its aspects concerns how science and scientific enterprise formed part of and facilitated colonial development. The other deals with how the colonial experience affected science and the contemporary scientific enterprise.[19]

Here we shall pursue, though only briefly, the second part of this story.

Two features of the flowering of postcolonial, single-stream history conflict with the histories of science most of us learned. These accounts tell the history of Europeans as part of the history of the peoples of the Americas, Africa, Asia, and the rest of the world, and vice versa. Moreover, these accounts do not restrict their perspective to the way such histories tend to appear from the dominant European discourses. They start off their accounts from the lives of the peoples whom Europeans encountered, and from their histories prior to the arrival of the Europeans on their shores. In doing so they are able to provide more balanced, less Eurocentric accounts of the encounters and interminglings of peoples throughout human history. From the beginnings of recorded history, they report, cultures have been interacting with each other and exchanging shells, beads, women, cattle, and scientific and technological information and ideas.

One distinctively Northern feature of modern sciences that becomes visible from the perspective of this kind of account is the selection of modern sciences' problematics. Just which aspects of nature European sciences describe and explain, and how they are described and explained, have been selected in part by the purposes of European expansion. Of course, these are not the only purposes shaping these sciences, but they are significant ones. The problems that have come to count as scientific ones in the modern North are disproportionately ones that expansionist Europe needed solved. One historian points out that, during the British occupation of India, in effect "India was added as a laboratory to the edifice of modern science."[20] We can generalize the point; the world was added as a laboratory to modern science in Europe through European expansion, and continues to so function today through the science and technology components of "development" that are controlled by the cultures of the North. It is not that everything done by these cultures is done for exploitative reasons or has such effects in the South. Rather, the claim is that the projects that Northerners are willing to sponsor and contribute to funding tend to be only those conceptualized by those in the North who get to participate in making "development" policy and their allies elsewhere. The majority of peoples who bear the consequences of the science and technology decisions made through such processes do not have a proportionate share in making them – to adapt John Dewey's formulation of a fundamental democratic ethic to the world of sciences and technologies. For example, with respect to European expansion, the picture of nature produced by solving the expansionist North's problems ignores or hides those aspects of nature that are assumed to be irrelevant to success at expansion. Thus culturally distinctive patterns of both systematic knowledge and systematic ignorance are easily detected from the perspective of cultures with different purposes.

For example, modern science answered questions about how to improve European land and sea travel, mine newly needed ores, identify the economically useful minerals, plants, and animals of other parts of the world, manufacture and farm for the benefit of Europeans living in Europe, the Americas, Africa, and India, improve their health and occasionally that of the workers who produced profit for them, protect settlers in the colonies from settlers of other nationalities, gain access to the labor of the indigenous residents, and do all this to benefit only local European citizens – for instance, the Spanish vs the Portuguese, French, or British. But they have not been concerned to explain how the consequences of interventions in nature for the benefit of Europeans would change the natural resources available to non-Westerners, or what the other social, psychic, environmental, economic, and political costs of such interventions might be. They have not been concerned to explain how to eradicate diseases that do not much affect peoples of European descent, and, especially, the already advantaged within this group, or how to use effectively renewable energy sources. Even physics, supposedly the most value-neutral of sciences, is far more shaped by its pursuit of militarily useful knowledge than is generally recognized.[21]

Thus, the distinctive patterns of knowledge and ignorance characteristic of modern sciences are in significant part products of both the needs of and resources provided by European expansion. The cognitive successes of modern sciences are importantly due to, and in their representations of nature bear the distinctive historical marks of, European expansion. This five-century pattern remains visible today.

4.3 Northern distribution and accounting practices

Third, modern sciences' distribution and accounting practices – the ways Northerners distribute and then account for the consequences of modern sciences – appear distinctively European or Northern. The accounting practices mask the actual distribution of sciences' benefits and costs. The benefits of modern scientific and technological change are disproportionately distributed to élites in the North and their allies in the South, and the costs disproportionately to everyone else. Whether it is sciences intended to improve the military, agriculture, manufacturing, health, or even the environment, the expanded opportunities that sciences make possible have been distributed predominantly to already privileged people of European descent, and the costs to the already poorest, racial and ethnic minorities, women, and Third World peoples.

The causes of this distribution are not mysterious or unforeseen. For one thing, the SCSST point out that it is not "man" whom sciences enable to make better use of nature's resources, but only those already advantageously positioned in social hierarchies. It is such groups that already own and control both nature – in the form of land with its forests, water, plants, animals, and minerals – and the means to extract and process such resources. Moreover, these people are the ones who are in a position to decide "what to produce, how to produce it, what resources to use up to produce, and what technology to use."

> We thus have this spectacle, on the one hand, of the powerful development of technological capacity, so that the basic and human needs of every human being could be met if there were an appropriate arrangement of social and production systems; and, on the other hand, of more than half the world's population (and something like two-thirds the Third World's people) living in conditions where their basic and human needs are not met.[22]

Such critics thus confirm how the opportunity to construct the most powerful representations of nature – to turn knowledge into power through science – is available only to already-advantaged groups.

However, they go on to point out that it is through science's accounting practices that this distribution is kept invisible to most of those who benefit from modern sciences and to many who do not. All consequences of sciences and technologies that are not planned or intended are externalized as "not science."[23] Thus military applications of sciences, or environmentally destructive consequences of sciences, their applications and technologies, can be excluded from what counts as science. Such an accounting need not even be intended; critics argue that such an "internalization of profits and externalization of costs is the normal consequence when nature is treated as if its individual components were isolated and unrelated."[24] Thus they argue that, at their cognitive core, modern European sciences are constituted in ways that have distinctive political dimensions and consequences.

4.4 *Value neutrality is not value-neutral*

A fourth distinctively European component of the cognitive core of modern science to which the Southern SCSST point is the claim to, and valuing of, cultural neutrality. Even if it were the case, impossible though it be, that modern sciences bore no such cultural fingerprints as the kinds marked above, their value neutrality would itself mark them as distinctively European. Of course, this is paradoxical: "if it's value-free, then it's not value-free." The point is that trying to maximize cultural neutrality, as well as claiming it, expresses a culturally specific value. Most cultures do not value neutrality; they value their own Confucian, or Indigenous American, or Islamic, or Maori, or, for that matter, Judaic or Christian values. So one that does is easily identifiable. Moreover, the claim to neutrality is characteristic of the administrators of modern cultures that are organized by principles of scientific rationality, as feminist and other analysts have argued.[25] Abstractness and formality express distinctive cultural features, not the absence of all culture. Thus when modern science is introduced into other cultures, it is experienced as a rude and brutal *cultural* intrusion because of this feature, too, say the Southern SCSST analysts. Claims for modern sciences' (value-neutral, internally achieved) universality and objectivity are "a politics of disvaluing local concerns and knowledge and legitimating 'outside experts.'"[26]

Much more could and should be said about the distinctive European enculturation of modern sciences. It will be useful here, however, to step back and reflect on some of the issues such accounts raise.

5 What Makes the Local a Resource for the Growth of Science?

Such Southern SCSST join Northern and feminist accounts in identifying distinctively local characteristics of modern sciences, some of which have advanced and others that have retarded the growth of knowledge. Are there any guidelines to be drawn from such studies as to which social and cultural features can advance the growth of knowledge and which do not? This question may sound like the old "rational reconstruction" projects of the internalist epistemologies to which all of these recent SCSST schools object. However, here we are interested not in "internal," cognitive features of science that transcend cultural differences, but in cultural features that become internalized in sciences' cognitive cores.

No doubt there are many illuminating ways to organize answers to this question.[27] Here is one that has the advantage of drawing on familiar resources of established science studies disciplines. First of all, geography and biology report how cultures are distributed through nature's diverse configurations, and how nature's configurations (diseases, genetic traits) are distributed through cultures. Cultures develop biological traits to deal with their environments: lungs to accommodate high-altitude conditions, inherited resistances to malaria, dark or light skins to deal with the effects of differing exposures to the sun, etc. People tend to be interested in their immediate surroundings and conditions – in what possibilities for food, shelter, medicine, disease, or other threats to life one finds in, over, or under oceans, deserts, rain forests, sub-Arctic environments, etc. Of course, cultures are not restricted to just one spot on the globe: Portugal-to-China or Cape Canaveral-to-the-moon also name culturally distinctive "natural" environments. Nor are cultures only these kinds of traditional objects of ethnographic examination; new cultures are continuously at the interstices of older cultures, through diasporas, the Internet, and many other ways. These "cultural differences" create possibilities for different cultures all to contribute to the expansion of knowledge about the natural world. The claim here is not that belief based on some set of local interactions is always more accurate; very often it is not. The fact that knowledge is local is no guarantee that it is the most accurate. Rather the claim is that cultures' different locations in heterogeneous nature expose them to different regularities of nature, and that exposure to such local environments is a valuable resource for advancing collective human knowledge. Cultures are repositories for historically developed and continually refined knowledge about different parts of nature.

Second, different cultures have different interests and desires even when they are more or less "in the same environment." Bordering the Atlantic Ocean, one culture will be interested to fish it, another to use it as a coastal highway for trading, a third to use it for emigration, a fourth to desalinize it for drinking water, a fifth to use it as a refuse dump, a sixth to use it as an underwater military highway for submarines and torpedoes, and a seventh to mine the minerals, gasses, and oil beneath its floor. Such distinctive interests have created culturally distinctive patterns of knowledge about this particular part of nature's regularities and their underlying causal tendencies.

Third, cultures approach or "see" local environments and their interests in them through distinctive discursive traditions; how the environments and interests appear to them – and that they appear at all – is in part due to their characteristic metaphors, models, and narratives of nature and social relations. As the Needham example suggests, Christianity and Confucianism enabled in some ways, and made invisible in other ways, possibilities for representing and interacting with the natural world.

Last, the cognitive content of sciences is shaped by culturally distinctive forms of social organization and, especially, of work. Scientific research is social labor, carried out in culturally distinctive kinds of organization – laboratories located in industries, universities, physicians' offices, federal institutes, computer-connected collections of such sites, field stations, farms, collecting and observing expeditions, conferences, learned societies, journals, hospitals, routine visits to healers with diverse credentials, etc. Different projects use different technologies and research methods. This is a heterogeneous category containing all of the culturally differing elements of organizing scientific activities. The "Voyages of Discovery" were one such social organization of scientific work. The Northern and Southern SCSST are full of historical and ethnographic studies of how other such forms of doing science have created distinctive patterns of scientific knowledge and ignorance.

Thus the local provides different kinds of continuously renewed resources for understanding nature. Cultures' interests, discursive resources, and ways of organizing the production of knowledge are not static and fixed, but continually changing as cultures transform themselves and are transformed by their interactions with each other and with nature. But neither is nature fixed and unchanging; species disappear, mutations appear, other configurations pass away and come into existence. Nature evolved, and there is no reason to think such evolution has ended. Thus there is no end to the resources that the local can contribute to human knowledge.

In the preceding discussion, I have been using the language of "social and cultural" features, though, of course, political and economic relations are always a central part of the social and cultural features of any society. Such political and economic relations are always a starting point of the Southern and feminist SCSST, often of the comparative ethnoscience approaches, but only sometimes of the Northern SCSST.[28] Thus the distribution of cultures and subcultures through natural environments, of natural conditions through populations, the interests of a culture and of its subgroups, their access and relation to discursive traditions, and their ways of organizing scientific work – all of these are always shaped by political and economic as well as other social and cultural relations.

Reflecting on such culturally distinctive resources enables us to begin to envision some possibilities for epistemological standards other than the kinds of internalist ones to which the various schools of SCSST have rightly objected.

6 "Strong Objectivity," Inclusive Rationality, and Universally Valid but Local Knowledge Claims

6.1 Objectivity and rationality

Southern SCSST's relocation of science and technology studies on to the historical maps generated by the postcolonial, single-stream global histories is clearly intended to provide not just another, culturally local account on an epistemological par with Eurocentric, single-stream histories of science and technology, but, instead, an account that is more objective and rational. However, to claim such an epistemological status does not require denial of the fact that Southern SCSST are constituted by their local cultures and practices. Instead, such a claim recognizes that at some moments in history and culture, certain locally generated cultures and practices can provide knowledge of interest far beyond the locations where it was generated. It is not just that such "local knowledge" travels well and far, but that it travels in a determinate historical relationship to other knowledge claims: it overtly contests them, claiming that they lack maximal accuracy and comprehensiveness. It claims greater objectivity, in that it can identify distorting or limiting features of the claim it contests.[29]

It is the feminist science theory and epistemology that has most directly and extensively articulated just how the older epistemological appeals can be appropriated and their standards strengthened for such projects. Feminist accounts, like the Southern SCSST, have not had the luxury of abandoning appeal to such notions as objectivity and rationality on the grounds that they were only socially constructed. Instead, such accounts had to socially negotiate their own status as objective and rational as a condition of even coming into existence. The status of feminist projects in the social and natural sciences was continually challenged – deprived of funding, refused publication, feminist researchers not hired, etc. – on the grounds that it was "only politics" and therefore not maximally objective or rational. Questions of the adequacy of the empirical evidence for the feminist claims have frequently been ignored and avoided entirely by the judgment that such a kind of evidence could not possibly be adequate, since it was by definition lacking prerequisites for objectivity and rationality – namely, the value neutrality that only men and/or non-feminists could bring to research. Thus the luxury of simply abandoning appeals to objectivity and rationality was never available to these researchers. Feminists had to work out how analyses that could identify sexist and androcentric presuppositions were more objective, more rational, than work that lacked such ability. They had to show how identifying and removing gender presuppositions advanced the growth of knowledge. However, those who had learned from and contributed to the Northern SCSST had to do so without claiming that feminist claims were thereby transculturally valid.

Thus, feminist standpoint theory, to take one example of such a postpositivist, anti-internalist, socially located epistemology, showed how starting off research from the perspective of women's lives enabled the identification of the "conceptual practices of power," as sociologist Dorothy Smith[30] put the point. The conceptual frameworks for sociology, or philosophy, or the law, or standard interpretations of evolutionary theory that were simply assumed by the conceptual frameworks of the disciplines as natural, or transcultural, became visible as historically determinate from the perspective of the lives of women. To the extent that they could identify such socially determinate elements, the feminist accounts were, then, more objective, more rational in the same kinds of ways that anti-Eurocentric accounts are. In such epistemologies, appeals to objectivity and rationality are justificatory claims additional to the classes of empirical claims (about, say, female roles in human evolution) that they would justify and with which they are enmeshed in a belief network. They neither stand "over" any and all empirical claims, nor can they simply be replaced by them – the positions of internalist, on the one hand, and the other postpositivist SCSST, on the other hand, respectively.[31] I shall not pursue further here these accounts which are available elsewhere of the stronger standards for objectivity and rationality that are needed to identify presuppositions, paradigms, conceptual frameworks, and epistemes that are culture-wide, or virtually so.

Instead, let us turn to the issue of universally valid scientific claims – one of the internalist epistemological notions not much examined in the feminist science studies, but central to the Southern SCSST that we have been exploring. Is there anything that remains useful in this notion for those who could agree that all sciences are local knowledge systems?

6.2 Universally valid claims

The conventional, internalist epistemologies hold that modern science, the only universally valid science, can successfully predict and explain nature's regularities because its internal procedures enable transcendence of the inevitable local values and interests of the individuals and cultures that have generated such sciences. In contrast to the case with only local knowledge systems, people from other cultures who do not share each other's values and interests can nevertheless understand and use such real sciences, and whether or not they understand and use them, the universally operative natural forces that shape their lives can be predicted and explained by the laws of nature that real sciences articulate. In such accounts, terms such as "universal science", "universally valid claims", and "universally operative forces" call up a number of different meanings originating, evidently, in everyday uses of the term, as any dictionary reveals. Are there any meanings of "universal science" to which there are still good reasons to appeal, if all scientific claims are inextricably embedded in local knowledge systems? At least the following four deserve such scrutiny.

Let us begin with the one that must be rejected: namely, that only value-neutral sciences can be universally valid. Clearly this neutrality condition must be rejected, for all scientific and technological knowledge claims are culturally local, constituted through the cultures and practices of the knowledge-projects of which they are a part. The Northern SCSST already show how claims to a distinctive transcultural scientific method, to reliance on the abstract language of mathematics, to a distinctive metaphysics (such as that of primary and secondary qualities), to a distinctive kind of scientific community, or to any other purportedly neutrality-insuring scientific practice cannot insure the cultural neutrality of a science. Sciences cannot possibly be completely culturally neutral. In the case of the notions of objectivity and rationality, abandoning this prerequisite for deploying the epistemological notion actually enabled the production of more accurate and comprehensive accounts of how knowledge advances. Rejecting the neutrality condition permitted the development of "strong objectivity" and inclusive rationality. It showed the "strong methods" necessary to detect at least some of those cultural frameworks that shape entire belief systems. To identify such frameworks, of course, cannot be regarded as requiring the further step of considering them as defects to be eliminated, for, as we saw in the preceding section, many culturally local features – interests, discursive resources, etc. – advance the growth of knowledge. So if the neutrality condition is rejected here, too, what is left?

A second meaning of universally valid science is that its makers have come from many different cultures and espouse different religious and other culturally specific beliefs. They are British, Japanese, French, Indian, Brazilian, Danish; they go to churches, temples, mosques, shrines, or no religious centers at all. But they have been able to agree to scientific claims even though there might well be little else upon which they could agree. Of course, it turns out that they have all been agreeing to scientific claims that were, in fact, distinctively European (and French, Protestant, etc.), as the diverse SCSST have pointed out. So why could they not all also agree to scientific claims permeated by Confucian, Brazilian, or African "cultures and practices"? This meaning of "universally valid" has been thought trivial, but it may not be so. Thinking about it draws our attention to the fact that it need not be only scientific claims embedded in European cultures and practices to which scientists from many different cultures can agree. Indeed, one focus of the Southern SCSST has been how European science borrowed from other cultures many still-important scientific and technological ideas – from Arabic numerals and Indian mathematical concepts to medical treatments such as, now, acupuncture. Some cultural uses of local resources have become particularly attractive to other cultures around the globe; this "globalization" or "universalization" of different cultures' local scientific and technological resources will continue in the future.[32]

A third, related meaning focusses on the indubitable fact that people from many different cultures want modern sciences, or, at least, to borrow parts of them for local use in cultures far from their origin. These sciences, the way they work, are transculturally appreciated. This meaning of universality functions like the first one. It draws our attention to the fact that people from many different cultures could and, in some cases, do want the benefits of scientific claims developed in other scientific and technological local knowledge systems. For example, Europeans wanted the Arabic numerals, and people of European descent today do want the benefits of acupuncture's pain management whether the explanations of its efficacy are given in terms of European or Chinese medical theory; they are indifferent to what explanations are offered.[33]

Finally, a fourth meaning of "universally valid science" is that modern sciences' descriptions and explanations of nature's regularities and their underlying causal determinants "hold true" far distant from their sites of original observation, and for phenomena that may be described and explained very differently in other cultures. They enable accurate prediction and, often, control of nature. "Science works" refers to this meaning of "universal science." Of course, as the preceding discussions have pointed out, the same can be said of other cultures' scientific claims. Acupuncture can effectively control pain for non-Chinese. For that matter, Ptolemaic astronomy and Aristotelian physics "work" to predict accurately a great deal that Copernican astronomy and Newtonian physics (respectively) also predicted. Even though these different explanations of nature's regularities presuppose very different culturally local theories of nature (and the supernatural), their sciences can make claims that "are true" everywhere.

Moreover, we saw in the last section that different cultures have access to different natural and social resources for the advance of scientific and technological knowledge. They are located in different environments, and bring to their thinking about nature different interests, discursive resources, and culturally distinctive ways of organizing the production of knowledge. Southern SCSST authors point out that not only is it the case that important scientific and technological ideas have come from non-European cultures in the past; they will also come from such places in the future. As the Northern SCSST themselves recognize now, such culturally distinctive resources are of great value to the growth of knowledge, for they enable us to "see" nature in yet additional ways.

A number of Northern and Southern SCSST accounts have explored just how some sciences achieve such an ability to make accurate predictions far from the sites of their original emergence. Thus, Latour[34] examines how successful sciences establish "obligatory passage points," "technoscience networks," and "centers of calculation" for subsequent scientists. Watson-Verran and Turnbull[35] show how medieval European cathedral builders, the Anasazi, the Inca, Australian aborigines, and the Pacific navigators, like modern scientists, developed "social strategies and technical devices" that enabled them to create "equivalences and connections whereby otherwise heterogeneous and isolated knowledges are enabled to move in space and time from the local site and moment of their production and application to other places and times."[36] These processes can be explored for science claims originating in other cultures that become "universally valid," in the sense that Newton's or Boyle's laws achieve that status. As one Southern contributor to SCSST puts the point:

> [I]f we were to picture physical reality as a large blackboard, and the branches and shoots of the knowledge tree as markings in white chalk on this blackboard, it becomes clear that the yet unmarked and unexplored parts occupy a considerably greater space than that covered by the chalk tracks. The socially structured knowledge tree has thus explored only certain partial aspects of physical reality, explorations that correspond to the particular historical unfoldings of the civilization within which the knowledge tree emerged.
>
> Thus entirely different knowledge systems corresponding to different historical unfoldings in different civilizational settings become possible. This raises the possibility that in different historical situations and contexts sciences very different from the European tradition could emerge. Thus an entirely new set of "universal" but socially determined natural science laws are possible.[37]

We can summarize four of the features of the practices and culture of European sciences that have enabled the latter to appear not just universally valid, but, as the arguments above indicate, uniquely so. The first three were created by resources provided by European sciences' links with European expansion. As European expansion turned the world into a laboratory for emerging European sciences, Europeans could test the hypotheses they developed about how to explain nature's regularities over vastly larger and more diverse natural terrains than could other cultures. Moreover, second, European sciences could "forage" in other cultures for elements of those cultures' ethnosciences to incorporate into European sciences. "Native informants" taught Europeans about the local flora and fauna, minerals and ores, climates, diseases and other threats to health, pharmacological remedies, agricultural, fishing, and engineering practices, land and sea routes, and much of the rest of the knowledge traditions developed and stored in local cultures. At the same time, third, European expansion suppressed or destroyed – intentionally and unintentionally – competitive local knowledge systems. Whether a culture that the Europeans encountered was wiped out by plagues or by intentional genocide, it took its repository of traditional knowledge about nature with it to the grave. And then there were the many examples of the Europeans' intentional destruction of local craft traditions, with their knowledge of nature and their technologies, to make way for the European practices that were more profitable to the Europeans – for example, Indian textile manufacturing,[38] and diverse agricultural and environmental practices around the globe. So three aspects of Euorpean expansion historically produced the illusion that only European sciences were and could be universally valid: European expansion as travel, as foraging, and as conquest.

A fourth feature is what one could refer to as European sciences' predatory conceptual frameworks. Persistent substitution of abstract for concrete, locally situated, and historical concepts of nature and the processes of science sucks up local features of local knowledge systems into apparently universal features of "real sciences." For example, features of local environments become aspects of omnipresent "nature" to be explained adequately only by universally valid laws of nature. Again, such everyday practices as induction, deduction, and "trial and error" reasoning – found in every farmer's, merchant's, and mother's repertoire – become elevated in the philosophies of modern sciences into distinctive features that distinguish "real sciences" from mere ethnosciences. So this type of conceptual framework also contributes to the illusion that only modern sciences can generate knowledge claims that are useful far from their site of original production. This kind of conceptual framework, too, is a local feature of the philosophies of European sciences.

It must be stressed that the interest of Southern SCSST is not primarily to contribute to the science and technology knowledge of Northern international cultures, but rather to develp ones that serve their own cultures. These theorists and policy analysts want to reinvigorate their own cultural traditions in ways that will enable the local scientific and technology projects better to satisfy local physical and cultural needs.

> Only when science and technology evolve from the ethos and cultural milieu of Third World societies will it become meaningful for our needs and requirements, and express our true creativity and genius. Third world science and technology can only evolve through a reliance on indigenous categories, idioms and traditions in all spheres of thought.[39]

They do so not to "go forward to the past" in a romantic revolt against modernity, but, rather, to update, modernize (postmodernize?) their cultural legacies, so that they, too, are capable of functioning effectively in a world containing – among other ethnosciences – modern Northern ones.

7 Conclusion

This chapter has been developing three arguments. First, Southern SCSST should be counted among the schools of contemporary science studies that are contributing uniquely illuminating analyses of modern sciences and other local knowledge systems. Second, different SCSST schools, like the sciences that they analyze, are all themselves local knowledge systems, with different locations in nature and global social relations, interests, discursive resources, and ways of organizing the production of knowledge – here about scientific and technological traditions, past, present, and future. Third, though Southern as well as other SCSST all criticize the internalist forms of epistemologies that appeal to universally valid scientific claims, from the perspective of Southern SCSST one can also identify residual elements available in the older internalist epistemologies that can be transformed into useful resources for the growth of knowledge.

This chapter is thus in a difficult position, in a critical stance not only to the conventional internalist philosophies and epistemologies of science, but also to most contemporary schools of science studies. I cannot hope that my arguments here will meet with widespread agreement. Perhaps they can contribute to fruitful reflection and dialogue about how in our own, local ways, each approach can more effectively contribute to democratic linkings of knowledge and power.

Notes

1   The phrase "science as practice and culture" is from Andrew Pickering (ed.), *Science as Practice and Culture* (University of Chicago Press, Chicago, IL, 1992). For a few of the many examples of other such studies, see John Dupre, *The Disorder of Things: Metaphysical Foundations for the Disunity of Science* (Harvard University Press, Cambridge, MA, 1993); Nancy Cartwright, *How the Laws of Physics Lie* (Oxford University Press, New York, 1983); Paul Forman, "Behind quantum electronics: national security as bases for physical research in the US, 1940–1960," *Historical Studies in Physical and Biological Sciences*, vol. 18, pp. 149–229; Ian Hacking, *Representing and Intervening* (Cambridge University Press, Cambridge, 1983); Donna Haraway, *Primate Visions: Gender, Race and Nature in the World of Modern Science* (Routledge, New York, 1989); Sandra Harding, *The Science Question in Feminism* (Cornell University Press, Ithaca, NY, 1986); Mary Hesse, *Models and Analogies in Science* (University of Notre Dame Press, Notre Dame, IN, 1966); Evelyn Fox Keller, *Reflections on Gender and Science* (Yale University Press, New Haven, CT, 1984); Keller, *Secrets of Life, Secrets of Death: Essays on Language, Gender and Science* (Routledge, New York, 1992); Thomas S. Kuhn, *The Strucure of Scientific Revolutions*, 2nd ed (University of Chicago Press, Chicago, IL, 1970); Bruno Latour, *Science in Action* (Harvard University Press, Cambridge, MA, 1987); Latour, *The Pasteurization of France* (Harvard University Press, Cambridge, MA, 1988); Latour and Steve Woolgar, *Laboratory Life: The Social Construction of Scientific Facts* (Sage, Beverly Hills, CA, 1979); Carolyn Merchant, *The Death of Nature: Women, Ecology and the Scientific Revolution* (Harper and Row, New York, 1980); Andrew Pickering, *Constructing Quarks* (University of Chicago Press, Chicago, IL, 1984); John A. Schuster and Richard R. Yeo, *The Politics and Rhetoric of Scientific Method* (D. Reidel, Dordrecht, 1986); Steven

Shapin, *A Social History of Truth* (University of Chicago Press, Chicago, IL, 1994); Shapin and Simon Schaffer, *Leviathan and the Air Pump* (Princeton University Press, Princeton, NJ, 1985); Sharon Traweek, *Beamtimes and Life Times* (MIT Press, Cambridge, MA, 1988); Bas Van Fraassen and Jill Sigman, "Interpretation in science and in the arts," in George Levine (ed.), *Realism and Representation* (University of Wisconsin Press, Madison, WI, 1993).

2   An early version of this approach can be found, for example, in C. Frake, 'The ethnographic study of cognitive systems," in T. Gladwin (ed.), *Anthropology and Human Behaviour* (The Anthropology Society of Washington, Washington, DC, 1962). A recent illuminating use of such ethnographic materials by philosopher/ historians working also with the resources of thirty years of SCSST can be found in David Turnbull, "Local knowledge and comparative scientific traditions," *Knowledge and Policy*, vol. 6, nos 3–4, 1993, pp. 29–54; and Helen Watson-Verran and David Turnbull, "Science and other indigenous knowledge systems," in S. Jasanoff, G. Markle, T. Pinch and J. Petersen, *Handbook of Science and Technology Studies* (Sage, Thousand Oaks, CA, 1995), pp. 115–39. See in the latter essay also an account of the difference between their work and the earlier comparative ethnoscience approaches.

3   However, we cannot follow through with the apparent analogy to the internalist vs externalist histories that I may appear to be headed into. The anti-epistemologists, in contrast to the externalist historians, hold that there is no transcultural "inside" to scientific processes and the claims they produce to which the social world is "external." The epistemological status of a scientific claim is socially achieved, but there is no value-neutral, cognitive core of science to which it is thereby external, since that, too, is socially negotiated.

4   "Southern" and "Northern" SCSST refer to schools of science studies, their themes, interests, resources, and ways of organizing the production of science studies, not to the ethnicity, nationality, or residence of their practitioners, which is diverse.

Just a few examples of the many Northern feminist studies seeking more robust epistemological stances are: Anne Fausto-Sterling, *Myths of Gender: Biological Theories about Women and Men* (Basic Books, New York, 1985, 1992); Haraway, *Primate Visions*; Harding, *Science Question in Feminism* and *Whose Science, Whose Knowledge?* (Cornell University Press, Ithaca, NY, 1991); Harding and Jean O'Barr, *Sex and Scientific Inquiry* (University of Chicago Press, Chicago, IL, 1987); Keller, *Reflections on Gender and Science* and *Secrets of Life*; and Dorothy B. Smith, *The Conceptual Practices of Power: A Feminist Sociology of Knowledge* (Northeastern Univesity Press, Boston, MA, 1990). Among the many such Southern, postcolonial, single-stream history SCSST writings are: Michael Adas, *Machines as the Measure of Man* (Cornell University Press, Ithaca, NY, 1989); Claude Alvares, "Science, colonialism and violence: a Luddite view," in A. Nandy (ed.), *Science, Hegemony and Violence* (Oxford University Press, Delhi, 1990); Thomas Bass, *Camping With the Prince, and Other Tales of Science in Africa* (Houghton Mifflin, Boston, MA, 1990); J. M. Blaut, *The Colonizer's Model of the World: Geographical Diffusionism and Eurocentric History* (Guilford Press, New York, 1993); Lucille H. Brockway, *Science and Colonial Expansion: The Role of the British Royal Botanical Gardens* (Academic Press, New York, 1979); Susantha Goonatilake, *Aborted Discovery:*

Science and Creativity in the Third World (Zed, London, 1984); Goonatilake, "A project for our times," in Ziauddin Sardar (ed.), *The Revenge of Athena: Science, Exploration and the Third World* (Mansell, London, 1988); Goonatilake, "The Voyages of Discovery and the loss and rediscovery of the 'Other's' knowledge," *Impact of Science on Society*, no. 167, 1992; Harding (ed.), *The "Racial" Economy of Science: Toward a Democratic Future* (Indiana University Press, Bloomington, IN, 1993); David J. Hess, *Science and Technology in a Multicultural World: The Cultural Politics of Facts and Artifacts* (Columbia University Press, New York, 1995); George Gheverghese Joseph, *The Crest of the Peacock: Non-European Roots of Mathematics* (I.B. Tauris and Co., New York, 1991); Kok Peng Khor, "Science and development: underdeveloping the Third World," in Sardar (ed.), *Revenge of Athena*; R.K. Kochlar, "Science in British India," Parts I and II, *Current Science*, vol. 63, no. 11, vol. 64, no. 1, 1992–3 (India); Deepak Kumar, *Science and Empire: Essays in Indian Context (1700–1947)* (Anamika Prakashan, and National Institute of Science, Technology and Development, Delhi, 1991); James E. McClellan, *Colonialism and Science: Saint Domingue in the Old Regime* (The Johns Hopkins University Press, Baltimore, MD, 1992); Charles Moraze (ed.), *Science and the Factors of Inequality* (UNESCO, Paris, 1979); Ashis Nandy (ed.), *Science, Hegemony and Violence: A Requiem for Modernity* (Oxford University Press, Delhi, 1990); Joseph Needham, *The Grand Titration: Science and Society in East and West* (University of Toronto Press, Toronto, 1969); Patrick Petitjean et al. (eds), *Science and Empires: Historical Studies About Scientific Development and European Expansion* (Kluwer, Dodrecht, 1992); Xavier Polanco, "World-science: how is the history of world-science to be written?", in Petitjean et al. (eds), *Science and Empires*; Wolfgang Sachs (ed.), *The Development Dictionary: A Guide to Knowledge as Power* (Zed, Atlantic Highlands, NJ, 1992); Sardar, *Revenge of Athena*; Vandana Shiva, *Staying Alive: Women, Ecology and Development* (Zed, London, 1989); Third World Network, *Modern Science in Crisis: A Third World Response* (Third World Network, Penang, Malaysia, 1988).

5   One might point out here that, after all, central concepts of modern physics, chemistry, and biology are no less useful for having been socially negotiated, as studies such as those cited in note 1 have revealed.

6   The thumbnail sketch above of epistemological differences between various tendencies over the last three or so decades of SCSST cannot possibly do justice to the subtlety and complexity of the diverse thought within each tendency or "school," and differences between them on this topic. I have had to assume that readers are familiar with at least two or three of the literatures to which I referred – no doubt an unfair assumption for some readers.

7   Cf. Patrick Williams and Laura Chrisman (eds), *Colonial Discourse and Post-Colonial Theory* (Columbia University Press, New York, 1994).

8   Cf. Hess, *Science and Technology in a Multicultural World*, p. vi.

9   I thank Vincanne Adams especially for her helpful discussion of this point in her comment on an earlier version of this paper presented at the Penn Mid-Atlantic Seminar for the Study of Women and Society, October 20, 1994.

10 Goonatilake, "The Voyages of Discovery"; Harding, "Is science multicultural? Challenges, opportunities, uncertainties," *Configurations*, vol. 2, no. 2, 1994, reprinted in David Theo Goldberg (ed.), *Multiculturalism: A Reader* (Blackwell,

London, 1994); Needham, *The Grand Titration*.

11   Paul Feyerabend, *Against Method* (New Left Books, London, 1975); Harding, *The Science Question*; Kuhn, *Scientific Revolutions*; W.V. O. Quine, "Two dogmas of empiricism," in *From a Logical Point of View* (Harvard University Press, Cambridge, MA, 1953).

12   Van Fraassen and Sigman, "Interpretation in science and in the arts."

13   For that matter, they have not thought there was anything to be learned from Northern feminist science studies, where "high science" studies have made crucial contributions to feminist science theory, but most work has been concerned with biology and the social sciences. (For examples of the former, see N. Katherine Hayles, "Gender encoding in fluid mechanics: masculine channels and feminine flows," *Differences: A Journal of Feminist Cultural Studies*, vol. 4, 1992, pp. 17–44; Keller, *Reflections*; Keller, *Secrets of Life*.)

      In the 1980s SCSST literature, there were already cross-cultural studies of fully modern sciences (in contrast to the older comparative ethnoscience tradition of studies of modern vs ethnosciences) appearing in the writings of a few authors from the North, such as Haraway's chapter in *Primate Visions* comparing Anglo-American, Indian, Japanese, and African primatologies and Traweek's comparison in *Beamtimes and Life Times* of Japanese and US high-energy physics. By the mid-1990s, a few more "postcomparative ethnosciences" analyses by scholars participatory in the Northern SCSST circles have appeared: for example, Hess, *Science and Technology in a Multicultural World*; Turnbull, "Local knowledge;" and Watson-Verran and Turnbull, "Science and other indigenous knowledge systems." My point here is not to draw firm boundaries, but only to note that one can easily identify distinct clusters of postpositivist science study discussions that only rarely communicate with each other. Northern SCSST and South-originating SCSST (including some of the critiques of "development") would mark two such clusters. A third is Northern feminist SCSST, in which some scholars read much of the non-feminist SCSST (and some do not), and few non-feminist SCSST scholars read any of the feminist work except for Haraway's and Traweek's.

14   Needham, *The Grand Titration*, p. 302.

15   Ibid., p. 323.

16   Needham, Ibid., p. 237.

17   Does it also reflect the modern familiarity with large bureaucracies and corporations where individual responsibility for rules and regulations is often unlocatable? That is, would the idea of characterizing nature's order merely through statistical regularities have been comprehensible or attractive to people living in absolute monarchies? Would it have been perceived to be (and, perhaps, actually be) politically threatening to such monarchies?

18   Keller, *Reflections*, pp. 131, 132.

19   McClellan, *Colonialism and Science*, pp. 1, 7.

20   Kochhar, "Science in British India," p. 694.

21   Forman, "Behind quantum electronics." Cf. also: Adas, *Machines as the Measure of Man*; Samir Amin, *Eurocentrism* (Monthly Review, New York, 1989); Alfred Crosby, *Ecological Imperialism: The Biological Expansion of Europe* (Cambridge University Press, Cambridge, 1987); Goonatilake, *Aborted Discovery* and "The Voyages of Discovery;" Harding, *The "Racial" Economy of Science*; Kochhar,

"Science in British India;" Moraze, *Science and the Factors of Inequality*; Nandy, *Science, Hegemony and Violence*; Petitjean et al., *Science and Empires*; W. Rodney, *How Europe Underdeveloped Africa* (Howard University Press, Washington, DC, 1982); Sardar, *Revenge of Athena*.

22 Khor, "Science and development," pp. 207–8.

23 Alvares, "Science, colonialism and violence," p. 108.

24 J. Bandyopadhyay and V. Shiva, "Science and control: natural resources and their exploitation," in Sardar (ed.), *Revenge of Athena*, p. 63.

25 Smith, *Conceptual Practices of Power*; Alfred Sohn-Rethel, *Intellectual and Manual Labor* (Macmillan, London, 1978).

26 Bandyopadhyay and Shiva, "Science and control," p. 60.

27 Note that a number of the Northern SCSST analyses have asked a somewhat different question: how should we account for the differing power of modern and other local knowledge systems? I return to this question below. My question here is a different one that focusses on the value of the local for locals and for others.

28 For examples of the latter, see Forman, "Behind quantum electronics;" Robert Proctor, *Cancer Wars: How Politics Shapes What We Know and Don't Know About Cancer* (Basic Books, Boston, MA, 1995); Joseph Rouse, *Knowledge and Power: Toward a Political Philosophy of Science* (Cornell University Press, Ithaca, NY, 1987).

29 See, for example, Blaut, *The Colonizer's Model*, for an account of the historical emergence of single-stream histories from 1930s and 1940s Indian and Caribbean historians, through postcolonial 1960s and 1970s world-systems theory, and then in the 1980s and early 1990s case studies of how the practices and culture of European scientific and technological institutions advanced the practices and cultures of colonialism, and vice versa (e.g., Brockway, *Science and Colonial Expansion*; McClellan, *Colonialism and Science*; and now Kumar, *Science and Empire*; Petitjean et al., *Science and Empires*, etc.)

30 Smith, *Conceptual Practices of Power*.

31 Cf., for example, Harding, "After the neutrality ideal: science, politics and 'strong objectivity,'" *Social Research*, vol. 59, 1992, pp. 567–87; Harding, "'Strong objectivity': a response to the new objectivity question," *Synthese*, 1996; Keller, *Reflections*; Phyllis Rooney, "Recent work in feminist discussions of reason," *American Philosophical Quarterly*, vol. 31, 1994, pp. 1–21.

32 Perhaps some readers would want to say that now Arabic numerals and acupuncture are no longer Arabic or Chinese, respectively; they have become European – and so they have, while remaining also Arabic and Chinese in their cultures of origin. From this perspective, one might prefer to speak of "universalizing" scientific practices and claims, and some as more "universalized" than others, while simultaneously becoming embedded in more and more local scientific cultures and practices.

33 Ted J. Kaptchuk, *The Web That Has No Weaver: Understanding Chinese Medicine* (Congdon and Weed, New York, 1983); C. P. Li, "Chinese herbal medicine: recent experimental studies, clinical applications and pharmacology of certain herbs," in Revolutionary Health Committee of Hunan Province, *A Barefoot Doctor's Manual*, revised edn (Madrona, Seattle, WI, 1977).

34 Latour, *Science in Action*.

35   Watson-Verran and Turnbull, "Science and other indigenous knowledge systems."

36   Turnbull, "Local knowledge," p. 29.

37   Goonatilake, "Project for our times," pp. 229–30.

38   Cf. Kochhar, "Science in British India."

39   Third World Network, *Modern Science in Crisis*.

3

African Philosophy and Modernity

Peter Amato

1 Introduction

There are two trends that have developed in opposition to the documentary orientation in conceptualizing African philosophy, in which the most interesting new work is being done. The first of these Serequeberhan identifies as the "scientific," or "scientistic" trend.[1] Writers who take this approach reject the "ethnophilosophical" standpoint of the documentary orientation, in the quest for an African philosophical attitude that is methodologically rigorous and universalistic. Philosophy as such is conceived as a rigorous scientific discipline which must necessarily overcome the narrowness of any particular historicosocial context and ethnic or national tradition. Anything less than this would represent the invasion of philosophical thinking by provincial concerns which are to be methodologically excluded from this as from any science.[2] Writers in this school "share in the criticism of ethnophilosophy and see philosophy in Africa as the 'handmaid' of science and [uncritical] modernization."[3]

The second approach which opposes itself to ethnophilosophy is the one with which Serequeberhan aligns himself. This he calls the "historico–hermeneutical" approach. Here, the contemporary reconsideration within Western thought of some of the central assumptions of classical modern philosophy is invoked in order to make sense of the intercultural situation of understanding:

> Any discourse on philosophy is necessarily implicated in an already presupposed conception of philosophy. As Martin Heidegger and Hans–Georg Gadamer tell us, reading or interpreting a text means being already involved with it. What needs doing then, is not to try to avoid this unavoidable "circle" of interpretation/

philosophy, but to engage it fully. In other words, to bring to the fore – as much as possible – the operative pre-judgements at work in one's philosophical engagement.[4]

As the precondition and the result of engagement in the attempt to come to understanding between African and Western European cultures, each may deepen its own self-awareness, since assumptions and prejudgements that are commonly unquestioned rise to the fore in the process. There is thus always a critical moment in any sufficiently broad project of understanding.

In what follows I use Serequeberhan's position as a starting point from which to facilitate the intercultural project implicit in the discussion of African thought and its relation to the European traditions of Western thought.[5] Wrapped up in the question regarding African philosophy is a whole series of questions regarding Africa and European modernity, and the ways that conceptions of modernity have been employed to facilitate colonization. The relation of African thought to the Western philosophical tradition turns upon a series of deeper considerations which have to do with the relations between African cultures and the European cultures which have substantially molded the latter tradition up until the present. Thus, most of this chapter presents a critical discussion of the relation between tradition and philosophy as it has been posed within Western philosophical discourse, attempting to push the self-established boundaries of "modernism" outward.[6] I try to interpret these issues in such a way as to show that the continuities or convergences between African and modern Western philosophy can become visible when the individuality and history of each of these traditions is "engaged" rather than ignored or displaced by dichotomies and distinctions that reflect traditional prejudices.

Such prejudices persist, for example, in the many attempts by Western scholars to apply dichotomies such as "open/closed," "rational/traditional," and "modern/premodern" in the discussion of intercultural understanding.[7] These dichotomies are normative and represent prejudgements implicit in the discourse of Western modernity which its confrontation with other cultures brings to the fore. Recent decades have seen the traditional superiority complex of Western culture brought under critical examination and, to some extent, questioned and rejected. The details of this "self-implosion"[8] will not be directly examined in this chapter. The interested reader can now draw upon a large number of broad-ranging and sophisticated sources. This chapter is instead concerned with the philosophical dimensions of the relationship as they bear upon African philosophy, and will examine "modernity" and "premodernity" in terms of the conceptualization of "tradition" in Western intellectual culture.

Previous approaches to the question posed by "intellectual modernization"[9] have tended to assume what they set out to show – that there is something about Western thought that makes it *modern* and something about African thought that is *not modern*. I wish to raise issue with this dichotomy itself. I will not be concerned, as Robin Horton and many others have been, to characterize the intellectual tendencies of the thousands of cultures of more than two continents and fit them into a previously conceived scheme, whether it be modern/premodern, open/closed, or rational/traditional. Instead, I wish to examine how it is that thinkers in the West still typically assume that these and similar dichotomies have anything to do with philosophical understanding, understanding philosophy, or understanding each other. In fact I believe that the confusion is generated by the application of economic and political categories as if they had philosophical, anthropological, or psychic import, an assumption which I reject.[10] The modern/traditional dichotomy expresses the economic and political reality that the West *has closed* African societies, and undermined their indigenous economic and political systems. Where it has not utterly destroyed them, it has spent several hundred years attempting to wipe out what has remained of indigenous intellectual culture, in order to substitute its own. It has regarded *their traditional authorities* as its enemy, and as the enemy of intellectual culture as such, since they have been an obstacle to *its own authority*, which has been understood as carrying forward the inevitable march of universal, traditionless human history.

There is a cynical and perhaps more common version of this type of perspective which regards itself not as evolutionist *per se*, but rather as the sober realism of a postmetaphysical, postevolutionist view. This position holds that, whether or not the substitution of other cultures by Western forms of life is seen as ultimately the expression of a rational process in history (as Hegel believed), in any event, it is now largely an historical *fait accompli*.[11] The rational thing to do if you are in a "premodern" culture is jump on the bandwagon and leave your cultural backwater behind, since *West* is the direction history has taken, whether it had to or not. Instead of being inevitable because it is rational, evolution toward "modernity" and away from "traditionalism" is seen as rational because inevitable. Thus, forces that might question or derail such inevitabilities are foreclosed. The question of what African modernity might represent is glided over as if to be "modern" necessarily required broad-scale cultural replacement, and as if the economic and political realities of the modernization of Europe had to create modern Africa only insofar as it is their byproduct.

The implication that I hope will become clear is that African philosophers need not ask non-African Westerners permission to be deemed legitimately modern or legitimately philosophical. They need not accept that only by conforming to the central methodological tenets of Western philosophy do they earn the right to philosophize.[12] The intellectual culture of a people expresses its substantive concerns, which cannot legitimately be reduced to their form or method of thematization. It is not and has never been through the use of a particular method either in the West or anywhere else that "philosophy" has earned whatever right it may claim to speak for and to humanity. It is rather philosophy's connection to central human concerns that legitimizes any such claims, and in each case this connection takes the form of a set of modalities, methods, or genres of discourse. Broadly speaking, it is philosophical in reflecting the close, careful pursuit of wisdom through dialogue and critical research. It may be modern, as well, to the extent that it engages in the ongoing dialogue regarding the principal issues of modern thought.[13]

As a Western non-African, I am proud of a modern philosophical tradition that holds human dignity, liberty, and pluralism among its stated ideals, and I believe that the attempt to make that tradition responsive and responsible to these goals requires steady and serious work. We cannot hope to successfully communicate interculturally until the deep-seated asymmetries that currently characterize our cultural practices and our thinking are critically engaged and dismantled from within as well as from without. These may sound like platitudes. My concern here will not be simply to invoke them, but rather to sketch some historical and philosophical considerations that seem relevant to the project of retaining the liberating elements of modernism while rejecting its tendencies toward homogeneity, élitism, complacency, and intolerance. Such internal criticism on the part of Western thought will not of itself answer the question of African philosophy about where its focus should be – that is finally a task to be accomplished by African thinkers. My comments here are aimed at undermining a significant obstacle to intercultural intellectual understanding that lingers in some deep and enduring prejudices of the Western intellectual tradition which are implicitly carried on in the rhetoric of "modernity" and "modernism."

Here, I present a two-part thesis. First, I try to establish that the concept of modernity has been used rhetorically and to bad effect by Western intellectuals both with regard to their own self-understanding and with regard to those whom they have considered as their "Other." I suggest that ideas of intellectual "modernity" and "traditionality" have tended to be used in an exclusive fashion, and that in the modern era of European philosophy, modernity appropriated knowledge for itself along with science, and left only dogma, mysticism, and mythology (also excluded from knowledge) for culture and tradition to be concerned with. Thus, it has tended to cover over rather than clarify the individuality of different societies, and continues to do so today.[14] The only horizon that Western intellectuals have allowed to non-Western cultures has been, and I would argue largely remains, the horizon reflected in its favored mythology of scientific progress, technological admin-istration, and capitalism as the future of humanity.[15] To the extent that a society can be placed somewhere in *this* narrative, it has merited a place in "History." To the extent that a society has not seemed to be moving along, however, it is to be considered another victim stuck in place along the universal horizon of development, destined to be undermined by the inevitable progress around it. It would either adapt to Western ways, die to itself, or die completely.

In short, Western intellectual culture has defined its "Other" as the traditional and non- or premodern by presenting its own self-described but inadequately clarified "modern" horizon as the universal horizon for humanity. A host of related questions regarding the respective roles of religion, myth, and scientific method in relation to thought were indefinitely deferred in the distinction between "modern" and "traditional" ways of life and thought. As the result of this, all intellectual forms and forms of discourse that may have existed in any culture were subsumed into an economic and political metanarrative. And despite this, self-described European modernity has only recently come around to consider what exactly its own achievement amounts to.

The second part of my thesis here is that an important step toward mutual understanding between African and non-African intellectual traditions therefore may be taken by addressing these questions critically and directly. When it becomes clear that the modern/traditional dichotomy has played a negative rhetorical role in Western self- and Other-designations, as I believe it has, the myth of a universal horizon for humanity can be retold in a fundamentally different and, I believe, positive way. Rather than a rhetorical device that allows one cultural tradition to subsume the individuality of all others in a homogenous and self-serving narrative of supposed intellectual and material progress, the idea of a universal human horizon may become simply the generalized location for the overlapping conceptualizations of human nature that our different intellectual cultures may produce through real dialogue. The focus would need to shift from a putative universal horizon, to the many actual and differentiated horizons of different cultures and different writers. Rather than being assumed at the outset, convergences would need to be seen as the hoped-for result of a pluralistic dialogue that could not be guaranteed (or imposed) beforehand.

Part of the problem here is that the scientific perspective that has dominated Western intellectual culture over the last few centuries has been rather unscientific in seeing its own expectations through: if some convergences were to result from close encounters between free peoples seeking mutual understanding, this would be both a predictable and a beneficial result. But the encounters between Europe and Africa have been anything but free and mutual. Instead of admitting the truth that it saw no purpose in and would not really pursue such understanding, Western intellectual culture blessed its political atrocities with lies. One of those lies has been that it could dictate the terms of human convergence and impose them upon the recalcitrant.

Today, there remain real reasons to see the political and economic disparities between Africa and Europe as significant obstacles to such mutually free discourse. Thus, I conclude with some comments on this, the immediate goal of all forms of current philosophy in this and related areas: the persistent and principled attack on all obstacles to free and mutual relations between cultures, of which philosophical-disciplinary disputes are a reflection and a distraction. At the root of such obstacles are the social, political, and economic relationships which continue to deny to people worldwide the dignity and freedom to appropriate their own horizons and control their own destinies.

2 Traditional European Modernism

It has been a fundamental premise of the modern philosophical attitude to place religious and social values outside of what it considers legitimate philosophical thought. Modern philosophy, taking its cue from science, has seen itself as an adventure in the explosion of myths of all sorts and independence from all authorities. Thus, religious-inspired conceptions of reality and mythic conceptions of reality have been seen as merely the elements of superstition and obfuscation, having no place in philosophical reason. In the past, writers on these subjects have moved from this premise of modern thought to the assessment that societies in which mythicoreligious ideas and social traditions play a significant role in intellectual culture must not, therefore, be rational or capable of "philosophy." In the case of African cultures, Westerners have tended to identify them as traditional or "closed" in just this sense, and to deem them unphilosophical and irrational. Much ink has been spilled to challenge the second premise of this argument, taking issue with the claim that African thought should be considered "traditional" or "closed," as opposed to "modern" or "open."[16]

I will here take issue with the first premise, however, which claims that philosophical reason must, or in any case can only ever truly, operate independently of some basis in the mythic or religious life of a community. As a result of this, I believe it to be the case that Western thought is in some ways as poorly prepared to understand itself and the experience of Western non-Africans as it is to appreciate the experience of African peoples and people in what are often thought of as "traditional" and modernizing, as opposed to "modern" cultures. In Italy, France, Germany, Britain and the United States, as well as in the various cultures of Africa, the experiences of diverse peoples are in many ways misunderstood and covered up by the homogenizing blanket of an undefined and generalized idea of intellectual modernism.

It was a long-unquestioned prejudgement in Western culture that its technological progress from the Middle Ages to the Enlightenment was the trace of the universal historical evolution of humanity. Despite the great caution exercised today by writers and speakers to avoid the language of evolutionism, as an overarching pattern through which culture is understood, something like this idea has persisted in modern Western thought.[17] It is certainly true that such assumptions are not as frequently taken for granted in academic circles today as they were only thirty years ago. But much of the discussion of cross-cultural philosophy seems to have an argument about evolutionism as its subtext. The continuing political and economic relationship between the industrialized nations of the "North" and the non-industrialized nations of the "South" is understood today as the result and not the cause of what Westerners in both popular and academic circles still consider a form of cultural "backwardness" or, as it is more commonly known, "traditionalism."

Evolutionism is often associated with explicit nineteenth-century exponents like E.B. Tylor and Herbert Spencer, and is popularly thought to have died out some time back in the 1950s, eons ago in the era of ignorance before the Johnson administration. But the roots of evolutionist thinking lie much deeper, and its influence extends further than I think is frequently recognized.[18] By evolutionism I do not refer only to the "hard" version which claimed that there are "steps or levels through which . . . people must have passed in the process of evolution: most usually savagery, barbarism, and civilization, the latter being considered a 'higher' stage."[19] For the most discredited among the generally discredited theories of evolutionism have been versions which proposed that a logic of necessary stages exists in history that rigidly determines the development of cultures and the direction of their development. Full-blown schemes of universal human development complete with charts and tree diagrams now seem to be a thing of the past. In current discourse, few sensitive writers use terms like "civilized" or "primitive." Yet, we have rested content to merely find felicitous alternative terminologies by which to designate a similar content.

As a theory about developmental stages in human history, evolutionism has been dropped, but the hierarchy it described has remained below the surface of our revised vocabulary. "Civilization" has been defined as "A human condition or state of being presumably elevated in some way above other states or conditions of being . . . A qualitatively high level of cultural or technological complexity.[20] Nobody wants to call African cultures "uncivilized" today. But many will use terms like "closed" or "traditional" instead. In the case of both of these latter terms, an elevated or qualitatively high level of cultural complexity is ascribed to modern cultures in contrast with "premodern" or "traditional" cultures. The ease with which Western thinkers still translate the fact of their technological complexity into intellectual modernity is a sign of the lasting influence of the hierarchical conception of human cultures rooted in evolutionist thinking. But Western culture did not *think* its way to technological and scientific advance.

In modern Western thought, this evolutionism has been reflected in the idealized relation of individual autonomy versus traditional authority. The key statements of modernism assert that philosophy is a liberated and liberating discourse. It is liberated in relation to myth, superstition, tradition, political power, irrationality, passion, etc. Complete freedom from these hindrances to rationality having been attained, philosophy frees the individual to exercise his or her natural powers to their fullest and most beneficial extent. Yet, key statements of the modern attitude fail to show that these conditions can be met and, if so, how. Modern thought does not escape the mythic dimensions of its own cultural setting. This failure is not objectionable in itself, and I suggest with Heidegger and Serequeberhan that it is unavoidable to some extent in philosophy, a case that has been well made before. But from the standpoint of Western philosophy's own expectations regarding its cross-cultural encounters, it is a failure that nullifies the sense of any significant intellectual difference between being modern and being premodern, a distinction upon which much political, philosophical, and scientific discourse still relies. To this extent, it is as if Hegel and Heidegger had had no effect at all on the dominant attitudes of Western thinkers.

A great portion of the discourse of modern thinkers in the Western tradition rests upon distinctions which make very little sense outside of rhetorical considerations. If this is true, then our dichotomies of modern/premodern, open/closed, and rational/traditional as they are commonly used are ill-conceived, and will distinguish very little that is of sociological or philosophical use. There may thus be no sense to the claim that African culture is traditional, and modern Western European culture is non-traditional. This would undermine the assumption that Western culture and its typical patterns of thought and behavior represent what other cultures should be measured against. "Modernity" would then be only the particular label by which we have come to identify the most lively and enduring element of the Western European philosophical *tradition*, rather than a normative category applicable to other cultures, measuring the degree of their escape from their own traditions.

The motif of individually exercised reason in confrontation with organized political and social authority is as old as Western philosophy, predating modernism, and is rooted in the abiding concern in Western culture regarding the relations between individuals and the state. The common problem of Plato's *Euthyphro* and *Republic* can be understood as a version of the general problem of whether the authority of social and political norms can be grounded rationally. If we can rationally ground them, then we will have defined virtue and will know what piety and justice mean, and why they must be followed. If we cannot rationally ground these, social order is merely authoritarianism, whether exercised by the *polis*, the populace, or the gods.[21]

In *Euthyphro*, ethicopolitical norms are considered from the standpoint of their rational basis. Without showing that there can be a purely rational basis for norms, Socrates undermines the rational coherence of Euthyphro's view that their mythicoreligious bases are absolutely certain and require no rational scrutiny. In the *Republic*, short of the attainment of virtue, the redeeming quality of states is simply the order they impose. The lowest form of political life is the complete lapse of political organization into anarchy and the political terror of arbitrariness and disorder. This set of concerns, implicit here and elsewhere in Plato's writings, sets an important paradigm for Western philosophy. As Socrates attempted to make of reason a tool to clear a path for thought amidst the decay and collapse of the Hellenic world, Renaissance Europeans would make the same attempt in the wake of the so-called Dark Ages. But the crucial difference that emerges between ancient and modern solutions revolves around where the locus of reason's authority would be seen to rest. For Plato and many of the ancients, to be rational meant tuning into a cosmological order that included values and natural hierarchies from which norms could be derived.[22]

This general type of solution survived in many forms in Christian philosophies through the Middle Ages, emerging in the revival of NeoPlatonism in Renaissance Florence.[23] The great families of Renaissance Florence attempted to breathe life into ancient political and philosophical attitudes on behalf of their own independence from the Church and Papal political authority. But resuscitation would not maintain them for long. The ideal of the polity in which the individuality of its members was submerged and liberty non-existent was to become the negative paradigm of "self-incurred immaturity"[24] as European capitalism took root. Advances in the sciences during the seventeenth and eighteenth centuries increasingly sharpened and generalized the antipathy between rational, scientific understanding and the world-view supported by the Church and associated political forces in Europe, driving home the philosophical point that the Church and political authorities necessarily stood in the way of science, reason, and social progress.

European humanists during the Renaissance had sought to shift intellectual authority away from the Church and the Papacy and toward ancient humanistic sources. But with the rise of capitalism and the values associated with entrepreneurship following the close of the fifteenth century, and the attendant exploration and colonial exploitation of "new" lands, the imperative would be to see the future as a project for humans as individuals.[25] Rather than merely replace intellectual authorities, philosophy in the new Europe would take nothing for granted. The prerogatives of the individual conceived of as a free capital in the market would provide the new basis for rationality, just as they were increasingly providing a new basis for social and economic relations. Even as they called for the "twilight of idols," to borrow Nietzsche's phrase, Western intellectuals did so without acknowledging that new idols and new authorities were introduced with the rise of the "Money Power" in the sixteenth century and the development of capitalism in finance and finally in production later.[26]

One can follow the emergence of these considerations into their modern form in Hobbes. For Hobbes, as for Plato, the state's embodiment of virtue is closely tied to its maintenance of order. In a peculiar way that reflects his materialism and empiricism, which are so much in contrast with ancient thought, Hobbes' *Leviathan* nonetheless is intended to describe the state as the *embodiment of virtue*: the commonwealth is "but an artificial man" with all the requisite analogous components including an artificial reason (its "equity"), will (its "laws"), and soul (its "sovereignty") to fulfill its one naturally ordained purpose, to protect and defend the subjects.[27] Yet, Hobbes' understanding of the relation between the individual and political authority is cast in terms which Plato would not appreciate. The "Christian Commonwealth" is not served by separate orders or classes of people, as was the Republic. In Plato, social order conceived as harmony was to be established between unequals and aimed at an all-encompassing conception of the good or virtuous life. What makes Hobbes so strikingly modern by contrast is that he proposes that the commonwealth is instituted to maintain an asocial peace between equals in a universe that reason knows only as matter in motion.[28]

It is axiomatic for Hobbes that "Nature hath made men equal." But this natural equality, reason tells us, has rather severe consequences for our understanding of human nature: "From equality proceeds diffidence . . . From diffidence war."[29] There is no morality and no "mine and thine" in this state of nature. The boundary zone between the cultural and natural realms is a moral periphery where "civilized morals" (the phrase is thus redundant) do not apply. The natural condition of humanity is a perpetual war of each individual against all, a situation of "continual fear and danger of violent death," as a result of which "the life of man [is] solitary, poor, nasty, brutish and short."[30] This idea works well for the colonial conscience. One literally can do no wrong at the economic-technological periphery of the West. Morality arises from the original contract, and thus excludes non-signatories. Virtue and justice do not exist at the boundary of "civilization," outside of which we are outside the domain of the contract. Nature hath made us all equal, but culture makes all the difference in the world. In this, Hobbes agrees with Rousseau's famous observation that humans are "born free, and yet . . . everywhere in chains."[31] Both see culture as an overlay upon the natural equality and freedom of humans. Where the local culture is thick with mythicoreligious obfuscation or slow and decrepit, it deserves to be overthrown on behalf of liberty and freedom. Such is the "revolution in permanence" against culture and tradition that is at the heart of modernity.[32]

Although for Hobbes the primary point at issue does not require that there be evidence that the "natural condition" ever actually prevailed as the general state of humanity in a real time before the organization of society, he does use empirical support for his argument. Speaking of the doctrine of perpetual war, he writes that

> [T]here are many places where [people] live so now. For the savage people in many places of America, except the government of small families, the concord whereof dependeth on natural lust, have no government at all; and live at this day in that brutish manner, as I said before.[33]

Thus, in the first instance, Hobbes' formulation of the natural condition of humanity rests upon the basis of a logical rather than a temporal priority, aiming at the philosophical and political points he wishes to make about the European commonwealth. Only in the second instance does he force the phenomena of living "savage" cultures to fit into this conception. This models the intellectual path of early modernism, from a narrative which it conveniently takes to be natural and for which it accepts no responsibility, to the extension of that idea to include all humanity; from its own horizon it deduces a universal horizon.[34]

Hobbes' principal political enemies were those he considered to be extremists of any kind. He counted Puritans and Catholics alike as dangers to the health and well-being of the commonwealth.[35]

> [T]here ought to be no power over the conscience of men, but of the Word itself, working faith in every one, not always according to the purpose of them that plant and water, but of God himself, that giveth the increase . . . [I]t is unreasonable in them, who teach that there is such danger in every little error, to require of a man endued with reason of his own, to follow the reason of any other man, or of the most voices of any other men, which is little better than to venture his salvation at cross and pile.[36]

Hobbes shows us here how the modern impulse, despite representing itself as a revolt against all authority, also contains a deeply conservative element in that it so easily may erect a new and more powerful type of authority over the individual. Europe had been through decades of bloody sectarian violence, and what Hobbes learned from this was the desirability of strong secularized political states whose primary interest lay in simply maintaining the institutional stability and peace that Plato had seen as the minimal benefit of political organization. Philosophy freed us from *traditional* authorities, liberating individual authorship from the authoritative claims of the "reason of any other man," and from the upheaval and tumult of revolt and rebellion. Philosophy thus had a conservative and controlling role to play on behalf of the new authority in stifling calls for change and allowing Europeans to settle down and pursue the prosperity that would accrue from social peace.

Hobbes casts the commonwealth as a human creation whose aim is to fulfill human needs and answer to human dictates, not metaphysical or ecclesiastical designs. Empirical, mechanistic science would provide the perfect rationale for legitimizing the sovereignty of the new power. Philosophy would thus stand in relation to political science as mathematics already stood to the new natural sciences:

> By Philosophy is understood the knowledge acquired by reasoning, from the manner of the generation of any thing, to the properties; or from the properties, to some possible way of generation of the same; to the end to be able to produce, as far as matter, and human force permit, such effects, as human life requireth

> . . . By which definition it is evident, that we are not to account as any part thereof, that original knowledge called experience, in which consisteth prudence: because it is not produced by reasoning . . . Nor to that which man knows by supernatural revelation; because it is not acquired by reasoning. Nor learning taken upon the credit of authors. Nor that which is gotten by reasoning from the authority of books; because it is not by reasoning from the cause to the effect, nor from the effect to the cause; and is not knowledge but faith.[37]

Philosophy is thus the handmaid of politics, its proper method drawn from geometry. In this role, it could be expected to lead us into confrontation with political, ecclesiastical, and academic authorities, passing through these and all authorities which might stand in the way of reason. But this is only because Hobbes has established the Leviathan as the model for the administration of society. This default authority Hobbes believes is necessary if liberty is at all a possibility. It is the most conservative and authoritative type of structure, whose only virtue is the order it maintains. In short, modernity, at its inception, seeks to make a virtue of necessity in the absence of any clear rational dialogue regarding virtue. In the abandonment of virtue as the organizing principle legitimizing authority, organization, i.e. authority itself, becomes the only virtue of authority. Any authority that might challenge the order imposed by the sovereign is a threat to order and therefore to liberty and to modernity. A perpetual state of suspicion is therefore necessary to maintain order, which is sanctioned by reason and science.

  This conception of philosophy is tied by Hobbes explicitly into an evolutionist conception of the cultural history of humanity that directly links technological complexity with cultural modernity, urbanism, and cosmopolitanism:

> The savages of America are not without some good moral sentences; but they are not, therefore, philosophers . . . [The natural plants of human reason] were at first few in number; men lived upon gross experience; *there was no method* . . . [I]t was impossible, till the erecting of great commonwealths, it should be otherwise. Leisure is the mother of philosophy; and Commonwealth, the mother of peace and leisure. Where there were great and flourishing cities, there was first the study of philosophy.[38]

In the natural condition, before the rise of philosophical method, human experience was merely uninterpreted "gross experience." Developing from the Greek states outward, the custom arose to "prate and loiter" in public spaces to discuss common concerns, which spaces gave their names to the earliest schools of philosophy, such as Academus, Lyceum, and Stoa. "[M]en were so much taken with this custom, that in time it spread itself over all Europe, and the best part of Africa; so as there were schools publicly erected and maintained, for lectures and disputations, almost in every commonwealth."[39] So it was not impossible for Africans to become civilized, it merely required the touch of Greek culture. The best part of Africa was the part so touched.

The programmatic element of Hobbes' philosophy is devoted toward furthering these processes which he thought had been set in motion historically. At each turn, philosophy had to broaden the struggle against "Errors from tradition" and the "Suppression of reason" through the "infirmity," "fraud," and "usurpation" practiced by ecclesiastical and illegitimate political authorities.[40] Reason was the only basis for *legitimate* authority. But the liberation so achieved ends quickly for Hobbes in the cruel irony that human nature, like a millstone, traps us beneath the shadow of the "overarching power" of the sovereign, the great Leviathan. It may be Hobbes who thus deserves to earn for political theory the label of the "dismal science," which has instead been given to Malthus' economics. Hobbes began with the notion that liberty consisted in the "absence of opposition" and ends sorting out what is left of liberty under the rule of the "unlimited power of the sovereign" which reason shows to be necessary.[41] Far from the absence of opposition, we are doomed to perpetual opposition and competition according to the universal horizon of human nature that reason and science have established as axiomatic. Humans are asocial individuals, in the first instance naturally opposed to one another and in the second instance liberated into subjection by the state. Although reason set us out for liberty, it seems curiously disposed to find liberty possible only on the condition of authoritarian government, whether it be that of a tyrant or of the majority.[42]

With the rise of humanism and advances in the natural sciences, Western thought had begun to escape the general tendency to see dark-skinned peoples as fated to subhumanity.[43] But the new attitude only said that their "backwardness" was the result of living under dehumanizing *conditions*. As Fanon wrote, "The effect consciously sought by colonialism was to drive into the natives' heads the idea that if the settlers were to leave, they would at once fall back into barbarism, degradation and bestiality."[44] This only made the general contempt for other *cultures* more pointed, even if it made the individuals in those cultures seem less blameworthy. Now there could be renewed hope to save the "savage," and sharper impetus to replace the savages' culture with a non-culture of philosophy, science, and reason. The traditionalism, religion, and naivety of other cultures made them positively harmful to their peoples. With the supposed escape of European culture from its own *darkness* into modernity and Enlightenment lay the hopes of the rest of humanity to follow, *or be led*, to freedom.

Descartes' philosophy provides another useful example of these stresses felt by the early modern philosophers, and their tendency to bracket or exclude tradition and culture from knowledge in the attempt to overcome them. For philosophy to develop in the modern era and become scientific it had to articulate itself as a *Discourse on Method*.[45] Descartes' first rule in Part II of the

Discourse is "never to accept anything as true unless I recognized it to be certainly and evidently such." But a few pages later he notes the impracticability of this in the first moral rule "derived from the method":

> The first [moral rule that I discovered] was to obey the laws and customs of my country, constantly retaining the religion which I judged best, and in which, by God's grace, I had been brought up since childhood ... For then I was about to discard my own opinions in order to re-examine them, and meanwhile could do no better than to follow those of the most reliable judges.[46]

And yet, it is clear from both the *Discourse* and the *Meditations* that this is not just a temporary holding action, but the condition in which humans find themselves, modern or otherwise. Descartes establishes in both works that the human mind is essentially a thinking being or *cogito*. It is thus that he can entertain rational, philosophical proofs for matters which the faithful will take on faith and from scripture. Without the cultural overlay of tradition and religion, humans are essentially thinking minds. "[C]ertainly it does not seem possible ever to persuade those without faith to accept any religion, nor perhaps even any moral virtue, unless they can be first shown these two things by means of natural reason."[47] Thus, the movement of Descartes' methodical doubt is to cast doubt upon the Other, it is not the radical self-purgation that Descartes presents in the *Meditations*. In the narration of that procedure, Descartes instructs the *faithless* upon their minds' road to reason: that is, they are to disabuse themselves of error and superstition so as to arrive at the tenets of the true religion in a rational way. The methodical doubt is a program for thinking at the periphery of the Christian West – please check your culture at the gate.

By Hume's time, European thought had reached a crisis as the result of the deepening tensions between the advancing natural sciences and unscientific *Western* traditions. Hume amply shows, if only in a negative way, that the developing philosophical understanding of science required of Western philosophy the denial of its own non-empirical bases, which Descartes had been content to admit in, but which Hume refused to accept on scientific grounds. One of the great ironies here is that Hume, for all his empiricism, ultimately leads to the explicit conclusion that both science and moral thought ultimately rely on "customs" or "habits" (traditions) of the mind, for which a providential Nature has thankfully outfitted humans. Hume relies upon a mythical entity in trying to account for philosophical thought in the absence of mythic entities, so he defers and clouds the issue. Again, the modernist call to regard all religious authority, myth, and tradition as having only a negative influence on thought refuses to recognize the extent to which this has never been possible.[48]

Kant provides us with perhaps the clearest and most sophisticated statement of Classical Modernism in its thinking about the relationship between tradition, modernity, and knowledge. Again, even if only negatively, Hume had shown how problematic the reconstruction of Western intellectual culture was going to be if it limited itself to only the tools which Newtonian science seemed to offer. Philosophy had to be reconceived as a critical project: that is, it had to begin with a critique of reason venturing beyond its proper self-imposed limits. In doing so it could discover how much more than simple mechanistic empiricism was involved in knowledge, even if this led it to discover that reason's scope needed to be limited.

Kant seeks to discover reason in the discovery of its limits – to tell what reason is by telling what reason is not. The new path of modern philosophy culminates in a *via negativa*; if reason is to be capable of success in the tasks which are appropriate to it, it must admit which questions are not appropriate to it. Unsurprisingly, these forbidden questions are all the areas most involved in myth and religion, and most deeply inscribed in cultural tradition – cosmology, psychology, and theology.[49] For Kant, it is the downfall of reason when reason is applied to such questions, as they are concerns regarding non-empirical and *noumenal* realities. Metaphysics is the repository for such ill-conceived projects of reason venturing into and trying to satisfy the demands of cultural traditions. Reason must abandon such projects to find itself and fulfill its promise. It can do this once it has cleared intellectual culture of the dialectical illusions fostered by religion and scholasticism. Kant gives perhaps the best summary of the conclusions of this aspect of Enlightenment thought when he declares that

> Enlightenment is man's emergence from his self-incurred immaturity. Immaturity is the inability to use one's own understanding without the guidance of another. This immaturity is called "self-incurred" if its cause is not lack of understanding but lack of resolution and courage to use it without the guidance of another. The motto of Enlightenment is therefore: *Sapere aude!* Have courage to use your own understanding! . . . Laziness and cowardice are the reasons why such a large proportion of men, even when nature has long emancipated them from alien guidance, nevertheless gladly remain immature for life . . . It is so convenient to be immature![50]

On the most obvious level, Kant identifies Enlightenment with the revolutionary renovation of Western culture as it emerged from the Middle Ages and the Renaissance, and the religious preoccupations and political formations which still survived in his era. But the reference here is not simply to "Europeans" releasing themselves from tutelage, or to some oppressed group of Europeans. The reference is to "man," and the implication is that the European revolution has world-historical significance for humanity. Enlightened Europe has a natural global agenda, and, unsurprisingly, it is the agenda of colonialism and cultural replacement. Under the guise of seeking complete freedom from authorities of any sort, Classical Modern philosophy had merely ushered in *new* authorities. With great frequency, but unsurprisingly, these programs of radical escape *returned* to the central ethical and epistemological tenets of Christian

Western Europe, even if they did ditch their outmoded scholastic metaphysical supports in the process.

Kant allows us to identify both the liberating implications in modernism and also the depth of its reductionism with regard to tradition, culture and humanity. Kant admits that the process, having begun, was far from complete in Europe in his time. But the development of modern philosophy did not stray far from the traditional Christian conceptions of humanity, offering finally new skins for all its old and bitter wines. There were new ways to be developed, some of them more malignant than the old biblical ones, for Europeans to justify what they had believed for centuries about other peoples, and which they would now enforce in a *modern* way, using pseudo-scientific and quasi-historical rationalizations. The Enlightened eighteenth-century attitude saw Europeans as *normal humans*, if not God's chosen ones, and the inhabitants of other continents

> as variants resulting from degeneration under different climatic conditions. At the same time, however, the nascent campaign for the abolition of the slave trade led to the identification of blacks as slaves, at the furthest remove from whites on the social scale . . . For the mere fact that so many Africans though physically strong had been bought, transported across the Atlantic, and forced to work for no more than a few whites was cited as an instance of their mental inferiority by many Europeans, including Voltaire who deplored all forms of slavery.[51]

Classical Enlightenment thinkers saw "modernism" as the denial of their own and others' conditions of life and circumstances in the interest of achieving rationality, at a time when reason took on the overtones of sciences that had not even been established or methodologically articulated. Yet, in the hope of achieving a standpoint from which the universal and scientific truth might appear, they cut themselves off from the lifeline of human cultural experience, not recognizing that they themselves would thus also be cut off from what had inspired many of them. Because in its attempt to be more scientific and universal, Western thought had only became more incestuous and homogenous, the central tenets of Enlightenment were to become dogmas of *lightenment*, which associated intellectual progress and human advance with the economic regime and the scientific and political program of European colonialism and imperialism. As the enduring legacy of this idea of modernism, it has been difficult for scholars educated in the traditions of Western philosophy to easily recognize that cultural productions and forms of thought from beyond its self-imposed boundaries can be legitimately philosophical, rational, or even modern, in an important sense.

During the nineteenth century, the West was continuing to profit from its unbalanced relation to the rest of the world in several ways, now justifying its superiority with a scientific aura.[52] The nineteenth century is littered with projects aimed at scientifically codifying the economic and political relationship that Westerners held to Africa and people of color around the world. Now, evolutionist assumptions would receive their strongest "scientific" support ever in the works of Malthus, Spencer, Darwin, and many others. Economically, the resources both in human labor and raw materials that Western nations now commanded would be essential to fuel the industrial revolution. In the arts and literature, the plunder of Africa and India was widely accepted as the badge of the "white man's burden," and not of his avarice. Showing great flexibility in thus presenting its irresponsibility as its duty, the bards of capital provided an important justification for the relations that existed even in the face of an official ideology of individual freedom, human equality, and political liberty.

In this way, modernism defined "traditional" societies out of its philosophical project to accord with their place in the political and economic project of colonialism and imperialism. But as authorship free of authority, Western thought has never lived up to this standard, to which it has nonetheless held other cultures as it has held them down. Yet, believing in its own modernism has allowed Western culture to fulfill the function of boundary maintenance. Defining "the West" as modern or Enlightened would be impossible without a premodern or un-lightened "Other." In the sense that Frantz Fanon and others have suggested, Africa has thus been the "invention" of Western authors, defined in relation to Westerners' own preferred image of themselves.[53]

Classical Modernism reached its highpoint with Kant, and, in many ways, attitudes about the status and the fate of modernity still often go back to and stake out their positions in relation to Kant.[54] While there are few orthodox Hegelians left any more, it is in Hegel's challenge to Kant that we find the roots of many assumptions which have been taken for granted by twentieth-century philosophers.[55] Among these perhaps the most important has been the recognition that, to some extent, reason is situated in some kind of history and is entwined with, while perhaps not being reducible to, the trajectory of perspectives that are accessible to humans in time. Yet, despite the many clear ways in which modernism has taken leave of key pre-Hegelian assumptions, and despite the broad-scale questioning of rationality that this has sparked within Western philosophy itself, it is also clear that there has yet been no coherent accomplishment of a post-Hegelian philosophical perspective that successfully fuses the plurality of perspectives that is generated in the abandonment of the Kantian ahistorical ideal of knowledge.

Movements in such a direction hold out the prospect of an idea of knowledge that does not foreswear its own roots in the history, tradition, and culture of a people. If "modernism," in its prospect for something like a universal horizon and in its trust that rational and free dialogue among the cultures of humanity can and should produce that result, has any life left, then it is only in the abandonment of its own self-imposed obstacles to such discussion that Western intellectual culture prepares the way for the fulfillment of its own modernity. Unsurprisingly, it cannot fulfill this promise by itself or on its own. It is only in the broadening and filling-out of the full picture of human rationality from all possible sides that a coherent, convergent idea of knowledge and truth fitting humanity could possibly be produced.[56] It is thus only in the prospect of African modernity that the hopes of European modernity may have any chance of success.

3 Sagacity and Hermeneutics

In thinking about African philosophy, it is useful to keep these aspects of modernism in mind. If the Western tradition moves toward a more convergent as opposed to an evolutionistic picture, conceptions of truth are helpful which offer the possibility of bringing the temporal and horizontal aspects of a cultural standpoint into connection with the vertical dimensions which we have traditionally attributed to conceptions of truth. It is such a description of the problematic that Gadamer suggested, and which Serequeberhan believes marks out the current philosophical actuality of African philosophy, within which current debates about its scope and immediate future are being carried on.

Much of the discussion of where and with what African philosophy should presently be concerned implicitly or explicitly reflects this. In distinguishing themselves one way or another from the tradition of ethnophilosophy and its variants, contemporary African philosophers register the uneasy place of the concept of tradition in relation to philosophical discussion, and the difficulty of fusing a horizontal tradition with a vertical notion of truth. Henry Odera Oruka has distinguished between three ideas of African philosophy that would not be circumscribed in the way that ethnophilosophy or "folk philosophy" is.[57] The first of these is what Oruka calls "philosophic sagacity," the second "nationalist-ideological philosophy," and the third "professional philosophy." These three notions represent a range of viewpoints which refer directly to the issue of the relation between tradition and philosophy. Ethnophilosophy, which Oruka sees as widely discredited, is at the extreme "right wing" in relation to tradition. It posits the "myth of a *unique* philosophy [for Africa], a specialized and wholly customs-dictated philosophy."[58] Any such "philosophy" is going nowhere, but merely repeating, preserving, and conserving some aspect of the unique cumulative wisdom of the people at large. Such a philosophy would be purely horizontal, and would lack any significant vertical dimension. The main point of what Oruka calls "philosophic sagacity" is to define African philosophy *with reference to* African tradition, and to show that they are not mutually exclusive. Sagacity is or can be philosophical when it is closely connected to individual or dialogical reflection in distinction from religion and other non-reflective aspects of culture. Such reflection provides enough of a vertical dimension to escape the apparent threat of remaining locked within a cultural perspective that only makes sense from within. It also, so Oruka believes, avoids abandoning all horizontality in the manner of the "professional" or scientific philosophy school.

Oruka's sage represents a possibility of moving beyond "folk philosophy" and "culture philosophy." But the mere existence of sages is not itself a sign that a philosophical tradition exists, for this would return us to ethnophilosophy:

> Being a sage . . . does not necessarily make one a philosopher. Some of the sages are simply moralists and the disciplined diehard faithfuls to a tradition. Others are merely historians and good interpreters of the history and customs of their people. In short, they are *wise* within the conventional and historical confines of their culture. But they may not be wise [rational] in understanding or solving the inconsistencies of their culture nor coping with the foreign innovations that encroach on it . . . They are spokesmen of their people, but they speak what after all is known to almost every average person within the culture.[59]

The crucial difference between a sage and a philosopher is that the former is a vessel for tradition and the latter accepts only that part of traditional belief that can satisfy rational scrutiny. The sage somehow knows more than the average person within the culture. Sagacity thus has two levels or "orders." The first order is that of the culture philosophy (or *mythos*) which underlies the sage's ideas, the knowledge of which links the sage with cultural tradition. This is the order of beliefs that the sage in most circumstances merely "explains and maintains" uncritically. But while this first order of sagacity is "purely absolutist and ideological," the second order, which Oruka describes as a "critical reflection on the first order," is "generally open-minded and rationalistic. Its truths are given as tentative and ratiocinative, not as God-sent messages."[60] According to Oruka, religion, myth, and custom are activities of the social group, not the individual, and are conventional and unreflective. Philosophical reason can have its beginnings here, but it must become individually or dialogically reflective in order to escape the snare of traditionality.

Against the claim that this formulation does not really find much that may be called a philosophical tradition in Africa,[61] Oruka replies that there is a difference between an established literary-academic tradition of philosophy (which contemporary African philosophers can develop), and a tradition of African philosophical reason among its sage-philosophers which preceded the widespread use of writing in African societies. A tradition of "organized, philosophical reflections," developing spontaneously on the basis of sagacity, has existed in Africa as long as there have been oral traditions maintained among African peoples. But the problem now faced is appropriating that tradition and assessing its place within the ongoing development of a literary-academic philosophical tradition in Africa.

Curiously, however, the philosophical sage is to develop a "rational" departure from prevailing wisdom which is, nonetheless, not a departure from the prevailing *mythos*, or general philosophy of the people. "The sage

philosopher produces a system within a system, and order within an order."[62]
Yet, the philosophical sages are typically in a "clash with the diehard adherents
of the prevailing common beliefs;" they "transcend the communal wisdom;"
the few philosophical sages "make a critical assessment of their culture and its
underlying beliefs."[63] In short, they seem to have a fairly strong *antipathy*
toward the prevailing wisdom, and the prevailing *mythos*, which stance seems
to *define* their status as philosophical:

> [Philosophic sagacity] shows that the problem in traditional Africa is not lack of
> logic, reason, or scientific curiosity, since we can find many sages there with a
> system of thought employing a rigorous use of these mental gifts. It shows that
> communal consensus, a fact typical of most traditional societies, should not be
> seen as a hindrance for individual critical reflection. Just as religion and all kinds
> of religious fanaticism did not kill philosophy in the West, traditional African folk
> wisdoms and taboos left some room for real philosophic thought.[64]

The second order, philosophical and rational, seems fairly deliberately defined
in opposition to the first order, which is mythicoreligious and "traditional."
The *via socratica* that Oruka describes as developing out of first-order sagacity
seems almost exclusively critical with regard to tradition and religion.

Socrates is offered as an example of an "unrecognized sage who failed to keep
silent" – the sage of the second order. Yet, Socrates certainly said his mission
was inspired by the gods, and the mystical element of his and related
philosophies cannot completely fit into the dichotomies Oruka utilizes.[65] The
point is that he is right, perhaps more right than he realizes – religion did not
kill philosophy in the West. It spurred it in ancient times, protected it in the
Middle Ages, and reinvented it in the Renaissance, until Enlightenment
thinkers determined that religion and culture were *nothing but* obfuscation,
superstitious magic, conformity, fetishism, and "fanaticism."

There is, of course, much that is ambiguous about Socrates' philosophical
life and mission. It is common today to claim that, where Socrates' apparent
positions seem very unlike our own ideas, he is (just) being literary or ironic.
But when we think of Socrates' mysticism as a kind of holdover from an earlier
epoch (or order) of thought, out of which Socrates and Plato dragged humanity
kicking and screaming, however this is phrased, we are indulging in something
similar to the long-established Western European philosophical origin myth.
Accepting this, we would then become obliged to make similar assertions for
almost all Renaissance philosophers, for Descartes and most continental
philosophers, and for many scientists and philosophers of science in the
twentieth century. Each similar interpretation then seems more plausible
because of the ubiquity of instances that seem to confirm it: there is always an
uncomfortable holdover, there is always a drag on thought, reason cannot escape
its prison-masters, all science and reason are polluted . . . philosophy is over.

It is all-too-familiar to see philosophy defining myth as "*purely* absolutist and ideological" and itself as something qualitatively distinct, capable of operating with circumspection and of dealing with ambiguity – "*generally* open-minded and rationalistic." It is as easy to make the claim that myth *fails* epistemically *because* it is too open-minded about questions of fact and shifting and arbitrary with regard to its own answers, and that it is rationalism that has been intolerant, ideological, and absolutist in its quest for certainty.[66] Socrates may be seen as an important ancestor or patron-saint through whose life story philosophers have had their practical ideal shown to them for several centuries. But it does not follow that he or any sage somehow necessarily steps outside tradition whenever he or she is carrying out a project of rational criticism with respect to existing norms. No culture is monolithic, and there are many places within culture to stand from which to view and criticize the others. Oruka recognizes this, suggesting that it would be "absurd" to suggest that African philosophers can be authentically philosophical while being "indifferent to traditional Africa."[67] He seems interested precisely to locate this (rational) ground within culture upon which the African philosophical tradition *may develop further* in a dialogue with its history and tradition.

I suggest there may be a final aspect of Oruka's formulation that may be somewhat at odds with these wishes. In introducing philosophic sagacity in contrast with ethnophilosophy, Oruka suggests that the former offers a superior conception of what "the problem in traditional Africa is," yet, he does not expressly address (at least here) the issue of whether there is or was a problem with traditional Africa.[68] As I hope has become clear from the foregoing, I think the assessment *that traditional Africa is problematic* is itself partially a register of political and economic realities imposed by the West, and begs several deeper questions. When we see this, we see also that it is *modernity* that should be considered unusual from the standpoint of humanity, and problematic from the perspective of a philosophical anthropology that is independent of, because broader than, the assumptions of traditional European Classical Modernism. One must, in this context, take care that the "development" *toward* philosophy on the *basis* of sagacity does not end up as a movement away from the particularity of real traditions with roots in a lived way of life toward a purported universality outside and independent of any tradition with roots in an Enlightenment dream. Instead, the movement that is based on sagacity should become a conscious movement from one particularity toward an inclusive plurality of particularities seeking convergences.[69]

This would be a kind of movement toward philosophy that was itself already a movement within philosophy, or a philosophical kind of movement like that which Serequeberhan describes as the immediate prospect of the hermeneutical situation of African philosophy:

The hermeneuticity of African philosophy – as is the case with the hermeneuticity of philosophical discourse as such – consists of the interplay of horizon and discourse. The interplay is grounded on the concrete and lived historicalness of a specific horizon . . . [I]t is out of the concerns and needs of a specific horizon that a particular philosophic discourse is articulated.[70]

If it is discourse which makes us capable of any vertical ascent to a higher hill for a more comprehensive perspective and a greater perspective on our own and possibly others' horizons, there is still always the hill there below us which makes such a viewpoint possible. If by ascending our hills we become more cognizant that a larger landscape surrounds and connect us all, perhaps it is in the valley that we will find our thoughts *and lives* converging. We all have to go back down our hills at the end of the day.

Why, after all, should it be a problem for non-African Western philosophers to accept that there could be an African philosophical "hill" just as there are German, French, British and American philosophical "hills" and schools?[71] Part of the reason is that the common part of the intellectual culture of Germany, France, Britain and North America is burdened with ambiguities about its own intellectual modernism, which developed during the Enlightenment and has only recently been subjected to broad and careful scrutiny. Both Analytic philosophy and Continental philosophy share a common social-historical basis in the modernization of European life over the last three hundred years. From the Western philosophical point of view, understanding African philosophy will require the renunciation of the relationship that the West has held toward Africa for centuries, a relation which has been encoded into its philosophical assumptions.

African philosophy must be considered only as uniquely African as American philosophy is considered uniquely American, and French and German philosophical attitudes are considered "unique" to their own cultures. No philosopher currently writing would think to claim that there are not significant differences in the accepted methods and the content of these historicogeographical regions, but that these represent lines which are easily crossed by individuals who have worked toward understanding the language, tradition, and literature of the philosophies under consideration. To become conversant with other traditions in lieu of having been formed by them should become a working model for intercultural understanding, rather than the requirement that all aspire to speak with no dialect, or that legitimate philosophy only consider certain specific topics. Both within any culture and between any two cultures, understanding is a matter of bringing traditions into active correspondence, not pretending to "speak reason," and waiting for the Other to learn its language.

African philosophers face a situation in which the claims made upon them by their traditions and the claims of "traditionalism" coming from Western philosophers must be sorted out in a way that does justice to their philosophy *because* it does justice to their cultural traditions. Historicohermeneutical conceptions of philosophical activity can play an important role in African philosophy as it develops in the context of a broadening and mutually challenging dialogue among African philosophers and with philosophers in other parts of the world who share responsibility for what they bring to that discussion.

Notes

1 Tsenay Serequeberhan, "Introduction," in T. Serequeberhan (ed.), *African Philosophy: The Essential Readings* (Paragon, New York, 1991), p. xix. Serequeberhan calls this the "school of Professional Philosophy" in his more recent book, *The Hermeneutics of African Philosophy* (Routledge, New York, 1994), p. 5, following the usage of some of its adherents.

2 Serequeberhan, *African Philosophy*, p. xxi.

3 Serequeberhan, "African philosophy: the point in question," in *African Philosophy*, p. 21.

4 Ibid., p. 3.

5 It is to some extent the legacy of historical distortion to counterpose "Western" and "African" too rigidly. As many authors have shown conclusively, the constitution of Western culture has involved the contributions of Africans from its earliest emergence. Here, I use the distinction in a rough and ready sense to denote the historical fact of the divergences between the cultures that emerged in the European context and those that have emerged in Africa.

6 This text will probably have many among its readers who, like me, have been educated entirely within the bounds of the Western canon. Thus, the present essay may be seen as trying to facilitate the hermeneutical process of understanding from the side of that tradition.

7 Karl Popper set the now infamous dichotomy between "closed" and "open" societies, reflecting the more general distinction between "dogmatic" and "critical" attitudes, within the context of the philosophy of science. Popper wrote in 1962 that "an uncontrolled wish to impose regularities, a manifest pleasure in rites and in repetition as such, are characteristic of primitives and children; and increasing experience and maturity sometimes create an attitude of caution and criticism rather than of dogmatism." *Conjectures and Refutations* (Harper, New York, 1968), p. 49. E.E. Evans-Pritchard suggested that the same distinction is crucial for understanding Durkheim's thought, in *Theories of Primitive Religion* (Oxford University Press, Oxford, 1965), pp. 53–61. Jürgen Habermas, in *The Theory of Communicative Action*, vol. I., trans. Thomas McCarthy (Beacon Press, Boston, MA, 1983), endorses a more sophisticated version of the "open/closed" dichotomy in relation to his conception of what it means to be "rational," through a critique of the debate between Robin Horton and Peter Winch. (See chapter I, "Introduction," pp. 1–142). Horton, in many works, has discussed the issue in terms of the common understanding of African thought as "traditional," and what this term should be taken to mean. (See, for example, "Tradition and modernity

revisited," in Martin Hollis and Steven Lukes (eds), *Rationality and Relativism* (MIT Press, Cambridge, MA, 1986), pp. 201–60.

8   Serequeberhan uses this phrase in paraphrase of Lucius Outlaw in *Hermeneutics of African Philosophy*, p. 3. To describe twentieth-century Western philosophy as in a protracted state of "internal self-implosion" is apt in general with respect to the rise of postmodern issues about rationality as such, as well as in particular with respect to the degree to which the discussion of African philosophy forces Western *ratio* to confront the collapse of its own self-description as "modern," "rational," etc.

9   The phrase is from Horton, "Tradition and modernity revisited," p. 204.

10 I am critical of how the fact that the global economic system *has* undermined and superseded many other forms of life and economy is implicitly taken as a marker of the intellectual or human progress reflected by one people as opposed to another. By gliding thus so easily from material facts which spell out *domination* to intellectual attributions which spell out *superiority*, Westerners have long been able to placate their own consciences. By attributing their domination not to their own traditions but to their *modernism*, Westerners misrepresent themselves and their own particularity, and refuse to accept any responsibility for the domination and oppression they exercise. The West then attributes everybody else's uniqueness to *their* traditions and any convergence is described as "Westernization."

11 See Serequeberhan's discussion of this in "The point in question," pp. 7–8. Also see Horton, "Tradition and modernity revisited," p. 204.

12 Interesting is the extent to which Western philosophy has not itself resolved this issue independent of the discussion of African philosophy and non-European philosophy in general. Analytic philosophy does not exactly distinguish itself from Continental philosophy regarding the choice of one method from among others. It differs more in the insistence that method itself be a fundamentally determining factor in distinguishing between philosophy and other forms of discourse and literature. Continental philosophy does not select a different method for philosophy than Analytic philosophy does. Rather, it emphasizes that the content of philosophical works should be a determining factor in the judgement that a work is of philosophical significance. In short, the "Continental" and "Analytic" (also known as "Anglo-English") philosophical subtraditions are themselves cases in point of the fact that the Western philosophical tradition contains a broad range of ideas about what constitutes philosophy, and that it routinely employs geographical–linguistic designations to identify different groupings. Those who would deny such a range to any African thinker should be expected to do the same with respect to all those who wrote in French, German, English, and Latin before the nineteenth century. To do so would eliminate 90 percent of the so-called Tradition with one stroke.

13 It would be out of place to develop in detail the many themes that are now involved in the broad questioning of "modernity" that has dominated philosophy over the course of at least the last half-century. Among those themes are certainly the question of the scope of subjectivity and autonomy, the relationship of science to knowledge, the status of the individual in relation to social structures, the social construction of knowledge in general, and many other issues. Whether hermeneutics is itself the signal feature of postmodernity or the latest stage of modernism remains

an open question. I think that hermeneutics should be understood as a modern attitude, and as presenting to modern philosophy its most challenging and lively questions. In fact, I believe that mainstream Western philosophers should realize that these are questions which African philosophers may be particularly well situated to contribute to an understanding of.

14　This could and should be said of the individualities of ethnic, sex, gender, class, and other groups as well. The rhetoric of modern/traditional has such deep roots in Western intellectual culture that it has been invoked in many types of social battle, despite and because of its ambiguity and incoherence. Manipulating the second thoughts that have emerged about an image of modern American life that has substance and is an appealing choice, contemporary American politicians, for example, exploit the ambiguities of "moving ahead" to "return to traditional values." Contemporary politicians urge the embrace of a brave new world by teasing the social memory with images from a utopian past that never existed. The message of the American right plays off and exploits the disaffection and exhaustion felt by the American people with (undefined) "modernism" as a basis for social policy. In its nostalgia the right is thus eminently modernist, in a negative and manipulative way.

15　While disavowing this, with its rhetoric of underdevelopment every report of the International Monetary Fund or the World Bank retells this myth. Like all myths which continue, it has some basis in fact. Like many myths, the factual basis can be overinterpreted and overextended. In this myth, technological and economic facts are interpreted as if they imply broadly self-serving anthropological conclusions, and as if they were natural.

16　Horton gives a good sense of this in his responses to criticisms and review of the literature, "Tradition and modernity revisited," pp. 201–27.

17　See Serequeberhan's "Introduction," in *African Philosophy*, especially at pp. 3–8.

18　"The relationship of anthropology to the notion of evolution is a fact of great importance in the study of culture, not only because all of the early anthropologists were influenced by the belief in evolution, but also because it continues to affect the ways we think about ourselves to the present day . . . [Such theories in their modern form were] suggested fairly early (1748) by Montesquieu, then elaborated by both Turgot (1750) and Adam Ferguson (1789)." L.L. Langness, *The Study of Culture*, revised edn (Chandler and Sharp, CA, 1987), p. 14. Langness goes on to discuss the "high evolutionism" of the nineteenth century like that of L.H. Morgan, E.B. Tylor, and James Frazer. An excellent source on the roots of evolutionist thinking in Western thought is Marvin Harris, *The Rise of Anthropological Theory* (Crowell, New York, 1968). Excellent sources which focus on the continuing legacy of evolutionist thinking in the sciences can be found in S. J. Gould, *The Mismeasure of Man* (Norton, New York, 1981); and *Ontogeny and Phylogeny* (MIT Press, Cambridge, MA, 1977).

19　Langness, *Study of Culture*, p. 221.

20　Ibid., p. 219.

21　References to the writings of Plato in this paper are to the translations found in *Plato: The Collected Dialogues*, ed. by Edith Hamilton and Huntington Cairns (Princeton University Press, Princeton, NJ, 1987).

22　Robert J. O'Connell, S.J., *Plato On the Human Paradox* (Fordham University

Press, New York, 1987).

23 A thorough discussion of the history of these ideas is out of place here. The reference, chosen for its contemporaneity with developments in other parts of Europe, is to Marsilio Ficino. The Platonic Academy of Florence, which Ficino founded in 1462, peered over the rubicon of European modernism by attempting to inject a humanistic element into revived NeoPlatonism.

24 Immanuel Kant, "What is Enlightenment?," in *Kant: Political Writings*, ed. Hans Reiss, 2nd edn (Cambridge University Press, Cambridge, 1991), p. 54.

25 Instead of humans "revolving around" a steady cultural tradition, as it were, Western thought would come to see the biological nature of humanity at the center of the cosmos, with cultural tradition decentered and detached from them, spinning and revolving around. This "Copernican Revolution in thought" had its roots much closer to Copernicus' time than to Kant's, although the latter coined the phrase to identify the perspective of his own epistemology.

26 Leo Huberman, *Man's Worldly Goods* (Monthly Review Press, New York, 1968); Fernand Braudel, *Civilization and Capitalism, 15th–18th Century*, vol. I: The Structures of Everyday Life, trans. Siân Reynolds (Harper and Row, New York, 1985); W.T. Jones, *A History of Western Philosophy*, vol. III, 2nd revised edn (Harcourt, Brace, Jovanovich, New York, 1975).

27 Thomas Hobbes, *Leviathan*, ed. Michael Oakeshott (Collier MacMillan, New York, 1962), p. 19.

28 James MacPherson, *The Political Theory of Possessive Individualism* (Oxford University Press, New York, 1964).

29 Hobbes, *Leviathan*, pp. 98–9.

30 Ibid., p. 100.

31 Hume would later use Hobbes' reasoning in laying the foundations for utilitarianism in the "Essay concerning the principles of morals," Section III: "Of justice," part I, in *Enquiries Concerning Human Understanding and Concerning the Principles of Morals*, reprinted from the 1777 edition with Introduction and Analytical Index by L.A. Selby-Bigge, 3rd edn with text revised and noted by P.H. Nidditch (Clarendon Press, Oxford, 1985), pp. 183–92.

32 The phrase is from Marx.

33 Hobbes, *Leviathan*, p. 101.

34 One can even see this as the essential move of Locke in his famous metaphor of the soul as a *tabula rasa* or an "empty cabinet" which is filled up by the effects of experience. In a certain sense, this way of thinking about the soul is at the center of the controversy regarding the status of culture and tradition in regard to the modern autonomous self. If we are, as Locke believed, blank slates to be written on by experience, then there is an irreducible and culture-free core or center, which can be regarded as the seat of reason. A version of this notion appears as well in Descartes and in Kant. This center is the heart of reason as ahistorical and noncultural. If this self can be conceived to exist in some respect or form, whether it be logical or temporal, then there is a hope for the Classical Modern conception of reason as unsituated and purely autonomous; there is a ground zero for reason. But if there is no constituted self without culture and history, without language and experience, without physicality and situatedness, then there cannot be a conception of reason that relies upon a cipher or an irrational posit: i.e., the Lockean

self. Hegel seems to have realized this in his rejection of Kantian abstract reason.

35 See Michael Oakeshott's "Introduction" to Hobbes, *Leviathan*.

36 Hobbes, *Leviathan*, p. 499.

37 Ibid., p. 478. The chapter is entitled "Of Darkness from Vain Philosophy, and Fabulous Traditions."

38 Ibid., p. 479; my emphasis.

39 Ibid., p. 480.

40 Ibid., pp. 492–3.

41 See particularly in this regard chapter 21, "Of the Liberty of Subjects," pp. 159–68.

42 See chapter 18, "Of the Rights of Sovereigns by Institution," pp. 134–41.

43 Langness reports that there is good evidence that "Rousseau's famous portrait of the 'noble savage' was actually based upon descriptions of the orangutan." *Study of Culture*, p. 8.

44 Frantz Fanon, *The Wretched of the Earth*, trans. Constance Farrington (Grove Press, New York, 1963), p. 170.

45 René Descartes, *Discourse on Method and Mediations*, trans. Laurence J. Lafleur (Bobbs-Merrill, Indianapolis, In, 1960), p. xvii.

46 Ibid., p. 18.

47 Ibid., p. 61.

48 Leszek Kolakowski, in *The Presence of Myth*, trans. Adam Czerniawski (University of Chicago Press, Chicago, IL, 1989), develops this point.

49 See Immanuel Kant, *Prolegomena to any Future Metaphysics*, trans. Paul Carus (Hackett, Indianapolis, IN, 1977), especially the "Preface," pp. 1–9; and Kant's critique of metaphysics in the "Transcendental Dialectic" portion of *The Critique of Pure Reason*, which is aimed at scholastic and neoscholastic attempts to apply reason to these categories of being. Immanuel Kant, *The Critique of Pure Reason*, unabridged edn, trans. Norman Kemp Smith (St Martin's Press, New York, 1965), "Second Division," pp. 297–549.

50 Kant, "What is Enlightenment?," see n. 24, above.

51 Hugh Honour, *The Image of the Black in Western Art* (Harvard University Press, Cambridge, MA, 1989), p. 12.

52 Langness recounts how "The first anthropological society – the Société des Observateurs de L'Homme – was formed in Paris in 1800. Although it had a distinguished membership including Cuvier, Lamarck, Geoffroy Saint-Hilaire, Pinel, Bougainville, and others equally famous, it lasted only until 1804 when Napoleon apparently withdrew his support . . . A major effort during the short-lived existence of the Society was collaboration in a grandiose but ill-fated scientific expedition to the south coast of Australia. One of the expedition members was François Péron, a medical student and self-styled "anthropologist." Interestingly enough, although information was sadly lacking, both doctors and travelers were asserting at this time that "savages" were superior in health, strength, and general physical perfection to Europeans. Simultaneously, however, it was also commonly accepted that the same "savages" were almost totally lacking in manners, religion, and, above all, morals. Thus, Péron set out to test his hypothesis that "moral perfection must be in inverse relation to physical perfection." *Study of Culture*, p. 9.

53 In a sense, Africa and "premodernity" can be seen as the "vanishing point" of
    civilization that Westerners have used to give definition to themselves and place
    their reality in a clearly understandable and systematic perspective. Kwame
    Anthony Appiah develops related views in *In My Father's House* (Oxford
    University Press, New York, 1992).

54 As perhaps the clearest case, (ed.), I cite Foucault's important essay on Kant's
    answer to the question "What is Enlightenment?," in Paul Rabinow (ed,), *The
    Foucault Reader* (Pantheon, New York, 1984), pp. 32–50. Rorty's version of
    pragmatism has many disparate roots, but the roots of pragmatism have often been
    said to lie in Kant. In the camp opposed to postmodernism, there is, of course,
    Habermas, whose affinities with Kant have been noted by McCarthy in *Ideals and
    Illusions* (MIT Press, Cambridge, MA, 1991), especially chapter 5.

55 See the editors' "General introduction," in K. Baynes, J. Bohman and T.
    McCarthy (eds), *After Philosophy: End or Transformation?* (MIT Press, Cambridge,
    MA, 1987), pp. 1–18.

56 Western intellectual culture has tended to maintain the promises of complete
    freedom as they had been offered on face value during the Enlightenment: i.e.,
    continued to believe that freedom meant liberation from all tradition and influence
    and to lose hope for freedom, since this no longer seemed viable after Hegel. It
    was only after Heidegger that a possible route *through* tradition and history toward
    a different conception of freedom started to be seriously considered.

57 Henry Odera Oruka, "Sagacity in African philosophy," in Serequeberhan (ed.),
    African Philosophy, p. 48. The first two of these fit into Serequeberhan's
    "historicohermeneutical" category, the last he considers "scientific" (p. xix).

58 Ibid., p. 47.

59 Ibid., p. 51.

60 Ibid., p. 53.

61 The article by Oruka is aimed at refuting this and other of Peter Bodunrin's
    criticisms of the concept of philosophic sagacity.

62 Oruka, "Sagacity in African philosophy," p. 52.

63 Ibid., p. 51–2.

64 Ibid., pp. 49–50.

65 Socrates, at a trial during which he seemed to do everything to provoke the jury
    against him, and showing no signs of wishing to mollify their own misguided
    religiosity, expressly identifies himself as the gadfly sent by the gods, on a divine
    mission to save Athens, even if it was to cost him his life. In *Apology*, we see most
    clearly and persistently a theme of sacrifice for the good of the polity on behalf of
    a divine will of some sort. Several of his *Phaedo* arguments and the strongest *Crito*
    arguments that try to establish that going to his death is the right thing to do seem
    almost secondarily concerned with the rationality of that choice from the
    perspective of Socrates as an individual, having much more to do with duty to the
    gods and to the polity.

66 For example, Alfred North Whitehead develops such ideas in *Science and the
    Modern World* (Macmillan, New York, 1966).

67 Oruka, "Sagacity in African philosophy," p. 60.

68 Ibid., p. 50.

69 Serequeberhan identifies Oruka's position as "ambivalent . . ., caught between the

claims of traditional African wisdom [sagacity] and the claim that philosophy is a culture-neutral universalistic discipline" (Serequeberhan, *African Philosophy*, p. xx). Yet it is not clear that the historicohermeneutical conception advances much further if it forces the surrender of the culture-connecting aspect of philosophy that Oruka seems concerned with here. Okonda Okolo presents an even more concrete form of involvement with tradition, and stresses the universalistic calling of philosophy much less than does Oruka in an article, "Tradition and destiny: horizons of an African philosophical hermeneutics," in the same volume (pp. 201–10), with which Serequeberhan explicitly identifies.

70 Serequeberhan, *Hermeneutics of African Philosophy*, pp. 17–18.
71 Serequeberhan suggests this as well, in "The point in question," p. 14.

PART II
Africa and Modern Philosophic Reason

4

The Color of Reason: The Idea of "Race" in Kant's Anthropology*

Emmanuel Chukwudi Eze

1 Introduction

In his important book, *This Is Race*, Earl W. Count observes that scholars often forget "that Immanuel Kant produced the most profound raciological thought of the eighteenth century."[1] This scholarly forgetfulness of Kant's racial theories, or his raciology, I suggest, is attributable to the overwhelming desire to see Kant only as a "pure" philosopher, preoccupied only with "pure" culture- and color-blind philosophical themes in the sanctum sanctorum of the traditions of Western philosophy. Otherwise, how does one explain the many surprised expressions I received while researching this work: Kant? Anthropology? Race? The Kant most remembered in North American academic communities is the Kant of the *Critiques*. It is forgotten that the philosopher developed courses in anthropology and/or geography and taught them regularly for forty years from 1756 until the year before his retirement in 1797.[2] Speaking specifically about anthropology, Kant himself wrote in the introduction to his *Anthropology from a Pragmatic Point of View*:

> In my occupation with *pure philosophy*, which was originally undertaken of my own accord, but which later belonged to my teaching duties, I have for some thirty years delivered lectures twice a year on "knowledge of the world," namely on

* The editor and publisher gratefully acknowledge permission to reprint this chapter from *Bucknell Review*, vol. 38, no. 2.

Anthropology and Physical Geography. They were popular lectures attended by
people from the general public. The present manual contains my lectures on
anthropology. As to Physical Geography, however, it will not be possible,
considering my age, to produce a manual from my manuscript, which is hardly
legible to anyone but myself.[3]

It was Kant, in fact, who introduced anthropology as a branch of study to the
German universities when he first started his lectures in the winter semester
of 1772–3.[4] He was also the first to introduce the study of geography, which
he considered inseparable from anthropology, to Königsberg University,
beginning from the summer semester of 1756.[5] Throughout his career at the
university, Kant offered 72 courses in "Anthropology" and/or "Physical
Geography," more than in logic (54 times), metaphysics (49 times), moral
philosophy (28), and theoretical physics (20 times).[6] Although the volume
Anthropology from a Pragmatic Point of View was the last book edited by Kant
and was published toward the end of his life, the material actually chronologi-
cally predates the *Critiques*. Further, it is known that material from Kant's
courses in "Anthropology" and "Physical Geography" found their way into his
lectures in ethics and metaphysics.

What was Kant's fascination for anthropology? What does Kant mean by
"anthropology"? How is this discipline connected to "physical geography,"
and why did Kant conceive of anthropology and geography as *twin* sciences?
More specifically, what are the substantive anthropological theories on race
propounded by Kant? In order to establish a framework for an adequate
appreciation of Kant's contribution to anthropology and the theory of race
in general, we will in this essay rely on copious but neglected works and
notes he prepared and used in his lectures in the area: *Anthropology from a
Pragmatic Point of View*,[7] *Physische Geographie*,[8] "Conjectural beginning of
human history" (1785),[9] "Bestimmung des Begriffs einer Menschenrace"
(1785),[10] "On the varieties of the different races of man" (1775),[11] and the
Observations on the Feeling of the Beautiful and Sublime (1764).[12] Although there
has been critical interest in Kant's anthropology among scholars as diverse as
Max Scheler,[13] Martin Heidegger,[14] Ernst Cassirer,[15] Michel Foucault,[16]
Frederick van de Pitte,[17] and so forth, there is no evidence that this interest
bears upon Kant's racial theories. Two recent articles, Ronald Judy's "Kant
and the Negro"[18] and Christian Neugebauer's "The racism of Kant and
Hegel,"[19] are relevant explorations of Kant's racial and racist statements, but
each of these discussions of the matter is either too theoretically diffuse and
unfocused on Kant's substantive themes on race ("Kant and the Negro") or
insufficiently rooted in the rich and definite anthropologico-conceptual
framework purposely established by Kant himself for his raciology ("The
racism of Kant and Hegel"). The following discussion, while relying on Kant's
texts and the critical literature, seeks to focus analytical attention on (1) Kant's

understanding of anthropology as a science, (2) his doctrine of "human nature," and (3) the idea and theory of "race" and racial classifications established on the basis of a specific conception of "human nature." In turn, we shall critique Kant on (1) through (3), and conclude with a general appraisal of the philosophical and the cultural-political significance of Kant's philosophy of race.

2 Kant's Understanding of Anthropology

The disciplinary boundaries established for "anthropology" by Kant and the eighteenth-century writers are radically different from whatever one may assume to constitute the contour of the discipline today.[20] One cannot understand the peculiar nature of "anthropology" as Kant understood it except in conjunction with his idea of "physical geography" – although his conception of "geography" is equally historically distant from us. According to Kant, "physical geography" is the study of "the natural condition of the earth and what is contained on it: seas, continents, mountains, rivers, the atmosphere, *man*, animals, plants and minerals."[21] "Man" is included in his study because humans are part and parcel of nature. But within "man," nature is manifest in two ways, or in two aspects: externally (as body) and internally (as soul, spirit). To study "man" in nature, or as part of nature, is therefore to study the two aspects of nature contained, revealed, or manifested in the human entity. While the one human aspect of nature (or natural aspect of the human) is bodily, physical, and external, the other is psychological, moral, and internal. In Kant's conception and vocabulary, "physical geography" and "anthropology" combine to study "man" in these two aspects; "geography" studies the bodily, physical, external aspect of "man," and "anthropology" studies the psychological, moral, internal aspect. This is why Kant called physical geography and anthropology "twin" sciences. Kant believed that, together, both disciplines would pursue and provide a full range of total knowledge on the subject of "man":

> The physical geography, which I herewith announce, belongs to an idea (*Idee*) which I create for myself for purposes of useful academic instruction, and which I would call the preliminary exercise in the knowledge of the world . . . Here before [the student] lies a *twofold field*, namely *nature and man*, of which he has a plan for the time being through which he can put into order, according to rules, all his future experiences. Both parts, however, have to be considered . . . not according to what their objects contain as peculiar to themselves (physics and empirical knowledge of soul), but what their relationship is in the whole in which they stand and in which each has its own position. *This first form of instruction I call physical geography . . . the second anthropology.*[22]

Thus while anthropology studies humans or human reality as they are available
to the *internal* sense, geography studies the same phenomena as they are
presented or available to the *external* sense. For example, in concrete terms,
since human *bodies* belong to the physical world and are perceptible to the
external senses (the eyes, for example), Kant's study of race and racial
classifications on the basis of *physical* characteristics (skin color, to be precise)
was done under the disciplinary domain of "geography."[23] On the other hand,
Kant's study of the *internal* structures which condition the human being as a
moral entity and which are therefore susceptible to development of character
(or moral perfectibility) comes under the disciplinary domain of "anthropology." While geography studies the human being as a physically given,
anthropology studies the human being as a moral agent (or "a freely acting
being").[24]

In his book *Anthropology from a Pragmatic Point of View*, Kant focused on
the study of the human being as a moral agent. The human individual is a moral
agent because one is capable of experiencing oneself as an ego, an "I," who
thinks (self-reflects) and wills. It is this capacity for consciousness and agency
that elevates the human being beyond the causality and determinism of physical
nature in which the individual is nevertheless implicated by embodiment:

> The fact that man is aware of an ego–concept raises him infinitely above all other
> creatures living on earth. Because of this, he is a person; and by virtue of this
> oneness of consciousness, he remains one and the same person despite all the
> vicissitudes which may befall him. He is a being who, by reason of his
> preeminence and dignity, is wholly different from *things*, such as the irrational
> animals whom he can master and rule at will.[25]

What confers or constitutes the ego, or "personhood," for Kant, is therefore
the ability to think and will, and this ability, in turn, is what makes the person
a moral agent. As a moral agent, the person is majestically raised not only above
mere (bodily) physical nature but indeed "infinitely above all other creatures
living on earth." Thus, for Kant, the domain of the body (physical) is radically
(qualitatively and otherwise) different from the domain of the soul (spirit, mind)
or of moral agency.

Kant recognizes that the moral domain, or that sphere which constitutes the
individual as "person" and as beyond mere thing, is also part of nature. But
Kant argues that the unique quality of this (human) aspect of the world
transcends mere nature. A recognition of the reality and the uniqueness of the
moral domain therefore justifies Kant's designation of his anthropology as
"pragmatic":

> A systematic doctrine containing our knowledge of man (anthropology) can either
> be given from a physiological or pragmatic point of view. Physiological knowledge
> of man aims at the investigation of what Nature makes of man, whereas pragmatic

knowledge of man aims at what man makes, can, or should make of himself as a freely acting being.[26]

The distinction between "what Nature makes of man" and "what man makes of himself" is central to understanding the relationship between Kant's anthropology and geography. While one generates pure (scientific, causal) knowledge of nature, the other generates pragmatic (moral, self-improvement) knowledge of the human. In the study of the human, however, both disciplines merge, or rather intersect, since "man" is at once physical (bodily) and spiritual (psychological, moral). Thus, for Kant, "geography" can be either *physical* or *moral*. In its physical aspect, geography studies humans in their physical/bodily (for example, "racial," skin-color) varieties, whereas in its moral aspects, geography studies human customs and unreflectively held mores which Kant calls "second nature."[27] "Anthropology," too, can be either *pragmatic* or *physiological*, as it studies humans as moral agents or as part of physical nature. In sum: pragmatic anthropology studies the inner realm of morality, the realm of freedom; physiological anthropology encompasses humans as part of unconscious nature; and geography studies humans both in their empirical (bodily/physical) nature and in their collective, customary aspects. Or stated otherwise, physical geography studies outer nature and provides knowledge of humans as external bodies: race, color, height, facial characteristics, and so forth, while pragmatic anthropology provides knowledge of the inner, morally conditioned structure of humans (practical philosophy provides moral knowledge and orientation as to what the destiny of human existence and action *ought* to be). The interrelatedness of geography and anthropology and moral philosophy is evident throughout Kant's lectures. As late as 1764, Kant himself had not separated anthropology from geography and thus included "moral anthropology" under the broader designation of "moral and political geography." Moral philosophy presupposes physical geography and anthropology, for while the first two observe and provide knowledge of "actual behavior of human beings and formulates the practical and subjective rules which that behavior obeys," moral philosophy seeks to establish "rules of right conduct, that is, what ought to happen."[28]

Kant's study of anthropology is not peripheral to his critical philosophy. We recall that Kant often summarized his philosophy as the attempt to find answers to the "two things that fill the mind with ever new and increasing admiration and awe, namely: the starry heavens above and the moral law within."[29] While the "starry heavens above" refers to physical nature, under the causal law (and studied by physics), "the moral law within" is the domain of freedom, of the human individual as a moral entity. For Kant, Newtonian physics had achieved spectacular success in terms of understanding the deterministic laws of physical nature, but philosophy had been unable to establish an equivalent necessary and secure grounding for morality and moral action. Faced with the metaphysical "dogmatism" of the rationalists (Descartes, Spinoza, Leibniz) on the one hand,

and the debilitating skepticism of Hume's empiricism on the other, Kant, against the rationalists, argues that the mathematical model they propose as ideal for metaphysical and moral inquiry is untenable primarily because mathematics studies ideal entities, moving from definitions by purely rational arguments to apodictic conclusions. Metaphysics, Kant argues, must proceed analytically (especially after Hume's attack on metaphysical dogmatism) in order to clarify what is given indistinctly in empirical experience. "[T]he true method of metaphysics," Kant concludes, "is basically the same as that introduced by Newton into natural science and which had such useful consequences in that field."[30]

But there is a problem here: unlike physical nature, the object of Newton's physics, God, freedom, and morality, and the immortality of the soul – the traditional "objects" of metaphysics – are *not* objects of empirical experience. This situation, potentially, would, in metaphysical matters, lead to radical skepticism *à la* Hume. However, while insisting with Hume that speculation must be based on experience, and always checked against experience, Kant rejected Hume's radical skepticism and sought within the structures of human experience fixed, permanent, and enduring structures that would ground moral actions as law. The *Critique of Pure Reason* and the subsequent *Critiques* can be studied not only from a negative standpoint of showing what is impossible to pure reason but, from this anthropological perspective, as a positive attempt to find in the subjectivity of the human structure a specifically human, inner *nature* upon which to found moral existence as necessity.[31] It was from the writings of Jean-Jacques Rousseau that Kant was inspired to locate this "fixed point of nature [from] which man can never shift."[32]

3 Kant's Doctrine of "Human Nature" Based on His Reading of Rousseau

Kant succinctly defines "nature" as "the existence of things under law."[33] In the announcement of his anthropology lectures for the academic year 1765–6, Kant stated that he would set forth a "new" method for the study of "man," a method based not just on the observation of humans in their varying historical and contingent forms, but on that which is fixed, permanent, and enduring in human nature.[34] In this announcement, Kant does not mention Rousseau by name, but he describes the method he would teach as a "brilliant discovery of our time,"[35] and, in the comments on the lecture notes, he explicitly states that "Rousseau was the very first to discover beneath the varying forms which human nature assumes the deeply concealed nature of man and the hidden law in accordance with which Providence is justified by his observations."[36] It is certain that Rousseau's most influential writings were already published in the 1770s when Kant was grappling with the problems of necessary foundations for metaphysics and morality. Rousseau's *Discourse on the Arts and the Sciences* was published in 1750. The second "Discourse," *Discourse on the Origin of Inequality among Men*, was published in 1758. The most famous Rousseau work, the *Social Contract*, appeared in 1762, the same year as *Émile*, the book on education. The *New Héloïse* appeared in 1761. These texts contain Rousseau's extensive speculations on "human nature," and evidence abounds that they impressed Kant greatly and influenced his own philosophical development.[37] *In order to understand Kant's positive articulation of the permanent and enduring "human nature," we must examine his reading of Rousseau.* Kant found in Rousseau's writings the idea of a fixed *essence* of "human nature," which provided the needed shore for grounding metaphysical and moral knowledge. What were Rousseau's views on "human nature"? Rousseau writes in the opening paragraph of *On the Origin of Language* that "speech distinguishes man among animals." In the same text, Rousseau links the origin of speech with the origin of society: language is "the first social institution."[38] Language and society are linked and inseparable because "as soon as one man was recognized by another as a sentient, thinking being similar to himself, the desire or need to communicate his feelings and thoughts made him seek the means to do so."[39] But in Rousseau's view language and society, as human creations, are not natural: they are *artificial*, invented. Language and society come into being when, and are signs of the fact that, a "pure state of nature" has been transgressed and a radically different dispensation, state of *human* nature, has dawned. For Rousseau, a "pure state of nature," the condition of *l'homme naturel*, is radically different from a "state of human nature," which is the condition of the civil, socialized *l'homme de l'homme*. Speech and society are *proper* to civilized humanity. Rousseau admits that it is conceptually impossible to grasp the cause or the origin and the nature of this revolutionary transition from non-articulate speech (gestures, hollering) to articulate speech (languages, symbols) as a means of communication.[40] Given the fact that one cannot obtain factual information or explanation of the transition from *l'homme naturel* to *l'homme de l'homme*, Rousseau proposes to imagine such a state as a hypothesis for explaining the origin and development of civilization. According to him:

> We will *suppose* that this . . . difficulty [of explaining origin] is obviated. Let us for a moment then take ourselves as being in this vast space which must lie between a pure state of nature and that in which languages had become necessary.

When Rousseau can locate himself in the "vast space" between a "pure state of nature" and human nature, he can *imagine* the moment when society was constituted and postulates that from one side of the divide to the other there was "a multitude of centuries" marked by distinct evolutionary steps. One cannot, however, ascertain factually what, when, or where, these stages were.[41] Both in the *Origin of Language* and in the *Origin of Inequality*, Rousseau postulates that one stage that ought to have existed between the "pure state of nature" and the constitution of society was the "age of huts."[42] The "age of huts" is the age of the "primitives," and Rousseau describes the primitive age as a time when "spare human population had no more social structure than the family, no laws but those of nature, no language but that of gesture and some inarticulate sounds." It is only after this primitive stage that communication grew from gesture to language, and community life from family to civil society, giving rise to morality, law, and history.[43]

Now, in his anti-Enlightenment writings, Rousseau employed his hypothetical views of the evolution of humans for critical purposes. In the *Social Contract*, for example, Rousseau states that "man is born free; and everywhere he is in chains." By this he means that in nature, or in the state of nature, humans are born free, independent, self-sufficient, innocent, and uncorrupted. It is society and culture that have put humans in bondage: ruled by laws not of one's own making, oppressed by others, wretched, and torn between one's natural inclinations, on the one hand, and social and conventional duties on the other. By nature, human existence is raw and rustic, but good and happy. Culture and civilization have imposed constraints and domesticated the individual so that development of the mind in the arts and the sciences has made humans civilized and dependent, oppressed, unhappy, and immoral. In fact, Rousseau's first *Discourse* was written for an Academy of Dijon essay competition on the question: "whether the progress of the arts and sciences has tended to the purification or the corruption of morality."[44] In his essay, which won the first prize, Rousseau argues that culture and civilization are destroying human nature because achievements in the arts and the sciences are blindly rewarded at the expense of and to the detriment of moral cultivation. Society and civilization breed evil and therefore are enemies of "true" (read: natural) humanity and mores. Using this hypothetical and ideal image of *natural*, Rousseau claims to have uncovered the disfigurements that human nature has undergone in the name of civilized society:

> Deep in the heart of the forest [of Saint Germain] I sought and found the vision of those primeval ages whose history I barely sketched. I denied myself all the easy deceits to which men are prone. I dared to unveil human nature and to look upon it in its nakedness, to trace the course of times and of events which have disfigured man (*l'homme de l'homme*) with natural man. I pointed out the true source of our misery in our pretended perfection.[45]

Rousseau's contention is that civilization may have added many dimensions (such as articulate language and the culture of arts and sciences) to the reality of human existence, but, as "artifical" overlays, they do not add anything of worth to the moral vocation of the human; in fact they may detract from it. Because civilization is artificial and superficial, it burdens that which is truly human in the individual.

Although some aspects of Rousseau's writings seem to advocate a rejection of civilization and a return to the "natural state," others (such as found in the main arguments of the *Social Contract*) refuse a wholesale rejection of civil society, attempt to justify the transition from nature to culture and organized society, and inquire into what kinds of social structures would be appropriate to develop, rather than corrupt, the "true" nature of "man," which is human freedom and "natural goodness."[46]

But if *artificial* civilization corrupts the "natural state" and natural goodness in "man," what, precisely, constitutes this "original," good, and uncorrupted "natural state" of humanity? In Kant's reading of Rousseau's *Origin of Inequality*, the "nature" to which "man" ought to return is not some precivilization, happy, primitive state, but a genuine cultivation of those high capacities that are specific to humans. Likewise, in his interpretation of *Émile*, Kant did not think that Rousseau intended to alienate humans from civilization or suggest that humans return to the Olduvai gorge. In his lectures in anthropology, Kant declares that:

> One certainly need not accept the ill-tempered picture which Rousseau paints of the human species. It is not his real opinion when he speaks of the human species as daring to leave its natural condition, and when he propagates a reversal and a return into the woods. Rousseau only wanted to express our species' difficulty in walking the path of continuous progress toward our destiny.[47]

After he had accurately given a summary of three of Rousseau's major works (*Discourse on the Arts and the Sciences*, *Discourse on the Origin of Inequality*, and *Julie*) as lamenting "the damage done to our species by 1) our departure from Nature into culture, which weakened our strength; 2) civilization, which resulted in inequality and mutual oppression; and 3) presumed moralization, which caused unnatural education and distorted thinking," Kant proceeded to deflate any positive, self-sustaining, and autonomous significance one might attribute to the three texts and their claims. In Kant's reading, the three works are merely a prepadeutic to Rousseau's later works, which give more positive humanizing characterization and value to society, culture, and civilization. According to Kant:

> [The] three works which present the state of Nature as a state of innocence . . . should serve only as preludes to his [Rousseau's] *Social Contract*, his *Émile*, and his *Savoyard Vicar* so that we can find our way out of the labyrinth of evil into which our species has wandered through its own fault.[48]

Obviously operating from the premise that the "state of nature" is (at least) *also* a realm of "evil," Kant interprets the thrust of Rousseau's body of work not as suggesting that we return to a "pure," innocent human "state of nature," but rather as inviting us to *make* humanity and goodness out of ourselves. In Kant's words: "Rousseau did not really want that man should go back to the state of nature, but that he should rather look back at it from the stage he has now attained."[49]

There is, then, in Kant, a clear distinction between a raw "state of nature" and a "state of *human* nature" which "man . . . has now attained." Indeed, for Kant, if the "state of nature" is a state of evil, it is "human nature," as moral nature, which offers the possibility of the overcoming of evil.[50]

For Kant human nature, unlike natural nature, is, in essence, a *moral* nature, so that what constitutes human nature *proper* is not, as the ancients may have believed, simply intelligence or reason, but moral reason – the capacity to posit oneself rationally as a moral agent. Humans, in the state of nature, are simply *animale rationabile*; they have to make of themselves *animale rationale*. The idea and the effort of "making of oneself" is a specifically historical and moral process. Moral capacity means that humans can posit goals and ends in their actions because they make choices in life, and choices are made in the function of goals. Intimately connected with the idea of moral reason, then, is the capacity for action directed toward self-perfectibility, or the faculty of self-improvement. Kant writes that the individual "has a character which he himself creates, because he is capable of perfecting himself according to the purposes which he himself adopts."[51] The "goal" of society and civilization is therefore tied to the destiny of the species: "to affect the perfection of man through cultural progress."[52]

Kant's peculiar appropriation of Rousseau was, and still is, controversial.[53] Kant's Rousseau is not the Rousseau who became known as advocating a return to the life of the "noble savage" – that is, the Rousseau who advocated passion and instinct against reason and became the hero of the Storm and Stress movement. Rather, Kant found in Rousseau a "restorer of the rights of humanity"[54] – but a humanity defined as social, civilized, and moral. In the *Anthropology*, Kant explicitly writes:

> Man, on account of his reason, is destined to live in a society of other people, and in this society he has to cultivate himself, civilize himself, and apply himself to a moral purpose by the arts and the sciences. No matter how great his animalistic inclination may be to abandon himself passively to the enticements of ease and comfort, which he calls happiness, he is still destined to make himself worthy of humanity by actively struggling with the obstacles that cling to him because of the crudity of his nature.[55]

Humanity is clearly demarcated away from and against the natural state and elevated to a level where it has necessarily to construct in freedom its own culture. For Kant, it is this radical autonomy that defines the worth, the dignity, and therefore the essence of humanity. Pragmatic anthropology as a science has as its object the description of this essential structure of humanity and its subjectivity. Anthropology's task is to understand and describe "the destination of man and the characteristic of his development"[56] as rational, social, and moral subject. Pragmatic anthropology is meant to help "man" understand how to make himself worthy of humanity through combat with the roughness of his state of nature.[57] Kant's anthropological analysis of the "essence of man," accordingly, starts not from a study of the notion of a prehistorical or precivilization "primitive" human nature, but rather from the study of the nature of "man" *qua* civilized. To study animals, one might start with the wild, but when the object of study is the human, one must focus on it in its creative endeavors – that is, in culture and civilization – for "civilization does not constitute man's secondary or accidental characteristic, but marks man's essential nature, his specific character."[58]

In the *Anthropology from a Pragmatic Point of View*, in which he draws a radical distinction between "inner" and "outer" nature, Kant argues that humans are essentially different from brutes because humans possess an inner nature, or character. He defines character in three senses: as natural disposition, as temperament, and as rational/moral. The first two refer to humans in their passive, bodily capacity, as subject to physical/causal laws of external nature (or "what can be done to man"), while the last refers to the human "as rational creature who has acquired freedom" and relates to "what he himself is willing to make of himself" through categorical self-regulation.[59] It is "character" in this moral sense which distinguishes human nature from animal nature:

> Here it does not matter what nature makes of man, but what man himself makes of himself, for the former belongs to the temperament (where the subject is merely passive) and the latter shows that he has a character.[60]

A moral character is conscious of itself as free: free to choose or to posit/ orient oneself and one's actions toward specifically human goals and destiny. The ability to posit specifically human goals signifies and reveals a teleologically compelling process that transcends the world of pure causality or causal inclinations. Freedom, as a horizon for destined action, places humans under another kind of "law," over and above the determinism of external nature. The destiny of the individual is to realize fully one's freedom by overcoming the "rawness" of nature, which, in moral terms, means to realize good out of (inherent) evil.[61] Exploiting his running dialogue with Rousseau for the explication of what he assumes to be the fundamental human condition, Kant states:

> The question arises (either with or against Rousseau) . . . whether man is good by nature or bad by nature . . . [A] being endowed with the faculty of practical reason and with consciousness [is] . . . subject to a moral law and to the feeling (which is then called moral feeling) . . . This is the intelligible character of

humanity as such, and thus far man is good (by nature) according to his inborn gift. But experience also shows that in man there is an inclination to desire actively what is unlawful. This is the inclination to evil which arises as unavoidably and as soon as man begins to make use of his freedom. Consequently the inclination to evil can be regarded as innate. Hence, according to his sensible character, man must be judged as being evil (by nature). This is not contradictory when we are talking about the character of the species because it can be assumed that the species' *natural destiny* consists in continual progress toward the better.[62]

The human project, then, is to overcome the state of nature by human nature, to overcome evil by good. In this project of overcoming "raw" nature and the inherent condition of evil, history, Kant implies, is on the side of humanity – for humans are the only animals with history; indeed history or historicality, and arts and culture, are the reality and the outcome of the human moral essence and condition. The possession of moral character therefore "already implies a favorable disposition and inclination to the good," while evil (since it holds conflict with itself and does not permit a permanent principle) is truly without character.[63]

To conclude, it should be obvious from the foregoing exposition of the theoretical groundwork of Kant's philosophical anthropology that the disciplinary and conceptual boundaries Kant established for his practice of physical geography cum anthropology follow closely upon his general procedure of philosophical inquiry. Maintaining the distinction between what in his system is the "phenomenal" and the "ideal," Kant, in his reception of Rousseau, seems to split Rousseau's ideas into the "historical" (the phenomenal) and the "hypothetical" (the ideal). Rousseau's ideas about the "primitive" origin and development of human nature, for example, are interpreted by Kant to be merely hypothetical, not theoretical. For Kant, such a hypothetical ideal (in this case, a model of humanity) is useful only for the regulation of moral life or, as he read it into Rousseau's work, the functional critique of modern society. One cannot fail to notice, however, that Kant himself elevated and reinterpreted Rousseau's supposedly hypothetical, or ideal, assumptions as to the origin and development of *European civilization* into a general statement on *humanity as such*.

Yet for Kant, human nature, or the knowledge of human nature, does not derive from empirical cultural or historical studies. History and culture are inadequate to understanding human nature because they deal only with the phenomenal, accidental, and changing aspects of "man," rather than with the essential and permanent. And "through the work of Rousseau, Kant did grasp the essential element in man: his ethical . . . nature."[64] Thus, according to Kant, while physical and racial characteristics as aspects of the physical nature are studied or established by "scientific reason," moral nature, or rational character, which constitutes humanity proper, is the domain of pragmatic anthropology leading to practical/moral philosophy.

4 Kant's Idea of "Race"

4.1 The taxonomy

We saw in the preceding sections of this chapter that for Kant physical geography, in conjunction with anthropology, is supposed to provide a full range of total knowledge on the subject of "man." Specifically, physical geography, which studies outer nature, provides knowledge of humans as external bodies: color, height, facial characteristics, and so forth, while pragmatic anthropology provides knowledge of the inner, morally conditioned structure of humans. In the *Observations on the Feeling of the Beautiful and Sublime*, especially section 4 ("Of national characteristics"), which essentially belongs to geography and anthropology, Kant, following Hippocratic lines, outlines a *geographical* and *psychological* (moral) classification of humans. From the geographic standpoint, just as other biological phenomena such as animals are divided into domestic and wild, land, air, and water species, and so forth, different human races are also conceived of as manifesting biologically original and distinct classes, geographically distributed. Taking skin color as evidence of a "racial" class, Kant classified humans into: white (Europeans), yellow (Asians), black (Africans) and red (American Indians). "Moral" geography (which might as well be called "cultural" geography) studies the customs and the mores held collectively by each of these races, classes, or groups. For example, some elements in the "moral geography" taught by Kant included expositions on culture, such as the "knowledge" that it is customary to permit theft in Africa, or to desert children in China, or to bury them alive in Brazil, or for Eskimos to strangle them.[65] Finally, it is the domain of moral philosophy to show, for example, that such actions, based upon unreflective mores and customs, natural impulses (or "the inclination to evil"),[66] and/or the "commands of authority," lack "ethical principles" and are therefore not *properly* (i.e., essentially) human.[67] Unreflective mores and customs (such as supposedly practiced by the non-European peoples listed by Kant) are devoid of ethical principles because these people lack the capacity for development of "character," and they lack character presumably because they lack adequate self-consciousness and rational will, for it is self-reflectivity (the "ego concept")[68] and the rational principled will which make the upbuilding of (moral) character possible through the (educational) process of development of goodness latent in/as human nature.

From the *psychological* or moral standpoint, then, within Kant's classification the American (i.e., in the context of this discussion, American Indian), the African, and the Hindu appear to be incapable of moral maturity because they lack "talent," which is a "gift" of nature. After stating that "the difference in natural gifts between the various nations cannot be completely explained by means of causal [external, physical, climatic] causes but rather must lie in the [moral] nature of Man himself,"[69] Kant goes on to provide the psychological-moral account for the differences on the basis of a presumed rational ability or inability to "elevate" (or educate) oneself into humanity from, one might add, the rather humble "gift" or "talent" originally offered or denied by mother nature to various races.[70] In Kant's table of moral classifications, while the Americans are completely uneducable because they lack "affect and passion," the Africans escape such a malheur, but can only be "trained" as slaves and servants:

> The race of the American cannot be educated. It has no motivating force, for it lacks affect and passion. They are not in love, thus they are also not afraid. They hardly speak, do not caress each other, care about nothing and are lazy.[71]

However,

> The race of the Negroes, one could say, is completely the opposite of the Americans; they are full of affect and passion, very lively, talkative and vain. They can be educated but only as servants (slaves), that is they allow themselves to be trained. They have many motivating forces, are also sensitive, are afraid of blows and do much out of a sense of honor.[72]

The meaning of the distinction that Kant makes between ability to be "educated" or to educate oneself on the one hand, and to "train" somebody on the other, can be surmised from the following. "Training," for Kant, seems to consist purely of physical coercion and corporeal punishment, for in his writings about how to flog the African servant or slave into submission, Kant "advises us to use a split bamboo cane instead of a whip, so that the 'negro' will suffer a great deal of pains (because of the 'negro's' thick skin, he would not be racked with sufficient agonies through a whip) but without dying."[73] To beat "the Negro" efficiently requires "a split cane rather than a whip, because the blood needs to find a way out of the Negro's thick skin to avoid festering."[74]

The African, according to Kant, deserves this kind of "training" because he or she is "exclusively idle," lazy, and prone to hesitation and jealousy, and the African is all these because, for climate and anthropological reasons, he or she lacks "true" (rational and moral) character:

> All inhabitants of the hottest zones are, without exceptions, idle. With some, this laziness is offset by government and force . . . The aroused power of imagination has the effect that he [the inhabitant] often attempts to do something; but the heat soon passes and reluctance soon assumes its old position.[75]

From the foregoing, it is obvious that Kant is able to hold the above views about the African because, thanks to transatlantic mercantilist slave trades, Kant *sees* and *knows* that, in fact, African slaves are flogged, "trained" in his words, as European labor. More generally, and from a philosophical perspective, and perhaps in a more subtle way, Kant's position manifests an inarticulate subscription to a system of thought which assumes that what is different, especially that which is "black," is bad, evil, inferior, or a moral negation of "white," light, and goodness. Kant's theoretical anthropological edifice, then, in addition to its various conscious and unconscious ideological functions and utilities, had uncritically assumed that the particularity of European existence is *the* empirical as well as ideal model of humanity, of *universal* humanity, so that others are more or less less human or civilized ("educable" or "educated") as they approximate this European ideal.

In his "orientalist" inscription of the Asian into his system, Kant writes of "the Hindus" that they

> do have motivating forces but they have a strong degree of passivity (*Gelassenheit*) and all look like philosophers. Nevertheless they incline greatly towards anger and love. They thus can be educated to the highest degree but only in the arts and not in the sciences. They can never achieve the level of abstract concepts. A great hindustani man is one who has gone far in the art of deception and has much money. The Hindus always stay the way they are, they can never advance, although they began their education much earlier.

And just in case anybody missed it, Kant reminds us that "the Hindus, Persians, Chinese, Turks and actually all oriental peoples belong" to this description.[76]

It is, therefore, rather predictable that the only "race" Kant recognizes as not only educable but capable of *progress* in the educational process of the arts and sciences is the "white" Europeans. In an important single sentence, Kant states: "The white race possesses *all* motivating forces and talents *in itself*; therefore we must examine it somewhat more closely."[77] Indeed, in his lectures and in the *Anthropology*, Kant's preoccupation can be summarized as: an exercise in the sympathetic study of European humanity, taken as humanity *in itself*, and a demonstration of how this "ideal" or "true" humanity and its history is *naturally* and qualitatively (spiritually, morally, rationally, etc.) and quantitatively (bodily, physically, climatically, etc.) superior to all others.

The position on the psychological-moral status of the non-Europeans assumed by Kant in his lectures and in the *Anthropology* is consistent with his more explicitly *color*-racial descriptions in other writings. We recall that for Kant the ultimate *scientific* evidence for racial groups as specie-classes is manifest and obtained primarily externally by the outer sense, from the color of the skin (thus the suitability of the discipline of physical geography for this branch of study).[78] Physical geography, according to Kant, deals with "classifying things, with grouping their external attributes, and with describing what they are in their present state."[79] In the essay "On the varieties of the different races of man," Kant gives a variation on the classification of races he

had done in the *Observations* by making explicit the geographic element of
climate, but the dominant variable here is the color of skin. Kant's hierarchical
chart of the superior to the inferior hues of the skin is as follows:

STEM GENUS: *white brunette*
First race, very blond (northern Europe), of damp cold.
Second race, Copper-Red (America), of dry cold.
Third race, Black (Senegambia), of dry heat.
Fourth race, Olive-Yellow (Indians), of dry heat.[80]

The assumption behind this arrangement and this order is precisely the belief
that the ideal skin color is the "white" (the *white brunette*) and the others are
superior or inferior as they approximate whiteness. Indeed, all other skin colors
are merely *degenerative* developments from the white original.[81] That Kant
seriously believed this can be seen in a story he tells about the process by which
the "white" skin turns "black." In the *Physische Geographie*, Kant states that
at birth the skin color of every baby of every race is white, but gradually, over
a few weeks, the white baby's body turns black (or, one presumes, red or
yellow): "The Negroes are born white, apart from their genitals and a ring
around the navel, which are black. During the first month blackness spreads
across the whole body from these parts."[82]

When Kant waxed more "scientific," and over a period of more than ten
years, he switched from this to other kinds of "theory" to explain why the non-
European skin colors are "red," "black," and "yellow" instead of "white." In
1775 he attributed the causes of "red," "black," and "yellow" skin colors to the
presence of mineral *iron* deposits at the subcutaneous level of the body.[83] Then
by 1785 he argues that the presence of an inflammable "substance," *phlogiston*,[84]
in the African's blood makes the skin color "black" and, by analogy and
extrapolation, is assumed to be responsible for the skin color of other "races"
as well.[85] To whatever cause Kant attributed the differences in skin color and
therefore of "race" or "racial" distinctions, he nevertheless maintained
throughout a hierarchical extrapolation of these color differences.[86] Kant
attributes the presumed grades of superiority or inferiority of the race to the
presence or absence of "true talent," an endowment of "nature" which marks
as well as reveals itself as marker of race in/as skin color. While maintaining
the usual four categories of the species (Europeans, Asians, Africans, and
Americans), Kant explains:

In the hot countries the human being matures earlier in all ways but does not
reach the perfection of the temperate zones. Humanity exists in its greatest
perfection in the white race. The yellow Indians have a smaller amount of Talent.
The Negroes are lower and the lowest are a part of the American peoples.[87]

This hierarchical color/racial arrangement is clearly based upon presumed differing grades of "talent." "Talent" is that which, by "nature," guarantees for the "white," in Kant's racial rational and moral order, the highest position above all creatures, followed by the "yellow," the "black," and then the "red." Skin color for Kant is evidence of superior, inferior, or no "gift" of "talent," or the capacity to realize reason and rational-moral perfectibility through education. Skin color, writes Kant, is the marker of "race" as specie-class (*Klassenunterschied*),[88] as well as evidence of "this difference in natural character."[89] For Kant, then, skin color encodes and codifies the "natural" human capacity for reason and rational talents.

Kant's position on the importance of skin color not only as encoding but as *proof* of this codification of rational superiority or inferiority is evident in a comment he made on the subject of the reasoning capacity of a "black" person. When he evaluated a statement made by an African, Kant dismissed the statement with the comment: "this fellow was quite black from head to foot, a clear proof that what he said was stupid."[90] It cannot, therefore, be argued that skin color for Kant was merely a physical characteristic. It is, rather, evidence of an unchanging and unchangeable moral quality. "Race," then, in Kant's view, is based upon an ahistorical principle of reason (*Idee*) and moral law.

4.2 *"Race": a transcendental?*

Kant's classificatory work on race, however, ought to be situated within the context of prior works in the area, such as the descriptions of the "system of nature" that the natural historians Buffon, Linnaeus, and the French doctor François Bernier had done in the preceding years. Buffon, for example, had classified races *geographically*, using principally physical characteristics such as skin color, height, and other bodily features as indices.[91] According to Buffon, there was a common, homogeneous human origin so that the differences in skin and other bodily features were attributable to climatic and environmental factors that caused a single human "specie" to develop different skin and bodily features. In Buffon's view, the concepts of "species" and "genra" applied in racial classifications are merely artificial, for such *classes* do not exist in nature: "in reality only *individuals* exist in nature."[92] Kant accepted the geographical classification of races, but he rejected Buffon's idea that "races" were not specie-classes – in which case the distinctions would be historical, contingent and ungrounded as logical or metaphysical necessity. According to Kant, the geographical distribution of races is a fact, but the differences among races are permanent and fixed, and transcend climatic or any other environmental factors. Race and racial differences are due to original specie- or class-specific variations in "natural endowments" so that there is a natural "germ" (*Keim*) and "talent" (*Anlage*) for each (separate) race.[93]

Kant's racial theories, then, follow more closely those of Linnaeus than of Buffon. Linnaeus had classified races on the basis of a variety of characteristics: physical, cultural, geographical, and "temperamental" (melancholic, sanguine, choleric, and phlegmatic).[94] Kant essentially reproduces this schema in his *Anthropology*.[95] In many favorable references to Linnaeus's *Systema naturae*, Kant shares with Linnaeus a passion for architectonics in taxonomy: nature is classified into the universe, humans, plants, rocks and minerals, diseases, etc. Yet, Kant regarded Linnaeus's classificatory "system" as "artificial." Kant criticized the "system" for being a mere synthetic "aggregate" rather than an analytically, logically grounded system of nature. After mentioning Linnaeus by name, Kant critiques the taxonomist's work:

> [O]ne should call the system of nature created up to now more correctly an aggregate of nature, because a system presupposes the idea (*Idee*) of a whole out of which the manifold character of things is being derived. We do not have as yet a system of nature. In the existing so-called system of this type, the objects are merely put beside each other and ordered in sequence one after another . . . True philosophy, however, has to follow the diversity and the manifoldness of matter *through all time*.[96]

For Kant, in short, Linnaeus's system was transcendentally ungrounded. In Kant's view, scientific knowledge has to have a transcendental grounding, for it is such a foundation that confers upon scientific knowledge the status of universality, permanence, and fixity. Linnaeus's system also needs to be provided with such universal, necessary reason, which would give it the required transcendental foundation. Indeed, Cassirer is of the opinion that in his *Critique of Judgment* Kant was supplying precisely that which he found lacking in Linnaeus: logical grounding for natural and racial classification.[97]

Over and beyond Buffon or Linnaeus, Kant, in his transcendental philosophy (e.g., *Critique of Pure Reason*), describes ways of orienting oneself geographically in space, mathematically in space and time, and, logically, in the construction of both categories into other sorts of consistent whole. In the *Observations on the Feeling of the Beautiful and Sublime*, a work which ought to be considered as primarily anthropological, Kant shows the theoretic transcendental philosophical position at work when he attempts to work out and establish how a particular (moral) feeling relates to humans *generally*, and how it differs between men and women, and among different races.[98] For example, "feeling" as it appears in the title of the work refers to a specific refinement of character which is *universally* properly human: that is, belonging to human nature as such. And we recall that for Kant "human nature" resides in the developmental expression of rational-moral "character." Since it is character that constitutes the specificity of human nature, "human nature *proper*," then whatever dignity or moral worth the individual may have is derived from the fact that one has struggled to develop one's character, or one's humanity, as universal. Kant states:

> In order to assign man into a system of living nature, and thus to characterize him, no other alternative is left than this: that he has a character which he himself creates by being capable of perfecting himself after the purposes chosen by himself. Through this, he, as an animal endowed with reason (*animale rationabile*) can make out of himself a rational animal (*animale rationale*).[99]

"Character," as the moral formation of personality, seems to be that on which basis humans have worth and dignity, and one consequence of this is that those peoples and "races" to whom Kant assigns minimal or pseudo rational-moral capacity – either because of their non-"white" skin color (evidence of lack of "true talent") or because of the presence of phlogiston in their blood or both – are seriously naturally or inherently inferior to those who have the "gift" of higher rational attainments, evidence of which is seen in their superior "white" skin color, the absence of phlogiston in their blood, and the superior European civilization.[100] While the non-European may have "value," it is not certain that he or she has true "worth." According to Kant:

> everything has either a value or a worth. What has value has a substitute which can replace it as its equivalent; but whatever is, on the other hand, exalted above all values, and thus lacks an equivalent . . . has no merely relative value, that is, a price, but rather an inner worth, that is dignity . . . Hence morality, and humanity, in so far as it is capable of morality, can alone possess dignity.[101]

If non-white peoples lack "true" *rational* character (Kant believes, for example, that the character of the *Mohr* is made up of *imagination* rather than reason)[102] and therefore lack "true" *feeling* and moral sense,[103] then they do not have "true" worth, or dignity. The black person, for example, can accordingly be denied full humanity, since full and "true" humanity accrues only to the white European. For Kant European humanity is *the* humanity *par excellence*.

In reference to Kant's *Critique of Judgment*, a commentator has observed that Kant conceptualized reflective judgment as constitutive of and expressing a structure of properly *universal* human "feeling" rather than merely postulating a regulative idea for knowledge. This position that reflective or the properly human expression of judgment is *constitutive of feeling* "is tantamount to introducing an anthropological postulate, for *constitutive of feeling which is universal* implies a *depth-structure of humanity*."[104] Whether this "depth-structure" of humanity is understood as already given or as potential, it is obvious that the notion derives from Kant's appropriation and reinterpretation of Rousseau, for whom there is a "hidden" nature of "man" which lies beyond the causal laws of (physical) nature, not merely as an abstract proposition of science, but as a pragmatically realizable moral universal character.

Kant's aesthetics both in the *Observations* and in the *Critique of Judgment*, therefore, harbor an implicit foundation in philosophical anthropology.[105] The discussions presented in Kant's texts on feeling, taste, genius, art, the agreeable, the beautiful, and so forth, give synthesis to the principles and practices that Kant had defined as immanent to and constitutive of human inner nature *as such*. A transcendentally grounded structure of feeling, for Kant, guarantees the objectivity of the scientific descriptions (distinction, classification, hierarchization, etc.) by conferring upon them the quality of permanence and universality, and it is on this score that Kant believed that his own work overcame the philosophico-logical weakness he detected and criticized in Linnaeus.

Kant's idea of the constitutively anthropological *feeling* thus derives from his conception of the reality of "humanity itself," for "feeling" reveals a specific, universal character of the human essence. Kant stated: "I hope that I express this completely when I say that [the feeling of the sublime] is the feeling of the beauty and worth of human nature."[106] Accordingly, in his racial classifications, when he writes in the *Observations* that the "African has no feeling beyond the trifling," Kant, consistent with his earlier doctrines, is implying that the African barely has character, is barely capable of moral action, and therefore is less human. Kant derived from Hume "proof" for the assignment of this subhuman status to "the Negro":

> Mr Hume challenges anyone to cite a simple example in which a Negro has shown talents, and asserts that among the hundreds of thousands of blacks who are transported elsewhere from their countries, although many of them have been set free, still not a single one was ever found who presented anything great in art or science or any other praiseworthy quality; even among the whites some continually rise aloft from the lowest rabble, and through superior gifts earn respect in the world. So fundamental is the difference between the two races of man, and it appears to be as great in regard to mental capacities as in color.[107]

Although Kant cites Hume as the confirming authority for his view of the black, a careful reading shows that Kant, as with Linnaeus' system, considerably elaborated upon Hume by philosophically elevating Hume's literary and political speculations about "the Negro" and providing these speculations with transcendental justifications. For example, when Hume argues that "the Negro" was "naturally" inferior to "the White," he does not attempt a transcendental grounding of either "nature" or "human nature," while Kant does. "Human nature," for Kant, constitutes the unchanging patterns of specie-classes so that racial differences and racial classifications are based a priori on the reason (*Vernunft*) of the natural scientist.

5 Critique of Kant's Anthropology and Raciology

5.1 The doctrine of "human nature"

Although he did not borrow blindly from Rousseau, Kant's conception of human nature is problematic on many grounds, and the development of some of the problems in Kant can easily be traced to their sources in Rousseau's original conceptions. An example of such a problematic is the distinction between the *primitive* "man in a state of nature" and the *civilized* European "state of human nature" – a typical Rousseauean distinction – upon which Kant capitalized, in his admittedly peculiar reading of Rousseau, to articulate and ascribe a specifically *moral* essence to human nature.

Now, in his own writings, Rousseau was never clear, or at least consistent, as to whether his distinctions between *l'homme naturel* and *l'homme de l'homme* are grounded or not in factuality. In one place, Rousseau writes that his notion of the "natural man" is simply an invention of the imagination that leaps beyond ascertainable facts in order to make possible the construction of an ideal past with which to critique the present "enlightened" European society. According to *this* Rousseau (in *On the Origin of Inequality*, for example), the idea of the primitive, uncivilized "natural state of man" is *imaginary* because we cannot observe humans in "a pure state of nature": there simply is not such a *human* state, for we have always known humans *in* society and can observe them only as such. If this is the case, if follows that the primitive condition eludes empirical investigation and therefore must be imagined, and the interpretation of human nature that flows from the fictional posit of "the primitive" must, of necessity, be merely hypothetical. In Rousseau's own words:

> Let us begin, then, *by laying facts aside*, as they do not affect the question. The investigation into which we may enter, in treating this subject [of the idea of primitive "man" in the state of nature], *must not be considered as historical truths*, but only as mere conditional and hypothetical reasonings, calculated to explain the nature of things rather than to ascertain their actual origin, just like the hypothesis which our physicists daily form about the formation of the world.[108]

Rousseau, then, was aware of the fact (as he expressly declared) that he was supplying an imaginative description and interpretation of a "state of nature" and a state of "primitivity" that perhaps never existed. He was simply positing an idea that might help the European man to interpret his current civilization.

But there is *another* Rousseau, a Rousseau who claims to be a natural historian who has given a scientific and *factual* historical description of the evolution of humanity. In fact, earlier in the same text quoted above, Rousseau states: "O man, whatever country thou belongest to, whatever be thy opinion, hearken: *behold thy history, as I have tried to read it*, not in the books of thy fellows who are liars, but *in nature*, which never lies."[109] Rousseau in this passage implies that he is doing a scientific description of "nature" – a "history" of nature as natural historians (such as Buffon, Linnaeus, or Bernier) did. Furthermore, at the end of his life, in a general review of his own work, in *Rousseau: Judge of Jean-Jacques*, Rousseau explicitly maintains this position of the natural historian when he describes himself as the first *truthful* "historian of human nature."[110]

Despite Cassirer's argument that Kant "never attributed" such historical "value" to Rousseau's doctrine of the origin of the nature of "man" (Cassirer's argument is based on the claim that Kant "was too acute a critic not to see the contrast between ethical truths based on reason and historical truths based on facts"), the case is not that clear. While it might be granted to Cassirer that "Kant framed no hypotheses concerning the *original* state of mankind," there is no evidence that he did not *use* one in his anthropology and raciology. Kant, I argue, *used* both the first and the second Rousseau. In 1786, when he wrote the "Conjectural beginning of human history," Kant explicitly put a disclaimer in the preface: he was doing a "mere excursion" of the imagination accompanied by reason.[111] But as in Rousseau, Kant's writings are neither clear nor consistent on this position. While his *theoretical* considerations concede that his own and Rousseau's account of the origin and development of history and humanity are "conjectural," Kant's *practical* uses of the same theories thoroughly ignore and blur such distinctions between the conjectured and the factual. In both Rousseau and Kant, theoretical and the methodological prudence are quickly overrun by the pragmatics and the exigencies of either social criticism or anthropological and geographical knowledge production. For example, despite the theoretical disclaimer in the "Conjectural beginning," Kant in his geography and anthropology (see *Physische Geographie*) uses the conjectured, hypothetical speculations ("mere excursions" of reason) as resources for establishing the supposed evidentiality of "race" as a transcendental, ahistorical idea of specie-class. Thus, "race" as an a priori idea is founded on *nature*, where "nature" is defined as "the existence of things under law."[112]

Kant contradicts himself because, on the one hand, he insists (theoretically speaking) that his conjectural narrative about the beginnings and development of "human history" is what it claims to be: conjectural. But, on the other hand, in his raciology Kant hierarchically posits first the American Indian, then "the Negro" and the Asian as "primitive" and inferior stages of humanity, for humanity *proper* is embodied only in the history of European life-formation (or, more accurately, in the existence of the white European male). How could Kant assume that this classification of humans according to race and racial distinctions (skin color assumed as external proof and evidence) is based on an idea "inevitably inherited by Nature" – that is, a priori, transcendentally grounded and immutable? If "race," according to Kant, is a principle of nature, a natural law, then, the so-called subhuman, primitive, and characterological inferiority of the American Indian, the African, or the Asian is a biologically *and* metaphysically inherited (arche)type.[113]

Christian Neugebauer seems to have in mind the impossibility of consistently justifying Kant's elevation of the concept of "race" to a transcendental, even from within the infrastructures of Kant's *Critiques*, when he argues that Kant's raciology is at best "ambiguous" on the question of whether or not Kant's idea of race is transcendentally hypostatic. According to Neugebauer:

> It is *a priori* impossible that the term *race* is an idea much less a principle or law. If it is an idea then Kant has produced the fallacy of hypostatizing an idea. In conclusion, race cannot be a well-established term in reason without ambiguity in regard to Kant's [theoretical] edifice.[114]

Just as Rousseau recognized the hypothetical nature of his "man in a natural state," but proceeded to build historical and social-political sciences upon them, Kant, building upon this tradition of contradiction or confusion, undermines his enunciated principles through an overtly prejudicial and tendentious interpretation of non-European "races," peoples, and cultures. Neugebauer clearly points out that, because of such inconsistencies and contradictions, "the Kantian can no longer hold firm to Kant's statements on the Negro [or other "races"] and further cannot expect further support from the master" on the issue.[115]

5.2 Essentialism

The issue raised above by Neugebauer as to whether or not Kant "hypostatizes" the idea of race should lead us to ask two related but more controversial questions: namely, (1) is Kant's theory of "human nature" essentialist? and (2) is Kant's conception of "race" essentialist? The answers to these two different questions need not be the same. Regarding the first, if we mean by "essentialism" the postulation of a *substance* or a *thing* as the inherent, permanent, inalienable reality that makes an object what it is, then Kant may not be an essentialist. But insofar as one can speak of ideals and ideas, particularly transcendental ideas, as *essentialized*, then Kant is an essentialist. Kant is not an essentialist in the first sense because, although he characterizes human nature as permanent, fixed, and unchanging or enduring, the interpretation of "human nature" derived by Kant from Rousseau (unlike other interpretations, perhaps) does not advocate any substantic or substantified condition *in which* humans existed, from which they have fallen, or to which they are supposed to return or recover. Rather (the essence of) "human nature" for Kant is a teleology, a goal, a destiny – or that which humans *ought to become*.[116]

Thus, Kant may be an "essentialist," but what he essentializes is not a specific *what of* "man," but – albeit, a specific – *what for*. Although Kant believed that Rousseau had discovered "the 'real man' beneath all the distortions and concealment, beneath all the masks that man has created for himself and worn in the course of his history," this "real man," the "true" nature of "man," for Kant does not consist in what one *is* but in what one *ought to become*. What is essential here is the *end* of "man."[117] Humans do not have an already given, or ready-made, static essence; they have an ethical one: transcendental, universal, transcultural, and ahistorical. Kant, if anything, is a *normative essentialist*. He appropriated from Rousseau the idea that *l'homme naturel* has an essence, but interpreted this "essence" in a teleological and ethical sense.

But, if Kant's doctrine of "human nature" is only normatively or prescriptively (rather than descriptively) essentialist, what about his *racial* theories? What for Kant is the "essence" of race? When Kant argues on the subject of race that the seed of "talent," or higher rational achievement, is what distinguishes the "white" from the "black" race,[118] what does he mean by "talent?" Is it something acquired, subject to historical contingency and transformation, or is it a substance fixed, permanent, and inherently present or absent in the races? Kant's long citation from Hume's "Essay on national character" in the *Observations on the Feeling of the Beautiful and Sublime* is supposed to "prove" that the Negro lacks "talent" – "talent" here understood as an "essential," natural ingredient for aptitude in higher rational and moral achievement. According to Kant: "among the whites some continually rise aloft from the lowest rabble, and through superior [natural] gifts [of "talent"] earn respect in the world," while no Negro has "presented anything great in art or science or any other praiseworthy quality."[119] Kant is hereby suggesting that there is an essential and natural "gift" that those who are "white" inherently have and those who are "black" inherently lack – and the evidence for this "natural endowment" or the lack thereof is the skin color, "white" or "black."[120] This natural "gift," a racial essence the presence and absence of which distinguishes the white from the black, according to Kant is "fundamental" and "appears to be as great in regard to mental capacities as in color."[121] Since skin color seems to be the empirically determining factor of the presence or absence of the natural "gift" of talent, and talent constitutes the racial essence, it is fair to conclude that the essentialism of Kant's raciology is *biologically* rooted. Thus, Kant's idea of "race" is not only transcendentally hypostatized but also biologically essentialized. Because "race" is an idea as well as a substan(ce)tified *natural* (color) reality, Kant is able to claim that the mixing of races is a contravention of the laws of nature. According to Kant: "Instead of assimilation, which was intended by the melting together of the various races, Nature has here made a law of just the opposite."[122] If we recall that for Kant "Nature" is ahistorically conceived as a quasi-Platonic archetype and, like the Platonic Ideas, it constitutes unchanging patterns of specie-classes, then Kant's essentialism becomes patent.[123] Racial differences and racial classifications, Kant claimed, are based a priori on the reason (*Vernunft*) of the natural scientist so that what the natural scientist does (a biologist, for example) is simply categorize species into their "Natural" (read: a priori, prefixed, rational) classes (such as race).[124]

5.3 Critique of sources

One must ask: what were Kant's sources of information on non-European peoples and cultures? As a philosopher notorious for his provincialism, how did Kant manage to accumulate so much "knowledge" of Africa, Asia, and the Americas? One obvious source is books – and there were in Kant's time numerous published accounts of "other lands" in travel literatures, both serious and light, as well as fictions and novels that exploited emerging interests in the exotic stories of explorers, missionaries, and fortune seekers.[125] As van de Pitte reminds us, Kant was a voracious reader who was just as comfortable with the scientific speculations of his time as with "the light novels."[126] From Kant's own writings, we have evidence at least that he read travel novels, such as Captain James Cook's *Voyages* (1773), and Kant's readings of such material found their way, and of course as confirming "evidence" and "proofs," into his lectures in anthropology and geography.

For example, in one of his lectures, Kant found in Cook's travel writings on Tahiti evidence to prove the veracity of a "Russian" wisdom that (1) wives enjoy being beaten by their husbands because it proves to the women that their husbands are jealous, and (2) jealousy is proof of marital fidelity on the part of the husband. Conversely, if the man does not show sufficient jealousy and sufficient attention, the woman, so Kant's story goes, becomes a public property for all men who inevitably want to "gnaw" at the now free "bone."

> The old Russian story that wives suspect their husbands of keeping company with other women unless they are beaten now and then, is usually considered to be a fable. However, in Cook's travel book one finds that when an English sailor on Tahiti saw an Indian chastising his wife, the sailor, wanting to be gallant, began to threaten the husband. The woman immediately turned against the Englishman and asked him how it concerned him that her husband had to do this! Accordingly, one will also find that when the married woman practices obvious gallantry and her husband pays no attention to it, but rather compensates himself with drinking parties, card games, or with gallantry of his own, then, not merely contempt but also hate overcomes the feminine partner, because the wife recognizes by this that he does not value her any longer, and that he leaves her indifferently to others, who also want to gnaw at the same bone.[127]

It seems to be that overall, insouciant of the exaggerations and the sensationalisms of European mercantilist, civilizationalist, and missionary-evangelist heroics fiction that pervade much of eighteenth-century accounts of European encounters with the rest of the world, Kant believed that travel stories provided accurate or factual information for academic science.[128] While acknowledging that "travel" by the scholar him or herself (or what one might call "fieldwork" today) is an ideal way to gather knowledge of other cultures, Kant argued that reading travel books (regardless of their Eurocentric audience-appeal and their intended purpose: namely, propagandistic justification of foreign expansionism and exploitation) can legitimately substitute for fieldwork. It did not seem to matter for Kant's anthropology or physical geography courses whether the research-scholar simply *read* in a travel novel, or actually *saw in situ*, that it is customary to desert children in China, to bury them alive in Brazil, for the Eskimos to strangle them, or that "the Peruvians are simple people since they put everything that is handed to them into their mouths."[129] Kant writes: "Travel is among the means of enlarging the scope of anthropology *even if such knowledge is only acquired by reading books of travel*."[130] It is common knowledge that one of the reasons why Kant never left Königsberg throughout his professional life was because he wanted to stay in the seaport town to meet and gather information from seafarers. For even before the publication of any of the *Critiques*, Kant was already nationally known in Germany and he turned down attractive job offers from several universities, such as Halle and Berlin. Königsberg, as a bustling international seaport, was ideal for acquiring all sorts of information about the world and other cultures from travelers: merchants, explorers, sailors, etc. May writes that during Kant's time Königsberg "was well-situated for overseas trade, and for intercourse with different countries and with peoples of diverse languages and customs."[131] In the *Anthropology from a Pragmatic Point of View*, in what appears to be an attempt to justify why he is qualified to teach cultural anthropology, Kant states:

> A large city like Königsberg on the river Pregel, the capital of a state, where the representative National assembly of the government resides, a city with a university (for the cultivation of science), a city also favored by its location for maritime commerce, and which, by way of rivers, has the advantages of commerce both with the interior of the country as well as with neighboring countries of different languages and customs, can well be taken as an appropriate place for enlarging one's knowledge of peoples as well as of the world at large, where such knowledge can be acquired *even without travel*.[132]

Thus, with travel books and a city like Königsberg (through both of which Kant could look at the rest of the world from a pristinely neutral Eurocentric perspective) at his disposal, Kant must have felt that he had all the preparation he needed for academic understanding of and teaching about all the peoples and cultures of the world.

This highly unorthodox nature of Kant's sources for anthropological theories was common knowledge both within and outside of the university. In his lecture announcements, Kant frequently acknowledged that he would be lecturing from his private notes.[133] Furthermore, he was granted state permission to do this. In a letter from the Ministry of Education, and on the strength of the argument that the "worst" source was "better than none," von Zedlitz, the Minister of Education, wrote:

> The worst compendium is certainly better than none, and the professors may, if they are wise enough, improve upon the author as much as they can, but lecturing on dictated passages must be absolutely stopped. From this, Professor Kant and his lectures on physical geography are to be excepted, as it is well known that there is yet no suitable text-book in this subject.[134]

With this kind of backing, Kant had every institutional cover and caché that allowed him to transform, in lively and entertaining lectures meant to delight both the students and the public,[135] hearsay, fables, and travel lore into instant academic science. Kant's reliance on explorers, missionaries, seekers after wealth and fame, colonizers, etc., and their travelogues provided, or served to validate, Kant's worst characterizations of non-European "races" and cultures.

On one reading, then, we might be tempted to believe that Kant's "theory of race" as contained in his anthropological and cultural-geographical writings was simply a provincialist's recycling of ethnic stereotypes and prejudices, fueled during Kant's time by the travel narratives of eighteenth-century Europeans who had economic and imperial political and cultural ambitions in other lands. Under this reading, Kant would be merely carrying forward the tradition of racism and ethnocentrism familiar to us from the literary and political writings of a Montesquieu, Locke, or Hume. While this interpretation may not be totally without merit, I want to argue, however, that it would be a mistake to believe that Kant contributed nothing new or of original consequence to the study of "race" or to the problem of European ethnocentrism in general. Strictly speaking, Kant's anthropology and geography offer the strongest, if not the only, sufficiently articulated *theoretical philosophical* justification of the superior/inferior classification of "races of men" of any European writer up to his time. This is evident, for example, in the title of his essay "Bestimmung des Begriffs einer Menschenrace," which Kant explicitly states he was moved to write in order to clear the conceptual confusions that had developed in the field since the increase in the number of explorations and empirical observations on the different parts of the world.[136] Walter Scheidt is correct, I believe, when he notes that Kant produced "the first *theory* of race which really merits that name."[137]

The highly theoretical and transcendental nature of Kant's treatment of the idea of "race" makes it impossible to understand those (such as Willibald Klinke)[138] who would argue that Kant's writings on race should not be taken philosophically seriously because Kant's interest in anthropology and cultural geography was supposedly mere "pastime" or "mental relaxation" exercise.

This estimation of Kant the geographer and anthropologist is untenable because it is impossible to prove that Kant's physical geography and anthropology are marginal to the overall humanistic project of his critical philosophy. The geography and the anthropology writings may have been *marginalized* by the critical reception of Kant in our time, but they were neither marginal to Kant's teaching and professional philosophical career nor inconsequential in our day to any attempt at a coherent understanding of Kant as a cultural thinker. The attempt to trivialize Kant's contributions in anthropology and geography may stem either from the fact that the content of his speculations in the area – which were questionable in the first place – might have been superseded by subsequent and current disciplinary, methodological, and other advances in the fields. It may also be explained as a result of the embarrassing difficulty of ignoring the inconsistencies and the contradictions presented by the (supposedly) "non-critical" anthropology and cultural geography writings to the unity of Kant's better-known transcendental theoretical projects. On closer examination, however, Kant's racial theories, which he reached through a concern with geography, belong in an intimate way to Kant's transcendental philosophy, or at least cannot be understood without the acknowledgment of the transcendental grounding that Kant explicitly provides them.[139]

6 Conclusion

It should be obvious that what is at stake in our critique of Kant is, as Lucius Outlaw pointedly states, the "struggle over the meaning of man,"[140] or the project of defining what it means to be(come) human. In 1765 Kant wrote:

> If there is any science man really needs, it is the one I teach, of how to fulfill properly that position in creation which is assigned to man, and from which he is able to learn *what one must be in order to be a man*.[141]

It is clear that what Kant settled upon as the "essence" of humanity, that which one ought to become in order to deserve human dignity, sounds very much like Kant himself: "white," European, and male.[142] More broadly speaking, Kant's philosophical anthropology reveals itself as the guardian of Europe's self-image of itself as superior and the rest of the world as barbaric. Behind Kant's anthropology is what Tsenay Serequeberhan characterizes as "the *singular* and grounding metaphysical belief that European humanity is properly speaking isomorphic with the humanity of the human *as such*."[143] This universalist conjuction of metaphysics and anthropology is made possible by a philosophy which understands itself as the lieu of logos so that philosophical anthropology becomes the logocentric articulation of an ahistorical, universal, and unchanging essence of "man." The so-called primitives surely ought to be wary of such

Kantian "universalist-humanoid abstraction,"[144] which colonizes humanity by grounding the particularity of the European self as center even as it denies the humanity of others. And lest it be forgotten, nothing that I have said here is particularly new. Friedrich Gentz, who studied with Kant at Königsberg between 1783 and 1786, pointed out that, if the goal of Kant's anthropological theories were realized, it would "compact the whole species into one and the same form," a dangerous situation which would destroy diversity and the "free movement of the spirit" – for anyone who disagreed with Kant's compact would be "treated as a rebel against *fundamental principles of human nature.*"[145]

Notes

1 Earl W. Count, *This Is Race: An Anthology Selected from the International Literature on the Races of Man* (Schuman, New York, 1950), p. 704.

2 See Paul Gedan, notes to Kant's *Physische Geographie*, in Immanuel Kant, *Gesammelte Schriften*, 24 vols (Reimer, Berlin, 1900–66). Hereafter cited as *GS*. Citations from *Physische Geographie* are based primarily on the English translations contained in J.A. May, *Kant's Concept of Geography and Its Relation to Recent Geographical Thought* (University of Toronto Press, Toronto, 1970); some citations are from other sources (see n. 8, below). Some of the translations are either my own or my adaptation of other translations.

3 Immanuel Kant, *Anthropology from a Pragmatic Point of View*, trans. Victor Lyle Dowdell (Southern Illinois University Press, Carbondale, IL, 1978), p. 6n. Hereafter cited as *Anthropology*.

4 Ernst Cassirer, *Rousseau, Kant and Goethe*, trans. James Gutmann et al. (Harper, New York, 1963), p. 25. Hereafter cited as *RKG*.

5 May, *Kant's Concept of Geography*, p. 4. Hereafter cited as *KCG*.

6 Ibid.

7 See n. 3, above.

8 Of which only the introduction is available in English; see the appendix in May, *KCG*. Due to the fact that there is not available in English a complete compilation of Kant's texts of the *Physische Geographie*, I have relied on several sources for my references to the texts. In addition to May (see n. 2, above) these sources are Kant's *Gesammelte Schriften* (see n. 2, above); *Kants philosophische Anthropologie: Nach handschriftlichen Vorlesungen*, ed. Friedrich Christian Starke (Leipzig, 1831); Christian Neugebauer's quotations from Kant's *Physische Geographie*, which are cited from the Kant-Ausgabe der Philosophischen Bibliothek edition, ed. K. Vorlander (Leipzig, 1920). Neugebauer's selections are contained in his essay "The racism of Kant and Hegel," in H. Odera Oruka (ed.), *Sage Philosophy: Indigenous Thinkers and Modern Debate on African Philosophy* (Brill, New York, 1990), pp. 259–72. In the following notes, the source and, when applicable, the translator of each citation from the *Physische Geographie* is indicated.

9 In Immanuel Kant, *Kant on History*, trans. Emil L. Fackenheim, ed. Lewis White Beck (Bobbs-Merrill, New York, 1963), pp. 63ff.

10 *Kants philosophische Anthropologie*, ed. Starke.

11 Translated by Count in *This Is Race*, pp. 16–24.

12 Immanuel Kant, *Observations on the Feeling of the Beautiful and Sublime*, trans. John T. Goldthwait (University of California Press, Berkeley, CA, 1960). Hereafter cited as *Observations*.

13 See his reading of Kant in *Formalism in Ethics and Non-Formal Ethics of Value*, trans. Manfred S. Frings and Roger L. Funk (Northwestern University Press, Evanston, IL, 1973).

14 See his study of Kant in *Kant and the Problem of Metaphysics*, trans. Richard Taft (Indiana University Press, Bloomington, IN, 1990).

15 Cassirer, *RKG*; see also Cassirer, *Kant's Life and Thought*, trans. James Haden (Yale University Press, New Haven, CT, 1981).

16 Foucault translated the *Anthropologie* into French, and in the translator's notice announced that he would write a full-length book on the subject of Kant's anthropology. There is, however, no evidence that he accomplished this project.

17 Frederick P. van de Pitte, *Kant as Philosophical Anthropologist* (Nijhoff, The Hague, 1991). Hereafter cited as *KPA*. See also van de Pitte's preface to the 1978 Southern Illinois University Press edition of the *Anthropology*.

18 Ronald Judy, "Kant and the Negro," *Society for the Study of African Philosophy (SAPINA) Newsletter* 3 (January–July 1991).

19 Neugebauer, "The racism of Kant."

20 For example, Kant's work *Anthropology from a Pragmatic Point of View* is today routinely classified and catalogued in libraries under the subject heading "psychology."

21 Immanuel Kant, "Entwurf und Ankündigung. eines Collegii der physischen Geographie" (1757), *GS*, vol. 3; the section on man is on pp. 311–20.

22 Immanuel Kant, "Von den verschiedenen Racen der Menschen," *GS*, vol. 2, p. 443n.

23 In the *Anthropology* Kant writes that knowledge of the races of man, which he regards as "products of the play of Nature," is not yet pragmatic (anthropologic), but only theoretical (geographic) knowledge of the world" (p. 4).

24 Ibid., p. 3. Kant's "anthropology," then, emerges as having two aspects: the descriptive, empirical (geographical and cultural) and the moral, pragmatic (philosophical). While one aspect examines the human in its – in Kant's vocabularies – phenomenal, accidental, or historical aspect, the other looks at the human from the point of view of that which is *properly*, or essentially, human or moral. The latter (moral-philosophical) aspect of anthropology is therefore co-constitutive of Kant's more general quest to establish that which is permanently or enduringly human, and it is here that Kant's idea of anthropology is woven into his critical philosophy.

25 Ibid., p. 9.

26 Ibid., p. 3.

27 Ibid., p. 5.

28 Immanuel Kant, *Lectures on Ethics* (1765–6), trans. Louis Infield, ed. Paul Menzer (Methuen, London, 1930), p. 2.

29 See "Kant" in Samuel Enoch Stumpf, *Socrates to Sartre: A History of Philosophy*, 4th edn (McGraw-Hill, New York, 1988).

30 *GS*, vol. 2, p. 286.

31 Indeed, it can be argued from Kant's writings that anthropology is the key to any attempt at understanding the unity of his philosophy. In the lectures on logic, where he gives an integrated view of philosophy, Kant placed anthropology as the capstone of all the other branches of the discipline. While the question "What can I know?" belongs to metaphysics, "What ought I to do?" to moral philosophy, and "What may I hope?" to religion, the key question, "What is man?" belongs to anthropology. Kant explicitly comments that the first three divisions "might be reckoned under anthropology, since the first three questions refer to the last." See *Kant's Introduction to Logic*, trans. Thomas Kingsmill Abbott (Longmans, Green, London, 1885), p. 15. For a detailed study of anthropology as the key to a unitive view of Kant's critical philosophy, see van de Pitte, *KPA*, as well as his preface to the *Anthropology* (1978 edition).

32 Notes written into Kant's own copy of the *Observations* (1764): "Where shall I find fixed points of nature which man can never shift and which can give him indications as to the shore on which he must bring himself to rest?" (*GS*, vol. 20, p. 46).

33 Immanuel Kant, *Critique of Practical Reason*, trans. Lewis White Beck (Macmillan, New York, 1993), pp. 153–4.

34 *GS*, vol. 2, p. 311.

35 Ibid., p. 312.

36 Ibid., vol. 20, p. 58.

37 Kant biographers, such as Cassirer, record that in Kant's spartan study, there was only one ornament on the wall: the portrait of J.-J. Rousseau. It is also reported how Kant, the model of punctuality in his daily promenade, but engrossed in the study of Rousseau's *Émile* when it first appeared, forgot his daily walk (see Cassirer, *RKG*, pp. 1–2). Kant himself also poignantly testifies to the influence of Rousseau in setting the direction for his philosophical anthropology. For example, in the *Fragments* edited by Hartenstein, Kant writes: "I am myself by inclination a seeker after truth. I feel a consuming thirst for knowledge and a restless passion to advance in it, as well as satisfaction in every forward step. There was a time when I thought that this alone could constitute the honor of mankind . . . Rousseau set me right . . . I learned to respect *human nature*" (*GS*, vol. 7, p. 624; my emphasis).

38 J.-J. Rousseau, *Essay on the Origin of Language*, trans. John H. Moran and Alexander Gode (University of Chicago Press, Chicago, IL, 1986).

39 Ibid., p. 5. When Rousseau further reflects on the problem of the exact relationship between language and society, speech and community, he writes: "For myself, I am so aghast at the increasing difficulties which present themselves, and so well convinced of the almost demonstrable impossibility that languages should owe their original institution to merely human means, that I leave, to any one who will undertake it, the discussion of the difficult problem, which was most necessary, the existence of society to the invention of language, or the invention of language to the establishment of society" (p. 151).

40 Rousseau criticizes writers such as Condillac who erroneously believed that they understood the cause and the genesis of such revolutionary phenomena; they are wrong because they merely project into this unknown primordial past "ideas taken from society."

41 Robert Derathé, quoted in Jacques Derrida, *Of Grammatology*, trans. Gayatri

Chakravorty Spivak (Johns Hopkins University Press, Baltimore, MD, 1976), p. 231.

42 For a detailed analysis and critique of the discrepancies and similarities of Rousseau's views on the question of the different stages in the evolution of language and society in the *Origin of Language* on the one hand and in the *Origin of Inequality* on the other, see Derrida, *Of Grammatology*, esp. pt 2.

43 Our interpretation may be a little too tidy if we locate the "age of huts," the primitive time, as the *middle* point from "state of pure nature" to "society." In the *Origin of Language*, the "age of huts" was located by Rousseau much closer to the unknown and unknowable "pure state of nature." There he wrote: "I consider primitive the period of time from the dispersion of men to any period of the human race that might be taken as determining an epoch" (p. 31, n. 1). Hence, the "age of huts" is specifically defined out of history, and the "primitives" out of historicality, as they would lack historical consciousness. It is necessary to keep this in mind when we study Kant's appropriation of Rousseau in his definition of what constitutes "human nature" and in his hierarchical gradation of "races" and cultures as "primitive" or "advanced" under the influence of Rousseau's definitions.

44 Frederick Coppleston, *A History of Philosophy*, vol. 6, *Wolf to Kant* (Newman, Westminster, MD, 1964), p. 69.

45 J.-J. Rousseau, *The Confessions*, trans. W. Conyngham Mallory (Brentano, New York, 1928), ch. 8.

46 Since there is no "natural" right to legislate for society – for society is "artificial" or conventional, while individuals are "born free" – the only legitimate way to secure at the same time collective existence and freedom is through self-legislation. The *Social Contract* proposes a creation of a collective or "general will," a "corporate capacity" called the state, an embodiment of the collective, moral will. The individual "puts his person and all his power in common under the supreme direction of the general will," and, within the corporate capacity, where he is received as an indivisible part of the whole, one would share in the power of the state both as citizen and as subject, making as well as obeying laws in which one, as part of the "voice of the people," has legislated. See the discussion of Rousseau's *Social Contract* in Coppleston, *History of Philosophy*, pp. 81ff. The influence of Rousseau's *Social Contract* in Kant can be seen in Kant's ethical concepts such as the relationship between the universal "good will" and the "categorical imperative." See, for example, van de Pitte, *KPA*, p. 55. Cassirer also argues "that Rousseau not only influenced the content and systematic development of Kant's foundation of ethics, but that he also formed its language and style" (*RKG*, p. 32).

47 *Anthropology*, p. 243.

48 Ibid., pp. 243–4.

49 Ibid., p. 244.

50 In the *Anthropology* Kant stated: "What is characteristic of the human species in comparision with the idea of other possible rational beings on earth is this: Nature implanted in them the seed of *discord* [evil] and willed that from it their own reason would bring *concord* [good]" (p. 238).

51 Ibid.

52 Ibid.

53 See, for example, Peter Gay's preface to Cassirer's *RKG*, as well as the various interpretations of Rousseau in certain essays contained in this volume.
54 Cassirer, *RKG*, p. 13.
55 *Anthropology*, pp. 241–2.
56 Ibid., p. 241.
57 Ibid.
58 *GS*, vol. 20, p. 14. In fact, it is in society/culture/civilization that the human comes to its proper or essential own by revealing itself as an ethical and moral content (*Wesen*). See Cassirer, *RKG*, vol. 22, or van de Pitte, *KPA*, pp. 50–1.
59 *Anthropology*, 3. It is important to keep in mind this definition of "character" and the specifically human, as it is necessary not only for a full appreciation of Kant's theory of human nature, but also for his ranking-ordering of Asians, Africans, and American Indians as "inferior" rational/moral human beings in comparison with white Europeans.
60 Ibid.
61 Again, according to Kant, "What is characteristic of the human species in comparison with the idea of other possible rational beings on earth is this: Nature implanted in them the seed of *discord* and willed that from it their own reason would bring *concord*" (*Anthropology*, p. 238).
62 Ibid., pp. 240–1; my emphasis.
63 Ibid., p. 238.
64 Van de Pitte, *KPA*, p. 51.
65 See Immanuel Kant, "Bestimmung des Begriffs einer Menschenrace" (1785), in Fritz Schultze, *Kant und Darwin: Ein Beitrag zur Geschichte der Entwicklungslehre* (Dufft, Jena, 1875).
66 *Anthropology*, p. 241.
67 See *Lectures on Ethics* of the years 1765–6.
68 *Anthropology*, p. 9.
69 See *Kants philosophische Anthropologie*, ed. Starke, p. 352; my translation.
70 Kant writes: "When a people does not perfect itself in any way over the space of centuries, so it is to be assumed that there exists a certain *natural* pre-disposition (*Anlage*) that the people cannot transcend." "Wenn sich ein Volk auf keine Weise in Jahrhunderten vervollkommnet, so ist anzunehmen, daß es schon in ihm eine gewisse Naturanlage gibt, welche zu übersteigen es nicht fähig ist" (ibid.; my translation).
71 "Das Volk der Amerikaner nimmt keine bildung an. Es hat keine Triebfedern, denn es fehlen ihm Affekt und Leidenschaft. Sie sind nicht verliebt, daher sind auch nicht furchtbar. Sie sprechen fast nichts, liebkosen einander nicht, sorgen auch für nichts, und sind faul" (ibid., p. 353; my translation).
72 "Die race der Neger, könnte man sagen, ist ganz das Gegenteil von den Amerikanern; sie sind voll Affekt und Leidenschaft, sehr lebhaft, schwatzhaft und eitel. Sie nehmen Bildung an, aber nur eine Bildung der Knechte, d.h. sie lassen sich abrichten. Sie haben viele Triebfedern, sind auch empfindlich, fürchten sich vor Schlägen und thun auch viel aus Ehre" (ibid.; my translation).
73 Neugebauer, "The Racism of Kant," p. 264.
74 "Die Mohren . . . haben eine dicke Haut, wie man sie denn auch nicht mit Ruthen, sondern gespaltenen Röhren peitscht, wenn man sie züchtigt, damit das Blut einen

Ausgang finde, und nicht unter der Haut eitere" (ibid.; my translation). Given that whips do indeed break the skin, it is difficult to avoid the suspicion that Kant's promotion of the split cane is to ensure a larger, more gaping wound. If the passage just quoted by Neugebauer (n. 73) was drawn from the same source as mine, rather than from a combination of references, his interpretation would be understandable from this perspective.

75   Quoted in ibid., p. 264, my translation.

76   "Die Hindus haben zwar Triebfedern, aber sie haben einen starken Grad von Gelassenheit, und sehen alle wie Philosophen aus. Demohngeachtet sind doch zum Zorne und zur Liebe sehr geneigt. Sie nehmen daher Bildung im höchsten Grade an, aber nur zu Künsten und nicht zu Wissenchaften. Sie bringen es niemals bis zu abstrakten Begriffen. Ein hindostanischer großer Mann ist der, der es recht weit in der Betrügerei gebracht und viel Geld hat. Die Hindus bleiben immer wie sind, weiter bringen sie es niemals . . . Dahin gehören die Hindus, die Perser, die Chinesen, die Türken, überhaupt alle orientalischen Völker" (*Kants philosophische Anthropologie*, ed. Starke, pp. 352 and 353; my translation).

77   "Die Race der Weißen enthält alle Triebfedern und Talente in sich; daher werden wir sie etwas genauer betrachten müssen" (ibid.; p. 353; my translation).

78   One of Kant's earliest essays on race, "On the varieties of the different races of man," was written in 1775 as an announcement for his lecture on physical geography. See the text in Count, *This Is Race*, pp. 16–24.

79   Kuno Fischer, *A Critique of Kant*, trans. W.S. Hough (Swan, Sonnenschein, Lowrey, London, 1888), pp. 67–8; quoted in May, *KCG*, p. 6.

80   Kant, "On the different races of man," p. 23.

81   Kant may have got this idea from the work of Johann Friedrich Blumenbach (1752–1840), the German naturalist to whose work on racial classifications Kant refers on page 211 of the *Anthropology*. According to Blumenbach, who placed skin color as the highest racial category (see his treatise *On the Natural Variety of Mankind* (1775) (Longman, Green, London, 1865), there are five races, but only three of them are basic. The "Caucasian" is the "most beautiful . . . to which the pre-eminence belongs;" the "Mongolian" and the "Ethiopian" races are "the extreme degenerations of the human [read: white] species." The remaining two races, the "American" and the "Malay," are simply *transitory* stages of degeneration from the white to, respectively, the Malay and the Ethiopian (x–xi).

82   "Die Neger werden weißgeboren, außer ihren Zeugungsgliedern und einen Ring um den Nabel, die schwarz sind. Von diesen Teilen aus zieht sich die Schwärze im ersten Monat über den ganzen Körper." Quoted in Neugebauer, "The Racism of Kant," p. 265; my translation. Neugebauer, following V.Y. Mudimbe, accurately points out that a century and a half earlier, a missionary named F. Romano wrote the same opinion as the one held by Kant on the origin of the "black" skin: "I naturali del Congo sono tutti di color negre chi pui, e chi meno; . . . Quando nascendo, non sonso negri ma bianchi, e poi a poco a poco si vanno fecendo negri."

83   "For good reason," writes Kant, "one now ascribes the different color of plants to the differing amounts of iron precipitated by various fluids. As all animal blood contains iron, nothing prevents us from ascribing to the different colors of the human races the same cause. In this way the base acid, or phosphoric acid . . . reacts strongly with the iron particles and turns red or black or yellow." "Man schreibt

jetzt mit gutem Grunde die verscheidenene Farben der Gewächse dem durch unterschiedliche Säfte gefällten Eisen zu. Da alles Thierblut Eisen enthält, so hindert uns nichts, die verschiedene Farbe dieser Menschenracen ebenderselben Ursache beizumessen. Auf diese Art würde etwa das Satzsäure, oder das phosphorische Säure, oder . . . die Eisentheilchen im Reichtum roth oder schwarz oder gelb wiederschlagen." See Kant's "Von den verschiedenen Racen der Menschen," in Schultze, *Kant und Darwin*, pp. 58–79; my translation.

84   *Webster's Collegiate Dictionary* (1963) defines "phlogiston" as "the hypothetical principle of fire regarded formerly as a material substance."

85   "Now the purpose [of race] is nowhere more noticeable in the characteristics of race than in the Negro; merely the example that can be taken from it alone, justifies us also in the supposition of seeing an analogy in this race to the others. Namely, it is now known that human blood becomes black, merely by dint of the fact that it is loaded with phlogiston . . . Now the strong stench of the Negro, which cannot be removed through any amount of washing, gives us reason to suppose that their skin removes a great deal of phlogiston from the blood and that nature must have organized this skin in such a way that the blood can be dephlogistonized to a much greater degree than is the case with us." "Nun ist dieses Zweckmäßige zwar an der Eigenthümlichkeit keiner Race so deutlich zu beweisen möglich, als an der Negerrace; allein das Beispiel, das von dieser allein hergenommen worden, berechtigt uns auch, nach der Analogie eben dergleichen von den übrigen wenigstens zu vermuthen. Man weiß nämlich jetzt, daß das Menschenblut, bloß dadurch, daß es mit Phlogiston überladen wird, schwarz werde . . . Nun giebt schon der starke und durch keine Reinlichkeit zu vermeidende Geruch der Neger Anlaß, zu vermuthen, daß ihre Haut sehr viel Phlogiston aus dem Blute wegschaffe, und daß die Natur diese Haut so organisiert haben müsse, daß das Blut sich bei ihnen in weit größerem Maße durch sie dephlogistiren könne, als es bei uns geschieht" (Kant, "Von den Racen der Menschen," in Schultze, *Kant und Darwin*, p. 150; my translation). In the *Anthropology*, Kant speaks of "innate, natural character which, so to speak, lies in the composition of the person's bood" (p. 235).

86   Anyone interested in exposing or refuting, perhaps with recent developments in science as background, the bogus nature of Kant's ideas about "race" and "racial" differences should see some excellent work of Kwame Anthony Appiah: for example, his recent *In My Father's House: Africa in the Philosophy of Culture* (Oxford University Press, New York, 1992), esp. chs 1 and 2: "The invention of Africa" and "The illusions of race." I am here more directly concerned with Kant's hierarchical *interpretation* of skin colors, or "race," and his philosophical *justification* of the interpretation.

87   "In den heißen Ländern reift der Mensch in allen Stücken früher, erreicht aber nicht die Vollkommenheit temperierter Zonen. Die Menschheit ist in ihrer größten Vollkommenheit in der Rasse der Weißen. Die gelben Inder haben schon geringeres Talent. Die Neger sind tiefer, und am tiefsten steht ein Teil amerikanischen Völkerschaften" (Kant, *Physische Geographie*, quoted in Neugebauer, "The racism of Kant," p. 264; my translation).

88   Kant states: "that which the sun implants in the skin of the Negro in Africa, and thus that which is only accidental to him, must fall away in France and only the blackness will remain which is his by birth, and which he reproduces, and which

alone can thus be used as a *difference in class*." "Denn das, was in Afrika der Haut des Negers die Sonne eindrükte, und was also ihm nur zufällig ist, muß in Frankreich wegfallen, und allein die Schwärze übrigbleiben, die ihm durch seine Geburt zu Teil ward, die er weiter fortpflanzt, und die daher allein zu einem Klassenunterschied gebraucht werden kann" ("Bestimmung des Begriffs einer Menschenrace," in Schultze, *Kant und Darwin*, p. 136; my translation and emphasis).

89 In the same essay, Kant argues that skin color is also "die Spur dieser Verschiedenheit des Naturcharakters" (ibid., p. 138).

90 Quoted in Richard Popkin, "Hume's racism," *The Philosophical Forum*, vol. 9, nos 2–3 (Winter–Spring 1977–8), p. 218. See *Observations*, p. 113.

91 *Histoire naturelle* (1749–). See excerpts in Count, *This Is Race*, pp. 3ff.

92 Ibid.

93 Kant, "Bestimmung des Begriffs einer Menschenrace," *GS*, vol. 8, p. 98.

94 *Systema naturae* (1735). See the discussion of this work by Walter Scheidt in his essay "The concept of race in anthropology," in Count, *This Is Race*, pp. 354ff.

95 See *Anthropology*, pp. 196–202.

96 Quoted in May, *KCG*, pp. 260–1; my emphasis.

97 According to Cassirer, Kant, in the *Critique of Judgment*, was playing the role of "logician to Linnaeus' descriptive science." See Ernst Cassirer, *The Problem of Knowledge: Philosophy, Science and History since Hegel*, trans. William H. Woglom and Charles W. Hendel (Yale University Press, New Haven, CT, 1950), p. 127.

98 *Observations*, p. 1.

99 *Anthropology*, p. 239.

100 In moral terms, those considered "uncivilized" by Kant, since they do not have "true" moral character, also lack "true" historicality. They are therefore subhuman and inherently nearly totally evil. (Or as Rudyard Kipling would later put it poetically: the African is "half devil and half child." See T.S. Eliot, *A Choice of Kipling's Verse* (Doubleday, New York, 1962), p. 143.

101 Quoted in Cassirer, *RKG*, p. 11.

102 As set forth in *Physische Geographie*; see Neugebauer's exposition of this in "The racism of Kant," p. 264.

103 Kant writes that "the difference in the organization/structure of Negro skin from that of ours is apparent even in the realm of feeling." "Überdem ist die Verschiedenheit der Organisation der Negerhaut von der unsrigen, selbst nach dem Gefühle, schon merklich" ("Bestimmung des Begriffs einer Menschenrace," in Schultze, *Kant und Darwin*, p. 151; my translation).

104 Forrest Williams, "Anthropology and the critique of aesthetic judgment," *Kant Studien*, vol. 46, 1954–5, p. 173.

105 For an extended examination of the interrelation of anthropology, race and aesthetic theory in eighteenth-century German thought, see Peter Martin, *Schwarze Teufel, edle Mohren: Afrikaner in Bewußtsein und Geschichte der Deutschen* (Junius, Hamburg, 1993).

106 *Observations*, p. 51.

107 Ibid., pp. 110–11.

108 J.-J. Rousseau, *Discourse on the Origin of Inequality*, trans. Ilse Barande et al. (Payot, Paris, 1965), pp. 175–6.

109   Ibid., p. 170; my emphasis.

110   Quoted in Cassirer, *RKG*, p. 24. Scholars and critics of Rousseau have pointed out these inconsistencies in Rousseau's writing. For example, Derrida in his study of Rousseau in *Of Grammatology* writes that "the difference among all Rousseau's texts is subtle, perhaps unstable, always problematic to this point" (p. 231). Cassirer also addresses this issue by characterizing it as "an ambiguity which had always made it hard to understand [Rousseau], and still does today" (*RKG*, p. 24).

111   Kant, *On History*, trans. Beck, pp. 53ff.

112   See extensive discussion of this issue in the section titled "Kant's doctrine of human nature," above.

113   See the discussion in the section titled "Kant's idea of 'race,'" above.

114   Neugebauer, "The racism of Kant," p. 265.

115   Ibid.

116   Cassirer captures this succinctly when he states: "Kant looks for constancy not in what man *is* but in what he should be" (*RKG*, p. 20).

117   As Cassirer points out, "Kant esteems Rousseau for having recognized and honored man's *distinctive and unchanging end* (ibid., p. 23).

118   *Observations*, pp. 110–11.

119   Ibid.

120   Have the words "black" and "white" retained in English the moral ascriptions that they harbored for Kant and the natural historians? For example, *Webster's Third New International Dictionary* anthropomorphically ascribed to the term "black" connotations such as: outrageously wicked; a villain; dishonorable; expressing or indicating disgrace, discredit, or guilt; connected with the devil; expressing menace; sullen; hostile; unqualified; committing a violation of public regulation; illicit; illegal; affected by some undesirable condition, and so on. On the other hand, "white" is ascribed with connotations such as: free from blemish, moral stain or impurity: outstandingly righteous; innocent; decent; in a fair upright manner; a sterling man, and so on.

121   *Observations*, p. 111.

122   *Anthropology*, p. 236.

123   See also quotations from Kant's "Bestimmung des Begriffs einer Menschenrace" in this essay, in the first part of the section on "Kant's idea of 'race,'" above.

124   Neugebauer points out that "to Kant, race, as soon as it is established as such, contains an unchangeable quality" ("The racism of Kant," p. 253).

125   For an examination of the reception of travel literature in eighteenth-century German thought (especially Herder), see Uta Sadji, *Der Negermythos am Ende des achtzehnten Jahrhunderts in Deutschland: Eine Analyse der Rezeption von Reiseliteratur über Schwarzafrika* (Lang, Frankfurt, 1979).

126   Van de Pitte, *KPA*, p. 49.

127   *Anthropology*, pp. 217–18n.

128   For a study of the kind of "padding" for all sorts of purposes that travel narratives were subject to, see, for example, a study of the memoirs of Glückel of Hameln in Natalie Z. Davis, *Women on the Margins* (Harvard University Press, Cambridge, MA, forthcoming).

129   *Physische Geographie*; quoted in May, *KCG*, p. 262.

130 *Anthropology*, p. 4; my emphasis.
131 May, *KCG*, p. 5.
132 *Anthropology*, p. 4n.; my emphasis.
133 See May, *KCG*, p. 4.
134 Quoted ibid.
135 Van de Pitte points out that Kant's lectures in anthropology were "popular, in both senses" (*KPA*, p. 11).
136 See Schultze, *Kant und Darwin*.
137 Walter Scheidt, "The concept of race in anthropology," in Count, *This Is Race*, p. 372; my emphasis.
138 Willibald Klinke, *Kant for Everyman*, trans. Michael Bullock (Routledge and Kegan Paul, London, 1952), p. 22 and passim.
139 The cultural-ideological and the geopolitical significance of Kant's raciology – a topic which I am currently addressing elsewhere – must as well be situated within this larger theoretical context of Kant's transcendental philosophy.
140 Lucius Outlaw, "African philosophy: deconstructive and reconstructive challenges," in Guttorm Floistad (ed.), *Contemporary Philosophy: A New Survey*, vol. 5, *African Philosophy* (Nijhoff, The Hague, 1987), pp. 9–44.
141 *GS*, vol. 20, p. 45; my emphasis.
142 Kant's *homo rationale* is a "distinctive human type (found only among persons of the appropriate gender and racial/ethnic pedigree) in the historicity of a particular complex or tradition of discursive activities"; see Outlaw, "African philosophy," p. 219. For a critique of Kant's anthropological and ethical theories about women, see, for example, Jean Grimshaw's *Feminist Philosophers: Women's Perspecitives on Philosophical Traditions* (Wheatsheaf, Brighton, 1986) or the several excellent essays in Eva Kittay and Diana Meyers (eds), *Women and Moral Theory* (Rowman and Littlefield, Savage, MD, 1987).
143 Tsenay Serequeberhan, *African Philosophy: The Essential Reading* (Paragon, New York, 1991), p. 7.
144 Wole Soyinka, *Myth, Literature, and the African World* (Cambridge University Press, Cambridge, 1976), p. ix.
145 Quoted in Steven Lestition, "Kant and the end of the Enlightenment in Prussia," *Journal of Modern History* vol. 65, March 1993, pp. 57–112; see particularly pp. 95–6.

5

The Critique of Eurocentrism and the Practice of African Philosophy

Tsenay Serequeberhan

Philosophy has this universal mission, a mission based on the assumption that mind guides the world. Consequently, they [i.e., the philosophers] think they are doing a great deal for the terrestrial species to which they belong – they are the mind of this species.

The time has come to put them [i.e., philosophers] on the spot, to ask them what they think about war, colonialism, *the speed-up in industry, love, the varieties of death, unemployment, politics, suicide, police forces, abortions – in a word, all the things that really occupy the minds of this planet's inhabitants. The time has definitely come to ask them where they stand. They must no longer be allowed to fool people, to play a double game.*

Paul Nizan[1]

What is the critique of Eurocentrism and how does it relate to the practice of contemporary African philosophy? In answering this double question I hope to lay out, at least in outline, the negative and critical aspect of what I see as a grounding task of thought in the contemporary practice (i.e., writing and thinking) of African philosophy. In doing so I will suggest to the reader a way or path and supply an instance of what this critique would look like when applied to some of the classical texts of Western philosophy. The texts I have chosen to focus on are the historicopolitical writings of Immanuel Kant, sometimes referred to as his fourth critique.[2]

1

Broadly speaking, Eurocentrism is a pervasive bias located in modernity's self-consciousness of itself. It is grounded at its core in the metaphysical belief or Idea (*Idee*) that European existence is qualitatively superior to other forms of human life.[3] The critique of Eurocentrism is aimed at exposing and de-structuring[4] this basic speculative core in the texts of philosophy. This then is the critical-negative aspect of the discourse of contemporary African philosophy.

Specifically, in this chapter, I hope to present an instance of this de-structuring critique by systematically exploring Kant's texts indicated above. In reading Kant – and by extension the Occidental tradition – in this manner, my purpose is to understand it and grasp it in all that it has to offer. This, furthermore, I undertake in full cognizance of the fact that earlier readings have understood these texts differently, and, still more, others will understand them in their own way, in the time to come.

In this respect, our responsibility to the future is to hermeneutically elucidate that which has remained hidden: that is, "a relevant reading . . . that hasn't been addressed thus far"[5] by the dominant Euro-American scholarship on the philosophic tradition. For if the future is indeed to be a joint future, as Cheikh Hamidou Kane has aptly observed, then it is necessary to clear the air of false perceptions grounded in a spurious metaphysics.[6]

In the last decade of the twentieth century, the "time has definitely come to ask" philosophers "where they stand." This critically interrogative time is our postcolonial present, in which the colonial asymmetries of the past are – at least in principle – not defensible any more.[7] Thus, the "mind of [the] species," philosophers must not be allowed to "play a double game" any more. To query this "double game" in regards to the complicity of philosophy in empire and colonialism is thus the critique of Eurocentrism: that is, the critical-negative aspect of the contemporary discourse of African philosophy.

In what follows (section 2), I will situate the general thematic context in which I will engage Kant's texts. I will then (section 3) explore Kant's texts by letting them speak for themselves, as much as possible, and suggest the manner of reading which I refer to as the critique of Eurocentrism. In conclusion (section 4), I will comment on the importance of this critical-negative project for the contemporary discourse of African philosophy.

2

In his, by now famous book, *The Postmodern Condition*, the French philosopher Jean-François Lyotard puts forth the thesis that the "postmodern" is "incredulity toward metanarratives," the discarding of the lived and world-historical "'grand narratives'" through which modernity constituted itself.[8] And as Wlad Godzich has noted, for Lyotard, the global self-constitution of modernity is coterminous with "the unleashing of capitalism."[9]

In other words, modernity is, properly speaking, the globalization of Europe – triumphantly celebrated by Marx in the first few pages of *The Communist Manifesto* – which constitutes itself globally by claiming that its historicity has "at last compelled [Man] to face with sober senses his *real* conditions of life and his relations with his kind."[10] Before Marx, Hegel[11] in *The Philosophy of Right* and in *The Philosophy of History*, and before him Kant in his historicopolitical writings, had essentially maintained the same view: that is, European modernity grasps the *real* in contradistinction to the ephemeral non-reality of non-European existence.

In this respect, Marx, a conscious and conscientious inheritor of the intellectual legacies of Kant and Hegel, articulates in his own idiom, his "materialist conception of history" that which Hegel had already pronounced as the manifestation of *Geist* (mind and/or spirit) and, earlier still, Kant had envisaged and conceptualized as the providential working out of humankind's "unsocial sociability." In other words, for all three, no matter how differently they view the historical globalization of Europe, what matters is that European modernity is the *real* in contrast to the *unreality* of human existence in the non-European world. In this regard, Hegel and Marx specify systematically, in their own respective ways, the Idea of European superiority which Kant, long before them, enunciated as the centerpiece of his historicopolitical writings.

As Lyotard has observed, "[m]odernity," and in its concrete manifestation this term always means empire and colonialism, "whenever it appears, does not occur without a shattering of belief, without a discovery of the *lack of reality* in reality – a discovery linked to the invention of other realities."[12] Indeed, in its global invasion and subjugation of the world, European modernity found the *unreality* of myriad non-capitalist social formations, which it promptly shattered and replaced with its own replication of itself. Paradoxically, the profusion of differing and different modes of life was experienced, by invading Europe, as the "lack of reality in reality": that is, as the *unreality* or vacuousness of and in the *real*.

On the other side of this divide, among the subjugated aboriginal peoples, this European perception of vacuity was experienced as death and destruction – the effective *creation* of vacuity. As Kane puts it:

> For the newcomers did not know only how to fight. They were strange people. If they knew how to kill with effectiveness, they also knew how to cure, with the same art. Where they had brought disorder, they established a new order. They destroyed and they *constructed*.[13]

The subjugated experienced Europe as the putting into question of their very existence. In their turn, in the words of Chief Kabongo of the Kikuyu, the subjugated put forth their own interrogative to the vacuity "constructed" by Europe: "We Elders looked at each other. Was this the end of everything that we had known and worked for?"[14] Indeed it was!

But how did Europe invent, as Lyotard tells us, "other realities"? By violently inseminating itself globally, after having properly tilled, turned over and reduced to compost[15] the once lived actualities of the historicity of the non-European world. Or in the words of Kane:

> Those who had shown fight and those who had surrendered, those who had come to terms and those who had been obstinate – they all found themselves, when the day came, checked by census, divided up, classified, labeled, conscripted, administrated.[16]

Indeed, as Edward W. Said has pointedly observed:

> Imperialism was the theory, colonialism the practice of changing the uselessly unoccupied territories of the world into useful new versions of the European metropolitan society. Everything in those territories that suggested waste, disorder, uncounted resources, was to be converted into productivity, order, taxable, potentially developed wealth. You get rid of most of the offending human and animal blight – whether because it simply sprawls untidily all over the place or because it roams around unproductively and uncounted – and you confine the rest to reservations, compounds, native homelands, where you can count, tax, use them profitably, and you build a new society on the vacated space. Thus was Europe reconstituted abroad, its "multiplication in space" successfully projected and managed. The result was a widely varied group of little Europes scattered throughout Asia, Africa, and the Americas, each reflecting the circumstances, the specific instrumentalities of the parent culture, its pioneers, its vanguard settlers. All of them were similar in one major respect – despite the differences, which were considerable – and that was that their life was carried on with an air of *normality*.[17]

In both of the above quotations what needs to be noted is that Europe invents, throughout the globe, "administrated" replicas of itself and does so in "an air of normality." This *normality*, as Said points out, is grounded on an "idea, which dignifies [and indeed hastens] pure force with arguments drawn from science, morality, ethics, and *a general philosophy*."[18]

This Idea, this "general philosophy," is, on the one hand, the trite and bland *prejudice* that European existence is, properly speaking, true human existence *per se*.[19] And, as noted earlier, this same Idea or "general philosophy" is that which Hegel and Marx, among others, inherit from Kant, and specify in their own idiom. This Idea or "general philosophy" is the metaphysical ground for the "normality" and legitimacy of European global expansion and conquest:

that is, the consolidation of the *real*. Thus, trite prejudice and the highest wisdom, speculative thought, circuitously substantiate each other!

This banal bias and its metaphysical "pre-text"[20] or pretension, furthermore, lays a "heavy burden" ("The White Man's Burden"?) on Europe in its self-assumed global "civilizing" charade and/or project. For as Father Placide Tempels, a colonizing missionary with an intellectual bent, sternly and gravely reminds his co-colonialists:

> It has been said that our civilizing mission alone can justify our occupation of the lands of uncivilized peoples. All our writings, lectures and broadcasts repeat *ad nauseam* our wish to civilize the African peoples. No doubt there are people who delight to regard as the progress of civilization the amelioration of material conditions, increase of professional skill, improvements in housing, in hygiene and in scholastic instruction. These are, no doubt, useful and even necessary "values." But do they constitute "civilization"? Is not civilization, above all else, progress in *human personality*?[21]

Indeed, as Rudyard Kipling had poetically noted, Europe's colonizing mission was aimed at properly humanizing the "[h]alf devil and half child"[22] nature of the aboriginal peoples it colonized. This is indeed what Tempels has in mind with his rhetorical question regarding civilization as "progress in human personality,"[23] for it is this self-righteous attitude on which is grounded the "normality" of Europe's process of inventing globally "administrated" replicas of itself.

The "lack of reality in reality" which Europe finds, and displaces by its self-replication, is the "immaturity" of the "[h]alf devil and half child" humanity of aboriginal peoples. Now, in this gauging of the "lack of reality in reality," European civilization is both the standard and the model by which this deficiency is first recognized and then remedied. Or to be more accurate, it is the Idea or "general philosophy" of this civilization – or the way that it understands itself – that is the measure of the whole undertaking.

Now, as Rousseau noted in the first chapter of *The Social Contract*, force does not give moral or normative sanction to its effects. Thus for philosophy, which conceives of "mind" as the guide of the world, violence and conquest are masks for the rationality of the real. This then is how European philosophy in general participates in and contributes to the invention of "other realities" – that is, of the replication of Europe as its cultural, material/physical, and historical substratum. And, as we shall soon see, this is precisely what Kant's historicopolitical texts intend to and do accomplish.

This inventiveness is grounded, as Lyotard tells us, in "the Idea of emancipation,"[24] which is articulated in

> the Christian narrative of the redemption of original sin through love; the *Aufklärer* narrative [i.e., Kant's narrative] of emancipation from ignorance and servitude

through knowledge and egalitarianism; the speculative narrative [i.e., Hegel's narrative] of the realization of the universal Idea through the dialectic of the concrete; the Marxist narrative of emancipation from exploitation and alienation through the socialization of work; and the capitalist narrative of emancipation from poverty through technoindustrial development.[25]

Between "these narratives there is ground for litigation." But in spite of this family or familial conflict, "all of them" are positioned on a singular historical track aimed at "universal freedom," and "the fulfillment of all humanity."[26] In Tempels' words, they are all aimed at "progress in human personality."

It is not my concern, in this chapter, to explore the conflicts between these narratives, but rather to underline their foundational similitude: that is, they all metaphysically coagulate around Tempels' phrase, "progress in human personality." To this extent these narratives collectively underwrite the colonialist project of global subjugation and expansion. For "universal freedom" and "the fulfillment of all humanity" presuppose, on the level of foundational principles (i.e., metaphysics) a singular humanity or the *singularization* of human diversity by being forced on a singular track of historical "progress" grounded on an emulation and/or mimicry of European historicity.[27]

In other words, it requires us to look at humanity as a whole, in all of its multiple diversity and amplitude, *not* as it shows itself (i.e., multiple, differing, diverse, disconsonant, dissimilar, etc.), but through the "mediation or protection of a 'pre-text'"[28] that flattens all difference. This is tangibly and masterfully accomplished by elevating European historicity, the "pre-text" (i.e., the text that comes *before* the text of humanity, as it shows itself in its multiple heterogeneity) to the status of true human historicity *par excellence*.

The de-structuring critique of this "pre-text" – the Occidental surrogate for the heterogeneous variance of human historical existence – is then the basic critical-negative task of the contemporary discourse of African philosophy. It is the task of undermining the European-centered conception of humanity on which the Western tradition of philosophy – and much more – is grounded. The way one proceeds in this reading is to allow the texts to present themselves, as much as possible, and to try to grasp them without "anticipating the meaning"[29] or superimposing on them the accepted reading which they themselves help to make possible.

In reading Kant's speculative historicopolitical texts in this manner, my purpose is to track down the way this "pre-text" functions in his reading of our shared humanity. This "pre-text" (i.e., Idea or "general philosophy") is the shrine at which the great minds of Europe (past and present) prayed and still pray. It is that which serves as the buttress and justification and thus enshrines the "normality" of the European subjugation of the world. It is the figleaf of European barbarity which makes it possible and acceptable, and without which

Europe could not stand to face itself: that is, its history. As Joseph Conrad puts it:

> The conquest of the earth, which mostly means taking it away from those who have a different complexion or slightly flatter noses than ourselves, is not a pretty thing when you look into it too much. What redeems it is the idea only. An idea at the back of it; not a sentimental pretence but an idea; and an unselfish belief in the idea – something you can set up, and bow down before, and offer a sacrifice to.[30]

Indeed, as Nietzsche has remarked against Hegel, in *The Advantage and Disadvantage of History for Life*, the "idea" is that in front of which one prostrates oneself. But let us now turn to Kant and confirm what has been affirmed thus far by exploring the Idea or "pre-text" in the texts through which he conceptualizes our shared humanity. For Kant is one of the most distinguished fabricators – or should I say constructors – of the Idea, by far the most lucid and important, in the modern European tradition.

3

In his piece, "What is Enlightenment?" Michel Foucault poses the question of what the term "mankind" means in Kant's essay of the same title. Foucault notes that Kant's "use of the word 'mankind,' (*Menschheit*)" is rather problematic, and asks:

> Are we to understand that the entire human race is caught up in the process of Enlightenment? In that case, we must imagine the Enlightenment as a historical change that affects the political and social existence of all people on the face of the earth. Or are we to understand that it involves a change affecting what constitutes the humanity of human beings?[31]

Having raised the question of the "use of the word" *Menschheit*, and then postulating an either–or, Foucault bypasses the crucial question of whose humanity is at stake in the project of enlightenment articulated by Kant. To be sure, and to his credit, Foucault indicates (even if only in passing and in parentheses) that this emancipatory project does have a domineering and tyrannical effect in "respect to others"[32] – that is non-European peoples. But why is that the case? Foucault neither pursues nor responds to the question.

As we shall see, beyond Foucault's either–or, it is the speculative effort to sketch out "the process of Enlightenment" as it affects "the humanity of human beings" which "the entire human race" or "all people on the face of the earth" are "caught up in" which makes for this domineering inclination in "respect to others." In other words, the "'transcendentalization' of the historical fact of the *Aufklärung* – is necessary, if the semblance of an answer is to be given in 'universal' terms to the original question,"[33] the question, as Kant puts it, of "man's release from his self-incurred tutelage."[34] The veneer of universality is required and essential precisely because Kant is concerned with "the totality of men united socially on earth into peoples."[35]

To be sure, the answer to the question of whose humanity is at stake in Kant's conception of the Enlightenment is rather simple. Two decades prior to "What is Enlightenment?" (1784), Kant had given his categorical response to this question in his precritical work, *Observations on the Feeling of the Beautiful and the Sublime*. In this work, Kant unequivocally affirms that

> The Negroes of Africa have by nature no feeling that rises above the trifling. Mr Hume challenges anyone to cite a single example in which a Negro has shown talents, and asserts that among the hundreds of thousands of blacks who are transported elsewhere from their countries, although many of them have even been set free, still not a single one was ever found who presented anything great in art or science or any other praise-worthy quality, even though among the whites some continually rise aloft from the lowest rabble, and through superior gifts earn respect in the world. So fundamental is the difference between these two races of man, and it appears to be as great in regard to mental capacities as in color.[36]

Much could be written on these "enlightened" and "enlightening" remarks. Kant, who never left the security and cultural ambiance of his country and native city of Königsberg, makes light of being "transported elsewhere." Kant, who, as Hannah Arendt has noted, valued highly "one's community sense, one's *sensus communis*"[37] and saw it as the source of one's humanity and critical capacity to judge and communicate, makes light of being uprooted (i.e., the experience of enslavement) when this catastrophe befalls the "Negroes of Africa."

But to return to our main point: Kant recognizes a "fundamental" "difference" and correlates "mental capacities" to the "color" of "these two races." For him the distance between the "mental capacities" of "these two races" is as radically and qualitatively different (in the spectrum of colors) as between white (the absence of color) and black (the complete absorption of the same). It should be noted, furthermore, that it is not only the "Negroes of Africa" that are castigated in this manner. The passage is too long to quote; it includes all of the non-European peoples that Kant could have known about – the Arabs, the Persians, the Japanese, the Indians, the Chinese, and the "savages" of North America.[38]

The differing peoples listed are described in an extremely pejorative manner, and a few are "complimented" by being compared with Europeans. The Arabs and the Persians are the Spaniards and the French of the Orient respectively, and the Japanese are the Englishmen of this exotic place! The "Negroes of

Africa," on the other hand, stand at the highest point of this negative pinnacle, precisely because they are assuredly "quite black from head to foot."[39]

From all of this, then, it follows that, insofar as the project of the Enlightenment is concerned with "the totality of men united socially on earth into peoples" and is aimed at establishing the "humanity of human beings" in terms of and by reference to the use of a free and autonomous self-reflexive reason, the "Negroes of Africa" and the differing shades of the rest of humanity are and must be beyond the *pale* of such a project. In as much as enlightenment is seen as "man's release from his self-incurred tutelage" and is thus a self-reflexive and self-reflective project of critical and rational emancipation, it cannot – on its own terms – be inclusive of non-European peoples and most distinctly of *Negro Africans*. This is so precisely because, according to Kant, reason and rationality are not indigenous to these, and in particular black African, peoples.

Indeed, Kant says as much in his "Idea for a universal history from a cosmopolitan point of view," published in the same year (1784) as "What is Enlightenment?"

> [I]f one starts with Greek history . . . if one follows the influence of Greek history on the . . . Roman state . . . then the Roman influence on the barbarians . . . if one adds episodes from the national histories of other peoples insofar as they are known from the history of the enlightened [European] nations, one will discover a regular progress in the constitution of states on our continent (which will probably give law, eventually, to all the others).[40]

The "others" (non-Europeans) will receive the Law of Reason from Europe or, in Kant's words, "our continent . . . will probably give law, eventually, to all the others." Those who cannot reason – and, as Foucault points out, the word for "reason" that Kant uses is *rasonieren* (i.e., "to reason for reasoning's sake")[41] – cannot be expected to effect "man's release from his self-incurred tutelage," since they lack the faculty for this human possibility.

Thus, Europe has to give the "law" to "all the others." Indeed, *de facto*, we of the present – Europeans and non-Europeans alike – exist in a world in which Europe has bestowed the "law" by means of conquest and violent hegemony. This is the case even if this act of "bestowing" abrogates – in the very act of giving – the Enlightenment's own notion of the self-liberating capacity of human reason.[42] What we need to examine next is how Kant legitimates this *de facto* (i.e., historical and thus contingent) globalization of Europe and makes of it the *de jure* actualization of the Idea.

To be sure, Kant was not a person devoid of sympathy or compassion for non-European peoples. In "Perpetual peace" (1795), he is quite disturbed by the inhumanity of civilized commercial European states in their dealings and contacts with non-European peoples. In the section in which he discusses "universal hospitality" as the law of "world citizenship," and after noting how the "ship and the camel (the desert ship)" bring people together and can foster "peaceable relations," he makes the following remarkable and praiseworthy statement:

> But to this perfection compare the inhospitable actions of the civilized and especially of the commercial states of our part of the world. The injustice which they show to the lands and peoples they visit [which is equivalent to conquering them] is carried by them to terrifying lengths. America, the lands inhabited by the Negro, the Spice Islands, the Cape, etc., were at the time of their discovery considered by these civilized intruders as lands without owners, for they counted the inhabitants as nothing.[43]

The same Kant, however, does express the view that "if the happy inhabitants of Tahiti, never visited by more civilized nations, were destined to live in their quiet indolence for thousands of centuries," one could not give a satisfactory answer to the question "why they bothered to exist at all, and whether it would not have been just as well that this island should have been occupied by happy sheep and cattle as by happy men engaged in mere pleasure?"[44]

The force of Kant's rhetorical question is directed at stressing what he calls "the value of existence itself,"[45] which is not, in his view, manifested in the placid, sedate or idle pursuit of "mere pleasure." As we shall see, for Kant, "the value of existence itself," which is ontologically and/or metaphysically proper to human life, is manifested in the rational control of nature, both in the human being and in nature as such.[46] It is interesting and I think significant to note further that Kant sees a similarity between the Tahitians (and the rest of non-European humanity by extension) and sheep because – if one is to judge by the illustrations he uses – sheep, for him, typify the paradigmatic example of a passive resource to be exploited.

In his "Conjectural beginning of human history" (1786), Kant, freely utilizing the story of Genesis, lists the four likely steps by which reason extracts man from instinct and his original abode in the garden of paradise. The fourth "and final step which reason took," he writes, to raise man "altogether above community with animals," occurred when man realized that he himself was the "true end of nature."[47] As Kant depicts it:

> The first time he ever said to the sheep, "nature has given you the skin you wear for my use, not yours"; the first time he ever took that skin and put it upon himself ... that time he became aware of the way in which his nature privileged and raised him above all animals. And from then on he looked upon them, no longer as fellow creatures, but as mere means and tools to whatever ends he pleased.[48]

In the following page in his remarks on the above – leaving allegory and sheepish examples aside – Kant states bluntly that reason separates man from instinct/ nature by establishing total dominion over the natural realm.

[M]an's departure from that paradise which his reason represents as the first abode of his species was nothing but the transition from an uncultivated, merely animal condition to the state of humanity, from bondage to instinct to rational control – in a word, from the tutelage of nature to the state of freedom.[49]

In other words, those whose humanness – by its lack of differentiation from and dominion over nature – resembles the placid and carefree existence of sheep, cattle, and animals in general, are still within the realm of instinct and have not yet ascended to "the state of freedom" which reason makes possible. Thus, if "what is good for the goose is good for the gander," then those who have made the "transition" from "merely [an] animal condition" can treat those who have not – the animalistic "gander" of non-European humanity – "no longer as fellow creatures [i.e., human beings worthy of respect], but as mere means and tools to whatever ends"[50] they – Europeans – see fit.

Indeed, as we saw earlier, this is precisely how Said describes the project and practice of European imperialism and colonialism, which is undertaken in "an air of *normality*."[51] This too is what Kant finds reprehensible in the European contact with and conduct towards non-European peoples.[52] And yet, as we have seen thus far, he himself is one of the most important constructors of the Idea or "general philosophy" behind this brutish practice: that is, the "pre-text" that insures the confident and self-possessed "normality" of European conquest.

It is important at this point to emphasize that by "reason" Kant means exclusively the instrumental and calculative control (i.e., "rational control") of the natural environment and of the human person as a being of nature with the possibility for rational freedom, or the "state of humanity" beyond the "lawless freedom" of non-European "savages."[53] Now, within the context of European history, this "rational control" is established by the proper utilization/*control* of reason in its public and private domains. For as Kant confidently puts it, in "What is Enlightenment?": "Men work themselves gradually out of barbarity if only intentional artifices are not made to hold them in it."[54] This is the play of "the unsocial sociability"[55] of human nature within the confines of European history, which Kant wants to assist in its unhampered unfolding,[56] even if it means establishing "a sort of contract – what might be called the contract of rational despotism with free reason."[57] This, to be sure, is the core concern of "What is Enlightenment?" which clearly has Europe and Kant's own "contemporary reality alone"[58] as its direct object of reflection. This is what Kant refers to and designates as the *"age of enlightenment."*[59]

What then of non-European humanity? How is it to achieve "progress" and "enlightenment"? It is here that the idea of "unsocial sociability" comes into its own and, beyond the formal niceties and distinctions that Kant makes, presents itself in all of its awesome ferocity. As already noted, for Kant, the non-European world is incapable of engaging in the self-reflexive and self-reflective project of enlightenment on its own terms, since it is beyond the *pale* of reason;

just as the Tahitians, had they not been "benefited" by European contact/ conquest, would be little different than sheep or cattle in their existence.

Thus, the non-European has to be civilized or enlightened from the outside. And for this purpose, nature utilizes man's "unsocial sociability," just as Heraclitus tells us that "[e] very beast is driven to pasture by a blow."[60] In other words, Kant cannot be candid in his critique of the imperialistic practices of European states (i.e., "the inhospitable actions of civilized . . . states," see note 43 for the full citation), since he himself thinks that the Tahitians are "nothing" but mere sheep. He is hard pressed "to give a satisfactory answer to the question why they bothered to exist at all" except for the fact that they were "visited by more civilized [European] nations." As noted earlier, Kant's historicopolitical texts metaphysically substantiate the very attitude he finds reprehensible in Europe's contact with the rest of us.

Indeed, in his ample articulations of the notion of "unsocial sociability," Kant gives us further and more concrete evidence of the above. According to Kant, humanity achieves greatness not as a result of its own inclinations, but by the secret design of nature.

> Man wishes concord; but Nature knows better what is good for the race; she wills discord. He wishes to live comfortably and pleasantly; Nature wills that he should be plunged from sloth and passive contentment into labor and trouble, in order that he may find means of extricating himself from them.[61]

For this purpose, "a wise Creator"[62] has devised the nature of man such that it is inherently antagonistic – social and yet inclined to isolation.

> This opposition it is which awakens all his power, brings him to conquer his inclination to laziness and, propelled by vainglory, lust for power, and avarice, to achieve a rank among his fellows whom he cannot tolerate but from whom he cannot withdraw.[63]

It is in this manner that the first steps are taken from "barbarism" to "culture," and gradually by "continued enlightenment the beginnings are laid" through which "a society of men driven together by their natural feelings" constitutes "a moral whole."[64] Otherwise, says Kant: "Men, good-natured as the sheep they herd, would hardly reach a higher worth than their beasts; they would not fill the empty place in creation by achieving their end, which is rational nature."[65] As noted previously, by "rational nature" Kant means the *ratio* at work in the instrumental control of nature and of human life as a manifestation of nature. This refers to the "value of existence itself," which is lacking in the pursuit of "mere pleasure" and is actualized through the inherent strife in human nature placed there by "a wise Creator."

Thus Kant extols nature for imprinting this basic aggressiveness in man:

Thanks be to nature, then, for the incompatibility, for heartless competitive vanity, for insatiable desire to possess and rule! Without them, all the excellent natural capacities of humanity would forever sleep, undeveloped. Man wishes concord; but nature knows better what is good for the race; she wills discord.[66]

But then it should be noted that the imperialistic attitude of European states in their dealings with non-Europeans is driven precisely by this "insatiable desire to posses and rule," this "discord" which nature "wills."

Kant cannot have it both ways. He cannot, on the one hand, impute to nature these "divinely" bestowed violent expansionist drives and glorify her for making them possible, and, on the other hand, condemn the concrete effects of these very drives: that is, the villainous attitude of Europeans in their travels. In effect, to do so is, in the words of Nizan, "to fool people, to play a double game."[67] In Kant's own terms then, conquest and brutish imperialist expansion are part of the foresight and divine design of nature!

The "free federation"[68] of states, furthermore, which Kant sees as the ultimate purpose of humanity and the only way to avert conflict and perpetual war, is itself a result of the recognition by states that mutual destruction has to be avoided. Such a union of states presupposes that each is already constituted unto itself as a "civilized" nation under laws, and has thus given up its "savage . . . lawless freedom."[69] But this is possible, for the non-European world, only if, like the inhabitants of Tahiti, it is visited – or, more accurately, conquered – by "more civilized [European] nations."

It is important to emphasize that Kant's explicit endorsement of European expansion and conquest (as the beneficial effect of the providential and secret design of nature) is not due to his lack of sympathy for non-European peoples; nor is it an accidental or extrinsic aspect of his historical thinking – an easily excusable "blemish." It is rather, as I have argued in this paper, the effect of his universalistic and universalizing discourse grounded on the *Idee* that European history is the "'transcendentally obligatory' meeting point of all particular histories."[70]

Kant is not willing to say, with Cornelius Castoriadis, that as a matter of historical fact – *de facto* – "the earth has been unified by means of Western violence."[71] He wants to add that this violence – best exemplified in Europe's contact with the rest of the world – is the work of Providence and the *de jure* actualization of reason on a global scale. It is the secret design for the self-rationalization and actualization of true humanity, whose "guiding thread"[72] he – Kant – has discovered.

At this point it should be noted that Kant was well aware of the faulty character of the empirical travel literature and information about non-European peoples that was available to him. In his review of the second part of Johann Gottfried Herder's "Ideas for a philosophy of the history of mankind" (1785) he makes the following very revealing remark:

[W]orking with a mass of descriptions dealing with different lands, it is possible
to prove, if one cares to do so . . . that [native] Americans and Negroes are
relatively inferior races in their intellectual capacities, but on the other hand,
according to reports just as plausible, that their natural potentialities are on the
same level as those of any other inhabitants of the planet.[73]

Now then, in view of the above, why is Kant so categorical in his negative
evaluation of non-European peoples? As he himself candidly admits, the
"ethnic descriptions or tales of travel"[74] – which constitute the information at
his disposal – are clearly equivocal and uncertain at best. Why then did he not
"care" to consider the contrary and "just as plausible" view regarding native
Americans, Negroes and other non-European peoples?

As Kant himself tells us, what is at stake – *contra* Herder, for example – is
the making of "natural distinctions" and "classifications based on hereditary
coloration . . . [and] . . . the notion of race."[75] In all of this:

The philosopher [i.e., Kant] would say that the destination of the human race
in general is perpetual progress, and its perfection is a simple, but in all respects
very useful, Idea of the goal to which, conforming to the purpose of Providence,
we have to direct our efforts.[76]

We have now come full circle to the Idea – the imperious notion of Occidental
superiority – with which Kant begins, constructs, and concludes his
historicopolitical reflections. This is the same Idea or "general philosophy"
which ensures the "normality" of European empire and colonial conquest, by
serving as the "pre-text" through which the humanity of human beings *as such*
is conceptualized in Eurocentric terms. It is the Idea of "rational control" best
incarnated in European humanity and lacking in the non-European world. It
is calculative "rational control" that, unlike the Tahitians' pursuit of "mere
pleasure," is the *true* and proper embodiment of "the value of existence itself."
For why else would Kant turn a blind eye to the equally "plausible" reports
regarding the humanity of the non-European world?

4

From all of the above, then, Kant's historicopolitical texts – and, as I have
argued elsewhere, the historical thinking of Hegel and Marx[77] and, by
extension, the European philosophic tradition as a whole – is *grosso modo*
grounded, minus its "dark horses," on a Eurocentric "pre-text" of the
humanity/historicity of human existence as a whole. But why is it necessary
to de-structively engage this "pre-text" or *Idee*? Why is this critical-negative
project an indispensable aspect of the contemporary discourse of African
philosophy?

To begin with, as Kwame Anthony Appiah has correctly noted, we contemporary African philosophers,[78] and Westernized Africans in general, share, by our training and educational formation, in the intellectual heritage of Europe. Consequently, we "see" ourselves and our contemporary situation, at least partially, through the lenses conferred to us by the transmissions of this heritage. Thus, to explore this shared heritage in regards to how it *sees* and *conceptualizes* our lived humanity is a necessary precondition to critically appropriating it.

For as Frantz Fanon reminds us – lest we forget! – our sharing in this heritage is rather problematic, since it is transmitted to us through a dour stepmother who "restrains her fundamentally perverse offspring from . . . giving free rein to its evil instincts" – a harsh "colonial mother" who "protects her child from itself."[79] Today, that part of our heritage which is African – or its residual – is no longer (at least in principle) considered "evil." In order to begin appropriating to ourselves that from which we were thus far protected, it is first necessary to clear the metaphysical grounding of all the evil that was said of us and done to us.

It is not enough to say with Kwasi Wiredu that:

> Indeed an African needs a certain levelheadedness to deal with some of these thinkers at all. Neither Hume, nor Marx, displayed much respect for the black man, so whatever partiality the African philosopher may develop for these thinkers must rest mostly on considerations of the truth of their philosophical thought.[80]

Indeed, to give proper consideration and appreciation to the "philosophical thought" expressed by these and other thinkers in the European tradition presupposes the critical de-structive labor of seeing how "the truth" is skewed and skewered by the partiality it justifies and in which it is enmeshed.

The necessity for this undertaking, furthermore, is grounded in the fact that today Eurocentrism is the general consciousness of our age. It is not something that merely affects Europeans. As Marx noted in the *German Ideology*, the dominant ideas of the ruling strata in a society are always, at any particular point in time, the dominating ideas of an age or historical period. Today – in our global society – the dominant ideas are the ideas through which Europe dominates the world. As Jose Rabasa has appropriately noted:

> I must emphasize again that by Eurocentrism I do not simply mean a tradition that places Europe as a universal cultural ideal embodied in what is called the West, but rather a pervasive [metaphysical] condition of thought. It is universal because it affects both Europeans and non-Europeans, despite the specific questions and situations each may address.[81]

To critically engage in a de-structive reading of the texts of the Occidental tradition as regards their views on non-European cultures is thus to critically appropriate that part of our own heritage which was violently "bestowed" on us by Europe. Not to do so would be to continue to inhabit a defunct intellectual horizon, whose material embodiments – that is, overt imperialism and colonialism – have already been destroyed by the formerly colonized peoples of the world. Today, in our postcolonial present, we face a more covert hegemony which functions and implements global Euro-American domination through the Westernized segments of formerly colonized peoples.

For better or for worse, *we* who belong to the Westernized segments of formerly colonized societies occupy positions of relative power which can be utilized either to replicate Europe or to try and unleash the concrete and suppressed possibilities of our respective histories.[82] For example, as Lyotard has correctly observed: "The spread of struggles for independence since the Second World War and the recognition of new national names seem to imply a consolidation of local legitimacies." But this "spread of struggles for independence" only "seem[s] to imply" the "consolidation of local legitimacies;" it is only a *semblance*, an appearance that hides the actuality that "[n]ew 'independent' governments either fall in line with the market of world capitalism or adopt a Stalinist-style political apparatus."[83]

In a similar vein, Castoriadis tells us that the West asserts "not that it . . . [has] . . . discovered the trick of producing more cheaply and more quickly more commodities, but that it . . . [has] . . . discovered *the* way of life appropriate to all human society." In making such a grandiose metaphysical assertion, the "unease" that "Western ideologues" might have felt is "allayed by the haste with which the 'developing' nations" or, more accurately, the Westernized élites of these nations greedily "adopt the Western 'model' of society."[84]

What both Lyotard and Castoriadis are pointing to is the fact that the hegemonic replication of Europe, in our shared postcolonial present, is carried on by and incarnated in the human residue – that is, the Westernized élites – left behind by the retreating colonial empires of Europe. In other words, the "fact that, in some particular domain, and to some particular end [i.e., the scientific/technological control of nature],"[85] the West has achieved considerable success is taken, by the Westernized élites and their metropolitan mentors, as a sign of Europe's absolute metaphysical superiority to the rest of humanity. It is, *grosso modo*, this domineering theme that constitutes the Eurocentric consciousness of our postcolonial globe and, as we have seen in our reading of Kant, finds its speculative foundation in the Western tradition of philosophy.

More than through physical force, Euro-America today rules through its hegemony of ideas, "through its 'models' of growth and development, through the statist and other structures which . . . are today adopted everywhere."[86] This is why Fanon concludes *Les damnés de la terre* with a simultaneous call to leave "old" Europe behind and engage in the concrete inventing and creating of our own lived historicity. But to heed, or even hear, Fanon's call requires that we first recognize and de-structure the speculative metaphysical underpinnings of the Eurocentric constraints that have held us – and still hold us – in bondage. This, in my view, is one of the most important and basic tasks of the contemporary discourse of African philosophy; its critical-negative project – the critique of Eurocentrism.

Notes

All emphases in the original unless otherwise indicated.

1 Paul Nizan, *The Watchdogs* (Monthly Review Press, New York, 1971), p. 38; my emphasis.

2 Lewis White Beck's introduction to *Kant on History* (Bobbs-Merrill, Indianapolis, IN, 1963), p. xviii, n. 14.

3 The term "Idea" (i.e., the German *Idee*) designates a theoretical or practical construct of the imagination which serves to give guidance to the theoretical and practical efforts of human reason. On this point see the *Critique of Pure Reason*, trans. Norman Kemp Smith (St Martin's Press, New York, 1965), pp. 308–14; see also Lewis White Beck's introduction to *Kant on History*, pp. xix–xx.

4 I borrow the notion of "destruction" from Martin Heidegger's *Being and Time*, part I, section 6 (Harper and Row, New York, 1962). In brief, a destructive reading is one that undermines the text from within and in terms of the cardinal notions on which it is grounded, and in so doing exposes the hidden source out of which the text is articulated. The hyphen in the variations of this term – which I utilize – is meant to stress that what is intended is *not* the "destruction" (i.e., the elimination, annihilation, or demolition) of what is in question, but rather its critical un-packing or opening up to a radical inquiry and interrogation. On Heidegger's notion of a destructive reading of the texts of philosophy, see, J.L. Mehta, *Martin Heidegger: The Way and the Vision* (University Press of Hawaii, 1976). Mehta describes this aspect of Heidegger's work as a "metaphysical archaeology" (pp. 96–7). For an interesting discussion of this aspect of African philosophy, which takes its point of departure from Derrida's notion of "de-construction," see Lucius Outlaw, "African 'philosophy': deconstructive and reconstructive challenges," in Guttorm Floistad (ed.) *Contemporary Philosophy*, Vol. 5, *African Philosophy* (Nijhoff, The Hague, 1987).

5 Edward Said, *The Pen and the Sword* (Common Courage Press, Monroe, ME, 1994), p. 78.

6 Cheikh Hamidou Kane, *Ambiguous Adventure* (Heinemann Educational, Portsmouth, NH, 1989), pp. 79–81.

7 It is to be remembered that, of his own "time," Kant wrote: "Our age is, in especial degree, the age of criticism, and to criticism everything must submit. Religion through its sanctity, and law-giving through its majesty, may seek to exempt themselves from it. But they then awaken just suspicion, and cannot claim the sincere respect which reason accords only to that which has been able to sustain the test of a free and open examination" (*Critique of Pure Reason*, p. 9). By the term "postcolonial" I mean the contradictory situation left by colonialism and the

concrete political struggles and contradictions through which the formerly colonized – i.e., the peoples of the Third World – have constituted themselves as "independent" nation-states. For an interesting critique of the variegated use this term has been put to, see Aijaz Ahmad, "The politics of literary postcoloniality," *Race and Class*, vol. 36, no. 3, January–March 1995.

8   Jean-François Lyotard, *The Postmodern Condition* (University of Minnesota Press, Minneapolis, MN, 1989), p. xxiv, and *The Postmodern Explained* (University of Minnesota Press, Minneapolis, MN, 1992), p. 17. I would like to emphasize, since I cannot explore this issue here, that this "incredulity" is and will always remain suspect so long as it does not explicitly address itself to the colonial globalization of Europe, which is the concrete actualization of modernity. This is because capitalism, as Marx noted long ago, is from its inception and always a global phenomenon.

9   Wlad Godzich, "Afterword: reading against literacy," in Lyotard, *Postmodern Explained*, p. 127.

10 Karl Marx and Frederick Engels, *The Communist Manifesto* (International Publishers, New York, 1983), p. 12; my emphasis.

11 For my critique of Hegel and Marx, see "The idea of colonialism in Hegel's *Philosophy of Right*," *International Philosophical Quarterly*, vol. 29, no. 3, issue no. 115, September 1989; "Karl Marx and African emancipatory thought: a critique of Marx's Eurocentric metaphysics," *Praxis International*, vol. 10, nos 1/2, April and July 1990.

12 Lyotard, *Postmodern Explained*, p. 9. Lyotard makes the same point, with slight verbal variation, in *Postmodern Condition*, p. 77. This almost verbatim recurrence of this formulation indicates that Lyotard sees it as being of cardinal importance to his perspective, and yet, as indicated in n. 8, this formulation too is suspect so long as it does not concretely explore what "reality" modernity finds "lacking" in its self-constituting global escapades.

13 Kane, *Ambiguous Adventure*, p. 49; my emphasis.

14 Chief Kabongo, "The coming of the pink cheeks," in *Through African Eyes*, vol. IV, *The Colonial Experience: An Inside View*, ed. Leone E. Clark (Praeger, New York, 1973), p. 32.

15 The term "compost" is used because it suggests decomposing matter out of which elements are set free that can then be utilized in another cultural context. On this point, see, Marcien Towa, "Propositions sur l'identité culturelle," *Présence Africaine*, no. 109, 1st Quarter, 1979, p. 85.

16 Kane, *Ambiguous Adventure*, p. 49.

17 Edward W. Said, *The Question of Palestine* (Vintage, New York, 1980), p. 78.

18 Ibid., p. 77; my emphasis.

19 On this point, V.Y. Mudimbe writes: "Until the 1950s – and I am not certain at all that things have changed today for the general public in the West – Africa is widely perceived and presented as the continent without memory, without past, without history. More precisely, her history is supposed to commence with her contacts with Europe, specifically with the progressive European invasion of the continent that begins at the end of the fifteenth century." *The Surreptitious Speech* (University of Chicago Press, Chicago, IL, 1992), p. xx.

20 Jean-François Lyotard, *Peregrinations* (Columbia University Press, New York

1988), p. 27.

21 Placide Tempels, *Bantu Philosophy* (Présence Africaine, Paris, 1969), pp. 171–2; my emphasis.

22 *A Choice of Kipling's Verse*, ed. T.S. Eliot (Anchor, New York, 1962), p. 143. This is the last line of the first stanza of Rudyard Kipling's poem, "The White Man's Burden," composed in 1899, fourteen years after the Berlin Conference that sanctioned the European colonial scramble for the partition of Africa.

23 Starting from the first page of his book, and throughout, Tempels complains about the fact that Christianized *évolués* periodically and violently revert to their "savage" ways. This is what Tempels sees as the failure of colonialism: i.e., the failure to retain the political and cultural loyalty of the *évolué*.

24 Lyotard, *Postmodern Explained*, p. 24.

25 Ibid., p. 25.

26 Ibid.

27 Cornelius Castoriadis, "Reflections on 'rationality' and 'development,'" in *Philosophy, Politics, Autonomy* (New York, Oxford University Press, 1991). See also Amanuel Sahle, "Views on restructuring," *Eritrea Profile*, vol. 2, no. 18, July 15, 1995, p. 2.

28 Lyotard, *Peregrinations*, p. 18.

29 Ibid.

30 Joseph Conrad, *Heart of Darkness* (Pocket Books, New York, 1972), p. 7.

31 Michel Foucault, "What is Enlightenment?," in *Foucault Reader*, ed. Paul Rabinow (Pantheon, New York, 1984), p. 35.

32 Ibid., p. 47.

33 Castoriadis, "The Greek polis and the creation of democracy," in *Philosophy, Politics, Autonomy*, p. 100.

34 "What is Enlightenment?," *Kant on History*, p. 3.

35 Ibid., p. 137.

36 Immanuel Kant, *Observations on the Feeling of the Beautiful and Sublime*, trans. John T. Goldthwait (University of California Press, Berkeley, CA, 1960), pp. 110–11.

37 Hannah Arendt, *Lectures on Kant's Political Philosophy*, ed. by R. Beiner (University of Chicago Press, Chicago, IL, 1982), p. 75.

38 Kant, *Observations on the Feeling of the Beautiful and the Sublime*, pp. 109–16.

39 Ibid., p. 112. In these comparisons just as the non–Europeans are "elevated" by being compared to Europeans (i.e., the Arabs and Persians by being likened to the Spanish and the French) to the same degree the Europeans are degraded, relative to other Europeans. The Arabs are like the Spanish just as the Persians are like the French. And the last two stand in the same relationship of superiority to the Spanish and the Arabs within their respective continents. Notice that Spain occupies the southern most extremity of Europe and that it is the one section of the European mainland that was under Moorish/African control for any extended period of time. Notice also that the English are like the Japanese, but the Germans are not utilized as a unit of comparison. Are they above such comparisons? Thus, you have the Spanish, the French, or the English – depending on how one arranges the hierarchy between their Asiatic correlates – and then the Germans, above all the Europeans: indeed, *Deutschland, Deutschland über alles!* There is a certain diabolical consistency in all of this. As is well known, Hegel held the view that there

are four world historical realms. In the order of their hierarchy, starting from the lowest, these are: the Oriental, the Greek, the Roman, and the Germanic. In a similar vein (vain?) Karl Marx repeats this same self-flattering evaluation when he writes, of India, the following remarks: "At all events, we may safely expect to see, at a more or less remote period, the regeneration of that great and interesting country [India], whose gentle natives are, to use the expression of Prince Saltykov, even in the most inferior classes, *'plus fins et plus adroits que les italiens,'* whose submission even is counterbalanced by a certain calm nobility, who, notwithstanding their natural languor, have astonished the British officers by their bravery, whose country has been the source of our languages, our religions, and who represent that type of the ancient German in the Jat and the type of the ancient Greek in the Brahmin" (from "The future results of the British rule in India," published in the *New-York Daily Tribune*, no. 3840, August 8, 1853, collected in *On Colonialism* (International Publishers, New York, 1972), p. 86). Notice again that the Italian peninsula is located at the southern extremity of Europe and the Italians (especially those of the South) have been inordinately influenced by Moorish and Arab culture. So the Jat – a fiercely independent and thus "noble" Northern Indian peasant group – is like the ancient Germans, and the ancient Greeks are like the Brahmin. All of this in spite of the "natural languor" of the "gentle natives." Such revealing remarks need no explicative commentary!

40   "Idea for a universal history from a cosmopolitan point of view," *Kant on History*, p. 24.
41   Foucault, "What is Enlightenment?," p. 36.
42   In other words, the project nullifies itself the moment that it sanctions "enlightenment by conquest," but this is, in effect, what Kant advocates.
43   "Perpetual peace," *Kant on History*, p. 103.
44   "Reviews of Herder's ideas for a philosophy of the history of mankind," *Kant on History*, pp. 50–1.
45   Ibid., p. 50.
46   Kant is ontologizing the ontic manifestations of instrumental rationality (manifest in the unfolding capitalist – as opposed to the feudal – relations of production) as a partisan of this rationality within a social formation in the historical process of embodying or being engulfed by the same. It should also be noted that Kant is expressing himself against Herder's conceptions of human life and history, which do not subscribe to the universalistic nature of Kant's position.
47   "Conjectural beginning of human history," *Kant on History*, p. 58.
48   Ibid., p. 58.
49   Ibid., pp. 59–60.
50   See n. 48 for the full citation.
51   See n. 17 for the full citation.
52   See n. 43.
53   "Perpetual peace," *Kant on History*, p. 98.
54   "What is Enlightenment?," *Kant on History*, p. 9.
55   "Idea for a universal history from a cosmopolitan point of view," *Kant on History*, p. 15.
56   "What is Enlightenment?," *Kant on History*, pp. 9–10.
57   Michel Foucault, "What is Enlightenment?," p. 37.

58 Ibid., p. 34.
59 "What is Enlightenment?," *Kant on History*, p. 8.
60 Philip Whellwright, *The Presocratics* (Bobbs-Merrill, Indianapolis, IN, 1975), p. 72.
61 "Idea for a universal history from a cosmopolitan point of view," *Kant on History*, p. 16.
62 Ibid.
63 Ibid., p. 15.
64 Ibid.
65 Ibid., pp. 15–16.
66 Ibid., pp. 16.
67 See endnote n. 1 for full citation.
68 "Perpetual peace," *Kant on History*, p. 101.
69 Ibid., p. 98.
70 Castoriadis, "The Greek polis and the creation of democracy," p. 100.
71 Castoriadis, "Reflections on 'rationality' and 'development,'" p. 200.
72 "Idea for a universal history from a cosmopolitan point of view," *Kant on History*, p. 12.
73 "Reviews of Herder's ideas for a philosophy of the history of mankind," *Kant on History*, p. 47.
74 Ibid.
75 Ibid. For an insightful discussion of race in Kant's thinking, see Emmanuel Eze, "The color of reason: the idea of 'race' in Kant's anthropology," in this volume.
76 "Reviews of Herder's ideas for a philosophy of the history of mankind," *Kant on History*, p. 51.
77 See n. 11.
78 Kwame Anthony Appiah, *In My Father's House* (Oxford University Press, New York, 1992), p. 85.
79 Frantz Fanon, *The Wretched of the Earth* (Grove, New York, 1968), p. 211.
80 Kwasi Wiredu, *Philosophy and an African Culture* (Cambridge University Press, Cambridge, 1980), p. 49.
81 Jose Rabasa, *Inventing America* (University of Oklahoma Press, Norman, OK, and London, 1993), p. 18.
82 For a detailed exploration of this point, see my book, *The Hermeneutics of African Philosophy* (Routledge, New York, 1994), chapter 4.
83 Lyotard, *Postmodern Explained*, p. 35.
84 Castoriadis, "Reflections on 'rationality' and 'development'" pp. 181–2.
85 Ibid., p. 193.
86 Ibid., p. 201.

6

Critic of Boers or Africans? Arendt's Treatment of South Africa in The Origins of Totalitarianism

Gail Presbey

Hannah Arendt misrepresented Africans at the same time that she criticized the actions of those who harmed them. Arendt's 1951 work, *The Origins of Totalitarianism*, aimed to show how Hitler's (and Stalin's) practices of totalitarian rule in Europe could be understood in the context of its predecessors, anti-Semitism and imperialism. As a middle stage in her argument, she focussed on the case of the Cape Colony in South Africa. Arendt's study includes: the distinctions she made between colonization and imperialism; her comments on race-thinking and racism; and her evaluation of labor practices, or the lack of labor, among the indigenous Africans, the trekboers, and the gold diggers. While making some valuable points regarding each of these topics, she nevertheless on occasion repeats some of the popular misconceptions regarding Africa. In addition, she advocates a position regarding labor that calls indigenous African practices into question as much as the adventures of the colonizers.

1 Race and Nation in Africa

Arendt draws a distinction between race-thinking and racism, based on its status in a given society; the former is one opinion among many, whereas racism is an ideology which seeks to persuade or already does motivate the behavior of the majority of people.[1] Arendt's categories differ interestingly from Anthony Appiah's more recent distinctions between "racialism" and "racism." For Appiah, racialism is a belief that there are races, whereas racism goes farther and argues that different races deserve different treatment. According to Appiah, the mere belief in races is not necessarily dangerous, if it results in "separate but equal" treatment.[2] On this point Arendt disagrees; she insists that the notion of race would never have come into existence except for political struggles. In other words, people turn to the idea of race because they need its explanatory power to achieve a goal. Race-thinking and racism have been created and developed as political weapons, not a theoretical doctrine; we know so because they appeal to experience and/or desires for credence.[3]

Even early race-thinking was tied by Arendt to political privilege. In France, for example, aristocrats like Boulainvilliers considered themselves of a different origin than the French people, belonging instead to an international caste not tied to the soil of France. In Germany, references to "blood relationship" and unmixed origin were needed as an ideological basis for national unity as a substitute for political nationhood, which was weak. The notion of "blood" helped secure national identity by creating a wall around the people as a substitute for a frontier.[4]

Like Appiah, however, Arendt does not think that "race" really exists in the world. While Appiah and others go into detailed criticisms of biological and anthropological pseudo-proof of the existence of "race," Arendt contents herself with noting that the idea of a difference in people's "blood" is a notion that has no scientific evidence.[5] Like Appiah, Arendt concludes therefore that the correct thing to do, both epistemologically and politically, is to give the notion of race no more credence, to admit that it is a bankrupt and troublesome category. She prophesies doom when Germans become Aryans and Englishmen become "white men," because individuals thereby lose "all natural connections with their fellow men" and destroy not only "the Western world" but all of human civilization.[6]

Connected to criticisms of race are criticisms of nationality and the rampant nationalism that Arendt thought could only destroy politics. Rather than defining themselves culturally or ethnically, states should instead embrace all individuals within their borders with equal rights. Arendt clarifies the difference between state and nation: states exist to protect the rights of everyone within their borders, while nations are based on national consciousness, the identity of people with the same genes and the same culture. Advocates of nationalism argued that, since states were impermanent, but nations permanent, the state should serve the nation.[7] A focus on national identity, however, led to problems insofar as there were always minorities who were then not considered full citizens, and had to be protected by minority rights. Dissatisfaction felt by minorities led to their clamoring for independence so that they could have their own nation.[8] Arendt's rejection of nationalism extended to her criticisms of the idea of the Jewish state of Israel, and she deplored the chauvinism that Jews show towards Arabs. Arendt insists that homogeneity of past and origin, although important for the nation-state, is not needed for the joint effort of political action. She prefers a government that depends upon law, which she explains connects persons whom external circumstances have brought together.[9]

Arendt's criticism of nationalism and its effects on personal identity were summed up succinctly by her husband, Heinrich Blucher, in correspondence to Karl Jaspers. Blucher states that, in contrast to Jaspers' interest in the "German essence," he no longer sees himself as a "German," since nationalism as an idea is out of date. He was disillusioned by nation-states that pretended to be "fatherlands" just to convince their people to sacrifice their lives for its greed. He prefers the USA, which he sees as a federal, not national, state.[10]

Blucher's concerns in 1960 for the future of the newly independent states in Africa are a mixture of insight, genuine concern, and condescension. As Blucher explains:

> With the aid of the national concept, genuine attachment to one's native people and land was distorted into the lies of racism and national superiority . . . Nationalism has always led to imperialism by way of jingoism and chauvinism. The new, small nations that are springing up out of the jungle soil like mushrooms are, by their nationalistic shrieking and all manner of mass hysteria, being driven into the hands of the imperialists . . . And so the necessary struggle for freedom, namely, the struggle of the federative principle against the imperialistic principle of all stamps, is made almost impossible by the fog of social and national drivel.[11]

Blucher's relationship to his own ethnic identity is problematic. Although excessive clinging to ethnic identity can be harmful insofar as one learns to care only about others who are like oneself, his willingness to shed his own identity as German as if it were an outmoded fashion is surely not realistic. Although we are not completely determined by our ethnic identity, we cannot be unaffected, becoming a "neutral" identity person. Perhaps instead, Blucher was happy to become an "American" – and the willingness of many Americans to downplay their ethnic heritage may come from a desire to assimilate and "fit in" to "mainstream" society.

Today, an emphasis on "nationhood" and national identity in Africa is often a move away from the centrality of ethnicity. While clarifying that present-day Kenya as a nation is made up of several older nations thrown together by the Europeans according to European interests, D.A. Masolo nonetheless suggests that all citizens of the nation overcome excessive loyalty to their own ethnic group, and learn to work together for the benefit of the new nation.[12] This description of nationalism would overcome Arendt's and Blucher's criticisms.

It might not be unreasonable to expect, given their political analysis, that Arendt and Blucher would approve of Nkrumah's Pan–African ideal of a "United States of Africa", which would escape neocolonialism by fostering the interdependence of African countries, and their coordination into a continent-wide federation. However, Appiah argues that Pan–Africanism is another form of racism, since it suggests that all peoples of common racial descent should stick together to protect their mutual interests.[13] Just what counts as "Africans sticking together" would differ depending whether one stressed that Africa was a continent or a race.[14] Appiah's suggestion of a "continental" rather than a racial version of Pan–Africanism would more closely fit Arendt and Blucher's paradigm of a federation where all individuals had equal rights and notions of race were delegitimated.[15] Despite African independence movements being constantly in the news during Arendt's lifetime, she does not analyze the phenomenon in her works, and passing mentions of it are rare.

2 Imperialism: Global Capital and South Africa

Arendt distinguished the case of African colonization from those of America and Australia, the latter which she called "the two continents that, without a culture and a history of their own, had fallen into the hands of Europeans".[16] She asks us to bear in mind that colonization in America and Australia was accomplished by use of "short periods of cruel liquidation".[17] South Africa's situation was different, she suggests, because "the land beyond the Cape's borders was not the open land which lay before the Australian squatter," but instead was "settled by a great Bantu population."[18] She greatly condemns the millions slaughtered in the Congo and elsewhere by European lust for power. However, regardless of her attempt at distinctions, many historians would now dispute the accuracy of the above historical claims, and stress instead the similarities of the various colonization attempts rather than the differences.

For example, Arendt's comments on population are inaccurate: while conventional wisdom in the 1950s thought that the entire population of the American hemisphere prior to European arrival was about 8 million, historians today put the figure at 75–100 million.[19] However, the population levels plunged dramatically, down to 1.8 million in 1600.[20] Regarding Africa, population studies show Africa's population in 1600 at 55 million; there were only one million inhabitants for all of South Africa at the time Europe set up the Cape Colony, debunking Arendt's charges of "overpopulation." The "great Bantu population" entered into southern Africa only later, around 1800. In fact, the native African population of South Africa was decimated in a way similar to the native American population: part disease, part starvation resulting from being pushed off of their lands, and part slaughter in wars of conquest.[21]

In her book Arendt wants to separate out what she considers to be two radically different stages and strategies of European expansion in Africa. According to her, imperialism began in 1884. It was caused by the congruity of the nation-state system with economic and industrial developments. The earlier colonization efforts were marked by the setting up of trade stations, whereas imperialism goes much farther, to exhibit the following traits: (1) conquest and permanent rule; (2) decimation of the native population; (3) permanent settlement. With imperialism, there is a shift from localized, limited, and predictable goals of national interest to the limitless pursuit of power with no nationally and territorially prescribed purpose, and no predictable direction. Therefore imperialism was in her eyes infinitely more dangerous than colonization. In fact, imperialism set the example for Hitler's own goals in Europe, including plans to depopulate Poland and repopulate it with members of the Aryan race.[22]

Arendt's harshest criticisms of capitalism are found in her analysis of South Africa. In this case, superfluous money (savings of Europeans looking for investment) combined with superfluous people (the unemployed, who would be troublesome and press for reforms back home if there were no alternatives) to find economic success in mining gold and diamonds – materials that provide wealth mainly through speculation. The owners of superfluous capital accompanied the superfluous labor they themselves produced, to establish the first "paradise of parasites." Arendt concludes that the original sin of simple robbery which got capitalism started had to be repeated over and over again to keep the motor of accumulation going. This alliance of the unemployed with capitalists undermined the Marxist hope of united workers; proletarians now bought into the ideas of master and slave races, and believed that there were colored and white people.[23]

Despite the exponential increase of damage to Africa coming with imperialism, Arendt does not assign evil motives to the expansionists. Instead she accuses them of absent-mindedness; they did not know what they were doing. In several places while describing the British acquisition of their empire, Arendt insists that the road to hell can be paved with no intentions at all. She further asserts that the British "drifted" from being conscious founders of colonies to ruling and dominating foreign people all over the world, as they were swept up in their own legend of the British Empire.[24] This suggestion that the British were not "conscious" of what they were doing, although not intended to absolve them from the responsibility for the consequences of their actions, can sound very much like apologetics. A theme that recurs in Arendt's works later in reference to the Eichmann trial is that those who did evil deeds did not intend to. Is such a claim a truism, insofar as people from their own (however distorted) point of view always intend good by their actions? In contrast to the Eichmann case, where many intellectuals were outraged over her suggestion that Eichmann did not intend evil but was merely thoughtless, there has been little or no outrage in the intellectual community over Arendt's repeated suggestions that the British did not intend evil when they expanded their empire but were merely being thoughtless.[25]

3 Labor in Africa

In the section on imperialism, Arendt showed how conceptions of race (refined in South Africa) and practices of bureaucracy (developed in British-dominated Egypt) were later combined by the Nazis into the practice of the bureaucratic killing of a race. Obviously a critic of totalitarianism, she also criticizes the Boers and the British for using race and race privilege as a basis for informal and/ or legal discrimination. Nevertheless, the grounds on which she decides to criticize them are not the usual grounds.

For example, she does not say that what the Boers and British did was wrong because: (1) they practiced slavery; (2) they engaged in unfair and discriminatory labor practices; (3) they appropriated for themselves all of the land, which they acquired through use of force; (4) they committed massacres and conducted cruel and unusual punishments. These four points are historically true and could rationally be seen as the center of a strong moral argument against the practices of the Boers. But instead Arendt's moral analysis and condemnation are based on her observation that the Boers did not work – a criticism that she levels against the Africans as well. In other words, both Boers and Africans are to be found as not measuring up to an implicit work ethic; thereby they are either to be equally condemned, or, if the Boers deserve a worse criticism, it is because they, of European heritage, should have known better. The following is an example of Arendt's criticism:

> The Boers were the first European group to become completely alienated from the pride which Western man felt in living in a world created and fabricated by himself. They treated the natives as raw material and lived on them as one might live on the fruits of wild trees. Lazy and unproductive, they agreed to vegetate on essentially the same level as the black tribes had vegetated for thousands of years.[26]

Arendt's criticism of the Boers is muted here by suggesting that the Boers were no worse than the Africans. However, even if we grant for the sake of argument that Africans were "unproductive," the moral equivalence of the two scenarios is problematic. Is living off the exploited labor of other people the moral equivalent of living off the natural abundance of wild fruit trees? Even fruitarians (a strict subset of vegetarians who suggest that plants as well as animals should not be killed) believe that fruit trees are not harmed when their fruit is picked and eaten. But rare is the ethicist who would claim that a human being who is forced to labor for others is not being harmed.

Arendt is obviously critical of the Boers for living off the labor of others, but this is because it leads to their own laziness. As Arendt explains, the Boers were content with mere survival, as were the Africans in her view. We could speculate that, if the Boers used the time freed up from labor to engage in political activity (as did the Athenians whom she admires and uses as a paradigm in her work, *The Human Condition*), Arendt might have praise for them. But is it accurate to say that the Africans were content with *mere* survival? I think it can be argued, rather, that they were just as interested in continuing their traditions, their family ties, their ties to the land, and their way of life. However, because of the historical circumstances of the encroaching Boers and British, they had to forgo these latter values in order to cling to the meager chance for survival that was left to them.

Prior to the setting up of a European post at Cape Colony, South Africa was occupied by self-sufficient pastoralists, along with some hunter-gatherers. Insofar as they labored to take care of their herds, they labored under their own direction, in an occupation of their choice, and participated in furthering their own cultural community. With the encroachment of European settlers, that lifestyle changed. The Dutch Company, desperate for provisions for their sailors who stopped over on the way to India, forced Khoikhoi (called "Hottentots") to sell more of their cattle than they wanted to, as a "tribute" to avoid further harassment by the company.[27] European pastoralists and agriculturalists took key pastures and watering areas, and soon reduced Khoikhoi to farm laborers whose yearly wages barely exceeded their food rations. During this same time, Xhosa pastoralists lost 95 percent of their cattle to an epidemic of lung sickness. Soon 30,000 of the 40,000 impoverished Xhosa were signed up on labor contracts. Sir George Grey made sure that stockpiled food was given only to those who would sign contracts, and a soup kitchen set up by charitable whites was closed down.[28]

In addition to the above treatment of Africans indigenous to the area, Africans sold as slaves from Angola, Mozambique, and Madagascar, as well as slaves and convicts from India and Indonesia, were imported to join the laboring force, and all soon took on the many tasks of cook, nanny, handling flocks and herds, cultivating grapes and engaging in wine production, as well as mending roads and serving in the armed forces.[29] White settlers indulged in prejudices regarding the various ethnicities of slaves, and in short order were referring to the slaves from Angola and Mozambique as good at hard labor, while the East Indians were saved for skilled work.[30]

After slaves were emancipated in South Africa in 1834, many were forced by lack of land and capital as well as by labor contract laws to work for their former owners.[31] Khoikhoi were also denied access to land. An official at the time, Lord Glenelg, said that he thought Khoikhoi would be better off if they continued to work for wages as laborers than if they went back to the land.[32] In fact, part of the rationale behind freeing slaves in the first place was concern by some European settlers that slavery did not properly instill the work ethic in slaves. Slaves who were motivated to work for wages would be more industrious and less likely to wish to harm their masters.[33]

From the above brief historical account, we can see that the experience of labor was greatly changed by the arrival of Dutch and British colonizers. Before, labor was not avoided altogether; however, it was only a part of a typical day's activities. Indigenous groups had their own political structures, and engaged in craft work as well.

The occupational experience of Dutch and other Europeans who came to Africa was also changed by the political set-up in South Africa. In Europe, most had worked as farmers and laborers; some but not all had skills as craftspersons. However, trekboers who had claimed homesteads on the frontiers soon relied so much upon cheap Khoikhoi labor that they came to see themselves as above labor. They became overseers.[34] Historians note that, by adapting themselves to life in Africa, they lost the skills of their fathers. No towns were set up; they did without the services of physicians, teachers, blacksmiths, carpenters, wagon makers, and masons. Despite their role as rulers of households, trekboers remained poor and at subsistence level. Of course, this is just the sort of evidence Arendt is looking for when she suggests that trekboers went "down" to the level of Africans.[35]

Despite the trekboers' insistence on superiority over the Africans, based mostly on the supposed superiority of Christianity, and their dedication "to the maintenance of an exclusivist 'European' way of life," they in other ways took on some cultural traits of the Khoikhoi who worked for them.[36] Khoikhoi who worked for trekboers retained their culture even during employment. They brought their mat huts with them and lived in them; they dressed in traditional animal skins, greased their bodies, and continued their mythology, music, and religion. Soon some trekboers were living in mat huts too, needing the flexibility in location to follow their herds; they developed an "aesthetics of cattle" similar to Khoikhoi. Cape Town residents told Europeans that trekboers were becoming in manners and appearance like the Hottentots, and they were aghast at what they feared was "contamination."[37] Perhaps Arendt was influenced by these same fearful stories of the trekboers' degeneration. It is important to sort out which of the trekboers' traits should truly call for fear or repulsion, and which should be considered acceptable. In contrast to Arendt, I suggest that the lack of permanent dwellings or a storehouse of riches should not make one shrink in horror of the Boers; rather, their insistence on living off the labor of Khoikhoi and others is what is morally unacceptable.

In contrast to the trekboers, wealthier settlers who could afford the capital investment of slaves became involved in agriculture. On agricultural farms involved in the wine industry, farmers paid knechts (whites who signed up on labor contracts with the colony) as overseers of slaves. Backbreaking work and long working hours were the lot of these slaves.[38] It was by inserting themselves at the top of a pyramid of labor that white Europeans freed themselves of directly laboring for their own livelihood. Blacks were reduced to mere laborers by others, and their other capacities were denied.

Greatly problematic in Arendt's statement is the suggestion that Africans are different than "Western man" in their indifference to the value of changing their environment into a human one. This statement challenges the extent to which Africans possessed a culture, and produced objects and/or structures of durability. It also draws into question the hierarchy of human abilities which Arendt endorses. Which human capabilities are championed, and which are belittled?

4 Labor Theorized

Arendt's thorough outline of her conceptions of labor, work, and action appears in her 1958 work, *The Human Condition*. Her distinctions are more specific and technical than everyday usage, so I will quickly delineate the key attributes.

Labor is related to survival of the body. One labors to produce consumables to fill necessities of the body. Labor is cyclical, in that it involves producing, consuming, and producing again. It is close to nature, and leaves no permanent mark on the world.[39] In contrast, work involves building objects of durability according to a plan; the presence of human-made objects in the world changes the character of the world and the human experience of the world. Culture is heavily dependent on these distinctive objects, and cultures can be distinguished by looking at their fabrications. Through work, a durability and permanence are given to a world that is otherwise biological and cyclical. A sense of tradition relies on objects that are witnesses to the past: statues of heroes, Gothic cathedrals, and so on. The experience of work is more personally fulfilling than labor, since skill and a sense of accomplishment are involved, and a more complex level of thought is needed.[40]

A contrast between labor and work would find Arendt's description conjuring up popular stereotypes of the African (based on the actual experience of exploitation and slavery), while the worker would conjure up popular images of the skilled European worker: one works with one's hands, but labors with one's body; the former needs skill, while the latter needs endurance.[41] The experience of work is one of violence and self-assertion; the experience of labor is exhaustion and pleasure.[42] There is no natural rhythm to work; there is a rhythm to labor.[43] In work, there is specialization; in labor there is teamwork.[44] The worker destroys nature; the laborer is in harmony with nature.[45]

Before I look into Arendt's applications of these concepts to Africa, let me quickly note that she contrasts these first two categories to a third, action. Action is involved in bringing something entirely new into existence. Acts take place outside of a strict causal chain of forces, and instead are due to the agency of the actor. Action relies on a plurality of human beings who can relate to each other, dialogue with each other, and plan together. An action is a concerted effort of a group. Action goes beyond the necessities of the body, filling higher needs for meaning, purpose and self-definition. Political action is a particular instance of this more general category of action.[46]

From her above outline, it would seem that, if Arendt accused any group of living in harmony with nature, it would mean that they engage in either no labor at all (such as living off fruits and berries), or mere laboring without work and action. For, it is only thorough work, and the construction of permanent objects through violent manipulation of natural materials, that the human "world" comes into being. An important addition to this material aspect of the "world" is the public space that comes into being when people gather together to express themselves and act in concert. In contrast to some environmentalist groups which would encourage further harmony with nature, Arendt can only mean the comparison in the sense that humans are not living up to their full potentialities as humans, and are not enjoying the benefits of living in a world that has been humanized, an environment that has been permanently changed by the expression of human culture.

Therefore we can say that the three aspects of the *vita activa* that Arendt outlines in her study are ranked hierarchically, and are not equally important. However, various critics of Arendt over the years have not been happy with this ranking. Mildred Bakan suggests that the three parts of the *vita activa* be seen in their relationship of mutual dependence.[47] Bhikhu Parekh likewise emphasizes that all three are indispensable and interdependent.[48] Both authors question her abrupt distinction between work and labor. Bakan suggests that Arendt's description of labor is true only of exploited labor, and that world-building is indeed one of the accomplishments of labor *unless* it is done merely in the service of another.[49] She asserts that both Hegel and Marx saw labor and work as tied together, and emphasized that it was through labor and work that human individuals and communities expressed and accomplished their chosen goals, resulting in a changed world. Labor is not merely "natural" in a reductive sense, or driven by necessity or instinct, since labor "takes place in a world opened up as an arena for possible activity."[50] Humans distinguish themselves both by choosing the goal of their labor and by transforming animal desires to human wants.[51]

Parekh points out the ways in which Arendt underestimates Marx's comments regarding labor, as well as noting what he thinks are her valuable critiques of Marx. Parekh agrees with Marx that what is distinctively human about labor is the way in which people collectively take charge of their destiny and reshape the world. He thinks that Arendt has denied the capacity of humans to engage in purposive or rational labor. In this way, labor itself can become a kind of praxis.[52] Therefore he disagrees with Arendt's imagery that labor "only feeds objects into the consumptive furnace of the human organism."[53]

Nevertheless, he thinks Arendt's view is an important corrective to an excessive naturalism in Marx, where labor is so glorified that even the human creation of social institutions is reduced metaphorically to silkworms producing silk. This reduces the objective world to a mere extension of natural man. He agrees that this thoroughgoing naturalism would equal the "destruction of the world" in Arendt's terms.[54]

The solution therefore seems to lie not in ignoring Arendt's distinctions, or collapsing all of them into labor, but rather in seeing human actions as incorporating many of the three attributes simultaneously. Indigenous ethnic groups in Africa had experience of all three prior to their reduction to mere labor by a system of exploitation.

5 Distortions of Africa

Whether Arendt intended to reinforce stereotypes of Africa in her delineation is a controversial topic. Arendt's writing on Africa precedes her careful delineation of labor, work, and action by several years. To notice the implications requires a "reading back" of the categories into the earlier work, a procedure which, although possibly controversial, is not entirely ungrounded. George Kateb in his book on Arendt suggests that, if one reads back into the earlier *Origins of Totalitarianism* the clear delineations present in the *Human Condition*, one will come to the realization that she sees Africans as mere laborers, suggesting that Europeans upon contact with them are somewhat justified in their horror.[55]

It is also important to keep Arendt's critical remarks in context. While she gives her categories a hierarchy of value, with action being the best activity since it is most fulfilling, and labor being the lowest and least fully human, she does not merely single out Africans as representatives of labor. In fact, her book indicts contemporary Americans for sinking back into labor, becoming a society of jobholders where work degenerates into operating the machinery which produces less than durable consumer goods, and the past glories of American political action are forgotten and shoved aside by bureaucracy.[56] Nevertheless, indigenous Africans "keeping company" with mesmerized contemporary consumers should not be comforting; who wants to be lumped into the same negative category?

The most problematic passages regarding Africa are found on pp. 189–94 of the 1951 work, *The Origins of Totalitarianism*, in the section addressing imperialism. It must also be said that Arendt has harsh words to say regarding both the later wave of British opportunistic gold hunters and the earlier Boer settlers. However, once again, she words her negative assessment of the Boers as having to do with their denial of European traditions and approaching the lifestyle of the Africans.

In these pages, Arendt quotes copiously from Conrad's *Heart of Darkness* to describe the mindset of gold rush adventurers. It is unclear whether she quotes merely to describe how Africans seemed from the point of view of the new wave of opportunists, or whether she thinks in some objective sense that it is a description of the Africans as they are. Arendt begins her references to Conrad first in the description of the "adventurers, gamblers, criminals" who were attracted to South Africa because of gold. "Like Mr Kurtz," she explains, "they were 'hollow to the core,' 'reckless without hardihood, greedy without audacity and cruel without courage.'"[57] The section continues with Arendt pointing out all the (in her estimate) accurate parallels between Kurtz's characterization and the men who actually in history went to South Africa. This leads me to believe that she is citing Conrad because she thinks he gives a particularly apt and accurate account of what really happened in South Africa.

Because of this, it is disconcerting that she refers again to Conrad's depiction of the Africans, and paraphrases his ideas in her own words.

> The world of native savages was a perfect setting for men who had escaped the reality of civilization. Under a merciless sun, surrounded by an entirely hostile nature, they were confronted with human beings who, living without a future of purpose and a past of accomplishment, were as incomprehensible as the inmates of a madhouse.[58]

She notes further:

> Many of these adventurers had gone mad in the silent wilderness of an overpopulated continent where the presence of human beings only underlined utter solitude, and where an untouched, overwhelmingly hostile nature that nobody had ever taken the trouble to change into human landscape seemed to wait in sublime patience "for the passing away of the fantastic invasion" of man.[59]

Although Arendt in this section definitely wants to single out the European opportunists, and the capitalist system that spawned them, as the villains in this imperialist scenario, implicit in the above quotes is also a derogation of the Africans who lived in South Africa at the time. She suggests that the Africans had not turned their environment into a world; they had left it in the state of nature, a sure sign, according to her later criteria, that Africans had remained in the state of laboring, and had not progressed to the levels of work and action. As she states soon after, regarding the black race:

> What made them different from other human beings was not at all the color of their skin but the fact that they behaved like a part of nature, that they treated nature as their undisputed master, that they had not created a human world, a human reality, and that therefore nature had remained, in all its majesty, the only overwhelming reality.[60]

She continues: "they were, as it were, 'natural' human beings who lacked the specifically human character, the specifically human reality, so that when European men massacred them they somehow were not aware that they had committed murder".[61] Arendt states this not to condone the murder of Africans, but rather to attempt to explain its possibility psychologically. However, explanations like this sometimes sound like apologetics. And even if we admit that Arendt is not condoning the massacre of Africans, since they are not "truly" less than human, how can we dissociate the ability to make these judgments on the part of the adventurers, from the similar valuing of Arendt's own position, which sees Africans as capable of merely laboring? While she does not see them as less than human, and therefore fit for killing, she does see them as less than fully human. And according to her, Europeans that mimic Africans take a step down in their status.

Notions that Africans were animal-like or "less than human" have had a long history in the European intellectual tradition. European folklore was filled with ape men and were-animals. In the late seventeenth century, Hottentots were supposedly the link between man and apes. Their "brutish" appearance and bestial customs become stereotyped in the literature of the eighteenth century. In 1680, Morgan Godwyn "shrewdly observed" that it was in the interest of planters and traders to propagate the belief that Africans were not fully human.[62]

Arendt's text is also filled with statements that could be understood only as "blaming the victim." At one point she notes that the "senseless massacre of native tribes" was in the same tradition of the tribes prior to European invasion; they routinely killed each other.[63] Africans, according to her, regarded the Boers as "a kind of natural deity to which one has to submit; so that the divine role of the Boers was as much imposed by their black slaves as assumed freely by themselves."[64] Straight out of Conrad's description, we must puzzle: is Arendt outlining how the British and Boers justified their actions to themselves? Or is she suggesting that this is the fact of the matter? Her tone is definitely the latter.

In contrast to her assertions, careful historical accounts have shown that ethnic groups indigenous to South Africa had fought the presence of foreigners on their territory ever since they realized that their ability to thrive was being undermined. Although in the beginning they willingly traded cattle for tobacco and iron with the Dutch Company, their attitude changed once they realized their grazing lands were being encroached upon. When they finally did work for trekboers on the frontier and burghers in town, they did so because they had fewer and fewer options for survival, not out of inherent subservience and worship of their new masters. Regarding slaves: they had been taken by force, on long boat trips, against their wills. Often up to 40 percent of the company's slave holdings died in a year; in the 1740s settlers conducted a day of prayer for their slaves who were dying from an epidemic.[65] Since slaves were far from home, and taken from so many other countries that they had no common language between themselves, united resistance to enslavement was difficult. Nevertheless historical accounts refer to numerous attempts at escape over the years, with at least a couple of uprisings.[66] Such recurring resistance would not have happened if black Africans and others had internalized the view of whites as gods, as they do in Conrad's book.

The repeated use of Conrad's descriptions of Africa and Africans is problematic, and brings Arendt into a contemporary controversy surrounding the book. For example, Nigerian author Chinua Achebe claims that Conrad's book is racist, and his essay quotes copious examples of racist statements from the novel.[67] Does this mean that Conrad himself was racist, or promoting racist notions through his book? Or was Conrad himself being descriptive and critical of the racism present in Europeans, like his novel's character Marlowe? Ross Murfin notes that parallels between the novel and Conrad's own month-long experience in the Congo are so numerous that it is tempting to read the novel as autobiography, in which case Marlowe would be Conrad himself. However, Murfin hesitates to draw a complete parallel and suggests instead that Marlowe's comments about Africa and Africans should be taken as ironical. Murfin suggests that Marlowe is meant to be an unreliable narrator, and that readers should experience a distance between themselves and the narrator.[68] The question is: is Arendt repeating the phrases from Conrad's book with the irony Murfin suggests? A completely ironic reading must be discounted insofar as Arendt's criticisms of Africa go beyond the quoting of Conrad to the heart of her philosophical system as expressed in her major works.

As Arendt notes, the Boers were depraved because they did not want to live by labor, but rather purely by exploitation. Even the later wave of British gold miners were not industrious. Sir Charles Payton complained that most whites "felt disinclined" toward manual labor, especially in the summer. According to Payton, "It is quite sufficient for them to sit under an awning and sort, leaving the Kafirs to perform all the other stages of work."[69] Yet in the context of her criticism of the Boers and British, Arendt displays an underlying prejudice against Africans: their shiftless avoidance of labor and work, she claims, had continued to the early 1920s. She speaks of the poor whites in South Africa, whose "poverty is almost exclusively the consequence of their contempt for work and their adjustment to the way of life of black tribes."[70] Whereas natives were hired as cheap, unskilled labor, the poor whites clung to race privilege to avoid labor. Arendt here sees irony in that "their former slaves . . . are well on the way to becoming workers, a normal part of human civilization."[71] This sounds as if the complete disruption of African lives by the Dutch and British, the wholesale stealing of their land, and the concomitant enforcement of wage labor in mines is a step up the ladder of progress for Africans; or as if Western lifestyles were paradigmatically "normal" civilization. Arendt's quote is evidence of neglect for Africa's self-sufficient and prideful past.

6 World-creating

Do these charges against Africans hold? Is it true that they live in a state of nature, with no humanly constructed culture resulting in a "world," and no experience of political action? Surely abundant evidence exists to the contrary. First regarding work, archaeologists can support evidence of tool-making and crafting of art objects for hundreds and even thousands of years in Africa. Why is such general historical knowledge unconvincing for Arendt? Kenneth Frampton finds "architectural corollaries" in Arendt's conceptions of labor and work, since she insists that there is a relationship between built form and politics.[72] Politics requires a durable space created by permanent architecture: the piazza is one of her favorites, but the town meeting hall is also architecturally adequate. Without such permanent structures, she suggests, "human affairs would be as floating, as futile and vain as the wandering of nomadic tribes."[73] Arendt does suggest however, that a "mud hut" is stable enough to count as a home with the required rootedness needed for politics.[74] In context, her comments on Africa are casual examples; her real target of criticism, according to Frampton, is the rootlessness of contemporary America, with the creation of mobile homes and anonymous prefabricated houses, and entire communities whose closest resemblance to a piazza is the shopping mall.[75]

However, could Europeans landing on the shores of Africa, seeing no great monuments, not come to the same conclusions as Arendt? I think Arendt's description of "making" a "durable" world emphasizes architecture to too great an extent, and overlooks African ways of creating a cultural world that incorporates ritual, dress, ornamentation, and oral literature traditions. Pastoralists, who because of their life's vocation seasonally travel to green pasture and watering sites, and therefore do not have need for the bulky and permanent dwellings of Northerners who are trying to brave the winter's cold, nevertheless have roots in their communities, and set patterns that are not lightly disturbed. Regarding permanent works of art, Africans often use paints to adorn their bodies rather than canvas. Does the painting, washing, and repainting of the body model cyclical labor more than the durable "work" of canvas-painting? If we note that recurring patterns appear in self-painting, correlated with certain special events, and that the painting is imbued with cultural meaning, I would say that such recurring rituals produce the durability needed to support a culture. We must be careful not to impose European ideas of work and durability upon all countries of the world. Frampton notes that music is an art that does not lend itself to the model of reification that Arendt puts forward for the arts.[76] Dance is another category found abundantly in Africa that does not result in the stockpiling of durable objects (other than dance's accoutrements, masks and costumes). In fact, to see an African mask on a shelf behind glass in a museum is to see it out of its original, dynamic context.

Contrary to what Arendt implies in her comments in *The Origins of Totalitarianism*, many African communities had living traditions of political action, and practices of power, much like she describes and longs for. In fact, social anthropologists Arens and Karp, in reference to African notions of power, describe a view uncannily close to Arendt's conception: "The stress in Africa is not on the element of control but on the more dynamic aspect of energy and the capacity to use it." The emphasis is on engaging and creating the world, and the authors suggest that the African notions go beyond the Western social science concepts of power by their stress on transformative capacity. Whereas Foucault observes the negative view of power prevalent in the Western tradition,[77] Arens and Karp see African societies "by their recognition of the tenuous nature of their existence, place an undisguised emphasis on power as a means to forestall both the demise of extant social arrangements and create new forms of experience and activity."[78]

Further studies into African history and culture will surely show the richness of African traditions, regarding all aspects of the *vita activa*: labor, work, and action.

Arendt's analysis of South Africa has been challenging and exciting. She has laid bare the exploitative nature of the enterprise, and shown the destructive outcome of race thinking in practice. Arendt, however, neglected to get a clearer grasp of the real Africa, apart from its distortions in popular Euro–American representations. More to the heart of her theory, there is a need to rethink the value-hierarchy of the *vita activa*, looking instead for the integrity involved in all three actions when they are done free from an exploitative context.[79] And we need to look with fresh eyes to see value where it was earlier passed over, in African traditional cultures and economies.

Notes

1 Hannah Arendt, *The Origins of Totalitarianism* (Harcourt, Brace, Jovanovich, New York, 1951), p. 159.

2 Kwame Anthony Appiah, *In My Father's House: Africa in the Philosophy of Culture* (Oxford University Press, 1992), p. 13.

3 Arendt, *Origins of Totalitarianism*, pp. 159, 184.

4 Ibid., pp. 162–3, 166–7.

5 Appiah, *In My Father's House*, pp. 35–42; Arendt, *Origins of Totalitarianism*, p. 166.

6 Arendt, *Origins of Totalitarianism*, p. 157.

7 Ibid., pp. 230, 237.

8 Ibid., pp. 272, 275.

9 Hannah Arendt, *The Jew as Pariah: Jewish Identity and Politics in the Modern Age* (Grove, New York, 1978).

10 Lotte Kohler and Hans Saner, *Hannah Arendt and Karl Jaspers' Correspondence*

1926–1969 (Harcourt, Brace, Jovanovich, New York), pp. 278–9.

11 Ibid., p. 401.
12 D.A. Masolo, *You and Your Society*, Book 2 (Longman Kenya, Nairobi), pp. 82–7.
13 Appiah, *In My Father's House*, pp. 17–20.
14 Ali Mazrui, *The Africans: A Triple Heritage* (Little, Brown, Boston, MA, 1986), pp. 41–62.
15 Appiah, *In My Father's House*, p. 180.
16 Arendt, *Origins of Totalitarianism*, p. 186.
17 Ibid., p. 187.
18 Ibid.
19 David E. Stannard, *American Holocaust: Columbus and the Conquest of the New World* (Oxford University Press, New York, 1992), p. 11.
20 Douglas B. Ubelaker, "Disease and demography," in Silvio A. Bedini (ed.), *The Christopher Columbus Encyclopedia*, vol. 1 (Simon and Schuster, New York, 1992), p. 228.
21 Colin McEvedy, *The Penguin Atlas of African History* (Penguin, New York, 1987), pp. 80, 86, 90.
22 Arendt, *Origins of Totalitarianism*, pp. xvii, 186–7, 209.
23 Ibid., pp. 147–52.
24 Ibid., pp. xviii, 209.
25 Elizabeth Breuhl, *Hannah Arendt: For Love of the World* (Yale University Press, New Haven, CT, 1982), pp. 337–78.
26 Arendt, *Origins of Totalitarianism*, p. 194.
27 Richard Elphick and V.C. Malherbe, "The Khosian to 1828," in Richard Elphick and Herman Buhr Gilomee (eds), *The Shaping of South African Society, 1652–1840* (Wesleyan University Press, Middletown, CT, 1988), p. 16.
28 J.B. Peires, "Suicide or genocide? Xhosa perceptions of the Nongqawuse catastrophe," in Joshua Brown, Patrick Manning, Karin Shapiro, Jon Wiener, Bolinda Buzzoli and Peter Delius, *History from South Africa: Alternative Visions and Practices* (Temple University Press, Philadelphia, PA), pp. 31, 37.
29 Elphick and Malherbe, "The Khosian to 1828," pp. 28–9, 37, 45; James C. Armstrong and Nigel A. Worden, "The slaves, 1652–1834," in Elphick and Giliomee (eds), *Shaping of South African Society*, pp. 109, 112, 116, 122–3.
30 Armstrong and Worden, "The slaves," pp. 117, 147.
31 Ibid., p. 167.
32 Elphick and Malherbe, "The Kosian to 1828," p. 50.
33 Armstrong and Worden, "The slaves," pp. 164.
34 Ibid., p. 94.
35 Leonard Guelke, "Freehold farmers and frontier settlers, 1657–1780," in Elphick and Giliomee (eds), *Shaping of South African Society*, pp. 87, 89, 91.
36 Ibid., p. 93.
37 Richard Elphick and Robert Schell, "Intergroup relations: Khoikhoi, settlers, slaves and free blacks," in Elphick and Giliomee (eds), *Shaping of South African Society*, pp. 226–9.
38 Armstrong and Worden, "The slaves," pp. 136–8, 144–5, 153.
39 Hannah Arendt, *The Human Condition* (University of Chicago Press, Chicago, IL,

1958), pp. 7, 171–2.

40   Ibid., pp. 136–44, 171.

41   Ibid., pp. 79–80.

42   Ibid., p. 139.

43   Ibid., p. 145n.

44   Ibid., pp. 123, 161.

45   Ibid., p. 139.

46   Ibid., pp. 177–81.

47   Mildred Bakan, "Hannah Arendt's concepts of labor and work," in Melvyn Hill (ed.), *Hannah Arendt: The Recovery of the Public World* (St Martin's Press, New York, 1979), pp. 51, 63.

48   Bhikhu Parekh, "Hannah Arendt's critique of Marx," in Hill (ed.), *Hannah Arendt*, p. 70.

49   Bakan, "Hannah Arendt's concepts of labour and work," pp. 52, 54.

50   Ibid., p. 52.

51   Ibid., p. 53.

52   Parekh, "Hannah Arendt's critique of Marx," pp. 76, 85–6.

53   Ibid., p. 68.

54   Ibid., pp. 74–5.

55   George Kateb, *Hannah Arendt: Politics, Conscience, Evil* (Rowman and Allanheld, Totowa, NJ, 1984), pp. 62–3.

56   Arendt, *Human Condition*, pp. 320–5.

57   Arendt, *Origins of Totalitarianism*, p. 189.

58   Ibid., p. 190.

59   Ibid., p. 191.

60   Ibid., p. 192.

61   Ibid.

62   David Brian Davis, *The Problem of Slavery in Western Culture* (Cornell University Press, Ithaca, NY, 1966), pp. 453–4.

63   Arendt, *Origins of Totalitarianism*, p. 192.

64   Ibid., p. 193.

65   Armstrong and Worden, "The slaves," pp. 126, 130.

66   Ibid., pp. 146, 157–61.

67   Chinua Achebe, "An image of Africa: racism in Conrad's *Heart of Darkness*," in *Hopes and Impediments: Selected Essays* (Anchor/Doubleday, NY, 1988), pp. 3–20.

68   Ross C. Murfin, Joseph Conrad, *Heart of Darkness: A Case Study in Contemporary Criticism* (St Martin's Press, NY, 1989), pp. 13–16.

69   H.J. and R.E. Simons, *Class and Colour in South Africa, 1850–1950* (Penguin, Baltimore, MD, 1969), pp. 35–6.

70   Arendt, *Origins of Totalitarianism*, p. 194.

71   Ibid., p. 195.

72   Kenneth Frampton, "The status of man and the status of his objects: a reading of *The Human Condition*," in Hill (ed.), *Hannah Arendt*, p. 101.

73   Arendt, *Human Condition*, p. 204; quoted in Frampton, "Status of man," p. 105.

74   Frampton, "Status of man," p. 128n; from Hannah Arendt, "Thinking and moral considerations: lecture," *Social Research*, vol. XXXVIII/3, Fall 1971, pp. 430–1.

75   Frampton, "Status of man," pp. 106–7.

76   Ibid., p. 123.
77   Michel Foucault, *Discipline and Punish* (Pantheon, New York, 1977), p. 194.
78   W. Arens and Ivan Karp (eds), *Creativity of Power: Cosmology and Action in African Societies* (Smithsonian Institute Press, Washington, DC), p. xix.
79   Mary Dietz, " 'The slow boring of hard boards': methodical thinking and the world of politics," *American Political Science Review*, vol. 88, no. 4, December 1991, pp. 878–9.

PART III
Rebuilding Bridges

7

African Philosophy's Challenge to Continental Philosophy

Robert Bernasconi

There was a time, not so very long ago, when the question of "African philosophy" meant the question of whether such a thing was possible. The question was addressed at that time by asking whether African thought met certain criteria set from Europe that would justify the application to it of the name "philosophy." Today it is impossible to deny that there are a number of different schools of African philosophy and that, in some of them, not only the standards set by Europe, but also "Europe" itself, are now very clearly in question. It is with African philosophy as a question posed from Africa to Europe that I am concerned in this chapter. This already introduces considerable distortion because much of African philosophy is written by Africans for Africans. Tsenay Serequeberhan has written that "African philosophers need to formulate their differing positions in confrontation and dialogue and on their own, that is, minus foreign mediators/moderators or meddlers."[1]

Even though I do not have any pretence to making a contribution to African philosophy, it is perhaps presumptuous of me, a specialist in Continental philosophy, to be saying anything about it at all at this time. However, if it is foolhardy on my part to engage with African philosophy, it would be even more indefensible to ignore it. Although this paper invites response from African philosophers, its intention is to begin a discussion among Continental philosophers of the following question: what would it mean to do Continental philosophy in the light of African philosophy? My intention is that this question will serve as an invitation to these Continental philosophers to be more critical of the tradition in terms of which they define themselves, and thereby enable them to become more open to other traditions.

Continental philosophy is not quite the same as Contemporary European philosophy, although neither term has been used with sufficient precision to enable anyone to say easily what the difference is. "Contemporary European philosophy" is primarily a geographical designation referring to the philosophy done in continental Europe. The label only secondarily says something about the content and manner of philosophizing practiced. "Continental philosophy," by contrast, is a designation found almost exclusively in English-speaking countries to describe a specific style or way of interpreting a select group of philosophers largely drawn from the phenomenological tradition. Very few, if any, of the European philosophers called "Continental philosophers" by their readers in North America and Britain would feel comfortable with that label, just as academic philosophers within Europe who are not "Continental philosophers" are not being altogether disingenuous when they complain that they too are "Contemporary European philosophers." It is to the English-speaking Continental philosophers, those mainly North American philosophers who philosophize with at least one eye still directed to continental Europe and to such thinkers as Heidegger, Levinas, and Derrida, that I am primarily addressing this chapter. Although it will rightly be objected that these brief remarks about Continental philosophy are a gross caricature, they are no more of a caricature than the picture I shall draw of African philosophy. The labels "Continental philosophy" and "African philosophy" are problematic, not only because of the artificial uniformity they impose, but also because of the use to which these constructions are sometimes put. I should add that, by focusing specifically on the challenge of African philosophy to Continental philosophy, I am not denying the value and importance of other such challenges.

Continental philosophers in Europe and North America have shown little interest in African thought, except perhaps for what they culled from the works of Lévy-Bruhl without submitting them to the appropriate level of scrutiny. Heidegger did not even see fit to deny the existence of African philosophy at the same time that he insisted that there was no Chinese or Indian philosophy.[2] For Heidegger, philosophy was Greek in essence.[3] Of course, the equation of philosophy with Greek philosophy and its direct heirs was not original to Heidegger. Hegel made the argument in his *Lectures on the History of Philosophy*, drawing on a consensus established at the end of the eighteenth century.[4] In the eighteenth century, histories of philosophy written in Europe might consider the philosophy of the Chaldeans, the Persians, the Phoenicians, the Arabs, the Jews, the Indians, the Chinese, the Egyptians, the Ethiopians, the Druids or Celts, the Scythians, the early Romans, and the Etruscans, before finally arriving at the Greeks.[5] But even if European philosophers from Hegel to Heidegger insisted almost as a point of dogma that Chinese and Indian thought were not philosophy, those same European thinkers still tended to show interest in Chinese and Indian thought. By contrast, African thought was dismissed. At a time when the thought of Asia was generally being displaced by European scholars from philosophy into religion, Hegel presented Africans as barely capable even of religion, and in a gesture, repeated by Heidegger, placed Africa outside of history.[6] Europe's exclusion of Africa from history, from religion, and from philosophy has been so total, so extreme, so hysterical, and marked by such ignorance and prejudice that one cannot even say Africa was inscribed within Western metaphysics as its opposite. Africa was regarded as non-assimilable. To quote Tsenay Serequeberhan, "European culture – philosophy included – historically and thematically establishes itself by radically differentiating itself from barbarism – the Otherness of the Other – the paradigmatic case of which is the Black African."[7] There could be discussion of Africa, but not discussion with it.

The Eurocentric view of philosophy is still largely intact, both in the institutional presentation of philosophy and in the declarations of some of Western philosophy's finest minds. Take Levinas, for example. In spite of the pluralism that his thought celebrates, Emmanuel Levinas was quite explicit that he was not willing to look beyond the Bible and the Greeks as models of excellence: "I always say – but in private – that the Greeks and the Bible are all that is serious in humanity. Everything else is dancing."[8] Derrida does not exhibit the same prejudice, but insofar as Western metaphysics has from the outset been deconstruction's primary object, deconstruction has had little use for what falls outside Western metaphysics. Derrida was clear that even though a "radical trembling" could come only "from a certain outside," the trembling was already "requisite within the very structure that it solicits."[9] And again, "In order to exceed metaphysics it is necessary that a trace be inscribed within the text of metaphysics."[10] In other words, the excess over metaphysics which deconstruction sought was located by a logical necessity within metaphysics. The exclusions which deconstruction addressed were exclusions from Western metaphysics of what in some sense nevertheless belonged to it. Worse still, there is a serious question as to whether deconstruction, perhaps in spite of itself, has not paradoxically served to sustain the homogeneity of the tradition that it set out to displace. In spite of its textual rigor, the literature on deconstruction is replete with unsubstantiated generalizations about Western metaphysics that make insufficient allowance for the exceptions.[11]

The closing pages of Derrida's groundbreaking essay on Levinas, "Violence and metaphysics," show how the operation of deconstruction's strategical necessities serve to rein in claims to exceed it. At the end of "Violence and metaphysics," Derrida identified the dream of a purely heterological thought with empiricism. He noted that empiricism has always been determined by philosophy as "*nonphilosophy*: as the philosophical pretention to nonphilosophy, the inability to justify oneself, to come to one's own aid in speech".[12] However, Derrida, rehearsing gestures elaborated more fully earlier in the essay, quickly re-enclosed non-philosophy within the orbit of philosophy: "nothing can so profoundly *solicit* the Greek *logos* – philosophy – than this irruption of the totally-other." Hence Derrida could underwrite Aristotle's *Protrepticus* and say: "If one does not have to philosophize, one still has to philosophize." Recalling how Levinas's identification of the encounter with the Other as experience *par excellence* was overlaid with an ethical significance whose Judaic inspiration was undeniable, Derrida entertained the hypothesis that one might call "this experience of the infinitely other" by the name of Judaism. This established the schema in terms of which Judaism is non-philosophy, whereas philosophy is Greek. However, Derrida showed that this opposition inevitably collapses because Greece (philosophy) is the site of this "historical coupling" of Judaism and Hellenism: "The Greek miracle . . . is the impossibility for any thought ever to treat its sages as 'sages of the outside.' "[13] In raising this issue, Derrida was being faithful to a strain in Levinas's thought that was reflected in the latter's acknowledgement of "a fundamental contradiction between Athens and Jerusalem."[14] Derrida sought to negotiate this contradiction by focusing on the capacity of the Greek logos always to expand to include what opposes itself to it: "the Greek thought of Being forever has protected itself against every absolutely *surprising* convocation."[15] By appealing to the fact that the interpellation of the Greek by the non-Greek must always be said in Greek, Derrida accomplished his aim of showing that Levinas's contestation of Greek philosophy could not be designated as arising simply from the non-Greek.[16] However, in the last analysis, there seems nothing to stop this assertion of the Greek logos as the conceptual framework for any encounter between Greece (the West generally) and its Others from serving as a reassertion of the hegemony of Greek reason.[17]

The force of Derrida's strategies for addressing certain tasks inherited by Continental philosophy from Heidegger cannot be denied. It accounts for much of the appeal Derrida has had in philosophical circles, an appeal that is different in its basis from that which he has had in literature departments, where deconstruction is defined somewhat differently.[18] Although Derrida relied heavily on Heidegger for his account of Western metaphysics, there were some very important differences. For example, whereas Derrida focused on the seeming unavoidability of the closure of metaphysics, Heidegger's account of the end of Western metaphysics was directed to another beginning that would arise through remembrance of the first (Greek!) beginning. That this other beginning largely disappeared from Derrida's rewriting of Heidegger might have received greater attention had not Heidegger addressed it specifically to the Germans, so that its absence removes a potential source of problems. I shall suggest later that it is also very limiting. Furthermore, it leaves the question of where, for example, Chinese philosophy, Indian philosophy, and especially African philosophy stand in relation to deconstruction. One has to say *especially* African philosophy because of the nature and force of its historical exclusion from Western philosophy. It is true that the denial and distortion of African philosophy can be traced in Western philosophy: for example, in its imposition of the idea of fetishism on African and other religions. One could imagine Derrida giving a more sensitive treatment of this distortion than one finds in *Glas*, but the issue transcends the level of gestures that Derrida did make or might have made. It is a question of the axioms and strategies which have come to define deconstruction.[19] More intriguing still, one can imagine deconstruction reopening the question of the exclusion of African philosophy by addressing the debt of Greek philosophy to Egyptian philosophy. Many Greek sources acknowledged this debt and it was only at the end of the eighteenth century that it was dismissed without proper debate and for extrinsic reasons. However, given deconstruction's parasitic relation to Heidegger's conception of the unity of metaphysics, the ramifications of such a revision, which would also have to take account of other sources, such as Zoroastrianism, would be far-reaching and would not leave appeals to the Greek logos intact.[20] Furthermore, even after such revision, it is not clear what contribution deconstruction could make to the contemporary dialogue between Western philosophy and African philosophy.

In the face of this uncertainty, it is with some relief, I suspect, that the Continental philosopher will learn of Lucius Outlaw's "African 'philosophy': deconstructive and reconstructive challenges."[21] The term "deconstruction" is increasingly used in discussions of African philosophy, but, as is the case throughout the academy, it is not always used with precision. Outlaw, by contrast, has provided a detailed account of why he chooses this word, which makes his essay an indispensable reference point for any discussion of Continental philosophy's relation to African philosophy. His essay, written from within the North American context, is inviting to Continental philosophers because it seems to see a possible line of connection between Continental philosophy and African philosophy.

Outlaw distinguishes between *Philosophy*, as the enterprise "practiced by the dominant figures in the dominant traditions, throughout its western history," and *philosophy*, as

> an enterprise more critically self conscious of its own historicity in ways that inform its practices and thus make it possible to identify other discursive modalities and traditions as appropriate instances of a refined notion of what constitutes philosophy, especially when these traditions and modalities are situated in non-European cultures.[22]

Outlaw argues that African philosophy challenges the very idea of Philosophy in a way that can be called deconstructive because it can be associated with the complex set of practices within the enterprise of Western philosophy that goes under that name.[23] He insists with due caution that there is an association rather than an identity between African philosophy and classic deconstruction. This is important because, while Outlaw recognizes explicitly that deconstruction self-consciously borrows from within Western philosophy the resources necessary for the deconstruction of that heritage, he also recognizes that African philosophy did not adopt that strategy. Outlaw's thesis is that "contemporary discussions about 'P/philosophy' in Africa have been 'deconstructive' *as a function of the historical exigencies conditioning their emergence*".[24] Or, again, "the advent of discussions about 'African' P/philosophy is, by the force of historical contingencies, *necessarily* deconstructive."[25] The argument is that the strategic projects, especially of the "nationalist-ideological" philosophers, are "in a very real way, *classically* deconstructive, in a Derridan sense" because "they preserve (are constituted by) the structure of 'difference.'"

> For in each case, the object of the strategy – the articulation of a "text" of "African philosophy" – is constituted *within* the bounds of that which it challenges (i.e., Philosophy), but as both the *same* (philosophy) and *different* (African).[26]

It perhaps does not distort Outlaw's position too much if one restates it in the form of the claim that *within the framework of Philosophy* the phrase "African philosophy" embodies a contradiction, and that it is from this that it gains its deconstructive force.

Western philosophy traps African philosophy in a double bind: either African philosophy is so similar to Western philosophy that it makes no distinctive contribution and effectively disappears; or it is so different that its credentials to be genuine philosophy will always be in doubt.[27] That is why Outlaw is right to insist with respect of "the self-image of the brokers of Western history and culture" that "any discussion of *African* philosophy involves, *necessarily*, confronting this privileged self-image. It is this confrontation which problematizes 'African' and forces its deconstruction/reconstruction in its relation of difference with 'European.' "[28] This would be true for so long, but only for so long, as the term "African philosophy" has the force of a contradiction. The suggestion is that "African philosophy" as a term functions, in ways that a reader of Derrida's "Violence and metaphysics" would recognize, to expose the limits of the dominant framework as they are enshrined within the double bind, and thereby to displace them.

However, the deconstructive force of the phrase "African philosophy" is not of itself sufficient, even within the unique context to which Outlaw refers. That is why Outlaw focuses on "nationalist-ideological" philosophy, because it specifically addresses the question of colonialism and in some cases the role of Western philosophy in providing a justification for colonialism.[29] Outlaw privileges the example of the Negritude movement among the various "nationalist-ideological" philosophies, describing it as "one of the most deconstructive forms of African philosophy,"[30] even though it has also been one of the most contested. Outlaw praises the Negritude movement for its "efforts directed at reconstructing and rehabilitating the 'African' while forging an identity and authenticity thought to be appropriate to the exigencies of 'modern' existence."[31] However, if this is what is most valuable in Negritude, it is also what is most vulnerable about it. One need only recall Senghor's famous phrase: "L'émotion est nègre comme la raison hellène"[32] (Emotion is black as reason is Greek.)

Senghor accepts the classic opposition and appears only to re-evaluate the terms without disturbing the framework. In this instance at least, it does not even succeed in being deconstructive, let alone reconstructive. That is why it was almost impossible for Sartre to expound negritude without reducing it to a moment within the dialectic. Fanon criticized Sartre for this, but he also knew that Sartre was not being altogether unjust. Hence Fanon's comment on *Black Orpheus* was "I needed not to know."[33] Deconstruction would be left with a similar dilemma. As deconstruction, the Negritude movement barely gets started, but this does not exhaust its philosophical importance, which lies in its political challenge to Europe's self-image. Nevertheless, Fanon himself seems to be a better representative of the category of nationalist-ideological philosophy for Outlaw's purposes, along with Kwame Nkrumah and Amilcar Cabral. To understand how these other resources might be utilized, one can turn to the work of Tsenay Serequeberhan.

In the conclusion of *The Hermeneutics of African Philosophy*, Serequeberhan takes up Outlaw's formulation of a deconstructive and a reconstructive challenge, and develops an understanding of these terms that, partly because it is more Heideggerian than Derridan, introduces further resources from Continental philosophy to the issue of African philosophy's challenge to Continental philosophy. Serequeberhan describes the reconstructive challenge of African philosophy as "aimed at supplying a positive hermeneutic supplement to the concrete efforts under way on the continent".[34] To illustrate this process, he drew a parallel between Amilcar Cabral's project of a "return to the source" and Heidegger's account of a repetition or *Wiederholung*.[35] Serequeberhan did not conceive of this as "a 'return' to a primordial 'truth' or some uncontaminated 'African *arche*,'" but as the reawakening of the vigor and vitality of African existence. This vitality would express itself in the production of new concepts: "In thinking the historicity out of which it is being secreted, African philosophy is concretely engaged in doing precisely this – working out 'new concepts.'"[36] This is conceived of as part of an "indigenizing theoretic effort in the service of revitalizing the historicity of African existence within the contexts and the bounds of our contemporary world."[37]

Although Serequeberhan's reference to *Wiederholung* shows the relevance of Heidegger's early philosophy, the fact that Heidegger's later thought was specifically engaged in revitalizing the historicity of German existence suggests that it might also have resources to offer not found in either the early Heidegger or deconstruction. For example, by divorcing the character of philosophical thinking from *ratio* or calculative reason, Heidegger undoes many of the axioms that had been employed at the end of the eighteenth century to restrict the history of philosophy to Greece. Furthermore, Heidegger's conception of "another beginning," while not proposing a new beginning, suggests a way out of the apparent impasse into which deconstruction appears to lead its adherents. If one of the main insights guiding deconstruction is the impossibility of any straightforward exit from the Western metaphysical tradition, Heidegger, by contrast, sought to prepare for the possibility of another beginning. The fact that this possible future was supposed to arise from recollecting the first beginning of philosophy in Greece(!) and was supposed to lead to an opening of German philosophy might not make this a particularly auspicious precedent to which to turn, but, for all the dangers of misunderstanding and for all the differences, Heidegger's late thought shows the connection between the construction of the history of philosophy and the opening of future thinking.

The "deconstructive challenge" in Serequeberhan's double venture, which is more precisely a destructuring challenge, performs "the unmasking and undoing" of the Eurocentric residue inherited from colonialism. In the context of *The Hermeneutics of African Philosophy*, Serequeberhan's examples are "the grounding parameters and cultural codes inscribed in these political, economic, educational, and social organizations" that remain still oriented by colonial and European condescending attitudes. However, elsewhere, particularly in his studies of Kant, Hegel, and Marx, Serequeberhan has undertaken this same deconstructive task or, in the Heideggerian idiom, "destructuring" task, with respect to some of the classic texts of Western philosophy.[38] There are numerous examples of other Africana philosophers engaged in exposing the racism of Western philosophy. European thought in general and Continental philosophy in particular face a similar task. It is not simply a matter of setting the record straight at the antiquarian level. Continental philosophy does not have a merely external relation to its own tradition. To give just one example, certain ideas of history and particularly of development were in part fostered to address Europe's uncertainty in the face of the discovery of peoples whom Europeans later came to classify as other races. These ideas of history and development still permeate philosophy, as well as being instruments in contemporary world politics in programs of economic and social development.[39] This gives the task a clear urgency.

The various critiques of European philosophy provided by African philosophers have already begun to play an important part in the re-examination of European thought by Europeans, but one should not expect that these two critiques will always coincide. This is because there is an existential as well as a theoretical dimension to the task. African philosophical thought has and will continue to have an existential role to play in the overcoming of colonialism. It is perhaps no wonder that Masolo closes his book, *African Philosophy in Search of Identity*, by stating: "Philosophy is experience. It is a personal point of view insofar as it is mine, and because philosophy consists not in persuading others but in making our own minds clear."[40] Even though Masolo goes on to concede that philosophy can become more than merely personal when grounds are given, the formulation seems to betray the scars of too many conversations in which the author has listened without being heard in return. It is possible that the basis of dialogue is not the presumption of agreement, but the admission on the part of the hearer that he or she is incapable of understanding. "You don't know what I'm talking about," closes the conversation only if the listener wants to control what is said. It can also elicit further response.

Continental philosophers should be capable of further response once they recognize Masolo to be evoking what they know as the *existentiell*. It is no surprise that Masolo does not invoke it explicitly, because to do so might recall the fateful invocation of existential philosophy by Placide Tempels, which Masolo himself carefully documents.[41] In the same way, one would expect African philosophers to be hesitant about any appeal to the idea of the prephilosophical because Africans were at one time confined to that realm. However, once it is recognized that all philosophies draw on prephilosophical experience, the old dream of a scientific philosophy is *ausgeträumt*, it is exhausted. According to Heidegger, what necessitated fundamental ontology to proceed by existential analysis was the recognition that philosophy arises from and returns to prephilosophical experience.[42] For example, Heidegger devoted a great deal of energy, as part of the destructuring of ontology, to showing how the prephilosophical experience of making, *poiesis*, determined the conceptual framework of Greek philosophy. Although Derridan deconstruction tends to overlook this dimension, Levinas has also recognized both the prephilosophical and the non-philosophical sources of his own philosophy. In his life the non-philosophical was pre-eminently the experience of anti-Semitism. This was reflected at the very heart of his thought when, in *Otherwise than Being*, being persecuted provided the access for the philosophical discovery of absolute passivity, which was inaccessible to the oppressor.[43] Reference to this experience does not place limits on Levinas's philosophy, but shows how the particular experiences of a people, experiences often enshrined within a tradition, can constitute its universal significance.

The existential dimension of African philosophy's challenge to Western philosophy in general and Continental philosophy in particular is located in the need to decolonize the mind. This task is at least as important for the colonizer as it is for the colonized.[44] For Africans, decolonizing the mind takes place not only in facing the experience of colonialism, but also in recognizing the precolonial, which establishes the destructive importance of so-called ethnophilosophy and sage philosophy, as well as nationalist-ideological philosophy. Serequeberhan, explaining the fact that in his study there would be positive references and appropriations of the European philosophic tradition, as well as critical rejections of it, explained that "the antidote is always located in the poison."[45] But these are issues for African philosophers. For Europeans, decolonizing the colonial mind necessitates an encounter with the colonized, where finally the European has the experience of being seen and judged by those they have denied.[46] The extent to which European philosophy championed colonialism, and more particularly helped to justify it through a philosophy of history that privileged Europe, makes it apparent that such a decolonizing is an urgent task for European thought. So, although the European, recalling Derrida's *pharmakon*, may find an antidote amidst the position – or, in Hölderlin's idiom borrowed by Heidegger, they may find that which rescues (*das Rettende*) where the danger (*die Gefahr*) is – nevertheless, African philosophy is already making a unique contribution to the critique of European philosophy. One cannot say that African philosophy has already taken so much from European philosophy that its critique of the latter is, or at least is indistinguishable from, an internal critique. Even if this were true, and I have tried to show it is not, no debt of recent African philosophy to European philosophy could be said to reduce the former to a moment of the latter, unless the capacity of the Greek logos to envelop whatever threatens to resist it has already been conceded.

Depending on the occasion, African philosophers may or may not be addressing Europeans when they expose the racism of European philosophy, but the ideas of pre-philosophical and non-philosophical experience as expounded by Heidegger and Levinas open Continental philosophers to the particular value of critiques of Western philosophy written from Africa. Of course, such critiques can be written from within European philosophy itself, but this would seem to be a case where the external critique is stronger than an internal critique. The difference arises as soon as one acknowledges the role of experience in philosophy. The question of "who is speaking?" is one that has been outlawed from philosophy because it seemed to set up an opposition between the authority of the author and universal reason. The deafness of neutral reason arises from its proud boast that it refuses to give weight to the identity of the speaker or writer. However, the powerful critiques of Western philosophy by African and African-American philosophers exceed Western philosophy and cannot simply be reinscribed within it, even when they rely on the idiom of Western philosophy for their presentation. This is because these critiques spring from the prephilosophical experience of racism and colonialism to which neutral reason is inevitably deaf, just as it is deaf to the role of tradition within philosophy.[47] If Continental philosophers would open themselves to a critique from African philosophy and thereby learn more about their own tradition seen from "the outside," they would find that the hegemonic concept of reason had been displaced, and they would be better placed to learn to respect other traditions, including those that are not African.[48]

Notes

1   Tsenay Serequeberhan (ed.), *African Philosophy: The Essential Readings* (Paragon, New York, 1991), p. xviii.

2   Martin Heidegger, *Was heisst Denken?* (Max Niemeyer, Tübingen, 1956), p. 136; trans. F.D. Wieck and J. Glenn Gray, *What is called Thinking?* (Harper and Row, New York, 1968), p. 224. See further Robert Bernasconi, "Heidegger and the invention of the Western philosophical tradition," *Journal of the British Society for Phenomenology*, vol. 26, 1995, pp. 241–55.

3   Martin Heidegger, *Was ist das – die Philosophie?* (Neske, Pfullingen, 1965), p. 13; trans. William Kluback and Jean T. Wilde (Vision Press, London, 1956), p. 31.

4   G.W.F. Hegel, *Vorlesungen über die Geschichte der Philosophie: Einleitung*, ed. Walter Jaeschke, (Felix Meiner, Hamburg, 1993), p. 68.

5   I have taken as my example Joanne Ernesto Schubert, *Historia Philosophiae*, pars prima (Jena, 1742). I have discussed the question of the reinvention of philosophy as Greek in "Philosophy's paradoxical parochialism," *Reflections on the Work of Edward Said: Cultural Identity and the Gravity of History*, (Lawrence and Wishart, London, forthcoming).

6   G.W.F. Hegel, *Vorlesungen über die Philosophie der Weltgeschichte*, vol. 1, *Die Vernunft in der Geschichte*, ed. J. Hoffmeister (Felix Meiner, Hamburg, 1980), pp. 213–34; trans. H.B. Nisbett, *Lectures on the Philosophy of World History* (Cambridge University Press, Cambridge 1975), pp. 173–90. I have investigated Hegel's treatment of Africa in "Hegel at the Court of the Ashanti," forthcoming. Heidegger's remarks can be found in *Lógica: lecciones de M. Heidegger (semestre verano 1934) en el legado de Helene Weiss*, ed. Victor Farias (Anthropos, Barcelona, 1991), p. 40. I am grateful to Richard Polt of Xavier University of Cincinnati for drawing this text to my attention.

7   Tsenay Serequeberhan, *The Hermeneutics of African Philosophy* (Routledge, New York, 1994), p. 128, n. 30. Henceforth *HAP*.

8   Emmanuel Levinas, "Intention, Ereignis und der Andere. Gespräch Zwischen Emmanuel Levinas und Christoph von Wolzogen," *Humanismus des anderen Menschen* (Felix Meiner, Hamburg, 1989), p. 140. I have argued that, in spite of such statements of Levinas's personal attitudes, his philosophy can, after some modification, still provide a basis for cross-cultural encounter. See Robert Bernasconi, "Who is my neighbor? Who is the Other? Questioning 'the generosity of Western thought,'" *Ethics and Responsibility in the Phenomenological Tradition*, The Ninth Annual Symposium of the Simon Silverman Phenomenology (Center Duquesne University, Pittsburgh, 1992), pp. 1–31.

9   Jacques Derrida, *Marges de la philosophie*, (Minuit, Paris, 1972), pp. 161–62; trans. Alan Bass, *Margins of Philosophy* (University of Chicago Press, Chicago 1982), pp. 133–4. Henceforth *M* and *MP* respectively.

10 Derrida, *M*, p. 76; Bass, *MP*, p. 65.

11 See Robert Bernasconi, "On deconstructing nostalgia for community within the West: the debate between Nancy and Blanchot," *Research in Phenomenology*, vol. 23, 1993, pp. 3–21. However, this would be an appropriate point for me to confess that my own work is by no means always free from this same tendency to rely on

a caricature of Western metaphysics.

12 Derrida, *L'écriture et la différence* (Editions du Senil, Paris, 1967), p. 226; *Writing and Difference*, trans. Alan Bass (University of Chicago Press, Chicago, IL, 1978), p. 152. Hencefort *ED* and *WD* respectively.

13 Derrida, *ED*, p. 227; *WD*, p. 153.

14 Emmanuel Levinas, "Transcendance et Hauteur," *Bulletin de la Société française de Philosophie*, vol. 54, 1962, p. 103.

15 Derrida, *ED*, p. 227; *WD*, p. 153.

16 *ED*, pp. 122 and 196; *WD*, pp. 82 and 133.

17 Compare the rather different assessment offered by Robert Young in *White Mythologies: Writing History and the West* (Routledge, New York, 1990), pp. 12–20.

18 It should be emphasized that in addition to the technical sense of deconstruction that is found in Derrida's early texts and which is usually what is intended in this chapter, there are other senses that are certainly relevant in the context of postcoloniality, but which are not considered here. See, for example, Gayatri Spivak, "Interview with radical philosophy," in *The Postcolonial Critic* (Routledge, New York, 1990), pp. 133–7 and "Feminism and deconstruction again," in *Outside the Teaching Machine* (Routledge, New York, 1993), pp. 121–40. I should acknowledge that what I am here calling the technical sense of deconstruction conforms to an interpretation that I have often advocated because of its logical rigor.

19 Jacques Derrida, *Glas* (Galilée, Paris, 1974), pp. 232–6; trans. John P. Leavey, Jr and Richard Rand, *Glas* (University of Nebraska Press, Lincoln, NB, 1986), pp. 207–11.

20 I tried to show how this issue touches on one short essay by Derrida, "Scribble," in "The Anglican bishop and the pagan priests: Warburton and the hermeneutics of Egyptian hieroglyphs," *Archivio di Filosofia*, vol. 60, 1992, pp. 131–44. For African discussions of the place of ancient Egyptian philosophy in African philosophy, see, for example, Cheikh Anta Diop, "Does an African philosophy exist?" in *Civilization or Barbarism*, trans. Yaa-Lengi Meema Ngemi (Lawrence Hill, New York, 1991), pp. 309–76; and Theophile Obenga, *Ancient Egypt and Black Africa* (Karnak House, London, 1992).

21 Lucius Outlaw, "African 'philosophy': deconstructive and reconstructive challenges," in G. Floistad (ed.), *Contemporary Philosophy: A New Survey, vol. 5, African Philosophy*, (Nijhoff, Dordrecht, 1987), pp. 9–44. Henceforth *DRC*.

22 Ibid., p. 10.

23 Ibid., p. 11.

24 Ibid., p. 12.

25 Ibid., p. 26.

26 Ibid., pp. 30–1.

27 Even Hountondji, perhaps in an offguard moment, seems to fall foul of the double bind when he wrote that African philosophy "means the contributions which African thinkers make to the sorts of critical and reflexive discussions in which philosophy has traditionally been taken to consist." It is clear that by "traditional" Hountondji did not mean African traditions, but the formulation serves as a reminder of how difficult it might be for him to identify what that tradition is without assuming precisely what is in question in this debate (P. J. Hountondji,

"African philosophy," in J.O. Urmson and Jonathan Rée (eds.), *The Concise Encyclopedia of Western Philosophy* (Unwin Hyman, London, 1989), p. 5). Hountondji's position on the issues raised by this chapter are better represented by the following texts: "Comments on contemporary African philosophy," *Diogenes*, no. 71, Fall 1970, pp. 109–30; "Langues africaines et philosophie: l'hypothèse relativiste," *Les Études Philosophiques*, 1982, pp. 393–406; "Occidentalism, élitism: answer to two critiques," *Quest* (Lusaka, Zambia), vol. 3, no. 2, 1989, pp. 3–30.

28 Outlaw, *DRC*, p. 35.

29 Outlaw borrows the category "nationalist-ideological" from Odera Oruka, who in 1978 divided African philosophy into four kinds. The others were: ethnophilosophy, of which the foremost representative was the now much criticized Placide Tempels, the author of *Bantu Philosophy*; sage philosophy, the documentation of the ideas of individual sages or wise men, such as Ogotemmeli, who reflected critically on the beliefs and practices of their community; and professional philosophy, which was associated primarily with Hountondji. See Henry Odera Oruka, "Sagacity in African philosophy," in Serequeberhan (ed.), *African Philosophy*, p. 49.

30 Ibid., p. 28.

31 Ibid., p. 32.

32 See the discussion of this sentence in S. Okechukwu Mezu, *The Poetry of L. S. Senghor* (Heinemann, London, 1973), pp. 85–6 and Sylvia Washington, *The Concept of Negritude in the Poetry of Léopld Sédar Senghor* (Princeton University Press, Princeton, NJ, 1973), pp. 74–6. See also Serequeberhan's "destructuring reading of the essentialist *Négritude* of Leopold Sedar Senghor" (*HAP*, p. 131) at *HAP*, pp. 42–53.

33 Frantz Fanon, *Peau noire masques blancs* (Seuil, Paris, 1952), p. 109; trans. Charles Lam Markmann, *Black Skin, White Masks* (Grove Weidenfeld, New York, 1967), p. 135. See further, Robert Bernasconi, "Sartre's gaze returned: the transformation of the phenomenology of racism," *Graduate Faculty Philosophy Journal*, vol. 18, no. 2, 1995.

34 Serequeberhan, *HAP*, p. 119.

35 Ibid., pp. 126–7.

36 Ibid., p. 9. Frantz Fanon, *Les damnés de la terre* (Gallimard, Paris, 1991), p. 294; trans. Constance Farrington, *The Wretched of the Earth* (Grove Weidenfeld, New York 1991), p. 246. I propose Fanon's "new humanism" for a new humanity as an example of such a "new concept" in Robert Bernasconi, "Casting the slough: Fanon's new humanism for a new humanity," in Lewis Gordon, T. Denean Sharpley-Whiting and Renée T. White (eds), *Frantz Fanon: A Critical Reader* (Blackwell, Oxford, forthcoming).

37 Serequeberhan, *HAP*, p. 119.

38 See Tsenay Serequeberhan, "The idea of colonialism in Hegel's *Philosophy of Right*," *International Philosophical Quarterly*, vol. 29, 1989, pp. 301–18; and "Karl Marx and African emancipatory thought," *Praxis International*, vol. 10, 1990, pp. 161–81. The paper on Kant is still unpublished. I am grateful to Professor Serequeberhan for providing me with a copy.

39 See, for example, Joseph Ki-Zerbo, "Le développement clés en tête," in Joseph Ki-Zerbo (ed.), *La natte des autres. Pour un développement endogène en Afrique*

(Codesria, Dakar, 1992).

40 D.A. Masolo, *African Philosophy in Search of Identity* (Indiana University Press, Bloomington, In, 1994), p. 250.

41 Ibid., pp. 64–7. See Placide Tempels, *La philosophie Bantoue*, trans. from Dutch by A. Rubbens (Présence Africaine, Paris, 1949).

42 Martin Heidegger, *Metaphysische Anfangsgründe der Logik* (Klostermann, Frankfurt 1978), pp. 196–202; trans. Michael Heim, *Metaphysical Foundations of Logic* (Indiana University Press, Bloomington, IN, 1984), pp. 154–9.

43 See Robert Bernasconi, "'Only the persecuted . . .:' language of the oppressor, language of the persecuted," in Adriaan Peperzak (ed.), *Ethics as First Philosophy* (Routledge, New York, 1995), pp. 77–86.

44 Cf. Ngugi wa Thiong'o, *Decolonising the Mind* (Heinemann, Portsmouth, NH, 1986).

45 Serequeberhan, *HAP*, p. 11. One might think of the use to which Du Bois put Herder in his philosophical reflections on the future of blacks in the United States. See, for example, Ingeborg Solbrig, "Herder and the 'Harlem Renaissance'" of black culture in America: the case of the "Neger-Idyllen," in Kurt Mueller-Vollmer (ed.), *Herder Today*, (Walter de Gruyter, Berlin, 1990), pp. 402–14.

46 See Robert Bernasconi, "'Ich mag in keinen Himmel, wo Weisse sind.' Herder's critique of Eurocentrism," *Acta Institutionis Philosophiae et Aestheticae* (Tokyo), ed. T. Imamichi, vol. 13, 1995.

47 As with so many of the themes raised here, it strikes me that some recent feminist philosophy has trodden a similar path. However, to give an example from Africana philosophy I would mention Frederick Douglass' reference to "black reasons" that white reason will never know (*The Life and Writings of Frederick Douglass*, ed. P. Foner (International Publishers, New York, 1975), vol. 2, p. 414). This was not a specific mode of reasoning, a different logic, but a different perspective that, in this case, arose out of the shared experience of slavery and that, as such, would not tolerate the kinds of compromise being negotiated by whites who opposed slavery for their own reasons but within clear limits. See Robert Bernasconi, "The Constitution of the People: Frederick Douglass and the *Dred Scott* decision," *Cardozo Law Review*, vol. 13, 1991, pp. 1281–96.

48 This chapter is based on a presentation given at the Collegium Phaenomenologicum in Perugia, Italy in August 1995, where I was invited to show the direction of my "current research." This should help to explain why there are so many references to my own work. I decided to retain them, not only because of the programmatic character of what is proposed here, but also because I am well aware that many of the concepts and arguments introduced in this chapter rely on exposition that I have given elsewhere.

8

Understanding African Philosophy from a Non-African Point of View: An Exercise in Cross-cultural Philosophy

Richard H. Bell

Wittgenstein comments on Sir James Frazer's *Golden Bough*: "We might say 'every view has its charm,' but this would be wrong. What is true is that every view is significant for him who sees it so (but that does not mean 'sees it as something other than it is'). And in this sense every view is equally significant."[1] A central aim of philosophy is to "see something as it is." If this is achieved, we have a reasonable benchmark for approaching another "thing as it is." The effort to see another culture "as it is," a particular African culture for example, when one is alien to that culture, poses several difficulties. Overcoming the skepticism that grips our understanding when challenged to embrace an unfamiliar point of view requires that we first understand our own culture "as it is." This, as Cavell would say, is a "stepwise" process.[2]

The understanding of anything is always tied to its surroundings, which include language, customs, geography, iconic traditions, and especially the ordinary practices of its people. The difficulties are many, but there are fewer mysteries in this process than philosophers suppose. Clifford Geertz says succinctly:

> The truth of the doctrine of cultural relativism is that we can never apprehend another people's or another period's imagination neatly, as though it were our own. The falsity of it is that we can therefore never genuinely apprehend it at all. We can apprehend it well enough, at least as well as we apprehend anything

else not properly ours; but we do so not by looking *behind* the interfering glosses which connect us to it but *through* them.[3]

As human beings we can and do understand another culture's life forms and practices "well enough," more or less "as [they are]." We can describe another culture's different forms and features just as it can describe ours, and can also go on to understand the culture to a degree hindered only by particular limitations in our own point of view.

Wittgenstein characterizes "meaning something" as "like going up to someone."[4] Interpreting and understanding the meaning of another culture is not unlike "going up to someone" in our own culture. We can learn much by analogy about works of art and ceremonial practices in a radically different culture by how we go up to works of art and respond to them in our own culture. Our separation along lines of language, ethnicity, gender, and religious preferences increases skepticism about the possibility of mutual understanding between peoples and cultures.

Understanding African philosophy (and more generally aspects of African culture) from the point of view of a non-African requires that we establish a specific philosophical procedure that will (1) engage the discussion among African intellectuals about features of their own self-understanding and its relationship to our own self-understanding; (2) listen to the oral narratives and lived-texts of African peoples; and (3) attend to the iconic traditions of Africa, its visual art, ritual drama, literature, and religious practices.[5]

1 A Procedure from an Aesthetic Point of View

The mutual understanding we would like to achieve in "going up to" another human being may be easily thwarted. If the other person is a stranger, we may naturally turn away or only talk or dwell reticently in their company; we may fail to spend enough time or give enough attention to meet "face to face" or "eye to eye." Wittgenstein sees these as more important drawbacks in understanding a stranger than believing they have a different way of thinking or a different "rationality" from our own. He probes how *we could contemplate* the differences – "riddles," he calls them – we encounter in practices that seem alien to us, so that we would *connect up* these differences with something familiar or that we did understand.

In thinking about discussions in *The Golden Bough* of why children in European Beltane Festivals or elders in an African community's re-enactment of ancient regicide rites (e.g., in accounts we have about the Shilluk of Sudan) might burn a straw effigy or kill an aging king, Wittgenstein finds an uneasiness in Frazer's too-ready-to-hand causal and theoretical explanations. Frazer's emphasis on explanation seems misplaced. He fails to note the gravity of the events, even if they are only re-enactments or plays; he does not see the "darkness" in such events. Frazer's "eye" is cast not on the people's activity, but toward some explanatory hypothesis that might appear or sound "rational" to Western "eyes" and "ears."[6]

A major difficulty in such accounts as Frazer's, and others formed under our "modern" epistemological paradigms, is that they function to make thinking easier; they shift the burden of the investigation *on to* an abstracted level and *away from* the level where the ordinary human activity, with its language, stories, or ceremonial acts, is doing something: that is, its job. The burden of understanding is shifted from ourselves on to a theory.

There is little doubt that "the burning of a man" or the killing of a king are serious matters and strike deep roots in us. Matters of life and death beckon to us and demand some understanding. Wittgenstein insists that what gives these matters depth is not to be found in an explanation of their origin, but in how we connect them with our own thoughts and feelings.

> We also say of some people that they are transparent to us. It is, however, important as regards this observation that one human being can be a complete enigma to another. We learn this when we come into a strange country with entirely strange traditions; and, what is more, even given a mastery of the country's language. We do not *understand* the people. (And not because of not knowing what they are saying to themselves.) We cannot find our feet with them.[7]

It is difficult to "find our feet" or "find ourselves" with those who engage in certain ceremonial acts. With the fire-festivals or regicide we have "come into a strange country." With some attention we can find out what they are saying and how their actions have meaning within their life. Yet, we still may not *understand* clearly. Wittgenstein sees this as the really crucial issue; one that cannot simply be left at an impasse, with a culturally relativistic response to fix it in place. We cannot say "every view has its charm" and leave it at that! We must "find our feet" or "find ourselves in them" on the matter, and thus move toward a more comfortable (or disturbed) understanding.

Wittgenstein focuses on understanding "the character" of the people who performed the ceremony and on discerning "the spirit" of peoples' acts. We understand these, he says, by "describing the sort of people that take part, their way of behavior at other times, i.e. their character and the kinds of games that they play. And we should then see that what is sinister lies in the character of these people themselves."[8] Then one can imagine what might also be "sinister behavior" in one's own life and thus "find one's self in them." He concludes by asking "What makes human sacrifice something deep and sinister anyway?" and answers, "this deep and sinister aspect is not obvious just from learning the history of the external action, but *we* impute [or ascribe] it from an experience in ourselves."[9]

Where do we begin then? We first want to arrive at what Wittgenstein calls a "perspicuous representation" of how those who engage in the festivals stand toward them.[10] Of course, this is being done by numerous ethnographers – we have many careful and detailed descriptions, and those descriptions have been put together in ways that have made the representations of other cultures close to transparent. A good example is provided by Malcolm Ruel in his study of two East African rites. He shows that what people do in their lives, ceremonially, expresses their deepest values. Their rites are "metaphorical actions" which "carry meaning across different situations." The rites he examines are of a young Nyakyusa chief's "coming out" and the Kuria act of "opening" a slaughtered cow's stomach, a beer pot or a room. Both rites, when represented fully, link us with important mutually understandable notions of how ceremonial acts are tied to larger social processes, and how they are related to one's natural environment and biological life processes. The Kuria rite also provides a "perspicuous" example of how hospitality and family prosperity are common human sentiments, cutting across cultural boundaries. These rites, and other ceremonial acts, contain in them and commemorate the whole of a community's life. There is not something outside their acts which the people and their stories "wrongly" or "superstitiously" or only "partly" are said to "assert" or "represent." To *understand* their rites and ceremonies is where we must begin to understand the people.[11]

Wittgenstein believes that there is *a way of seeing* how those who engage in creating and transmitting stories actually stand in relation to their stories and practices. With such descriptions, however, the question remains: *is all this sufficient for our understanding?* How are we, for example, to become "convinced" that the gods of other people "have the same meaning" as our own gods?[12]

On this point – and *it is the more important one* – Wittgenstein provides us genuinely new insights. He poses a new question which links *us* with the people's life being described: how is it that "we impute" (or ascribe) "from an experience in ourselves" what is deep and sinister or fundamentally disquieting about another's action? It is "in ourselves" that we must see how we stand to the burning of a man; we must deal with our own feelings of guilt or anxiety – of disquiet – and find some analogous experiences where we do this or say that, and then feel satisfied. To contemplate the depth of the experience of others we must *look into ourselves for some analogous experiences*.

What kinds of analogous experience are these? What is this *understanding* without a hypothesis or theory? Here is the difficulty. We must think out the analogies for ourselves – no shortcuts or bypasses. In so doing we discover that "the religious actions or the religious life of the priest-king [or of a Nyakyusa chief] are not different in kind from any genuinely religious action today, say a confession of sins. This also can be 'explained' (made clear) and cannot be explained."[13] Wittgenstein points us in a different direction with his examples.

He wants me to come to some personal satisfaction regarding a disquieting situation – therein lies *my understanding*. He asks what kinds of experience I have which may bring my heart and mind to rest.

When the seriousness of death, for example, impinges on a person or community, *any* manner of action(s) may arise within the person or community to enable them to allay anxiety, dispel further fears, or celebrate a new confidence in the ongoing nature of life in death. We all want to keep our family and community healthy and ongoing. In all the emergent rites and commemorative stories, the aim is not to provide an explanation for death, but to express human life in all its paradoxicalness. In the case of East African Kuria people, Malcolm Ruel says, "The worst that can befall a person – man or woman – is for their descent line to be terminated or 'closed.'" We can connect with the hope of keeping our family alive and prosperous and celebrating family passages. Ruel says, "a generous, hospitable man is described as having 'a wide corral entrance.'" Again a common sign of hospitality – an open door – is an act we can easily connect with.[14] Thus we and others express ourselves.

Back to the strangeness of celebrating by burning a *man*. The sinister impression is carried with the act, metaphorically "carried over" with a host of connections related to the strangeness of one's own natural history. We come to the strangeness and to an understanding of it, says Wittgenstein, as we discover "the *environment* of a way of acting"[15] – both the environment of the strange happening and our own. In the end, like those who live out the stories and practices, we must acquire the capacity for the understanding, it cannot be given in the theory. We must look into ourselves and to what others are saying of themselves, and put together those links from what we have seen and heard, from what we have experienced and already understood. The *understanding* is something that an individual *does* and it is tied to what Søren Kierkegaard called a particular self-reflective "life-view".[16]

Wittgenstein's way of "finding our feet" or "finding ourselves in" another's way of life is both a more *universal* and a more *particular* way of understanding. It is more universal in that Wittgenstein sees the relevance of tying the feelings and actions expressed in one culture to similar feelings and actions in another: namely, in one's own. Meaning "is like going up to someone." It is more particular because the psychological phenomenon of understanding itself is deeply tied to a person or community and a particular life-view – though this does not mean it becomes purely subjective. Rather, understanding comes back to an aesthetic point of view – to the *place where I am* – and this place is always surrounded by some common ways of acting formed within and by a shared inherited background: my family and community, my language, my culture, my status, my gender, my uniqueness as a human being. It is against this background that our understanding of another culture arises and that the possibility of resonant chords is struck in us.

Finally, recognizing our own capacities, or lack thereof, helps us discover the lacunae in our own self-understanding. We may lack a developed life-view of our own, have few hopes, have suffered little, and our anxieties may be trivial. Not feeling what is sinister in the fire-festivals, or joyful in an installation of a Shilluk or Asante king, or tragic in Rwanda or in *Lear*, or beautiful in a Namibian sunset, may reflect our own bereft lives; it may reflect our own inability to understand something that is fundamental to others' lives and to our humanness. We may not be, or may never have been, hospitable, and thus fail to understand another's simple (or ritualized) gesture of hospitality. Our own horizons may be limited and our capacity to understand therefore impaired. In such cases it is better that we come to see our own limitations, the lacunae in our lives – only then will we be prepared to understand others.[17]

2 The Case of African Philosophy and Religious Practices

"There is greater excitement to be found in philosophical discussion of religion in Africa than in philosophy of religion in the West."[18] Lamentably, a true remark. We have much to learn from examining a culture different from our own, and in coming to realize our common pursuits. Africa is both far and near: far in that it retains an aura of the exotic and the strange; near in that it has been dominated by and has accommodated "Western" culture without having lost its own for nearly four hundred years. Differences between African and Western life are often blurred, but something very "African" stands fast.

Finding resonances with others' beliefs and practices – as strange as their particular way of acting or speaking might strike us – points to the common behavioral and natural reactions that all human beings have toward their life in the world, such as the common human desire for good, not harm, to come to them. Reactions of joy and fear, sorrow and pain, compassion and hope are responses to objects of a similar kind wherever these feelings or emotions find expression.

Character and *spirit* are features of human life that connect men and women everywhere. We might say that it is a feature of human character that stimulates our desire to have something good or just done to us and to avoid harm, or repels us from something "sinister" or unjust. This common moral feature of humankind finds expression in family structures and in communal and individual strivings. Character is a moral concept that runs deep in many philosophical traditions: (for example, in those following Aristotle and Confucius, in ancient biblical wisdom literature, and in those of early Ethiopian philosophers).[19] Spirit is that feature of life, usually understood as a religious concept and used widely and diversely, that stimulates a human "hunger for God" seen in virtually every culture and embedded in their many and varied religious practices.[20]

In Wittgenstein's account we see that religion *is not* grounded in the intellectual act of *belief*: that is, "believing that" God exists, or that the world is uniquely and purposely designed, and so on. Rather, religion and its "spirit" and "spiritual striving" are rooted in an ungrounded way of acting – in our reactions and responses to a world that "impacts us" or "is striking."

In terms of specific "spiritual" reactions to features in our world which are common to African and non-African alike, Wittgenstein writes:

> It goes without saying that a man's shadow, which looks like him, or his mirror-image, the rain, thunderstorms, the phases of the moon, the changing of the seasons, the way in which animals are similar to and different from one another and in relation to man, the phenomena of death, birth, and sexual life, in short, *everything we observe around us year in and year out, interconnected in so many different ways, will play a part in his thinking (his philosophy) and in his practices*, or is precisely what we really know and find interesting.[21]

What is spiritual in all human beings lies in the connectedness of such phenomena as death, birth, and sexual life, and in our way of acting that expresses the depth of joys, sufferings, hopes, and desires associated with these phenomena. These "play a part in" our philosophies and in what we come to know and find interesting. Both character and spirit are interconnected with and shaped by community, by its ceremonies, and in individual moral lives. "Everything we observe around us, year in and year out, interconnected in so many different ways," is the point of departure for all people. This forms the criterion for what is true, whatever the particular cultural point of departure might be. It is also what, as Wittgenstein says, allows us to identify the similarities (and differences) in meaning between one people's conception of God and our own. What are some features of *character* and *spirit* found in contemporary African communities – especially in their religious practices – that draw us closer to understanding them?[22]

First, we should dispense with the "them" and "us" distinction. There is not one "Africa" alien to our understanding – not culturally, or religiously, or politically, or geographically, or linguistically, or ethnically. Its many cultures are as diverse as those of American Indians, Latin Americans, African Americans, Asians, and English-Irish-German-Italian-Polish Americans which make up the United States. Sub-Saharan Africa claims only one thing that dominantly identifies it as "African" – a skin color common to about 85–90 percent of the population. But even if "black skin" is a common feature, it too is extremely diverse, since Bantu-speaking communities appear vastly different from Nama and Setswana-speaking communities in skin color and "racial" features, and much of the sub-Sahara Savannah region and southern Africa has highly "mixed race" people (with Arab, Semitic, Asian, and European integration).

The issue of "race" and "color" as identifying features of a society or continent is a highly divisive and problematic device used in discussing any modern society. Appiah gives an excellent critique of the term "race" and concludes:

> What we in the academy *can* contribute – even if only slowly and marginally – is a disruption of the discourse of "racial" and "tribal" differences. For, in my perfectly unoriginal opinion, the inscription of difference in Africa today plays into the hands of the very exploiters whose shackles we are trying to escape. "Race" in Europe and "tribe" in Africa are central to the way in which the objective interests of the worst-off are distorted.[23]

That African religious practices are homogenous and "animistic" is another myth to be dispelled.[24] Islam and Christianity *are* the dominant religions of Africa (and are so increasingly), in Ethiopia one finds Christianity's and Judaism's oldest continuous communities (Orthodox Christians and a "Jewish" tradition going back to Solomon and the queen of Sheba), and Durban, South Africa, hosts the largest Hindu community in the world outside of India. Furthermore, most larger "indigenous" religious movements are hybrid variations of either Islam or Christianity, or both, adapted to a traditional pattern of life.[25] The actual number of rural African communities that sustain a consistent and reasonably pure "traditional" (non-"world religion"-influenced) religion is relatively small, and they are rapidly dying out.

Moreover, in the practices of the remaining "traditional" religious communities there are as many differences as similarities. Some are more naturalistic and ritualistically oriented with a very minimalist notion of a god (like the Kuria and the Abaluyia in east Africa), some have a clear monotheistic orientation with more individualistic patterns for prayer and worship (e.g., the Dinka, Samburu, Masai, and Nuer – Nilotic peoples), and some have a highly developed cosmological religious system, with creation and the natural order, everyday living and ritual practices very closely and systematically interwoven (the Dogon in Mali and Burkina Faso, and perhaps Yoruba religion). Between these different types there seems, historically, to have been little or no contact. These cultures and their particular life-views arose from their own natural environments and their own way of acting. Yet, despite these differences in *how* they express themselves, *what* is expressed in their life has common features and reflects the connectedness each human community has with important natural, social, and biological features common to their ways of acting.

Although it is true that most Africans are Christian or Muslim, traditional life and indigenous religious movements remain important. There is within the diversity of African states and ethnic groups a considerable amount of commonality in belief and patterns of life. Mutual understanding *between* African people at the level of day-to-day life (whether Christian, Muslim, or neither) is more common and more easily found than between Africans and non-Africans. Akan people can *more easily* "find themselves in" Shilluk people, or Herero people "in" Abaluyia people, than I could find myself in any of these.

There is much to commend focusing on notions of "communalism" – deferring one's personal identity to one's community – as central to "pan-African" self-understanding, rather than on the Western notion of "individualism" with its emphasis on "individual rights." Also the spread of Christianity and Islam (setting aside issues of sheer colonial-religious imperial power, educational opportunities, and conversion for purely pragmatic reasons)[26] depended in part on long precolonial patterns of life that were favorable to monotheism, a spirit-centered cosmos, and a strong sense that God/gods have a direct effect on human life. The ordinary experience of Africans accepts "God being present" among, and sometimes within, the proximate environment of people's day-to-day lives. Divine aid and sanctions are simply understood as part of prayer and ritual actions of all sorts. Individual prayers and petitionary songs to God among Nilotic people (Masai and Samburu, for example) have direct bearing on the particulars of human life and the community – on the well-being of cattle, crops, marriage and fertility, on general health and prosperity.

African concepts of a creator and active "God" or "Divinity" itself, with many names, and manifest through many stories, are recognizable in virtually every culture in the world. Though by no means uniform or universal among traditional Africans, a concept of "God" is neither alien nor marginal to most communities, and human responses to various uses of "God" or "Divinity" are surely part of what enables non-Africans to "find themselves in" any number of African contexts.[27]

There is simply not an Africa that is "Other" than "we are" or the "West is," and the rejoinder of "more of less developed" is beside the point. A distinction grounded in "economic" measures created by Western capitalism in the twentieth century does not mean more or less rational, or more or less religious, or that Africans have a diminished conceptual capacity or a different "emotional" nature. Europe ruled Africa for over one-and-a-half centuries;[28] it bureaucratized and exploited natural and human resources; and even while consciously excluding its partnership in Western economic development, Europe unwittingly forced Africa's growing integration into the global community. There is little justification for identifying Africa as an "Other" to "Us".[29] Through all the trials and struggles that African peoples have had to endure, they have had relatively (or I should say remarkably) accommodative souls, and made numerous transformations in their life.[30]

More and more African intellectuals, however, are urging an understanding of themselves that stresses their plurality as well as of an Africa, as Appiah says, "already contaminated" by European culture with no turning back. Appiah goes on: "'Here I am,' Senghor once wrote, 'trying to forget Europe in the pastoral heart of Sine.' But for us to forget Europe is to suppress the conflicts that have shaped our identities; since it is too late for us to escape each other, we might instead seek to turn to our advantage the mutual interdependencies history has thrust upon us," and he concludes, "there is a clear sense in some postcolonial writing that the postulation of a unitary Africa over against a monolithic West – the binarism of Self and Other – is the last of the shibboleths of the modernizers that we must learn to live without."[31]

With such interdependencies, and the growing pluralism of African cultures, how can we speak of an epistemological relativism *or* the hegemony of a single epistemological narrative? Both alternatives for cross-cultural understanding are hopelessly flawed. The first (relativism) leaves us speechless, unable to talk critically about our differences, while the second (hegemony of a "race") fails to recognize our common humanness and the fact that "contamination" goes both ways. We must recognize what is common in our ways of acting, and awaken to the fact that what we share as human beings demands reciprocity in understanding. Whatever our differences, there are overriding moral and practical reasons why we should seek mutual understanding. On moral grounds Appiah says, "unless all of us understand each other, we shall not treat each other with the proper respect,"[32] and practically, we live in a time when only the invincibly ignorant could suppose that continents and cultures are not politically and economically connected and interdependent.

Finally, against any unitary notion of an Africa that is "Other" to European culture, there are new themes that run through recent African literature. These refocus our attention *away from* unique African "identity" themes of nationalism or negritude and liberation from the "Western Imperium," *toward* the alleviation of suffering that has, in fact, resulted from the poverty and suffering of postcolonial regimes of the last thirty years. Africans have become victims of their own postcolonial states[33] (along with drought, famine and the unprecedented migrations due to armed conflicts sponsored largely by "Western" cold war ideological and economic preoccupations). This terrible suffering brings forward again a common conviction – that something is terribly wrong when harm and not good is done to human beings.[34] Human spiritual striving is thwarted at too many points and harmdoing clouds human hope for some good. This theme cuts across cultures and continents. It resonates within the literature of "liberation theology" in Central and South America; it surfaces like a natural spring wherever evil and suffering are a commonplace experience, wherever oppression and economic injustices prevail.

"Forgiveness," "reconciliation," and "hope" are signs which, in a curious but profound way, grow out of Africans' long centuries of enduring poverty and privation. Africa, says South African-born, Botswanan author Bessie Head, "may be the only place on earth where [poverty] is worn with an unconscious dignity."[35] It is astonishing that the words "forgiveness" and "reconciliation" can even fall from the lips of black African leaders and communities in Namibia and South Africa, where the most vicious form of systematic racial oppression, apartheid, was practiced. Let me illustrate. An African–American college student from the south side of Chicago studying in Namibia and South Africa in 1994, while traveling in South Africa before the April elections, was both surprised and troubled to find these values being expressed. He noted that African–Americans, particularly those raised in urban areas of the United States as he had been, found little cause for hope, and that a deep anger and frustration made forgiveness of and reconciliation with American "whites" virtually unthinkable. He *could not* "find himself in" these black South Africans and had to search hard within himself to find a way to connect with those he otherwise had reason to call his "African" brothers and sisters.[36]

Even Bessie Head was unable to either comprehend or write creatively about the inhumaneness of South African society. She asked: "How do we write about a world long since lost, a world that never seemed meant for humans in the first place, a world that reflected only misery and hate?"[37] "You can't think straight about anything if you're hating all the time. You even get scared to write because everything has turned cockeyed and sour."[38] This fear drove her into exile from South Africa, as it did many others. Bessie Head found her moorings again in a different harshness, the harshness of a dignified poverty that pervaded the simple, village people of Serowe, Botswana – a place where "the shattered bits [of her life] began to grow together."[39]

Of the South Africa she left, and of which she could not write, she said, prophetically, in 1972:

> It is impossible to guess how the revolution will come one day in South Africa
> . . . It is to be hoped that great leaders will arise there who remember the suffering
> of racial hatred and out of it formulate a common language of human love for
> all people.[40]

Her hope was to be realized, but not before her death in 1986. Who could remember "the suffering of racial hatred" better than Nelson Mandela, and who but one who so suffered could "formulate a common language of human love for all people?"

Here, if we as non-Africans are to look for a point in our own understanding that might connect with the South Africans' experience, we might search the New Testament Beatitudes and take the teaching of Jesus at face value, that blessedness comes through love of those who persecute you. Through such a link we might begin "to find ourselves in" the spirit of the new southern Africa. This is, however, no easy matter, because loving those who persecute you is itself an alien idea to most Christians in the United States. White Christians generally have little background in poverty, have usually been on the side of persecutor, and have lost much, if not most, of their dignity to consumer-oriented lifestyles. Working through civil rights struggles or welcoming blacks or minorities or refugees into mainstream white churches or neighborhoods may help give meaning to this Beatitude; it may be a step toward connecting with southern African blacks or minorities. Just to wrestle with such scriptural texts as the Beatitudes is an entry point for understanding the difficulty of such a response and how one's "environment" is crucial to understanding. We confront our own limitations. Nowhere on the continent of Africa is hope among all people, blacks and non-blacks, so high as in South Africa, and one must continually ask: what is the "environment" of their self-understanding that makes such hope possible?

3 Finding Pictures and Narratives "Surprising"

Don't take it as a matter of course, but as a remarkable fact, that pictures and fictitious narratives give us pleasure, occupy our minds.[41]

How do we begin to construct a way of mutual understanding between cultures? How do we, "stepwise," undertake the task of "overcoming skepticism" about so-called different "rationalities" and incommensurable worlds? *First*, by sensitive and detailed observation and description of others' everyday practices, including their religious ceremonies, we can understand how they stand with respect to their life-view, and see what is similar to and different from our own. From such attention we discover our own limitations, the lacunae in our own self-understanding. As striking as the differences, are the resonances in fundamental features of human patterns of life. This is mutual discovery: though there are different points of view and environments, there are not different human "rationalities." *Second*, by examining several kinds of pictures and narratives found in the African context, we can rediscover our mutual innocence as human beings – the childlike "wonder" that enables us to find our varying pictures and narratives of life "surprising." In this discovery philosophy finds its original home, the place where a spiritual quest hopes to arrive. It is in these stepwise movements that skepticism dissolves and all humans meet face to face.

Much of our world strikes us as beautiful or terrifying, delicate or destructive, awesome or ordinary, mysterious or strangely complex. Whether we be a local artist or institutional scientist, sage or shaman, teacher or technician, woman or man, African farmer or restless explorer, the same world strikes us all with similar emotions and feelings. From these varied points of view, *different aspects* of the world are seen, and different ways of acting follow. Each point of view may generate different pictures of the world or construct a different narrative out of its responses. This world of ours, according to Wittgenstein, should be taken as "a remarkable fact": attended to with awe and respect, pictured, written about, dissected in a way that gives us pleasure and retains its surprise. Each day, in every way, we must "awaken to wonder."

What can we discover in the pictures and fictitious narratives from different parts of Africa that will enable us to see its self-image with the same "surprise" with which we might see our own? Those Western technical philosophies that have adapted to restrictive empirical norms have lost the capacity to find the world surprising. In reaction, Wittgenstein insisted we take pictures and fictitious narratives seriously. He believed pictures and narratives important to philosophy; indeed, philosophy should serve the same end as the pictures and narratives. Wittgenstein compares "propositions" (that well-understood term that was paradigmatic to "meaning and truth" among analytic philosophers) and their grammar, and *how* they "picture states of affairs," *with* "what a painting or relief [sculpture] or film does."[42] They are not so different in their application. "So why should not paintings and film be a part of our philosophy?" we might ask. In the two entries preceding our epigraph to this section, Wittgenstein says:

> If we compare a proposition to a picture, we must think whether we are comparing it to a portrait (a historical representation) or to a genre-picture. And both comparisons have point.
>
> When I look at a genre-picture, it "tells" me something, even though I don't believe (imagine) for a moment that the people I see in it really exist, or that there have really been people in that situation. But suppose I ask: "*What* does it tell me, then?" . . .
>
> I should like to say "What the picture tells me is itself." That is, its telling me something consists in its own structure, in *its* own lines and colours. (What would it mean to say "What this musical theme tells me is itself"?)[43]

What a picture tells us "consists in its own structure, in *its* own lines and colours." The same is true with a musical theme, or a ritual drama, or a novel, or a film, or an oral narrative – all tell us something about the world in a manner that attempts to preserve its surprise. And the better the "iconic" form is executed, the greater will be its "surprise" and "pleasure," and the more it will continue to "occupy our minds."[44] This is true of any culture's best iconic forms. Furthermore, I can read the pictures or fictitious narratives from the place where I am and connect them up with their own context as well as my own. There is a far smaller epistemological gap in such iconic representations and ordinary human responses than is often suggested by relativists. The Bushman rock art (thousands of rock engravings dating hundreds, and in some cases thousands, of years ago in north-western Namibia) is neither mysterious nor indecipherable in its own expression ("*its* own lines and colours"); it continues to "surprise" and "occupy our minds" in exciting and natural ways whether observed by me or a local herdsman.

Appiah has a devastating example against relativism and "postmodern" criticism in his account of an African Art exhibition in New York in 1987. Among several co-curators selecting works for the exhibition with Susan Vogel was Lela Kouakou, Baule artist and diviner, from the Ivory Coast. Vogel qualifies the process in the following way: "In the case of the Baule artist [the only native African artist co-curator], a man familiar only with the art of his own people, only Baule objects were placed in the pool of photographs." At this point, notes Appiah, we are directed to a footnote to Vogel's essay, which reads:

> Showing him the same assortment of photos the others saw would have been interesting, but confusing in terms of the reactions we sought here. Field aesthetic studies, my own and others, have shown that African informants will criticize sculptures from other ethnic groups in terms of their own traditional criteria, often assuming that such works are simply inept carvings of their own aesthetic tradition.

Appiah continues:

> Let me pause to quote further, this time from the words of David Rockefeller [another co-curator], who would surely never "criticize sculptures from other ethnic groups in terms of [his] own traditional criteria," discussing what the catalogue calls a "Fante female figure": 'I own somewhat similar things to this and I have always liked them. This is a rather more sophisticated version than the ones that I've seen, and I thought it was quite beautiful . . . the total composition has a very contemporary, very Western look to it. It's the kind of thing that goes very well with contemporary Western things. It would look good in a modern apartment or house."

Later Appiah concludes:

> This Baule diviner, this authentically African villager, the message is, does not know what *we*, authentic postmodernists, now know: that the first and last mistake is to judge the Other on one's own terms. And so, in the name of this, the relativist insight, we impose our judgement that Lela Kouakou may not judge sculpture from beyond the Baule culture zone because he will – like all the African "informants" we have met in the field – read them as if they were meant to meet those Baule standards.[45]

This exclusive Western "rational" point of view of Vogel (not to mention the "ethnic criteria" of Rockefeller) is just the kind of nonsense that passes as "scholarly" or "postmodern" criticism. What makes Rockefeller's "culture zone" – "the kind of thing that goes very well with contemporary Western things" – any more worthy than the Baule's judgment?

Many narrative situations in African fiction mark important moments in the life of its people. Wole Soyinka sees in the contemporary African novel the human struggles that so deeply wound and constrain the current African reality; the novel can be a creative instrument for expressing the anger, the suffering and the hope that is the African experience. Both the liberation struggle and the self-expression of the deepest values of its people are found in what Soyinka calls the culture's "iconic tradition."

An iconic tradition is more than a collection of artifacts, stories, symbols, and formalized ritual; it is a primary and reflective mode of human expression and, as such, is philosophical in nature – "compare a proposition to a picture." Contemporary African fiction, ritual drama, music, and visual arts are not a spontaneous eruption of raw emotion. They express a highly structured and reflective life-view. They are, in Soyinka's words, "material evidence of the integration and cohesiveness of a culture *in situ* ... they are celebrative instruments of an integrative world."[46] Part of the narrative consciousness of a culture is its aesthetic consciousness, and the aesthetic consciousness of a culture is expressed through its iconic traditions.

An aesthetic consciousness is itself a reflective consciousness – one step removed from the immediacy of sensible experience. An aesthetic consciousness orders sensible experience to express human hope and wholeness. When a work of art is produced from the aesthetic consciousness and displays only the fractured and suffering nature of human life, it is making a judgment on the culture which is itself fractured and hurting, pointing to the incompleteness of human life. Such a work of art presupposes a sense of what wholeness is and what the beautiful could be. Soyinka remarks that "the true icons of a people are themselves the repository of a worldly wise human history."[47] They have a sagacity that transcends time and cultures.

What is expressed in the art of a culture, in its iconic tradition, is not accidental; nor is it simply the spontaneous expression of emotions and feelings; it is, rather, the conscious creation of considered and often wise reflections of a people on its age, and as such deserves to be taken seriously as part of the narrative portrait of the people's most important concern. The "picture" and other iconic forms offer critical perspectives on our human nature; they enable us, from an aesthetic point of view, "to get down upon the flat level of experience and interpolate [human experience] piecemeal between distinct portions of [our] nature," as William James once said.[48] James was here commenting on his method of looking at the religious life of people. He called his method "crass" or "piecemeal supernaturalism" as opposed to "refined" supernaturalism. Refined philosophers of religion were *unable* "to get down upon the flat level of experience." Perhaps our approach to understanding the religious life, following Wittgenstein's way of trying to keep surprise alive in philosophy, is also "crass" and "piecemeal." But this approach is as much the stuff of philosophy as are the "critical" or "refined" reflections which are made upon it. Through such icons, the "spirit" of a people's concern is transmitted and the "wonder" and "surprise" of a culture is kept alive.

Soyinka also gives focus to the moral concerns of African people as expressed through their "pictures" and "fictitious narratives." He says that an African philosophy, in its narrative aspect, should "translate the inherent or stated viable values of a social situation into a contemporary or future outlook."[49] The "inherent or stated viable values" are those embedded in one's narrative situation, and the continuous translation of these values is, for Soyinka, a revolutionary activity. This translation is what he calls the "revaluation" of traditional values, and this revaluation requires the selective lifting up of the deeper (viable) traditional values of a community and recasting them to meet today's realities.[50] Let us see how values from one region in Africa are translated and revalued for our understanding today.

Author Bessie Head calls herself a "dreamer and storyteller." She says of those who dream and tell stories that they "have seen life" at eye level and are "drunk with the magical enchantment of human relationships," and she notes that one "always welcome[s] the storyteller." And what do such dreamers and storytellers provide for us? "Each human society," she says, "is a narrow world, trapped to death in paltry evils and jealousies, and for people to know that there are thoughts and generosities wider and freer than their own can only be an enrichment to their lives."[51]

Storytellers, with their pictures and fictitious narratives (both oral and written), enrich our lives beyond our own narrow world. Thus I can see something of southern Africa through the stories of Bessie Head, and she something of my familiar narrow world in the southern United States, with its "paltry evils and jealousies," through stories of Flannery O'Connor or William Faulkner.

Head's stories tell of human innocence and the individual desires of women and men to neutralize evil and to love beyond and grow beyond their traditional village customs of arranged marriages, clan struggles, and communal taboos (see her stories "The lovers," "Village people," and "Property"). She writes of the dignity found in poverty and humility – African virtues born of circumstances, and virtues, as we have noted, that free a human being for forgiveness and hope. "Poverty," she said, "has a home in Africa – like a quiet second skin. It may be the only place on earth where it is worn with an unconscious dignity."[52] The hope that grows out of this poverty may bring about some economic transformation.

This "unconscious dignity" among Africans is linked to their desire to avoid evil, whether by "spells" or "medicines," or by the avoidance of violence, or by accommodation to circumstances. Bessie Head's story "The power struggle," about the avoidance of evil and the maintenance of dignity, begins:

> The universe had a more beautiful dream. It was not the law of the jungle or the survival of the fittest but a dream that had often been the priority of Saints – the power to make evil irrelevant. All the people of Southern Africa had lived out this dream before the dawn of the colonial era. Time and again it sheds its beam of light on their affairs although the same patterns of horror would arise like dark engulfing waves.[53]

The picture/story then painted/told of two brothers, Davhana and Baeli, and their struggle for power is a story of good and evil. The way this story is presented has an interesting parallel to Kierkegaard's account of the parable of Jesus at the house of Simon the Pharisee (Luke 7: 36–50), when an un-named woman bursts in and weeps and anoints Jesus' feet with oil. Kierkegaard notes that the woman says nothing, that "she is what she does not say . . . she *is* a characterisation, like a picture: she has . . . forgotten herself, she, the lost one, who is now lost in her Savior, lost in him as she rests at his feet – like a picture."[54]

Davhana is also "like a picture" lost in life, forced to choose goodness over evil, peace over violence, life over power. It is his silent dignity that helps him avoid intrigue, and his actions to avoid evil are *his* "characterisation." We *see* Davhana, like a picture, and react to what we see. He frees himself from burdens of power, like a child, to maintain a sense of innocence. It is such pictures that give us pleasure and cast a "beam of light" on goodness rather than evil, thus keeping a dream alive.

A pragmatic consequence of the inherited value of "unconsious dignity" carries over from private experience to public life. It was clearly brought out to me while living in newly independent Namibia (which shares a common border and Kalahari culture with Head's Botswana) that the concept of "human dignity" is not just a bit of political or social rhetoric. Human dignity is the highest principle enshrined in the Namibian constitution – *not* "freedom of speech" or "individual rights" as in the United States constitution. Namibians, unlike even eighteenth-century American colonists, do not think in the manner of individual rights. I was told: "Individual rights is not in our way of thinking and our way of life." To have dignity means that each person commands the respect of all human beings – dignity is a sign of moral character achieved by one's particular contribution to the whole community.

This more pragmatic sense of dignity is tied to community, but this is not to say that "Africans" only think communally while "Americans" think individualistically. There are aspects of life among Africans and Americans that may emphasize these respective values more than others. But even as we hear the values of community being stressed within African societies, these communally based societies are usually structured hierarchically with the "Headman," then other *men*, then women, then children in order of rank value. Thus even the notion of "community" as an "African virtue" must be qualified and criticized – seen "*in situ*," as Soyinka says.[55] Like all values, it must be translated and revalued for today's reality.

The temptation to generalize about "world-views" – African or Western or Oriental – recurs and is strong, and must be resisted. Better that we sit and wait for the storytellers to remind us of our "narrow worlds" *and* of "thoughts and generosities wider and freer than our own." Such wider and freer "worlds" we can see only if we are "full of innocence" and are not "trapped to death" by the paltry games of our adult, self-centered lives. Is this not a "universal" idea, born of being human, and not a local or exclusive "rationality?" Are not the notions of love and dignity, poverty and power common to humanity and expressed by "dreamers and storytellers" everywhere? Should we not find our whole world "surprising," even those things we claim to know by reason of "scientific certainty?"

In African "iconic" traditions there are equally telling visual and aural arts where, as Wittgenstein said, "what the picture tells me is itself," and what these pictures tell us are *what that life-view is.* Let us look briefly at two iconic examples that are different in kind: one provided by Appiah from the New York City African Art exhibition, the other from a concert in October of 1994 in Namibia. These further illustrate the accommodative and integrative way in which African culture expresses itself and how it continues to widen its "thoughts and generosities," reflecting the "surprise" and "innocence" that underlie mutual understanding in human life. These two examples also reflect the mutual understanding found in a non-African (myself) observing an African rock concert in Namibia, and an African (Appiah) observing an American-jurored African Art exhibition in the United States.

African-American writer James Baldwin was one of the invited co-curators for a 1987 New York City exhibition entitled "Perspectives: Angles on African Art." He selected a piece that alone was not "in the mold of the Africa of the [earlier] exhibition Primitivism."[56] It was a piece labeled *Yoruba Man with a Bicycle.* Appiah notes what Baldwin said about it:

> This is something. This has got to be contemporary. He's really going to town. It's very jaunty, very authoritative. His errand might prove to be impossible. He is challenging something – or something has challenged him. He's grounded in immediate reality by the bicycle . . . He's apparently a very proud and silent man. He's dressed sort of polyglot. Nothing looks like it fits him too well.[57]

I have commented above on the attitudes toward this exhibition by co-curator David Rockefeller and also about the director, Susan Vogel's comments barring another co-curator, an African artist, Lela Kouakou, from selecting entries from outside of his own traditional area in Ivory Coast. What I want to lift up here is the liberating effect that this one piece, which seemed to break the mold, had on Appiah (an African) – as it did on Baldwin, an African-American – and the surprising effect it would probably have on most viewers, African or non-African, who were attentive to it. Appiah's comments speak for themselves:

> I am grateful to James Baldwin for his introduction to the *Yoruba Man with a Bicycle* – a figure who is, as Baldwin so rightly saw, polyglot, speaking Yoruba and English, probably some Hausa and a little French for his trips to Cotonou or Cameroon; someone whose "clothes do not fit him too well." He and the other men and women among whom he mostly lives suggest to me that the place to

look for hope is not just to the postcolonial novel – which has struggled to achieve the insights of a Ouologuem or Mudimbe – but to the all-consuming vision of this less-anxious creativity. It matters little who it was made *for*; what we should learn from it is the imagination that produced it. The *Man with a Bicycle* is produced by someone who does not care that the bicycle is the white man's invention – it is not there to be Other to the Yoruba Self; it is there because someone cared for its solidity; it is there because it will take us further than our feet will take us; it is there because machines are now as African as novelists – and as fabricated as the kingdom of Nakem.[58]

Baldwin's remark on this "picture" and Appiah's comment show something profoundly true about the contemporary African self-image; they capture the "surprise" in the not-so-surprising fact of how much alike all human beings are and how our mutual understanding is never far away.

Our *second*, and last, example is from the African musical world. In a recent live concert in the Katatura district of Windhoek, Namibia (a former "black" township while Namibia was under South African rule), the Malian singer, Salif Keita, and his band gave a remarkable performance full of paradoxes. Mali, in the north-west sub-Saharan region, is largely a Muslim nation, while Namibia, in the subcontinent's far south-west, is overwhelmingly Christian; Keita, himself an albino, born into an aristocratic, though poor, rural family, was outcast by his community; his band had musicians from Mali, Cameroon, Brazil, France, Guinea, Morocco, and Guadeloupe ("white" and "black"); the audience of some two to three thousand were nearly equally mixed "white" and "black" – all equally and enthusiastically "surprised" by this music.

This was an African "iconic" event of the first order; it was an example of the best of African contemporary music/art. Salif Keita is an idol in his own country, where his community once rejected him because of his skin color. His music is his own blend of African, Islamic, Carribean, jazz, and Western influences. It was described by the African press as "young and modern – a brilliant example of the cultural richness of the African Continent."[59] Salif Keita also reflects Africa's new pragmatism. To criticism of Peter Gabriel and Paul Simon for appropriating African music, he replies, "If you make a collaboration with a musician it is because you want something different from him. If you do it for the record company only to make money, then I don't like that. But you see, white people who collaborate with African musicians want the inspiration. It is not bad. They get inspiration and we get popularity."[60] Salif Keita's inspiration, he says, comes from God. "When I first come out and put my hands together in the prayer position, I do this because I want to go to God before the concert and I want the people to go with me . . . I come to sing to help them spiritually and magically."[61]

Salif Keita's art, like *Yoruba Man with a Bicycle*, is "polyglot." But this is not to say it was contrived, or artificial, or some ungainly patchwork. Both icons reflect a self-image of Africa *that is itself*; they reflect a self-image that is "surprising," "spiritual," and "magical," and that evokes a sense of "innocence" in all viewers and hearers.

The philosophical issues in cross-cultural understanding are complex and require attention to detail. In our "stepwise" approach we first established a philosophical procedure that would carefully help us overcome our natural skepticism and question the epistemological paradigms embedded in Western academic thinking. This enabled us, from a non-African point of view and from our aesthetic point of departure, to engage African points of view. We then focused on common features of our humanity as found in reactions to those things "we observe around us year in and year out" and "interconnected in so many different ways" that are found in contemporary African life and that resonate with our own life. This allowed us to see the basis for mutual understanding, and to show that, with all our pluralism and differences in points of view, there is more in common that unites human beings than divides them. With these discoveries made, and with examples from the everyday life of Africans, from their ritual and religious practices, their oral and iconic traditions, and from their literature and art, we can see what ties us to one another and what gives rise to mutual surprise and wonder in life.

Notes

1   Ludwig Wittgenstein, "Remarks on Frazer's *Golden Bough*," *The Human World*, no. 3, May 1971, trans. A.C. Miles and Rush Rhees, p. 36. Hereafter *RF*.
2   Stanley Cavell refers to "the stepwise overcoming of skepticism," in *This New Yet Unapproachable America* (Living Batch Press, Albuquerque, NM, 1989), pp. 116–17.
3   Clifford Geertz, "Found in translation: on the social history of the moral imagination," *The Georgia Review*, vol. 31, Winter 1977, p. 799.
4   Ludwig Wittgenstein, *Philosophical Investigations*, ed. G.E.M. Anscombe and R. Rhees, trans. G.E.M. Anscombe (Blackwell, Oxford, 1953), p. 457. Hereafter *PI*.
5   I started this process in my "Narrative in African philosophy," *Philosophy*, vol. 64, 1989, pp. 363–79, where I reviewed the current debate among African philosophers over whether philosophy must begin only with written, "scientific" texts of a culture, as Paulin Hountondji argues, or whether philosophy may also arise from within oral, literary, and iconic forms, as H. Odera Oruka and Wole Soyinka would claim. In this chapter, I extend the latter claim.
6   For a full discussion of the nature of Frazer's explanations and their difficulties, see my "Understanding the fire-festivals: Wittgenstein and theories in religion," *Religious Studies*, vol. 14, 1978, pp. 113–24; and Jonathan Z. Smith, "When the bough breaks," *History of Religions*, vol. XII, May 1973, pp. 342–71.
7   Wittgenstein, *PI*, part II, 223e. The German of this last sentence is: "Wir können uns nicht in sie finden." Although Ms Anscombe's phrase "find our feet" is a good one here, more literally the German means "We cannot find ourselves in them,"

which has a closer resonance with the point we are making. Fergus Kerr drew my attention to this point.

8   Wittgenstein, *RF*, p. 38.
9   Ibid., p. 40.
10 Ibid., pp. 34, 35, 38; Wittgenstein, *PI*, 90, 122.
11 See Malcolm Ruel, "Icons, indexical symbols and metaphorical action: an analysis of two East African rites," *Journal of Religion in Africa*, June, 1987, pp. 98–112.
12 Cf. Wittgenstein, *RF*, p. 34.
13 Ibid., pp. 30ff.
14 Ruel, "Icons, indexical symbols and metaphorical action," p. 107.
15 Wittgenstein, *RF*, p. 40.
16 Søren Kierkegaard, *On Authority and Revelation*, trans. Walter Lowrie (Harper and Row, New York, 1966), p. 8. See also pp. 163–5 and 171–3.
17 The argument in these last few paragraphs is developed more fully in my essay: "Wittgenstein's anthropology: self-understanding and understanding other cultures," *Philosophical Investigations*, vol. 7, no. 4 (October 1984), pp. 295–312.
18 Kwame Anthony Appiah, *In My Father's House: Africa in the Philosophy of Culture* (Oxford University Press, Oxford 1992), p. 108. For fifty years the philosophy of religion "in the West" was largely cast in the mold of positivism and responses to it. The full range of issues raised in the Wittgenstein–Frazer remarks can be found in the British and American philosophy of religion literature only if you go back to the Clifford–James exchanges at the turn of the century which are richly aired in William James', *Varieties of Religious Experience: A Study in Human Nature* (Longmans, Green, New York, 1902). Although most of the manuscript of Wittgenstein's remarks dates from 1931, it was not published until 1967 and appeared in English translation in 1971. The popular one-volume edition of Frazer's *Golden Bough* appeared in 1922. It was an essay by Peter Winch, however, in 1964 (with his awareness of Wittgenstein's kind of concerns in his remarks on Frazer) that newly engaged both social anthropologists and philosophers in the question of "cross-cultural understanding" – or "comparative rationality" – and renewed a long overdue discussion buried by the dominance of logical empiricism.

    Winch caught the philosophical significance of this cross-cultural debate as no other philosopher had done in his "Understanding a primitive society," *American Philosophical Quarterly*, vol. I, 1964, pp. 307–24. The larger debate among Western philosophers and social anthropologists was taken up by thinkers like Geertz, Gellner, Tambiah, Horton and MacIntyre. See collections: B. Wilson (ed.), *Rationality* (Harper Torchbook, New York, 1971); R. Finnegan and R. Horton (eds), *Modes of Thought: Essays on Thinking in Western and Non-Western Societies* (Faber, London, 1973); and S. Lukes and M. Hollis (eds), *Rationality and Relativism* (Blackwell, Oxford, 1982).

    Some of these issues have been taken up by African writers and philosophers in reflecting on the particularities of an African philosophy tied to its plurality of cultures, its traditional past, its colonial inheritance, and its postcolonial realities. See particularly the works by Robin Horton, in Wilson (ed.), *Rationality*, and Lukes and Hollis (eds), *Rationality and Relativism*; Wole Soyinka, *Myth Literature and the African World* (1976); Kwasi Wiredu, *Philosophy and an African Culture: The Case of the Akan* (Cambridge University Press, Cambridge, 1980); Paulin

Hountondji, *African Philosophy: Myth and Reality* (Indian University Press, Bloomington, IN, 1983); V.Y. Mudimbe, *The Invention of Africa* (Indian University Press, Bloomington, IN, 1988); and Appiah, *In My Father's House*.

19 Character and the moral life have been important in African life and are found in centuries-old written texts. They are central to the maxims found in *The Book of the Philosophers* from the early sixteenth century, and in *The Treatise of Walda Heywat* from the late seventeenth century in Ethiopia. These texts are found in Claude Sumner (ed.), *Classical Ethiopian Philosophy* (Adey, Los Angeles, CA, 1994).

20 The lineage of both "character" (the moral life) and "spirit" (the centrality of God in the world) is traced from African traditional thought to its effect on the African Diaspora, especially the African–American experience, by Peter J. Paris in *The Spirituality of African Peoples: The Search for a Common Moral Discourse* (Fortress Press, Minneapolis, MN, 1995).

21 Wittgenstein, *Philosophical Occasions* (1912–1951), ed. James Klagge and Alfred Nordmann (Hackett, Indianapolis, IN), pp. 127–8; my italics. Hereafter *PO*.

22 As a non-African trying to understand aspects of African cultures, in addition to attending closely to recent philosophical literature from Africa, especially those I have noted, I draw upon African fiction, poetry, and other "iconic" forms, fifteen years of teaching African philosophy and religions, as well as three extended research periods in eastern Africa (Kenya and Tanzania) and Southern Africa (Namibia, South Africa, Botswana, and Zimbabwe) which have contributed some first-hand observations.

23 *In My Father's House*, p. 179. See his chapter 2 for larger discussion.

24 This term "animistic" or "animism" is a catch-all euphemism for religious practices other than those found in "world religions" like Christianity, Islam, Buddhism, and Judaism, and is embedded in the vocabularies of such globally pervasive institutions as the Vatican and the US State Department.

25 Consider the following examples. In Namibia, 95 percent of the people claim to be Christian and well over 60 percent of those Christians are Lutherans! Several nations in the north of sub-Saharan Africa (excluding the Arab states of the Mediterranian) would boast being 95 percent Muslim, and many coastal nations, east and west, divide religious loyalties between Islam and Christianity.

26 See the excellent article by J.D.Y. Peel, "Conversion and tradition in two African societies: Liebu and Buganda," *Past and Present*, vol. 77, 1977, pp. 108–41.

27 See John Mbiti, *Concepts of God in Africa*, (Praeger, New York, 1970). This is a strong thesis in Paris, *Spirituality of African Peoples*, as well, using Mbiti and others' research. A significant number of contemporary African intellectuals – Hountondji and Appiah, for example – are very skeptical about how uniform this concept can be made.

28 It was four European states – Britain, France, Portugal and Belgium – which constructed the national geography of contemporary Africa.

29 The whole notion of a single African identity is a new thing – a construct of the colonial experience. Appiah writes:

> if we could have traveled through Africa's many cultures in [precolonial times] – from the small groups of Bushman hunter-gatherers, with their

stone-age materials, to the Hausa kingdoms, rich in worked metal – we should have felt in every place profoundly different impulses, ideas, and forms of life. To speak of an African identity in the nineteenth century – if an identity is a coalescence of mutually responsive (if sometimes conflicting) modes of conduct, habits of thought, and patterns of evaluation; in short, a coherent kind of human social psychology – would have been "to give to aery nothing a local habitation and a name" (*In My Father's House*, p. 174).

30 A similar point to this is made as part of a critique of Robin Horton's contribution to African philosophy by Mudimbe and Appiah in "The impact of African studies on philosophy," H. Bates, V.Y. Mudimbe and Jean O'Barr (eds), *Africa and the Disciplines: The Contribution of Research in Africa to the Social Sciences and the Humanities* (University of Chicago Press, Chicago, IL 1993), p. 129.

31 *In My Father's House*, pp. 72 and 155. Twenty-five years earlier, referring to "black" and "white" in South Africa, Ezekiel Mphahlele wrote: "The blacks have reconciled the Western and the African in them, while the whites refuse to surrender to their influence. This is symbolic of the South African situation. The only cultural vitality there is, is to be seen among the Africans; they have not been uplifted by a Western culture but rather they have reconciled the two in themselves." From "Remarks on negritude," in *African Writing Today* (Penguin, Harmondsworth, 1967), p. 248.

32 *In My Father's House*, p. 134.

33 This is a subject worthy of a whole book: first, to analyze the effects of "coldwar politics" on turning Africans against themselves, and creating "killing fields" with the importation of weapons for masses of people; second, to understand the roots in both colonialism and in traditional societies' hierarchical structures for how and why leaders exploit one another for their "individual" personal gain, and further impoverish their own people. Appiah and others have called attention to the fact that many postcolonial African states have become "kleptocracies" (ibid., p. 150).

34 For a further discussion of the point of this paragraph, see Appiah's discussion on pp. 150–5 of *In My Father's House* of the novels of Yambo Ouologuem, especially his *Le Devoir de Violence*. Appiah says that Ouologuem is appealing to an ethical universal . . . an appeal to a certain simple respect for human suffering, a fundamental revolt against the endless misery of the last thirty years." (p. 152). At the end of the novel, Ouologuem writes: "Often, it is true, the soul desires to dream the echo of happiness, an echo that has no past. But projected into the world, one cannot help recalling that Saif, mourned three million times, is forever reborn to history beneath the hot ashes of more than thirty African republics" (ibid.).

35 Bessie Head, *Tales of Tenderness and Power* (A.D. Donker, Johannesburg, 1989), p. 41.

36 This account was conveyed to me by my daughter, Rebecca Bell, who was on the same college study program in southern Africa, and who was a good friend of the African–American student. Even my daughter found this spirit of forgiveness and reconciliation surprising, but not as alien due to her experience.

37 Bessie Head, *A Woman Alone: Autobiographical Writings* (Heinemann, London, 1990), p. 66.

38 Ibid., p. 14.
39 Bessie Head, *Serowe: Village of the Rain Wind* (Heinemann, London, 1981), p. x.
40 Head, *A Woman Alone*, p. 103.
41 Wittgenstein, *PI*, 524.
42 Wittgenstein, *PI*, 520.
43 Ibid., 522, 523.
44 Ibid., 524.
45 *In My Father's House*. Appiah's point is here compressed from pp. 137–9.
46 The idea of an "iconic tradition" within African culture was developed by Soyinka in a lecture "Icons for self retrieval: the African experience," given at Oberlin College, Oberlin, Ohio, 14 November 1985.
47 Ibid.
48 James, *Varieties*, p. 409.
49 Soyinka, *Myth, Literature and the African World*, p. 98.
50 There is more than a hint here of Nietzsche's notion of the "transvaluation of values" central to his *The Genealogy of Morals* and *Beyond Good and Evil*. In my essay "Narrative in African philosophy," *Philosophy*, vol. 64, 1989, pp. 363–79, I discuss examples given by Soyinka from African literature on this point as well as other values which surface from African oral traditions like village palavers. See especially pp. 372–8.
51 Head, *Tales of Tenderness and Power*, p. 141.
52 Ibid., p. 41.
53 Ibid., p. 72.
54 As found in George Pattison, *Kierkegaard: The Aesthetic and the Religious* (Macmillan, London 1992), p. 167.
55 I heard this cautionary tale many times, especially among younger African intellectuals.
56 Appiah, *In My Father's House*, p. 139.
57 Ibid.
58 Ibid., p. 157.
59 From the Windhoek *Namibian*, October 15, 1994.
60 From an article by Quincy Troupe, "Beat King: Salif Keita," *New York Times Magazine*, January 29, 1995, p. 27
61 Ibid.

9

*Alterity, Dialogue, and African Philosophy**

Bruce Janz

Put on the string skirt
And some beads on your loin!

Okot p'Bitek, Song of Lawino[1]

African philosophy has been consumed with the question about its own identity. Is African philosophy nothing more than *mitumba*, used ideas imported or borrowed from the West? Is it exotic local fashion? Is it creative hybridity, or perhaps utilitarian appropriation? Is there another way to characterize it? What is the relationship of African philosophy to Western philosophy, to other versions of philosophy, to its own diverse strands and fractious history, to the life-world from which it springs, to those it claims to represent, to those it fails to represent? Is there a way of conceptualizing a philosophy that is rooted in the particular, the concrete experience of social and individual life?

Philosophy based on concrete experience has, of course, been a goal of theory as long as Africa has thought of itself as having a philosophy. Some attempts at Africanizing philosophy by rooting theory in a concrete life-world have been in one way or another derived from Western fashion. For a time existentialism had its appeal to negritude because it rooted philosophy in

* A number of people offered helpful comments on earlier drafts. These include Kieran Bonner, Idske Janz, John Johanson, and Paul Harland. I am grateful for their input, and want to assure them that they bear no responsibility for oversights or outright mistakes that may appear here.

a particular kind of subject. (Ironically, this ultimately turns into a kind of essentialism dictated by Western categories.) Marxism (at least in its African manifestations) had its appeal because it rooted thought in a struggle that has particular social, economic, and historical features. Freudian styles of analysis (e.g., Frantz Fanon) eschew universalizing rationalizations in favor of a particularized unmasking of power and desire. Deconstructive strains of postcolonialism (e.g., Gayatri Spivak) assert the radical diversity of perspectives, and in uncovering the metaphysics of presence and the coercive violence of its organizational strategies attempt to clear a field for the expression of the disenfranchised and the subaltern.

The problem for less subtle versions of these is that they can become nothing more than an African version of Western tools of thought. Merely Africanizing philosophy seems little better than importing *mitumba*. The problem arises because it is difficult to know what the particular or the concrete might be. Most attempts work not from individual experience, but from shared experience. And yet, that experience cannot simply be generalized from simpler units, because that does little more than establish a reductionist method which philosophizing from particulars is meant to overcome. The result is that particularized or concrete philosophy can look very much like universalist philosophy, only beginning from a non-European base.

The usual alternative to particularized philosophy, universalist philosophy, is also problematic. Philosophizing from particulars is spurred by deep concerns about universalism: that universalist philosophies (i.e., ones that emphasize universal metaphysics, epistemology, axiology, logic, and method – mainly those derived from the European Enlightenment, right-wing Hegelianism, or theology) ironically fail to represent all human experience, but rather generalize from one point. If the universalist philosophy does claim to represent all human experience, it is because that experience has been coerced or forced into the point from which generalization has occurred. Universalist philosophies are unable to radically critique their own presuppositions and grounding, much less recognize their own partiality; and the emancipation that universalist philosophies offer is no more than individual conformity to some ideal.

The concerns about the ability to represent and critique advocated by the universalists are legitimate. However, one might also argue that these concerns can only find articulation given the freedom and ability of the marginalized subject to understand his or her own situation. Of course, theorists may recognize that the violence of marginalization may have weakened both freedom and opportunity for the person or society that has been marginalized. In the most radical cases, the subaltern cannot speak, or at least cannot be heard.

One unintended effect of this may be that professional postcolonial voices emerge, who may have a vested interest in solidifying their own authority by removing their discourse from the possibility of access by the very marginalized for whom they are clearing a space. If the discourse is not translatable back to the lived situation and cognizance of those most directly affected, one wonders who the critic is really speaking for. More important, though, is the fact that the critique of universalism must have some basis or *telos* beyond the coherence imposed by strategies of domination. While this *telos* of coherence could look suspiciously like that of colonialist power/knowledge, the complexity of critique can also turn into a spiral of self-indulgence if not directed by the coherence implicit in the goal of emancipation. No theorist ever simply critiques for the sake of critiquing – the purpose is always greater freedom, self-representation, and equality. Even if these concepts are not taken in an essentialist or universalist manner, they represent an implicit and inevitable direction of thought. It is this tension between the coherence and the complexity of the concrete that must be investigated.

While the charge against universalist philosophizing is that it does not represent lived experience, or when it does, that it does so coercively, the charge by universalism to philosophies rooted in the particular must also be considered. In what way is the philosophy of a particular lived situation a philosophy at all, and not simply special pleading or glorified relativism? How does one know when the lived situation has been reached by the theory (and not some theoretical displacement of lived experience), and the critique has yielded a reliable sense of the situation itself? Is it not possible, so the critique goes, that there is still some moral bedrock that has not been and perhaps cannot be questioned – a commitment to freedom or equality, for example? One might argue that these must be defined in concrete terms, and that they have no meaning outside of that definition.

The problem is given form in the tension between the hermeneutic of trust and the hermeneutic of suspicion. A simple attempt to explicate a tradition or any culture does not come to terms with the subliminal aspects of power; on the other hand, a simple critique of power in Western categories does not come to terms with the specific local heritage of the African contexts, not to mention its inability to articulate a viable historical destiny. In fact, a truly African critical theory must also be self-critical at a deep level, or it becomes no better than the universalism that it attempts to overcome. That self-critique, I will argue, will not result in nihilism, but it will also not take refuge in foundationalism or essentialism.

This tension is one which some thinkers have tried to address by using another philosophical perspective, that of hermeneutics. The earliest investigation of hermeneutics in African philosophy was Theophilus Okere's *African Philosophy: A Historico-hermeneutical Investigation of the Conditions of its Possibility*,[2] and has its most recent expression in Tsenay Serequeberhan's *The Hermeneutics of African Philosophy: Horizon and Discourse*.[3] I wish to critically analyze the use that Okere and Serequeberhan make of hermeneutics, and suggest further possibilities for its use, both in conceptualizing African philosophy itself, and also in working through particular issues within African philosophy. Both Okere and Serequeberhan have identified important features of African philosophy, but also overlook certain aspects of hermeneutics that would be useful in theorizing African philosophy (in particular, the details of the tension between coherence and complexity). This oversight is part of the development of African philosophy itself, and needs to be accounted for. Dealing with both the continuities and the cracks in their accounts of coherence and complexity opens up a more nuanced explication of the traditions and peoples that African philosophy represents (and, perhaps, fails to represent), and the (self-)critical capacity of this philosophy.

1 Theophilus Okere and the Ontology of Non-philosophy

In *African Philosophy*, Okere appropriates hermeneutics by arguing that all philosophies must spring from and deal with non-philosophy. Hermeneutic philosophy is both the interpretive tool and the result of mediating and rationalizing lived experience. Most of Okere's work is an overview of the Western tradition of hermeneutics; it is only in the final chapter and conclusion that Okere explicates what he thinks is the hermeneutic nature of philosophy in general, and African philosophy in particular. It is this: philosophy must always deal with the non-philosophical features of lived experience and its expression, whether that be religion, culture, or even the irrationality of certain presuppositions.[4]

Okere is somewhat unclear about the nature of non-philosophy; sometimes, it is the irrational, sometimes the prerational, sometimes the transcendent. His definition is his interpretation of Gadamer's *Vorurteile*, or prejudgments: "non-philosophy must stand for the non-reflected, that unreflected baggage of cultural background . . ."[5] This definition, however, leaves open the question of the status of non-philosophy. Is it a necessary evil (he calls it "baggage," after all)? Is it the ur-thought, the inchoate beginning of Hegel's dialectic? Is he suggesting that ethnophilosophy simply requires another step, that of reflection and rationalization? Or, is it simply the Enlightenment hope made African, that the irrationality of religion or culture will finally be overcome by the rationality of philosophy?

For Okere, at any rate, the philosophical and hermeneutic moment is the appropriation or repetition of these non-philosophical roots without negating them. But why should Okere appeal to hermeneutics at all? The most likely explanation is that he wants to ensure that African philosophy has a unique starting point, since it is rooted in a particular tradition of non-philosophy. This means that African philosophy can be unique, not reducible to other philosophical systems, and at the same time can make use of all the rational tools that any other philosophical tradition assumes as essential. In other words, hermeneutics allows the ontological moment of self-understanding to emerge through repetition for African philosophy.

But the essential problem that Okere does not come to terms with is that he assumes that hermeneutics is nothing more than a method for uncovering meanings that are latent within the patterns of objectification that a culture employs. As such, two questions are not answered: (1) How does one find a method that can reflect on itself, so as to foreground its own prejudices? (2) How does one deal with meanings that are not simply there to be uncovered, but are the result of some violence that does not want itself to be named?

Of course, hermeneutic theory is well aware of the necessity of foregrounding its own prejudices, but in fact in Okere's case that theory has been worked out in a relatively limited context. The bulk of his work is taken up giving an account of the history of hermeneutics, with the barest of allusions to its applicability to the African situation.[6] As mentioned, the applicability only becomes evident in the argument that hermeneutics is the bridge between culture (non-philosophy) and philosophy. But what culture? Does he suggest that we can intuit this pure culture (and it must be pure, or it would not be an African philosophy that emerged), and that it can somehow provide the basis of a truly African philosophy? Or is the philosophy nothing more than the covert articulation of (neo)colonialism? Okere's problematic category of non-philosophy renders the possibility of philosophy into little more than the sketch of existing conditions, with no theoretical apparatus for their critique, for the conceptualization of the possibility of alternate conditions, or for proposing a philosophy of action that affirms what is important in the life-world while also working for change.

And yet, Okere recognizes that, for philosophy to be African, it must have some expression of the African life-world. His attempt to characterize African philosophy as hermeneutic comes shortly after Hountondji's seminal essay critiquing ethnophilosophy,[7] and he works toward a similar conclusion: that African philosophy will not be constructed out of nothing more than customs – it requires some apparatus for reflection. In fact, Okere takes a step beyond Hountondji, in that he also recognizes that universal method is as problematic a starting point as particular experience. One wishes that he had followed that insight further, and actually questioned hermeneutics itself, instead of just imposing it on an African life-world, as well as providing the possibility for critical reflection, rather than just explication.

2 Tsenay Serequeberhan and the Hermeneutics of Resistance

Tsenay Serequeberhan is clearly familiar with the implications of the argument to this point. In *The Hermeneutics of African Philosophy*, he argues that the

ethnophilosophers and the professional philosophers have both succumbed to
a universalism which would simply reinforce Africa's position as Europe's
Other. In ignoring the particular African historical life-world, those attempting
to appropriate Marxism as well as those attempting to argue for an African
essentialism end up philosophizing on non-African terms. He maintains that
this debate has been stultifying, and has not come to terms with the "failed
actuality of the promise of African independence."[8]

The answer to these latent and insidious universalisms is to "make one's
philosophic reflections sensitive to the historicity out of which they originate
– that is, to resuscitate and explore the concerns grounded in our own lived
historical existence."[9] Specifically, this means coming to terms with the
violence inherent in imperialist and colonialist projects of the past, in terms of
both description and emancipatory possibilities. If this is done, Serequeberhan
thinks, it should be possible to finally extricate Africa from the status of
Europe's "there, but for the grace of God, go I."

Serequeberhan's work implicitly attempts to come to terms with the
deficiencies in Okere's version of hermeneutics (although, interestingly, he has
nothing but good to say about Okere's work). Okere employed what Paul
Ricoeur called the hermeneutics of trust – the belief that there is something
present in the African experience that must be explicated, and it is our job to
uncover it. Serequeberhan is not so optimistic. Hermeneutics misses something
if it simply assumes that there is a coherent tradition that can be accessed. False
consciousness has its roots in the experiences of marginalization, slavery,
colonial oppression, the exploitation of resources, and the division of Africans
against Africans to serve the desires of the oppressor. This is not to suggest some
utopian existence before the encroachment of "civilization," of course; it is
simply to say that it is quite possible that the glowing face which appears in
the hermeneutics of trust is nothing other than the mask of the torturer.

Serequeberhan addresses this by proposing a horizon of discourse which
radically questions the construction of the self and society in African
philosophy. Taking his cue from Marxian theory (while at the same time being
deeply critical of its universalist espousers in Africa), and also from Mudimbe's
The Invention of Africa,[10] Serequeberhan tries to mitigate the possibly
conservative aspects of hermeneutic philosophy by giving the grounds for a
philosophy of action. This philosophy of action has its roots in, but is different
from, Fanon's psychoanalytic Marxism, in that it continues the dialectic
between theory and practice rather than supposing that right theory can give
rise to right practice in any linear manner.

Unlike Okere, Serequeberhan does not feel the need to give an outline of
Western hermeneutic theory. This is more than a difference of style. Okere
wants a hermeneutic method (he says as much in taking Ricoeur's path) which
will *apply to* the African situation. Serequeberhan wants a hermeneutic that
grows from lived African experience. It is not simply that hermeneutic theory

exists as a universal, and the variables simply need to be filled in (the way a doctrinaire Marxist might simply look for the means of production, labor market, level of technology, and so forth). Hermeneutic theory itself must be shaped by lived conditions.

While the project is by far the best attempt to theorize African experience through hermeneutics, it has its limits. These can best be summed up in an examination of Serequeberhan's use of two fundamental hermeneutical concepts: the concreteness of historicity and the fusion of horizons.

The limitation on the description of violence becomes evident in chapter 3, when Serequeberhan proposes to describe the neocolonial situation in its specific historicity. Fanon's work forms the basis of this, but Serequeberhan attempts to avoid the force of Hannah Arendt's criticisms of Fanon (that he advocated violence for violence's sake) by claiming that Fanon was merely describing an existing historical situation. Serequeberhan's appropriation of this description becomes one which has a Hegelian/Marxian ring to it, as it shows the necessary outcome of the history of violence implicit in the original colonial enterprises. Since that violence is necessarily present, and since the oppressor only understands the language of violence, the conclusion is that counter-violence is necessary, and anyone who denies this is in complicity with the original violence.[11]

The problem with this line of argument is that Serequeberhan takes seriously the need for the historical specificity of an account (although this is still generalized), but ignores the partiality of that account. All interpretation is closed down, as one description of the nature of history becomes the correct one, and the dissenter is implicated with an *ad hominem* argument. Violence is not *a* choice, but *the* choice, forced on the colonized by the colonizer, and therefore the only legitimate response.[12] It is the only route to existential release, and the only emancipation.

This seems to me to be a hermeneutics of convenience, which takes what is useful and ignores what is not. Historicity must come to terms with the concrete (and the meaning of "concrete" is very difficult to pin down in Serequeberhan's work, even though the word is ubiquitous), and that means not only avoiding universalist rationalization, but also highlighting the discontinuities in experience. None of this suggests that the history of violence should be downplayed; it simply means that the disease cannot be so easily scripted, or the cure so easily prescribed.

One might reply by saying that hermeneutic philosophy (the uncovering of the possible) must be preceded by hermeneutic method (the clearing-away of misunderstanding), and the critique of violence simply clears the space for true hermeneutic philosophy to happen. The problem is that the two moments cannot be separated so easily. Space is not cleared by simply maintaining that an unequal power relationship be rectified before dialogue and discovery can happen. That unequal power relationship must be addressed within the hermeneutic philosophy itself, or there really is no hermeneutics at all, but simply a modernist project of revolution founded on the uninterpretable given.

The closure that Serequeberhan invokes does not stop here. The fusion of horizons, the place where interpretation happens in all its complexity and coherence, is closely defined as the horizon between two and only two specific groups: the Westernized African, who has access to the education provided by the colonizer (the "urban"), and the non–Westernized African, who has access to tradition (the "rural").[13] These categories are created by the colonizer, and must be bridged if true liberation is to occur. The entirety of chapter 4, "The liberation struggle: existence and historicity," is meant to show forth some of the possibilities of the practice of freedom.

Again, Serequeberhan has used particular hermeneutic concepts to his own ends, without being very clear on them. The fusion of horizons is not just a mixing of the strengths of two groups. The fusion is a complex one in which each finds its own identity in finding the points of dialogue with the other. If hermeneutics is the process of finding out what is compelling in the claim of the Other in order to come to better Self- and Other-understanding, it is unclear how this goal can be achieved here. Fragmentation is overcome, which is a positive aspect of this process, but the possibilities of dialogue have been narrowly constrained to identify the only two legitimate groups, and their only legitimate topic of conversation. The rural must discover its African roots, or it is not authentic; the urban must philosophize about violence, or it is not authentic. Despite his comments to the contrary, it seems that this conversation does not open up as many possibilities of self-understanding as it could or should.

Now, it may be objected that an African hermeneutic can adjust traditional Western hermeneutic concepts to fit its own needs. Indeed, if it does not, it is not yet African, but still European, and still bears the marks of its own history. While I have been arguing all along that theory bears the marks of its own history, the answer is not to adjust the parts of the theory that are inconvenient. This is to regard hermeneutics as a method, with a particular set of assumptions and outcome. But if Gadamer is right, hermeneutic philosophy begins exactly where method ends. Serequeberhan's hermeneutics seems to be an attempt at description, explanation, and correction of a situation, but this attempt does not allow the complexity of the situation to show itself (because closure has been invoked), and does not allow the creative dialogue with the Other (because the Other has been defined, and the terms of the conversation have been laid down).

3 Mitumba, Again

Woman,
Shut up!
Pack your things
Go!

Take all the clothes
I bought you
The beads, necklaces
And the remains
Of the utensils,
I need no second-hand things.

Okot p'Bitek, *Song of Ocol*[14]

The problem for Ocol is that he is caught between worlds. He wants to reject *mitumba*, and yet his wife Lawino is deft at pointing out the incongruity of his position – while he vocally rejects "second-hand things" from his own culture, he has raised the collection of *mitumba* ways from Europe almost to an art form. The result has been that he has marginalized himself not only from his traditional ways, but also from his family and friends.

It would be nice if *Song of Lawino* and *Song of Ocol* could be read straightforwardly, the first as a robust defense of tradition, the second as a somewhat unbelievable valorization of modernity. If that was the case, of course, Lawino would win the argument. But things are rarely as straightforward as they seem, when it comes to *mitumba*. The either/or of African tradition vs Western modernity cannot be solved simply by reversing the binary opposition and favoring tradition over modernity.[15]

Lawino knows that, too. At times she rails against all things European, but at other times she seems to be saying that, while she wants to hold on to her ways, different ways are appropriate for different people. Lawino casts Europe as the Other, and in this way is able to bring her own tradition into sharp focus. Lawino herself is well able to see some implications of her own tradition that are brought into focus by the European Other (while seemingly either unaware of or accepting of others, such as gender roles and hierarchy). This is an important and necessary function of the Other in all cases, although it is a short path from defining yourself against the backdrop of the Other, to allowing the Other to define you. At some point, *mitumba* must cease being an external imposition, and start being a creative means of repetition and criticism. But how can the Other become one's own without simply succumbing to its coercive power? Can *mitumba* ever be one's own, or is it always borrowed, to be returned with interest?

4 The Self-image of African Philosophy

Philosophy can have a number of different methodological tropes for itself. It can regard itself as on a journey of discovery – laying bare what is already present, but latent. It can think of itself as the archaeologist, uncovering that which is hidden. It can see itself as inventor rather than discoverer, making the world in its image. It may be the midwife, the one who enables the birth of philosophy out of the stuff of culture and tradition. It might think of itself as the collector, the one that appropriates and adapts for its own use. Or it could be the interpreter, that which mediates, explicates, and translates what is significant in the claim of the other, and in the process discovers its own claim on itself.

Each of these models, or tropes, can be found in the recent history of African philosophy. One might argue that African philosophy has always been around, and simply needed to be "discovered," or foregrounded. In a way, this was the conviction of the ethnophilosophers.[16] Cheikh Anta Diop,[17] Isaac Osabutey-Aguedze,[18] and others could be considered the archaeologists, uncovering the traces of the influence of African philosophy on world philosophy. One might suggest that African philosophy is a recent invention, and exists in the historical conditions of oppression out of which arises the slave-consciousness (in the master–slave relationship), a kind of post-Hegelian position.[19] Fourth, one might suggest that the philosopher is the one who fosters an authentic African philosophy – sage philosophy is a case in point.[20] Fifth, the philosopher might be the collector of useful philosophical tools, wherever they originated – professional philosophy.[21] Or, finally, one might suggest that the philosopher's task is to interpret a tradition – this is the place of hermeneuticists such as Okere and Serequeberhan.

Instead of trying to decide which of these is "real" philosophy, it might be more useful to think of philosophy as the self-interpretive, self-critical, and self-emancipatory dialogue that emerges out of all these. In this sense, and along with Okere and Serequeberhan, I would like to suggest that hermeneutics describes not only the interpretation of existing conditions, but also the understanding of the rationalizations of those conditions. In fact, then, I would like to suggest that hermeneutics brings with it the capacity to make African philosophy into a process, instead of a group of positions on issues or a method. So, the call to stop talking about African philosophy and start doing it is a bit misleading, for African philosophy comes to self-understanding through the self-interpretation of dialogue about its own activities and traditions.

What tradition are we talking about? Clearly, in a culture whose traditions have been based on oral literature until recently, the recovery and repetition (in Kierkegaard's sense of the term) of that tradition must have a broad notion of the text. In that case, ethnophilosophy seems to be an ever-present possibility. But in a broader sense, African philosophy has its own tradition, which it also draws on to understand its own identity.

Perhaps more important, what is the goal of that interpretation? Are we laying bare a tradition to come to some sense of self-identity? For what purpose? Are we, on the other hand, explicating a tradition to come to some sense of explanation? Again, for what purpose? The answer to this problem is straightforward in Gadamerian hermeneutics – understanding supersedes explanation. However, most African hermeneuticists (other than Serequeberhan) rely on the work of Paul Ricoeur, for whom both explanation and understanding are important.[22] Ricoeur recognizes early on that the Diltheyan split between explanation and understanding cannot simply be recombined by fiat. His background in structuralism remains with him throughout his life, and accounts for his conviction that meaning can reside in structure of texts. But he also recognizes Gadamer's claim, that meaning is an ontological moment.

Traditionally, these two positions have undercut each other. Indeed, it is still the case – witness the debate between the poststructuralist Derrida and the hermeneuticist Gadamer. But what is the real conflict between the two? It is that structuralism makes possible a publicly criticizable account that can ideally form the basis of societal action (although the more radical the poststructuralist critique, the less likelihood there is of action), while hermeneutics makes possible the construction of an account of the self in society (although the greater the focus on this, the more likely it is that radical critique will undercut it).

This is the core of the problem for Okere and Serequeberhan: each only takes half of the understanding/explanation tension. Okere wants to understand, but there is little place for explanation here, or the consequent basis for change. Serequeberhan wants to explain (and therefore to change), but there is little place for understanding because the nature of the horizon has been predetermined by the need to change.

This distinction does not map directly on to the earlier distinction between coherence and complexity. Both positions strive for coherence, and the price they pay is the minimization of the range and contradictory nature of possibilities opened up by dialogue.

What is needed is a reminder of the multifaceted and contradictory nature of alterity. Understanding the Self through understanding the Other lies behind the tension between coherence and complexity. The Other both disrupts understanding and makes understanding possible. It is tempting to cast the Other in only one manner – Africa has been Europe's "Other" (meaning inferior), and must now extricate itself, making Europe the Other (meaning the hostile oppressor). But Otherness has many faces:

- *Fascination*. The Other can be the exotic, the foreign. It could be the object of idle curiosity, of collection, of pride.

- *Repulsion.* The Other can be the thing to be avoided, the leper. It could be that which reminds me of my own corrigibility, or that which just turns my stomach.
- *Desire.* The Other can be the thing to be owned or controlled. It is that which I believe fulfills a lack in my existence.
- *Dependence.* The Other can be the thing which makes my own existence possible. According to Karl Barth and Rudolph Otto (to use an analogy from theology), it is the Otherness of God that is the real point of religion. It could be the ground of my being, or it could be the transcendence of my being; either way, it is what I am not, but what makes me possible.
- *Smugness.* The Other could be the primitive (Lévy-Bruhl), the ones not like us because they lack Culture. They could be valorized (Rousseau) or vilified (Hegel), but they are always easily forgotten.
- *Appropriation/subsumption.* The Other could be that which is absorbed, that which is assimilated into my being, giving up its own being on my behalf.
- *Marginalization.* The Other is often that which is left out after coherent meaning is arrived at. It is that which makes no sense, from the point of view of the coherent center.
- *Horizon.* The Other might be that which holds the possibility of understanding by being the place where tradition and prejudice can be uncovered, at least in part.
- *Domination.* The Other could be that which is my servant, that which relieves me from the drudgery of my own existence by taking that drudgery on him-, her-, or it-self. The machine and the slave are both the Other.
- *Foil.* The Other could be that against which I test myself, or that against which I measure myself.
- *Mirror.* The Other could be that in which I find myself again and meet myself anew, the familiar in the alien, and the alien in the familiar.
- *Body.* The Other could be that part of me that is always subordinate, if I believe Descartes and hold that I am a thinking thing. It may simply reduce to a tool that I can use to control other thinking things, or it could be the thing that keeps me from true Enlightenment (Plato, Gnostics). It could also be that which requires interpretation, as it is my expression in the world and the world's interaction with me (Merleau-Ponty).

There are probably many more tropes which can be used for alterity. The point is that African philosophy is defined by its ability to set for itself Others for it to understand. The Other of (neo)colonialism is an important one, but not the only one. There is the Other of culture, as Okere argues. There is the Other of its own tradition, of other world traditions of philosophy, of religion. The Other may be relatively benign, as the trope of the mirror or the foil may suggest, or it may be insidious, as the trope of domination may suggest. It will always come with moral as well as epistemic and ontological implications, for the tropes do not exist in isolation. And, of course, there is the position of oneself as the Other of something else (a position African philosophy knows all too well). The Other may be insidious, but to assume that it is only that (just as to assume it is only benign) is to close down interpretive possibilities and flatten the possibilities of self-understanding.

The Other serves the function of making oneself coherent, either by mirroring or by alienating, and serves as the locus of complexity in any narrative of coherence. It establishes noetic possibilities through the making of distinctions, while unmasking the machinations of power behind knowledge through the questioning of the motives of those distinctions. The result is a move to the construction of coherence with the realization of complexity, the hope of repetition with the realization of power/knowledge, and the possibility of action with the realization of fallibility.

5 African Philosophical Hermeneutics?

Perhaps *mitumba* has had a bad rap. It may be nothing more than an attempt to deny one's heritage for another. On the other hand, it may be creatively used and appropriated to unfold new meanings and new understandings. Okere is right about at least one thing: hermeneutic philosophy is the process of understanding concrete prereflective practice. And Serequeberhan is right about at least one thing: hermeneutic philosophy must be transformative, or it is not true to its understanding of concrete experience.

The real value of heremeneutics for African philosophy is in pushing the issue of self-understanding to a new level. The conversation about the nature of African philosophy has tended to focus on certain specific kinds of question: What is the true object of African philosophy? Is there a unique method? In what way can African philosophy describe and prescribe based on its factical conditions? These are legitimate questions, but they are subquestions of something larger: is there an African way in which African philosophy can understand itself? My argument to this point has been that both Okere and Serequeberhan have recognized the significance of mediating between lived conditions and theory, but that both have not gone far enough to make African philosophy truly self-critical and self-understanding. What is needed is to have some sense of the elements of the conversation in which African philosophy finds itself.

The African philosophy conversation cannot ultimately be centered around finding a truly African methodology. While method may be necessary, it is also shot through with presuppositions, many of them inherited from a colonial or colonized past. Method privileges its own implicit goals, and chooses some modes of attaining those goals over other modes. This is why so many are uneasy with ethnophilosophy – it is a method that has built-in assumptions about the place of Africans in the world and the nature of African rationality. In any method, what you look for is what you will find.

The reverse of this, the search for a universal method, is found in so-called professional philosophy, which in most cases is little more than philosophy which happens to be done in Africa. If the method is Anglo-American analytic philosophy, African philosophy already comes subordinated to it, because it refers to another tradition as its arbiter. The same applies to Continental philosophy, more prevalent in Francophone Africa. This is why I have been at pains to distance heremeneutic philosophy from hermeneutic method, because that would be equally subordinationist. To require African philosophy to come up with a new and unique method in order to be called philosophy is an unfair requirement. In that case, African philosophers seem to have only two choices: recover Western method by showing that it was really African all along (the tactic of Cheikh Anta Diop and others who argue that European thought is really rooted in African thought), or find a new method (the tactic of H. Odera Oruka and others, who champion sage philosophy). Each case has its problems: in the first, one might ask what relevance the fact of history has, if it is a fact at all; and in the second, one might ask whether the knife-edge between ethnophilosophy and professional philosophy has really been walked successfully.

There is another way to think about the place of hermeneutics in African philosophy, and that is to implicate all theory in its own tradition. Consider the notion of freedom, for example. For a universalist philosopher such as Plato or various Enlightenment thinkers, freedom is a concept that has a single definition and is applicable everywhere. The critique leveled by both the structuralists and Wittgenstein is that freedom has no universal meaning, but refers either to other parts of a language, or to the background of meaning. While for the United States freedom has something to do with the Constitution and individual rights, and for Canada it has something to do with the tension between group and individual rights, for Africa it refers to the struggles in Liberia and South Africa, to the Mau Mau and to Oginga Odinga's *Not Yet Uhuru*, and to many other concrete historical events.[23] And, it takes seriously the fact that the English word "freedom" may hold a different place in the language than "Uhuru" does in Kiswahili.

The poststructuralist will argue that keying a term to its own history is better than supposing that it refers to a universal ideal, but then will point out how that history itself is not an unbroken web of definition and reference for the term. There can be no romantic notion of the good old days; nor can the deceit be maintained that a term such as freedom has any unequivocal meaning for those sharing a culture. The complexity of the subject, the culture, and the idea itself prevent meaning from taking hold. Indeed, that is the way it should be, because as soon as meaning takes hold, it becomes coercive, and always necessarily leaves someone out.

Of course, there are various strategies at this point for unmasking the complicity of theory with oppression, beginning with deconstruction, Freudian analysis, and feminism. These critiques are important and necessary, but they themselves need to be considered in light of their own histories. Each arises in the context of Western frustration with the hegemony of Western scientific reasoning and totalizing world-views. While each may be critical of traditional canons, each has its own canon. Indeed, each makes sense only in light of its own tradition. Terms, as well as other tools of meaning, are implicated in their own histories. The poststructuralist argument that there is fissure in all structures does not invalidate the observation that terms (and philosophies) are implicated in both the continuities and the cracks of tradition.

Most theorists realize this, which is why postcolonial theory is not just the simple-minded application of another Western method of thought. But the very fact that this application is not made betrays the fact that tradition cannot be deconstructed, bracketed, or dismissed so easily. In other words, for there to be a truly African philosophy, and not simply a series of used Western ideas adapted for an occasion, any appropriated theory must critique its own tradition, and to do that, it must admit that it has one.

For African philosophy, this means two things: first, that appropriation of the Other is possible, but only with the realization of the factical conditions of the emergence of what is appropriated; and second, that African philosophy itself can become self-aware through the uncovering of its own tradition seen in the analysis of the Other. This is the true fusion of horizons, for this process is an ongoing creative one on both sides. African philosophy has it within itself to critically appraise the Other as well as itself, and in so doing can contribute something unique to world philosophy while coming to self-understanding.

I am not suggesting that we replace one theory with another. Rather, I am suggesting that a truly African philosophy is not one which ignores outside influences, but one which is able to root them in its own soil. The Kierkegaardian notion of repetition is relevant here. The repetition is not recollection, but posing anew the question of what is significant, and how it can be remanifest in a different historical space. The plea is not to get caught up in the debate about what kind of philosophy is not truly African philosophy, but rather to transform the intuitions into African philosophy.

Ethnophilosophy may not be true philosophy, but it does have one useful observation – that African philosophy must be rooted in Africa, and not simply philosophy that happens to be done in Africa. The problem is that ethnophilosophers have assumed that the object of study must be African traditions. In fact, African traditions must inform African philosophy, but the object of study must be human experience as it manifests itself and as it comes to self-understanding. Philosophy, whether African or not, is the understanding of understanding in its specific historical and material conditions, in its hope and in its doubt.

The same applies to justifying African thought by arguing that it is the ultimate basis of European thought. The intuition that history is important is good, but causal lines of influence do not necessarily support the contention that Africa has a philosophical life. The real question is: are those lines of influence more than historical curiosities? Is repetition possible?

Professional philosophy holds the intuition that philosophy must be transferable outside of cultural boundaries, and must be able to critique a culture rather than simply reflecting the views of that culture. This observation is important as well, but does not necessarily need to result in universalism. It could mean that philosophy is irreducibly dialogical. Philosophies will have some points of contact outside of themselves, and philosophers can build on the rootedness in a particular culture to dialogue with and critique the philosophies that arise in other cultures.

One way to frame the hermeneutic project is that it raises the question of what is compelling in the claim of the Other. This "Other" has many forms, as postcolonial theory has pointed out. The question remains, though: how do we get past the tyranny of the Other constructing African philosophy, and allow African philosophy to construct itself in dialogue with its own Other? Hermeneutics does not offer a simple answer to this, and certainly does not want to minimize the masks of power and domination. It does, however, offer the possibility that the dialogue between different orientations of African philosophy is not a prelude to philosophy, but is philosophy itself, and is the process of repetition.

And this, I would suggest, is the other side of *mitumba*. African philosophy is not just cast-off or recycled ideas from the West. It is the appropriated, the stitched-together, altered, and tie-dyed, Africa in a new dress that seems somehow familiar, or perhaps in old clothes that take on new meaning in a new appropriation. At the same time, it is not derivative, for the meaning is not located in the sum of the parts, even if the parts could all be traced back to non-African origins (which they cannot). African philosophy is the repetition of Africa itself, and also the subversion of any simple recollection.

Notes

1   Okot p'Bitek, *Song of Lawino and Song of Ocol* (Heinemann, London, 1984), p. 116.
2   Theophilus Okere, *African Philosophy: A Historico-hermeneutical Investigation of the Conditions of its Possibility* (University Press of America, Lanham MD, 1983).
3   Tsenay Serequeberhan, *The Hermeneutics of African Philosophy: Horizon and Discourse* (Routledge, New York, 1994). It should be noted that these two are not the only African philosophers who have written on or incorporated hermeneutic

theory. Other sources include: Ngoma-Binda, "Pour une orientation authentique de la philosophie en Afrique: l'herméneutique," *Zaire-Afrique*, vol. 17, 1977, pp. 143–58; J. Kinyongo, "Essai sur la fondation épistémologique d'une philosophie herméneutique en Afrique: le cas de la discursivité," *Présence Africaine*, no. 109, 1979, pp. 12–26; N. Tsiamalenga, *Denken und Sprechen Ein Beitrag zum Relativitäts Prinzip am Beispiel einer Bantusprache (Ciluba)*, dissertation, Frankfurt/Main, 1980; Nkombe Oleko, *Métaphore et métonymie dans les symboles parémiologiques: L'Intersubjectivité dans les proverbes tetela* (Faculté de Théologie Catholique, Kinshasa, 1979); Okonda Okolo, "Tradition and destiny: horizons of an African philosophical hermeneutics," in T. Serequeberhan (ed.), *African Philosophy: The Essential Readings* (Paragon, New York, 1991), 201–210; translated from the French "Tradition et destin: horizons d'une herméneutique philosophique africaine," *Présence Africaine* no. 114, 1980.

4 Okere, *African Philosophy*, pp. 82ff.
5 Ibid., p. 88.
6 It is only in the conclusion, pp. 114–31, that Okere directly addresses the applicability of hermeneutic theory to the African situation. His application seems very close to ethnophilosophy, in that his example of the Igbo culture of Nigeria consists in the philosophical interpretation of symbols from the culture. If this is hermeneutics, it seems to be fraught with all the questions that can be leveled at ethnophilosophy.
7 Paulin Hountondji, "Comments on contemporary African philosophy," *Diogenes*, vol. 71, Fall 1970, pp. 109–30.
8 Serequeberhan, *Hermeneutics of African Philosophy*, p. 9.
9 Ibid., p. 53.
10 V.Y. Mudimbe, *The Invention of Africa* (Indiana University Press, Bloomington, IN, 1988).
11 Serequeberhan, *Hermenentics of African Philosophy*, p. 78.
12 Ibid.
13 Ibid., pp. 83–4.
14 Okot p'Bitek, *Song of Lawino and Song of Ocol*, p. 121.
15 Serequeberhan cites Cornel West's comment in *Prophesy Deliverance!* (Westminster Press, Philadelphia, PA 1982), p. 24: "In fact, ironically, the attempt by black intellectuals to escape from their Americanness and even go beyond Western thought is itself very *American*." Serequeberhan comments: "In the context of contemporary African philosophy, one needs only to substitute 'European' for 'American' and 'African intellectuals' for 'black intellectuals' to see the relevance of this sentence" (*Hermeneutics of African Philosophy*, p. 127, n. 28).
16 Many examples could be cited. The ones most often given are Placide Tempels, *Bantu Philosophy*, trans. Rev. Colin King (Présence Africaine, Paris 1959, 1969); M. Griaule, *Conversations with Ogotemmêli* (Oxford University Press, for the International African Institute, London, 1965); John S. Mbiti, *African Religions and Philosophy* (Heinemann, Nairobi, 1969).
17 Cheikh Anta Diop, *The African Origin of Civilization: Myth or Reality*, (Lawrence Hill, Chicago, IL, 1974).
18 Isaac D. Osabutey-Aguedze, *Principles Underlying African Religion and Philosophy* (Maillu Publishing House, Nairobi, 1990). Originally a thesis written in 1933, and

rejected as a master's thesis ("The rationale for African religious rites") by Syracuse University.

19   V.Y. Mudimbe's *The Invention of Africa* (Indiana University Press, Bloomington, IN, 1988) has some characteristics of this.

20   H. Odera Oruka (ed.), *Sage Philosophy* (African Center for Technology Studies, Nairobi, 1991).

21   Many have taken this name for themselves, or had it applied to them. Included in this list are Paulin Hountondji, P. O. Bodunrin and Kwasi Wiredu.

22   Charles Taylor has also put the problem well in "Understanding and ethnocentricity," *Philosophy and the Human Sciences: Philosophical Papers 2* (Cambridge University Press, Cambridge 1985), pp. 123–30.

23   Okot p'Bitek says it nicely, in the mouth of Lawino:

> He says
> They are fighting for Uhuru
> He says
> They want Independence and Peace
> And when they meet
> They shout "Uhuru! Uhuru!"
> But what is the meaning
> Of Uhuru?
> . . .
> Ocol dislikes his brother fiercely,
> His mother's son's hatred
> Resembles boiling oil!
> The new parties have split the homestead
> As the battle axe splits the skull!
> My husband has sternly warned me
> Never to joke
> With my husband–in–law:
> Not that joking may cause pregnancy,
> Not that I am a loose woman,
> But that the strong gum of the joke
> Will reconnect the snapped string
> Of brotherhood
> Between him and his brother!
>
> Is this the unity of Uhuru?
> Is this the Peace
> That Independence brings?

(Okot p'Bitek, *Song of Lawino*, pp. 103, 104–5)

PART IV

The Politics of the "Postcolonial"

10

Tragic Dimensions of our Neocolonial "Postcolonial" World

Lewis Gordon

O town of my fathers in Thebes' land,
O gods of our house.
I am led away at last.
Look, leaders of Thebes,
I am last of your royal line.
Look what I suffer, at whose command,
because I respected the right.

Sophocles, Antigone

Mr Smith said to his interpreter: "Tell them to go away from here. This is the house of God and I will not live to see it desecrated."

Okeke interpreted wisely to the spirits and leaders of Umuofia: "The white man says he is happy you have come to him with your grievances, like friends. He will be happy if you leave the matter in his hands."

"We cannot leave the matter in his hands because he does not understand our customs, just as we do not understand his. We say he is foolish because he does not know our ways, and perhaps he says we are foolish because we do not know his. Let him go away."

Chinua Achebe, Things Fall Apart

When I search for man in European technique and style, I see a succession of negations of man, an avalanche of murders.

Frantz Fanon, Les damnés de la terre[1]

African philosophy in American terrain faces postcoloniality as a question of location in the proverbial belly of the beast. However the question of cultural *Angst* may be formulated, as in Appiah's (in)famous problematic of the Europeanized African, the US-American reality is one of stringent, stratified political-economic domination, which is so aptly phrased today as "global capitalism." For global reality today is such that there is no viable cultural, economic, or military opposition to the hegemonic weight of the current "world order."[2] For example, by sheer force of its utility, the US dollar has become the primary currency of the world. Even in former enclaves, like Cuba, there is a direct correlation between access to US dollars and access to a higher standard of living. Such hegemony hardly signals a *post*, in the sense of former or passed, colonial relation of any kind, but instead a new or properly *neo*colonial relation. This neocolonialism, bolstered not only by the fall of its eastern European opposition, but also by years of successful political, economic, and military destabilization of Third World sites of resistance, finds itself facing a classical theodicean problem of legitimacy that has plagued many previous imperial orders: how can it legitimate its conquest without depending on conquest itself as its source of legitimation? In other words, "Now that we have conquered our opposition," it can be asked, "how do we assure that our victory isn't more than a case of might makes right?" The heart of the new regime must be demonstrated to be pure, to be good, in the midst of its contradictions. Its plight is a familiar performance of ideological legitimation. Its hopes are familiar hopes, hopes signalled by familiar politics of absorption, extermination, and pathology; is there any longer a place for the miscreants, the outcasts, the anomalies, the sites of contradictions – sites regarded as problematic terrain?

The current situation is a tragic situation.[3] It is marked by tragedy because of the classic, paradoxical conflicts of just injustice and unjust justice that emerge from its various relations of power. African philosophy, in the midst of the unjust justice of hegemonic capitalism, faces the question of formulating a just justice in a system that offers no recourse but a just injustice. The question of *formulating* a just justice, which is a just injustice to those who reap the benefits of the current world order, is made particularly acute in the situation of the intellectual of African descent:

> Essentially consumers during the period of tyranny, the intelligentsia becomes
> productive. Its literature is at first willingly confined to the poetic and tragic
> genres. Then they go to novels, short stories, and essays. It seems to be a sort
> of internal organization, a law of expression, which wills that poetic expression
> diminishes in proportion to the precise objectives and methods of the struggle
> for liberation. Themes are fundamentally renovated. In fact, there is found less
> and less bitter and hopeless recrimination, [less and less of] that blooming and
> sonorous violence, which, on the whole, reassures the occupiers. The colonialists,
> in earlier times, encouraged these efforts, facilitated their existence. Sharp
> denunciations, slackened misery, expressed passions are, in effect, assimilated by

the occupiers into a cathartic process. To facilitate such processes is, in a sense, to avoid dramatization, to loosen the atmosphere.⁴

Although Fanon is critical of the "tragic" and the "poetic" style, it is an ironic feature of his thought that his dramatization of colonial and neocolonial reality takes definite tragic forms in the violent face-off that he articulates.⁵ Fanon here points to a fundamental contradiction in an intelligentsia whose work brings about a catharsis in hegemonic instead of colonized communities: the tragic stage, or *skene*, has been turned over in such cases, the consequence of which is a preserved unjust justice.⁶ It is a dramatic tale in which Sophocles' King Creon is left assured of the rightness of his sentencing Antigone to her death.⁷ The intellectual, then, faces more than the urgent need "to build up his nation."⁸ The intellectual also faces the question of producing intellectual work that properly *dramatizes* the articulation of that need. It is the intellectual's role to set the stage, as it were, for the characters to unfold in their peculiarities.

It is argued, in what follows, that key features of classical tragedy suggest that there is a global political and spiritual context for tragedy in the contemporary world, and that role is one that centers liberatory texts like those of Frantz Fanon and C.L.R. James as contemporary loci of tragic literature. In that regard, in response to literary theorists like Henry Louis Gates, Jr, Homi Bhabha, Gayatri Spivak, and Manthia Diawara, and a philosopher like Kwame Anthony Appiah, who have argued against both liberatory and global theoretical descriptions of and prescriptions to the times, we will see that the present age is global, and indeed all-too-global, in a tragic way.

Aristotle defines tragedy as: "The representation of an action that is serious and also, as having magnitude, complete in itself; . . . with incidents arousing *pathos* and fear, wherewith to accomplish its *catharsis* of such emotions."⁹ He writes this after announcing that the context of tragedy is a conflict between virtue and vice, which divides "all of mankind." In pathos, one suffers from and with another's suffering; and in identifying the achievement of catharsis, which in ancient times (in both the Mediterranean and the Nile) referred to the medicinal activity of purgation and cleansing, we can see that tragedy presents actions to the community that elicit communal suffering. The tragic lesson is that setting things "right" or "just," and thereby setting the community right, often calls for horrible interventions. We find in these tragic interventions, with their historic resonance, the terror and disclosing possibilities of what has been ironically identified by both Kierkegaard and the more Marxist Sartre as a dialectic of "mediations."¹⁰

The terrifying, cathartic dimension of mediation signals the audience's role in tragic presentation, a role that has been a subject of considerable debate for over two millennia. It is the question of audience that has in fact raised the skeptical claim of whether tragedy is any longer possible, given the absence of both the audience and social conditions which it was designed to address. Oliver

Taplin has pointed out, however, in his *Greek Tragedy in Action*, that a great deal of that debate is mired in fallacies of decontextualized aesthetic claims.[11] A particularly egregious fallacy is to reduce the tragic setting to any one of its elements. Thus, it is important to respect what happens "on stage," as it were, as well as what happens in the audience. For matters of textual determination, understanding what happens on stage is vital. But to make it communicable requires understanding of what it is meant to achieve through what it is trying to say. Thus, the cathartic dimension of tragedy, placed in a contemporary context, presumes its relevance to contemporary audiences.

According to such Euro-philosophers as G.W.F. Hegel and Arthur Schopenhauer, classical tragedy holds themes that are of great relevance to modern audiences. For Hegel, the fundamental theme emerged through a performance of conflicting right, where two characters face each other in the midst of a just injustice. In *Antigone*, for instance, tragedy emerges as King Creon's rightful condemnation of a traitor and Antigone's rightful efforts to provide a proper burial for her brother, who, in spite of his act of treason, remained her brother to the end. Hegel's claim raises a question, however, of the accuracy of his egalitarian moral face-off, for the Greek (and even the Elizabethan) audiences had, after all, a definite *right* that was to be exemplified by the characters in the drama.[12] Although a just injustice elicits pathos, there was nevertheless a teleological context, *dikê* (order of the universe), which suggests a just justice in the dramatic unfolding of events.

Schopenhauer, on the other hand, presents tragedy as an indirect bringing to consciousness of that which we attempt dearly to avoid, and that is the failure of existence itself and the irretrievable fall of the just and the innocent: a conclusion that hardly embraces the modern taste for fairness and happy endings. Schopenhauer adds:

> What gives to all tragedy, in whatever form it may appear, the peculiar tendency towards the sublime is the awakening of the knowledge that the world, life, can afford us no true pleasure, and consequently is not worthy of our attachment. In this consists the tragic spirit: it therefore leads to resignation.[13]

Schopenhauer's description of tragedy aptly fits the colonialist mentality that Fanon was criticizing earlier. It is that type of tragedy that signals the pessimistic, resentful, anti-liberatory productions of an impotent élite. On the other hand, Schopenhauer's conclusion of quietude, resentment, and pessimism destroys the dynamism of tragedy as *human* and *political* presentations, and, in that regard, we can regard Schopenhauer as perhaps the first *postmodern* theorist of tragedy. For, like Lyotard (and, for that matter, Gates and Appiah), there is advanced rejection of both human–centrism and the politics of liberation within the material sphere (the place governed by what Schopenhauer called the *principle of individuation*).[14] What Schopenhauer fails to see, however, is that, by his ultimately making life itself tragic, not only would Greek audiences not recognize his pessimistic message, but neither would we. Pessimism is not a *goal* or an ally of tragedy, but a condition for which tragedy is supposed to be an adversary.

The etymology of the word 'tragedy' offers an alternative picture of tragedy. From the Greek words *tragos* (meaning goat) and *ôidê* (meaning song), tragedy is clearly linked to the proverbial burden-carrier itself: the scapegoat. On this basis, Eva Figes, in her *Tragedy and Social Evolution*, advances the following conclusion:

> The origin of the word 'tragedy' is thought to lie in the Greek word for a goat, and though the ritual associations are obscure one inevitably thinks of the Israelite scapegoat, which Aron was required to send into the wilderness with the sins of the community on its back. The rituals of cleansing and atonement did in fact require two goats, the second one being sacrificed for a sin-offering. We know that animal sacrifices were made at the start of drama festivals in Athens, as at other important public gatherings, such as the political assembly.[15]

Taplin has been rather critical of at least the "ritual" dimension of this view, which he regards as ultimately an effort to barbarize the Greeks to meet the political needs of the present.[16] Tragedy, he argues, is fundamentally an aesthetic affair. We need not resort to rituals, however, to support our thesis that the *content* of tragedy exemplifies political realities and values of the society in which it is composed. Aesthetic affairs are, after all, often rich with political and ethical content. That said, we can consider Figes's interpretation of tragedy. She writes:

> Tragedy in the theatre is the sad story of a central protagonist who, either deliberately or by accident, offends against the most fundamental laws of his society, those laws which are so basic as to be considered divine . . . In tragedy a community can see [that] . . . the central protagonist who has polluted his environment, *bringing disruption on himself and the community within which he lives*, is eliminated, whereupon peace and order are restored. Whether that protagonist intended to break the divine social laws or not is beside the point.[17]

It is easy to find support for Figes's view in actual tragedies, as the epigraph from *Antigone* attests. During the years of *de jure* and *de facto* colonialism, the "players" in the drama were also easily marked. I have argued elsewhere, for instance, that both Frantz Fanon's and C.L.R. James's writings exemplify powers of *pathos* primarily because of their status as tragic texts on violent, colonial realities.[18] In the present age, however, the violence and abject poverty persist, but the texts that are being produced by our avowed spokespersons on their theorization are of a different kind. We are therefore led to ask: what are the roles of contemporary theorists on the neocolonial scene? Unfortunately, like the mythological Hermes, they have acquired a hermeneutical role of bringing flawed messages, messages of, in a word, tricksters. This need not have been so. But perhaps the chief reason rests in their postmodern (un)commitments and the postmodern antipathy to materiality that underscore their message. The former god of the age, if both Richard Wright and Jean-Paul Sartre are correct, is the Enlightenment project of progress and a better world – a project at least once thought best exemplified in the ethical dimensions of Marxism.[19] As John O'Neill sardonically puts it:

> It is not the masses who have sickened of the injustice and exploitation that grinds their lives, weakens their families, starves their children, murders and terrorizes them each hour of the day and night in every corner of the world. No, it is not these people who have abandoned idealism, universalism, truth and justice. It is those of the others. The two sides, of course, never meet. Each remains on the other side of the great wall of class upon which there flickers the imagery of mass culture, on one side, and the imagery of élite, professional culture, on the other. No one appears to own the wall. This is why those on each side of the wall see only themselves in their own cultures. Worse still, since the masses have no reason to believe they own anything – let alone the wall – those on the élite side have persuaded themselves that the wall is culture rather than property. This idea appeals to the cultural élite since what they own – as well as what they disown – is largely symbolic capital, especially language and its professional practice.[20]

O'Neill is not alone. In the midst of this situation is Africa as project. The African divine was, and perhaps among some theorists and laypersons still is, *Pan*-Africa. And while Africa's cultural élite, comfortably situated in the élite expatriate's First World conditions, deconstruct away language with which to articulate very modern demands upon US–European hegemony, African conditions – whether on the continent itself or through the micro-African experiences that dot urban centers – continue to choke under the weight of material reconfigurations of the global economy. When such intellectuals "speak out," what is the scene that is being laid by such a gesture? To whom are they speaking?

It appears that some spokespersons within this faction have laid claim to absolution through denial of obligation in the first place. For them, the question of audience conceals insidious demands for cultural, and often racial, authenticity – that there is, in a word, a failure to acknowledge an African identity by way of recognizing the Africana people as the most morally relevant audience in this situation. "How can we speak to the African audience," they seem to say, "when we are also members of the European community?" This question serves as a response, admittedly, to the disdainful *ad hominem* of the "Europeanized African." The problem is not, however, a matter of the authenticity of the "Westernized African." That problematic only reflects naive and ultimately absurd forms of cultural anthropology. After all, cultural purity, if it ever existed, no longer functions as a lived reality. Global capitalism has seen to it that no stone has gone unturned, and, in that regard, the only accurate concern becomes one of which *dimension* of Western society is manifested by the Africana intellectual in Eurocenters. In those centers, the "distances," if you will, are not necessarily geographical; the boundaries are of the kinds described by Antonio Gramsci as *strata* – his euphemism for class, but also a convenient term for any socially separated segment of society. Tragic dimensions begin to emerge when we cut through the muck of obfuscating language, the morass of self-aggrandizing, narcissistic platitudes, and get to the point with the crass or properly vulgar language of the streets and logic of the concrete: "When all is said and done, my friends, whose side are you on?"

Since the scene is primarily a circumstance of speaking to the king while serving as a member of the palace, we may do well to return to the *Antigone*, where, after all, there is a lesson to be learned from a tragic heroine in a tragic situation of having "to choose sides." The lesson to be learned from Sophocles' *Antigone* is a lesson about flaws in the midst of obligation. Creon is, after all, a *flawed* king, and so is Antigone by virtue of her origin. She is progeny of the unholy marriage of a righteously flawed king to a righteously flawed queen.[21] All of these characters are oddly designed for suffering, for it is in fulfilling who they are, in fulfilling their publicly recognized roles of power and communal responsibility, in a word, their *characters*, that they encounter what they must do – or more pointedly, *who* they are. All of them bring calamity upon their community. For the community's demands to emerge, the kind of rightful action that must emerge is the reconstitution of justice. In other words, regardless of the characters' points of view, the world must be placed back into a certain order. The tragedy in tragedies is that the "innocence" of the characters who occupy a wrongful place in the drama is ultimately irrelevant. Thus, the tragic protagonist finds her or himself guilty by virtue of deed and circumstance, not intent, and suffers, ironically, for the sake of justice.

In a 1992 article, Jacques Derrida, a veritable guru of textual-poststructural cultural studies, and consequently textual-poststructural postcolonial studies, declared that "the 'sufferance' of deconstruction, what makes it suffer and what makes those it torments suffer, is perhaps the absence of rules, of norms, and definitive criteria that would allow one to distinguish unequivocally between *droit* and justice."[22] Derrida seems to advance textual poststructuralism as a tragic hero.[23] The stage is set by association, then, for the question of whether our Africana élite in First World castles face their flawed king as heirs to their revolutionary foremothers and fathers' ghosts – as suggested, for instance, by Homi Bhabha's foreword to the English edition of *Peau noire, masques blancs* or Henry Louis Gates, Jr's appointment (accompanied by Kwame Anthony Appiah) as W.E.B. Du Bois Professor at Harvard.[24]

In Derrida's claim that "what makes [deconstruction] suffer and what makes those it torments suffer, is perhaps the absence of rules, of norms, and definitive criteria that would allow one to distinguish unequivocally between *droit* and justice," a great many problems of audience ironically become clear. We have already seen O'Neill's remarks about delusions of criterial and normative "absence" – delusions that are apparently welcomed by Derrida in spite of Third World peoples being included in those whom it torments by the advocation of blurring ethical distinctions. Now, we may also add a dimension that separates tragedy itself from the sort of hero or antihero advanced by Derrida et al.[25] For although the conflict of "right" may emerge Hegelian style in most tragedies, the question of *audience* addresses a definite right: atonement, after all, had to be made for Oedipus and Jocasta's polluting Thebes. Although Chinua Achebe's Okonkwo was a strong man with flaws of tragic proportion, it is the Igbo people themselves who ultimately stand as the tragic heroes, like the Trojan women, in the face of calamitous unjust justice. Whether *Oedipus the King*, *Things Fall Apart*, or, for that matter, *Les damnés de la terre* or *The Black Jacobins*, a hallmark of actual tragedies, and consequently of actual tragic heroes, is the demand for recompense. Something must be set right. Although Derrida et al. may not be able to distinguish unequivocally between right and justice, that may be a consequence of realities (or, for that matter, unrealities) in which they live. The problem is in the bad-faith presentation of ideological commitment to begin with – signaled by a rightful, and often righteous, avowal against determining rightness and justice itself. The tragedy of the situation can be realized, however, through the question of ethical ramifications in the face of current, global possibility. Nothing can be said, that is, to a Third and growing Fourth World people's violent response to First World opulence and the ongoing violence unleashed for the sake of its preservation. The linguistic play of the African intelligentsia on American terrain becomes, then, a question of whose ideology they are protecting. Their attack on liberation that often accompanies the indecidability of *droit* and justice is all too obvious here.

Perhaps, then, the Westernized African should also take seriously a voice from the Western past:

> Our happiness depends
> on wisdom all the way.
> The gods must have their due.
> Great words by men of pride
> bring greater blows upon them.
> So wisdom comes to the old.[26]

It is a voice, as we can see, that is hardly alien to anything African.

Notes

1   Full citation of epigraphs: *Sophocles I: "Oeidpus the King," "Oedipus at Colonus,"* and *"Antigone,"* trans. (respectively) David Grene, Robert Fitzgerald, and Elizabeth Wykoff, ed. David Grene and Richmond Lattimore (University of Chicago Press, Chicago, IL, and London 1954), ll. 939–40; Chinua Achebe, *Things Fall Apart* (Fawcett Cress/Ballentine, New York, 1959), p. 175; and Frantz Fanon, *Les damnés de la terre*, preface by Jean-Paul Sartre, ed. Gérard Chaliand (Gallimard, Paris, 1991) pp. 372–3; *The Wretched of the Earth*, preface by Jean-Paul Sartre, trans. Constance Farrington (Grove, New York, 1963), p. 312. Although I will cite the pages in the English edition as well, all of the translations are mine.

2   For discussion, see Tsenay Serequeberhan, *The Hermeneutics of African Philosphy* (Routledge, New York and London, 1994); John O'Neill, *The Poverty of Postmodernism* (Routledge, New York and London, 1995); and Antonio Callari, Stephen Cullenberg, and Carole Biewener, *Marxism in the Postmodern Age: Confronting the New World Order* (Guilford Press, New York and London, 1995).

3   I have argued that both colonialism and neocolonialism are classically tragic situations in my book, *Fanon and the Crisis of European Man: An Essay on Philosophy and the Human Sciences* (Routledge, New York and London, 1995), ch. 4.

4   Fanon, *Les damnés*, p. 287; *Wretched*, p. 239.

5   Gordon, *Fanon and the Crisis of European Man*, ch. 4.

6   For discussion, see P.F. Shelley, "Africa, Frantz Fanon and the postcolonial world," *News & Letters*, June 1995, p. 8; Olufemi Taiwo, "On the pitfalls of national consciousness: a retrospect on Frantz Fanon's gift of prophecy," in Lewis R. Gordon, T. Denean Sharpley-Whiting, and Renée T. White (eds), *Frantz Fanon: A Critical Reader* (Blackwell, Oxford, 1996).

7   For an updated adaptation that suits our discussion perfectly, see Athol Fugard, *The Island*, in which black South African inmates stage a production of *Antigone* both as an act of protest and as a description of their situation.

8   Fanon, *Les damnés*, p. 307; *Wretched*, p. 247.

9   *Poetics*, 1449b 24–26. This is my revision of Ingram Bywater's translation of the *Poetics* in Richard McKeon (ed.), *The Basic Works of Aristotle*. The Greek text from which my revisions were determined is: Aristotle, *Poetics*, ed. and trans. S. Halliwell; Longinus, *On the Sublime*, ed. and trans. W. Hamilton Fyfe, revised by D. Russell; Demetrius, *On Style*, ed. and trans. D. C. Innes; based on the translation by W. R. Roberts (Harvard University Press, Cambridge, MA, 1995).

10   See Søren Kierkegaard's complex discussion of tragedy in Problemata II of *Fear and Trembling*, trans. and ed. by Howard V. Hong and Edna H. Hong (Princeton University Press, Princeton, NJ, 1983) and Sartre's *Search for a Method*, trans. by Hazel Barnes (Vintage, New York, 1968), ch. 2; in the French, "Question de méthode," preface to *Critique de la raison dialectique*, vol. 1 (Gallimard, Paris, 1960).

11   Oliver Taplin, *Greek Tragedy in Action* (Routledge, London, 1993), ch. 10.

12   For Hegel's discussion of tragedy, see his *Philosophy of Fine Art*, trans. F.P.B. Somaston, 4 vols (G. Bell and Sons, London, 1920) as well as *The Introduction to*

Hegel's Philosophy of Fine Art, trans. Bernard Bosanquet (Kegan Paul, Trench and Co., London, 1886).

13   Schopenhauer, *The World as Will and Idea*, vol. III, 7th edn, trans. R.B. Haldane and J. Kemp (Kegan Paul, Trench, Trubner and Co., London, 1883), p. 213.

14   For François Lyotard's ironically "classic" statement on postmodernism, see his *The Postmodern Condition: A Report on Knowledge* (University of Minnesota Press, Minneapolis, MN, 1984), and for Gates' most recent assault on liberation theorizing, see his "Critical Fanonism," *Critical Inquiry*, vol. 17, 1991, pp. 457–78. Appiah is placed in this equation primarily because of the assault on African philosophy of the liberatory kind that emerges in *In My Father's House: Africa in the Philosophy of Culture* (Oxford University Press, Oxford, 1992).

15   Figes, *Tragedy and Social Evolution* (Persea, 1976), p. 11.

16   *Greek Tragedy in Action*, pp. 161–2.

17   *Tragedy and Social Evolution*, p. 12, my emphasis

18   *Fanon and the Crisis of European Man*, ch. 4.

19   For some of Richard Wright's views, see "I tried to be a communist," in Richard Crossman (ed.) *The God That Failed* (Harper and Row, New York, 1965) and "How 'bigger' was born," his introduction to the 1940 and all subsequent editions of *Native Son* (Harper and Row, New York, 1966), and for discussion of Wright's complex transition from communism to existentialism and then black nationalism, see Cedric Robinson, *Black Marxism: The Making of the Black Radical Tradition* (Zed, London, 1983), ch. 11. Similar ethical and historical concerns launched Sartre's investigations into what became his *Critique of Dialectical Reason*. For discussion, see Ronald Aronson, "Sartre on progress," in Christina Howells (ed.), *The Cambridge Companion to Sartre* (Cambridge University Press, Cambridge, 1992). It can easily be shown, by the way, that in the cases of both Wright and Sartre, their later stages are more concrete forms of their existential stages. Wright's black nationalism and Sartre's existential Marxism are ultimately premised upon the demand for concrete foci of liberation struggles. For a discussion of philosophy of existence in the Africana context, see Lewis R. Gordon (ed.), *Existence in Black: An Anthology of Black Existential Philosophy* (Routledge, New York and London, 1996), and for a discussion of existence and historical specificity, see *Fanon and the Crisis of European Man*, ch. 2.

20   *Poverty of Postmodernism*, pp. 1–2.

21   For the entire story, see *Sophocles I*, ed. Grene and Lattimore.

22   Jacques Derrida, "Force of law: the 'mystical foundation of authority,'" in Drucilla Cornell, Michel Rosenfeld and David Gray Carlson (eds.), *Deconstruction and the Possibility of Justice* (Routledge, New York, 1992), p. 4. Derrida's guru status is well known, but his association with the textual-poststructuralist postcolonial studies set is based primarily on his influence on the individuals who emerge in the very influential Henry Louis Gates, Jr (ed.), *"Race," Writing and Difference* (University of Chicago Press, Chicago, IL, 1985, 1986).

23   If this seems far-fetched, I urge the reader to examine Derrida's advancement of deconstruction as a contemporary Hamlet, and hence "heir," to specters of Marx, in his book with the same title, subtitled *The State of the Debt, the Work of Mourning, and the New International*, trans. Peggy Kamuf, with an intro. by Bernd Magnus and Stephen Cullenberg (Routledge, New York and London, 1994). See also Aijaz

Ahmad's critical discussion of *Specters of Marx*, "Response to Derrida," in *New Left Review*, no. 208, 1994.

24 See Bhabha's "Remembering Fanon: self, psyche, and the colonial condition," foreword to 1986 (London) Pluto Press edition of that work. For a critical discussion of Bhabha's work, see P.F. Shelley, "Fanon, Africa, and the postcolonial world."

25 "Et al." refers not only to the individuals of *"Race," Writing, and Difference*, but also to Gates's very influential "Critical Fanonism," where the people of color contingent of Derridanism are unwarrantedly advanced as chief spokespersons not only of "Fanonism," but also of postcolonial criticism. For criticism and critique, see *Fanon and the Crisis of European Man*, ch. 5.

26 Sophocles, *Antigone*, ll. 1349–50.

11

*Honor, Eunuchs, and the Postcolonial Subject**

Leonard Harris

Jacobus Eliza Joannes Capitein (1717–47) is the quintessential postcolonial subject. Capitein's poetry and disputations are similar to exemplary postcolonial texts by such authors as Homi Bhabha, Abdul JanMohamed, and Gayatri Spivak. Capitein, I will argue, was an intellectual eunuch. He was incapable of being honored, I try and show, for reasons having to do with his ideas, the world which those ideas inhabited, and what it is to be honored. Why Capitein is the quintessential postcolonial subject reveals the deep limitations of postcolonial theory – a theoretical approach that relies on a way of explaining reality incapable of lending support for a world any different than the one we now inhabit.

Capitein was born in West Africa, sold to the slave trader Captain Arnold Steenhart, and given by Steenhart to Jacobus van Goch, chief trader in Guinea at Elmina.[1] He was soon taken to Holland for formal education. Ordained by the laying on of hands, May 7, 1742, ten months later he gave a public Latin oration on March 10, 1743, entitled "Dissertatio politico-theologica de servitute libertati christianae non contraria." Capitein argued that slavery was compatible with Christian doctrine. Booker T. Washington, in Tuskegee, Alabama, approximately a hundred and fifty years later, saw African Americans as having gone through the "school of slavery," a school that prepared its pupils for entrance into the Christian West as members and eventual co-equals in, and co-creators of, the new world.

Capitein arrived at Elmina, Ghana, on October 8, 1742, as chaplain and

* I am indebted to Vernon Williams, Purdue University, and Patricia Knox, Northern Kentucky University, for critical comments on an earlier version of this article.

reformed pastor for the West Indian Company. He requested permission from his superiors in Holland to marry a local African ward. However, this was denied and he was sent, as one of the most honored of Africans, a Dutch girl, Antonia Ginderdos, by the West Indian company. Capitein faithfully pastored at Elmina, with little success as a missionary. Laudatory poems were written about him in Europe, and as a man of great learning his reputation was highly regarded by the Asante King Opoku Ware. A portrait of Capitein bears the most telling description of the highest honor he could achieve: "Look at this Moor! His skin is black, but his soul is made white, since Jesus himself intercedes for him. He goes to teach the Moors in faith, hope, and charity, so that they, made white, may honour the Lamb together with him." The inscription accompanies the portrait of Capitein drawn by P. Van Dyek and etched by P. Tanje.

Capitein saw the world as posttribal, postagrarian, postfeudal, and postbarbarian. He could, like contemporary authors, see the world as postnationalist, postindustrial, postcolonial, and postmodern. Assuming that Capitein was right, his explanations for why "post" conditions existed allowed him to infer that his world was the teleology of world history: that is, the world of Christology was the only reasonable world to envision and, as such, the end of world history. Posttribalism existed because Dutch Christianity and its mode of commerce helped destroy tribalism. All laudable character traits – for example, love, piety, sobriety, and grace – were expressed in Dutch Christian terms by Capitein. His dress, the geography of slave castles, Latin, etc., were for him embodiments of Christian traits. Character traits, in effect, caused, created, and shaped dress, castles, and language. Power, postcolonial theory often holds in concert with Foucault, is pervasive in literature as well as in politics. The abiding beliefs underlying christological doctrines were for Capitein the source of power shaping the world and any future world.

Capitein could not explain reality in a way that allowed him to infer or require, from his explanation, radical action. Nor, from his explanation of reality, does he predict the possibility or likelihood of a fundamentally different world. He could, however, hope for revisions of his existing world; revisions that would help make the ideal of christology universal. The death of slavery for Capitein, for example, would be coterminous with the triumph of Christianity over all domains; a triumph identical with the triumph of the Dutch. And the death of heathen, barbaric, and all "pre" forms of antiquated social life – or at least their absolute subordination to the material, military, commercial, and religious will of "post" sectors of the new global agents – would be coterminous with the triumph of christology. Capitein, living in a condition of posttribal reality, is analogous to the condition of postcoloniality in a way that makes Capitein's role and theoretical stance quite similar to postcolonialist authors.

It is arguable that "Postcoloniality is the condition of what we might ungenerously call a comprador intelligentsia: of a relatively small, Western-style, Western-trained, group of writers and thinkers who mediate the trade in cultural commodities of world capitalism at the periphery."[2] In a perceptive critique of postcolonial theory, Kenneth Parker describes postcolonialist authors as performing a similar role – bearing Euro-American culture to the formerly colonized.[3] Appiah suggests that the condition of postcoloniality may not commit us to pessimism. Appiah writes:

> For what I am calling humanism can be provisional, historically contingent, antiessentialist (in other words, postmodern), and still be demanding. We can surely maintain a powerful engagement with the concern to avoid cruelty and pain while nevertheless recognizing the contingency of that concern.[4]

Appiah, however, expresses a hope that Capitein did not share: "This human impulse – an impulse that transcends obligations to churches and to nations" may be found in postcolonial literature, but it is in no way an obvious obligation. If there is an impulse to condemn suffering and pain, the forms of suffering and pain that deserve strenuous condemnation are tied to religious obligations and identities. As Capitein surely knew, what counts as undue suffering, pain, and misery is tied to one's religious obligations and identities. Such obligations help determine precisely whose suffering counts and for what. Thus, Capitein could consistently support slavery and continue as a good Christian ministering to the natives. He could hope for a better tomorrow because of the globalizing effects of such companies as the Dutch West Indian Company and the slave trade, which brought the unlettered in Latin and unChristian into the world of civility, albeit painfully. Hope, like Christian faith, is what postcolonial theory appeals to as a bulwark against pessimism. Such hope and faith are completely empty of content, since nothing that is being hoped for is structually different from what already exists. Capitein performed his role as mediator between Euro-Americans and the posttribal world admirably, lamenting the misery of the enslaved, having faith or hope in a better future, but having no way to fundamentally condemn the world that made that misery.

Parker and Aijaz Ahmad share an interesting insight about the reasoning strategy of postcolonial theory. They demonstrate that "theoretical eclecticism runs increasingly out of control"[5] in several ways: theories understood as offering a system or grand unified account of knowledge are rejected because they propose a finality (i.e., an ultimate end to capitalism in particular); grand unified accounts rely on collective agents and identities to explain, particularly, class and nation, when all such collectives are oppressive and all such identities falsely require or promote some notion of authenticity or origin. Yet, postcoloniality reintroduces collectives of class, race, nation, and gender as somehow collectives suffering from harm. Phenomena rejected for purposes of explanation are ironically accepted as recipients of concern. That is, "classes" are not treated as causal agents, but they are treated as groups suffering from a misery. These authors have done well to point out an explanatory incongruity of postcolonial theory – the use of social entities as impotent agents except in relation to fairly mundane expressions of sympathy and empathy.

I wish to point to how, if Parker and Ahmad are right, a postcolonial theory cannot make the misery suffered by starving immigrant workers, battered women, or enslaved children warrant concern more than the misery suffered by a multimillionaire exploiter of migrant workers who stubs his toe, the loneliness of rich lesbians, or the fear of bankruptcy by rich stockbrokers. There is nothing about any one of these categories that should require our commitment to the liberation of its members. The liberation of these categories and their members has no bearing on the benefit of any other category. Starving immigrant workers, for example, certainly want liberation from their misery; but their liberation cannot be taken as substantively capable of causing any other benefit. Postcolonial theory, in other words, rejects the idea of social entities as causal agents and it rejects the idea of social entities as peopled by a common subject. Thus, the liberation of women, for example, cannot mean any more than the liberation of the working class, lonely lesbians, or fearful rich stockbrokers. Mundane appeals to "humanity" will in no way explain why anyone should expect greater or less benefit from the relief of one misery over the other. It might be objected, however, that although Capitein, and authors employing postcolonial theory, consider social entities such as workers, women, nations, and classes as impotent causal agents, there are important differences between them.

Unlike Capitein, authors employing postcolonial theory disavow a totalizing narrative such as Christianity and deny envisioning the world as monocultural. However, these are not differences that matter. The world, for the postcolonialist, is already monocultural in the sense that it is an abiding tenet of postcolonial theory that we live in a postnationalist world of common cultural currencies. Consequently, by default, a totalized narrative already rules. To be against any new totalizing narrative is quite different from fighting against the one that already rules. One way to see this is by considering the contemporary status of religion.

The most important cultural movements in postcolonial nations are movements of religion. Never before has the world been so dominated by so few religions. There are no belief systems and associated social practices gaining more adherence than the religions of Christianity, Islam, Buddhism, and Hinduism. Capitein's desire is, to some degree, successful by default. That is, Christianity as a dominant force is undeniable. Yet, none of the authors associated with postcolonial theory supports an organization that advocates the absolute destruction of religion. To be against any new totalizing narrative could not warrant the same sort of radical organization required to seriously confront the existing totalizing narratives. Thus, any attack on the first is qualitatively different from an attack on the latter. There are other reasons besides Capitein's similarity to postcolonial theory, however, for why Capitein is the quintessential postcolonial author.

Of particular importance to my argument is that J.E. Capitein had no way of explaining global reality in a way that would allow him to find the world of Christian Europe irredeemable, or at least sufficiently wretched to warrant enslavement as a *modus vivendi* for eventual liberation. He could certainly describe his social condition using a multiplicity of variables: for example, the sinful character of the human spirit or the struggle to achieve grace occurring too often through dedication to earthly items of worship. He had no way, however, of providing a system of variables (of the sort used by banks, Marxists, consulting firms to major political parties, or tea manufacturers). Capitein could explain the world in structuralist or poststructuralist terms. Sobriety and reason or frugality and wealth, for example, could be used by Capitein to explain why the Dutch West Indian Company was more successful than other companies or why slavery was a conduit for bringing heathens into civility. Even if Capitein rejected the idea of "explaining" in favor of a postmodernist concept of depicting reality, the success of the West Indian Company would still be pictured as a reality which did not allow us to predict any alternative future.[6] His "post" world was, *ipso facto*, the end of all worlds.

Capitein was a voluntary intellectual eunuch. A genuine eunuch is incapable of creating progeny and is a member of a group that is generally despised. Eunuchs cannot create, control, or shape future generations. They cannot ascend above the trait that makes them generally despised – artificially delimbed and alienated from affiliate relations. Eunuchs, as a collective group, are without the ability to provide an ideology that future generations would want to immolate or revere.[7] There is no way to assure the transfer of assets, wealth, and authority across well-defined generations. They are a category that does not have, as a function of what eunuchs are, redeeming qualities. Eunuchs, as individuals and as a category, cannot receive the exalted regard of honor.

Honor is a good that is necessarily attributed to a representative of a kind; and simultaneously, it allows the honored to ascend above their kind. Courage, for example, is a good that a Zimbabwean soldier can have as a Zimbawbean, but the soldier has the good as a function of traits shared by all courageous persons. Honor is a good that can be held just in case one is a member of a group that is susceptible to honor.[8] Consequently, eunuchs cannot receive genuine honor because they cannot embody inviable virtues as eunuchs and they cannot escape, or be seen as something other than a eunuch. Although, for example, poems were written to praise Capitein's renown, he could never be honored. That is, he was prestigious but never revered. A voluntary eunuch, especially an intellectual eunuch, has the same limitations in relation to his or her ideas and lifestyles as a genuine eunuch.

Capitein is historically noteworthy solely because he represents a racial type encrusted in an intellectually respected cloak – a rare European-educated

African – a DeFoe's Friday who writes well. Capitein could proclaim in unison with Gayatri Spivak:

> When Benita Parry takes us – and by this I mean Homi Bhabba, Abdul JanMohamed, Gayatri Spivak – to task for not being able to listen to the natives or to let the native speak, she forgets that we [Capitein included] are natives too. We talk like Defoe's Friday, only much better.[9]

Capitein talks like Spivak, etc. He is concerned with the poetics of beauty and incongruity. He sees himself as beyond a representative of an origin, race, or authentic type. He too spoke better than DeFoe's Friday. He never saw himself as representing any social collective, other than the one he inherited. He was African by heritage, a heritage he did not choose; but he was happily Christian. He was never a patriarch of any African tribe or nation, never an intentional representative of any class, or a defender of any civilization other than the one he understood as Christian.

Capitein was a model of what missionaries might accomplish and, consequently, he could only be a subject – someone to be written on – or at best an agent of critique. Capitein was like a dissenting colonizer. He could never propose modes of thinking or acting that would destroy any social entity that stood in opposition to the only social entity he gave ontological status – the European Christian community.

One way to see why the subject of the postcolonial discourse (i.e., the authors of the discourse and the postcolonial culture of which the discourse is about), is incapable of being honored is to ask the following: In defense of what, and in pursuit of what, is it reasonable to imagine Capitein as ruthless? Why does "being ruthless" seem antithetical to the being of Capitein? Ruthlessness is something Capitein could be if defending Christianity, or, with a stretch of the imagination, if acting as a missionary. He could not be ruthless in pursuit of his own freedom because then he would have to kill other Christians, destroy their ill-gotten property, and make use of weapons of war. Capitein would have to act in opposition to the social realities that give him meaning: that is, Christianity and modeling what an otherwise heathen can become – de-racial, ethnic, national, and "de" any other trait threatening to Christianity as Dutch. It would be out of character for Capitein to be ruthless toward any European-based Christian community.

Analogously, postcolonial discourse can discuss the oppressive character of autocratic regimes in former colonies, but it cannot proffer an explanation, depiction, or prediction that recommends ruthlessness toward former colonizers. The social entities that give postcolonial discourse meaning – the imperialism of England, France, Germany, etc. – cannot be the object of justifiable ruthlessness, destruction, and death. They are the "post" world which the "pre" world of former colonies is destined to become identical with, or subservient to, save trivial differences of culture. That is, the "pre" world's only future is for its members to produce, distribute, value, and worship in the same fundamental ways as the "post" world. The route to the "post" world is either a school such as slavery leading to the "post" world or an unfortunate state of autocratic barbarism awaiting enlightenment. The very meaning of "postcolonial" is that nations in that position are no longer in the condition most definitive of colonialism: that is parasitism. Why things happen is explained by what caused "post" conditions, and those causes have reached their teleology. The lack of agency of classes, nations, races, ethnic groups, etc. leaves no reason to believe that any future world would differ from the present. To recommend ruthlessness toward former colonizers would be, for an author of postcolonial theory, as out of character as Capitein recommending or killing a Christian slave master, rapist, or thief.

There are no cases of someone having honor, – that is, having exalted regard and deference, and being understood as the possessor of enviable virtues such as courage, temperance, or sagacity – without that regard being a condition of "representing." No slave, eunuch, serf, or peasant was ever honored as slave, eunuch, serf, or peasant. When members of such groups attained honorable regard it necessarily had to be a function of behavior or attributes which made them exemplary as "above" their lowly station: that is, "post." In this "post" world, no group, according to postcolonial theory, is an agent capable of bringing into existence human liberation, no group embodies especially laudable character traits, all future social structures are already present, and we are to hope for a better future on the field of existing normality – a normality that allows totalizing visions such as Christian visions to flourish. Since there is nothing about social categories in the postcolonial theory that gives us reason to believe that there will be a radically different future, we are free to be like Capitein: an intellectual eunuch made so because his ideas could not help create a different future than the one that made him despised.

Notes

1 Hans Werner Debrunner, *Presence and Prestige: Africans in Europe* (Basler Afrika Bibliographien, Basel, 1979), pp. 80–1. Also see Sander L. Gilman, *On Blackness without Blacks* (G.K. Hall and Co., Boston, MA, 1982).
2 Kwame A. Appiah, *In My Father's House* (Oxford University Press, New York, 1992), p. 149.
3 Kenneth Parker, "Very like a whale: post-colonialism between canonicities and ethnicities," *Social Identities*, vol. 1, no. 1, 1995, p. 167.
4 Appiah, *In My Father's House*, p. 155.
5 Aijaz Ahmad, *In Theory* (Verso, New York, 1992), p. 200.
6 For an explication of explanation, as a causal account, and a depiction, unfolding,

or script as social science, see Pauline M. Rosenau, *Post-Modernism and the Social Sciences* (Princeton University Press, Princeton, NJ, 1992).

7   I argued elsewhere that categories such as class, race, and nation can function as agents of liberation if they possess arguably redeeming qualities: "Historical subjects and interests: race, class, and conflict," *The Year Left* (Verso, New York 1986), pp. 91–106.

8   I argue for this conception of honor in "Honor: empowerment and emasculation," in Larry May and Robert A. Strinkwerda (eds), *Thinking Masculinity* (Rowman and Littlefield, New York, 1992), pp. 191–208. Also see Orlando Patterson, *Slavery and Social Death* (Harvard University Press, Cambridge, MA, 1982).

9   M. Koundoura, "Naming Gayatri Spivak," *Stanford Humanities Review*, Spring, pp. 91–2.

12

Postphilosophy, Politics, and "Race"

John Pittman

I will juxtapose Richard Rorty's postphilosophic thought and practice to that of Cornel West, who is best known as the most prominent contemporary African-American philosopher, and is a writer in keeping with a conception of postphilosophy as a kind of cultural criticism. Both Rorty and West have pursued careers at variance, to different degrees and in different ways, with the traditional professional philosophical model. Rorty, after a career in the mold of the academic philosopher, has recently become more visible to a broader public than is normal for professionals of that mold. Though West had an academic philosophical training, and has occupied teaching and research positions in the academy since leaving graduate school, he has not taught in traditional philosophy departments. I will contrast some of the formulations concerning the vocation of a postphilosophy put forward by these two widely influential writers, and bring out the connections between these formulations and the politics of "race."

Rorty's "standing" as a postphilosopher and a brief account of what that means can be gleaned from his comments at a conference on "The Politics of Liberal Education" cosponsored by Duke University and UNC Chapel Hill in 1988, where he spoke of *Veiw of Rorty:*

the philosophical theses which Foucault and Derrida took over from Nietzsche: truth is a matter of useful tools rather than of accurate representation, the self is a nexus of relations rather than a substance, truth and power will always be inextricably interlocked, there is no point in trying for grand totalizing theories of history ("scientific socialism," for example), there is no such thing as "rationality" other than that contextually defined by the practices of a group, etc.

These theses are common to Nietzsche and Dewey, and as a Deweyan I am naturally happy to see them becoming entrenched.[1]

I want to take this list of five "philosophical theses" as providing a rough and ready initial account of what "postmodern" theorizing involves. And although Rorty in this context does not identify himself as a "postmodernist" but rather as a Deweyan, he has, in other contexts, and at other times, been content to affix the postmodernist label to his own views.[2]

Cornel West studied with Rorty as a graduate student at Princeton, and has, by his own admission, been deeply influenced by Rorty's work. In a brief autobiographical preface to the published version of his Princeton dissertation, West writes of his "eye-opening and horizon-broadening encounter" with Rorty, a "major influence" on his thought, whose "historicist turn was like music to my ears," as he puts it.[3] The evaluation and critical accounting of Rorty's work has been a continual theme in West's philosophical writing: though enthusiastic, West has not been uncritical of Rorty's neopragmatism, as we shall see. There are striking similarities in approach as well as deep differences in outlook.

At the same time, West has taken stock of and incorporated some of the same "postmodernist" themes that Rorty has been writing about. In a recent article on the "cultural politics of difference," West lists four "major historicist forms of theoretical activity" that provide resources for "black cultural workers":

> Heideggerian *destruction* of the Western metaphysical tradition, Derridean *deconstruction* of the Western philosophical tradition, Rortian *demythologization* of the Western intellectual tradition and Marxist, Foucaultian, feminist, antiracist or antihomophobic *demystification* of Western cultural and artistic conventions.[4]

Most significantly, West seems to embody in his own activity the idea – proclaimed by Rorty and displayed as well by those contemporary Continental thinkers who are generally taken as paradigmatic "postmodernists" (Derrida, Foucault, and Lyotard) –– of the irrelevance of traditional disciplinary boundaries, and specifically of the self-proclaimed foundational and legitimizing significance of academic philosophical activity.

There are several axes on which the contrast I want to make between Rorty and West can be drawn most sharply and, I think, most revealingly. These are the axes of their existential standpoint, their theoretical conceptions of the reality of the social, and their political views of the historical moment and of what is to be done.

5. Authors have different Existential Standpoints
- Shown in 4 ways
6. Race plays a role in perception - World of Humanities & African Studies

262   *John Pittman*

1

By "existential standpoint" I want to identify something involving a style, a manner of writing and of positioning oneself in relation to a readership and discipline/institution, as well as a more properly theoretical conception of the relation of self to the world. Here the contrast between Rorty and West can be drawn in a number of different ways. West has prefaced each of his major published books by situating the text he has produced in a brief account of his project and a personal narrative reprising how he has arrived at this point. The narrative is fixed through a scheme of sociological and historical terms to a vocabulary of political intent. Rorty's works typically are not given such a self-consciously personal-political provenance; to the extent that he provides any account of origins, it takes the more standard form of retracing the evolution of inquiry culminating in the current presentation of ideas. This difference might be – partly – characterized as that between a more traditionally detached academic voice and a more personally engaged political one. But this difference in voice is compounded with another, closely related one: Rorty has most often addressed a more philosophically refined audience, in a disciplinary sense, while West has written for laypersons as well as practitioners of the speculative arts. Both have readerships and institutional orientations beyond the strictly professional-philosophical: both have written for law journals, newspapers, and political magazines, as well as for professional journals. Rorty worked up to this ecumenicism from a traditional beginning as disciplinary sectarian; West neither sought nor gained the hard-core disciplinary credentials, pursuing more global ambitions from the start.

Those ambitions were never purely personal ones. For West, the personal is political in a way that it could not be for Rorty, who would also endorse the substance of that slogan: it's the difference between black and white. West has always identified himself as black, or, as he puts it now, a "New World African;"[5] Rorty has never identified himself racially, but only ideologically. That difference is a political one, surely, but it is also as surely a deeply personal one. It is a difference the possibility of which is inscribed in the American grain. It is a difference that plays in ramified ways: West's opinion pieces will be taken as those of a race-representative, almost in the nature of the case. It is almost impossible for Rorty's to be taken in that way. That is not something he has to think about. For West it must be a problem, or at least an issue, and has been raised as such by at least one black critic.[6] This difference has its institutional side, of course: while Rorty sits in a Chair of Humanities, West always has one foot in African-American Studies. This is not simply a matter of choice on West's part, for other distinguished black academics are in the same position.

These differing aspects of the "existential standpoints" of Rorty and West are not merely situational, objective givens, socially defined. They are shaded by theoretical reflection in different ways by these two thinkers, given coloration in different conceptual tones. Rorty's project is invested with an attitude of irony; West's begins with the experience of dread, despair, and the absurd. And for each of them, these positionings are responses to contingency, although in one case the contingency has more of a theorized, poetic import; for the other it has a lived, historical one.

In his second book, *Contingency, Irony, and Solidarity*,[7] Rorty develops his conception of "postmetaphysical culture" and of the tasks of philosophers in it. Rorty describes the postphilosophical philosopher as an ironist intellectual who continues to affirm particular values and beliefs even though recognizing that there is no justification of those beliefs, which are merely the contingent products of the socialization processes which constitute her as accepting those values and holding those beliefs. (Interestingly, Rorty consistently pronominalizes his ironist protagonist as "she," whereas her old-style metaphysical nemesis is consistently rendered as "he.") Rorty generally refuses to characterize the situation in terms of values and beliefs, preferring to "redescribe" the difference as one between the "final vocabularies" these two opponents employ. He defines an ironist as one who "has radical and continuing doubts about the final vocabulary she currently uses because she has been impressed by other vocabularies," rejects the idea that her vocabulary is "closer to reality" than others', and has given up the possibility of resolving her doubts because she recognizes that she has "no noncircular argumentative recourse" that would make such resolution possible.[8] *Thoughts of Ironist ↑*

The ironist is the person who insistently poses the question – "How can I continue to be the person I am, accepting the beliefs I do and caring about the things I do, in the face of the contingency of selfhood, thinking that what I am is simply the consequence of contingencies of birth and socialization?" As Rorty puts it, "The ironist spends her time worrying about the possibility that she has been initiated into the wrong tribe, taught to play the wrong language game," and has thus been socialized "into the wrong kind of human being. But she cannot give a criterion of wrongness."[9] This private dilemma would become generalized in "an ideally liberal polity;" indeed, Rorty wants "to suggest the possibility of a liberal utopia: one in which ironism, in the relevant sense, is universal." He goes on to add that "[a] postmetaphysical culture [that is, an ironist one] seems to me no more impossible than a postreligious one, and equally desirable."[10]

An ironist is, from this account, clearly entangled in high-literate forms of anxiety: such a being might be described as suffering from a chronic philosophical twitch-reaction to contingency. Of course, she is reacting not to contingency as such, but to a particular high-literate description of contingency. Though Rorty here plays at describing ironism as the practice of a particular (peculiar?) sort of intellectual, he is in fact *prescribing* a mode of conduct for postphilosophers. Ironism is the cure, metaphysics the malady. Since meta-

9. W/Ho recognition of future events which are possible but no/few certainty?
10. Doesn't provide answer. Recognizes other possible events, but does not care about the answer?
264   *John Pittman*

physics is a sort of denial of contingency (in the Freudian sense as well), ironism is the condition born of the recognition of it (or shall we say obsession with it?): or so Rorty would have it. But surely that is to make of contingency an extralinguistic fact, which, on his own view, would be a most unironic thing to do. It must for the ironist be a linguistic construction, a figment of a vocabulary. This is not just to say that what ironism cures is a cultural affliction, or that the culture in question is distinctly ivy-league. This affliction is not taken by the ironist as a "real" problem; nor is the cure a "real" solution, in the sense that ironism "leaves everything as it is."[11]

If the situation of the ironist is grounded in the carpet of the seminar room, the postphilosophical scene for West's protagonist is out on the street. This scene is extralinguistic, at least in the following sense: it derives its dimensions from experiences that challenge or subvert the possibility of description, that define the limit of a vocabulary. That is what makes it existential. In the introduction to his book on Marxism, West, in explaining why he is not a Marxist, writes that he

> stress[es] the concrete lived experience of despair and tragedy and the cultural equipment requisite for coping with the absurdities, anxieties, and frustrations, as well as the joys, laughter, and gaiety of life . . . Marxist thought does not purport to be existential wisdom – of how to live one's life day by day.[12]

Such existential wisdom is far from the concerns of the ironist, if only because its application with respect to despair and absurdity is not to redescribe but to cope with them. And coping with them is a necessity only because they are intransigent, "real" problems – problems that will not go away. They are problems that are felt, can only be felt, and that is an immediacy insusceptible to the cool distancing of ironism. The reality of these problems is that they are not susceptible to dissolution by redescription. Their contingency is brute, historical, and not merely linguistic. It may help here to cite West's characterization of why "existential issues . . . have always been fundamental" for him:

> It's a reflection of being a New World African and having to deal with the absurd: both the absurd in America and America as absurd. There was a need to come up with ways of imposing some kind of sense on the chaos coming at one, the chaos of a certain kind of white supremacist ideology, with its assault on black beauty and black intelligence . . . . It is part of the response to being perceived as sub-human in a particular historical epoch, the age of Europe.[13]

It is not the absurd in general or as such that West acknowledges by beginning with existential issues, but the absurd of race as a construct of what he calls "white supremacist ideology." The absurd of race is the absurd in America: while the ideology of race may have its roots in Europe, and be global in scope consequent to the global hegemony of Europe, that ideology has perhaps its

11. Referring back to point 6. Rorty view cannot (ironism) cannot be applied to West. b/c the language that is used amongst African-American cannot be used in a global context b/c the experience is only from black people.

Postphilosophy, Politics, and "Race" 265

Key differences between R & W

most insidious branch in the intestines of the "American empire." But the *experience* of race, the experience of the absurdity of race, is granted only to those who must confront it from the inside out, so to speak, those who have "the strange experience of being a problem – that is, being an American of African descent."[14] This experience is, as West puts it, specific to a particular historical epoch and, in the first place, to a particular group of people – black folk, as Du Bois put it. This should suggest how deeply the African-American tradition has been shaped by the concern with this experience as an existential issue. This is, in part at least, a source of the difference between Rorty's and West's responses to contingency, and the significance of that difference is thus a racialized one, deriving from the cultural construction of race. That cultural construction is a peculiar sort of contingency, with a logic all its own, eliciting not only a peculiar sort of experience in the racialized Other, but also a peculiar sort of silence from the ironist.

It might be objected that this passage is but a redescription of the context in which West as New World African had the experience of despair and absurdity. That is fair: it is a redescription that invokes race and history/white supremacy. But the objection also misses the point: it is a redescription indicating why it is unlikely that ironism could be an option for "New World Africans" who of necessity (albeit "contingent necessity") must cope "day by day" with the absurd in/of white supremacist America. And if I cannot say that this redescription corresponds better to reality, I do want to suggest that it is closer to the street. While the ironist spends a lot of time posing to herself the problem of "the possibility she has been initiated into the wrong tribe," socialized into the wrong kind of human being, for some of us the problem America poses is of being born into the wrong color of skin.[15] Now this problem *might* be redescribed by saying that a whole bunch of people – those in the white supremacist mainstream – have been socialized into the wrong kind of human being. But that, again, though probably fair, would be missing the point: for what is at issue here is not those people at all, but *our* experience, and the ways we have devised for describing *and* coping with it. We are consumed not with the contingency of self *as a theoretical problem* in the (inverted) form of metaphysics, West seems to be saying, but with the contingency of black skin *as a day-by-day practical problem* in the (institutional) form of American white supremacist ideology and practice. That is a problem, if there is any, requiring "existential wisdom" rather than ironist redescription. Who would say that the pursuit of such wisdom should not be called philosophy?

2

If one difference between Rorty and West is that between the assumption of irony and the confrontation with absurdity, this difference is not only that between the secular and the prophetic, the self-doubting and the faithful. There is a further difference between two ways of understanding the significance of the social. I will call these the libertarian and the socialist. These labels serve, of course, to mark a political divergence, and suggest something of the character of that political parting of ways. But these are also philosophical differences in an old, folk-philosophical sense. They are differing estimates of the reality and effectivity of the social. This is a difference not only in the conception of the social as such, but in the answer to the broader question of how sociohistorically dense – and in what way – must a vocabulary or set of narrative possibilities be? And between Rorty and West this question is most clearly posed in their differing descriptions of the decisive "historicist" turn in philosophy.

Rorty describes the controversy between traditional "metaphysical" philosophers and what he elsewhere calls the "post-Nietzschean" philosophers as one between different "final vocabularies," issuing in fundamentally different descriptions and self-descriptions. Rorty, in so redescribing the issue, advocates a new "paradigm" of what-was-philosophic-but-now-by-redescription-becomes-post-philosophic practice. He writes:

> I think of Hegel's *Phenomenology* both as the beginning of the end of the Plato–Kant tradition and as a paradigm of the ironist's ability to exploit the possibilities of massive redescription. In this view, Hegel's so-called dialectical method is not an argumentative procedure or a way of unifying the subject and object, but simply a literary skill . . . what Hegel actually did, by founding an ironist tradition within philosophy, was help de-cognitivize, de-metaphysize philosophy. He helped turn it into a literary genre.[16]

Rorty's redescription is, for all that, another description of the development of the "Western philosophical tradition." He calls it the Plato–Kant tradition because of how, on Rorty's redescription, the next man up to the plate changed the rules of the game. But Rorty still takes as the central players of that tradition the usual list of characters – Plato, Aristotle, Descartes, Locke, Kant. His account is, on the whole, fully in keeping with the expectations of the profession in this sense: the cast of characters is more or less the same, and the motions they are put through are familiar, almost predictable. The moral of the story, however, is different: the tradition's conception of philosophy is pointless and futile, it has exhausted its intellectual resources, and so philosophers should stop doing what they have been doing and do something else. But what is to be done?

Here Rorty returns us to the notion of ironism – specifically, the philosophical ironism of which his two paradigm cases are Nietzsche and Heidegger. Paradigms though they be, Rorty's redescription of the tradition includes a description of the insufficient cleanliness of these two thinkers: they were still too much philosophers (or, perhaps, Philosophers),[17] still tainted by metaphysics. For this reason, Rorty plays Nietzsche and Heidegger off against his model of the perfectly accomplished ironist, drawn from among the poets – Marcel Proust. Rorty produces a narrative of Proust's self-making as paradigm of ironist activity: ironism is no longer conceived as philosophical in the old way, it becomes a literary strategy for the achievement of personal autonomy through poetic self-overcoming. But the ironist's activities extend beyond self-perfection to a kind of liberal cultural criticism aimed at strengthening the bonds of solidarity. For a liberal ironist, solidarity is strengthened by inculcating in others and strengthening in ourselves "the ability to see more and more traditional differences (of tribe, religion, race, customs, and the like) as unimportant when compared with similarities with respect to pain and humiliation – the ability to think of people wildly different from ourselves as included in the range of 'us'."[18] This also is a literary activity, for Rorty, where literary is to be contrasted with theoretical: the force of his use of "redescription" is to deny "postphilosophical criticism" the conceptual tools – the vocabulary – of social analysis, and so, it could be argued, of any real critical teeth. This is for two related reasons: first, the model of poetic self-transformation, based as it is on the high Romantic image of the individual artist as cultural hero, conforms to what I have called a libertarian, or minimalist account of the significance of the social in the constitution of the individual; second, Rorty's postempiricist nominalism and skepticism regarding social-scientific explanations aggravate a predeliction for simplistic, almost mythic narratives that lack even a toehold for what could be called, borrowing from Bernard Williams, socially thick concepts.

The contrast with West's account of the decisive philosophical turn could not be sharper. West has always been concerned to contextualize philosophical discourses by situating them within broader historicist narratives. West first formulates his version of "radical historicism" in his dissertation, a study of the ethical dimensions of the thought of Marx and selected philosophical writers in the Marxist tradition. Significantly, West argues that the Marxist theorists he examines – Engels, Kautsky, and Lukács – all overlook a decisive feature of Marx's thought. Marx, West claims, became a radical historicist as a result of a crucial "metaphilosophical move":

> he becomes a radical historicist in ethics primarily because of his disillusionment and disenchantment with the conception of philosophy as the quest for certainty and search for foundations. His disillusionment and disenchantment is prompted by his acknowledgment of the importance of historical consciousness as found in Hegel's philosophy and by the significance of dynamic social practices and human activities as revealed by his political activism. The historical consciousness and the political activism finally lead Marx to reject the foundationalist conception of philosophy.[19]

This crucial step in Marx's thinking allowed him to give up, in good conscience, such "*philosophic* notions as status, validity, objectivity" in favor of "*theoretic*

notions such as role, function, description, and explanation." For the radical
historicist such as Marx, "the distinction between moral philosopher and social
critic breaks down." The historicist, by clearly distinguishing between
justification and explanation, and giving up the prospect of an ahistorical or
otherworldly justification of ethical principles, is able to focus on doing what
theoretical tools can do – providing analyses and explanations of the
"emergence, dominance and decline of particular moral principles under
specific social conditions in the historical process." These are the theoretical
tasks of the moral philosopher turned radical historicist social critic. Since
critical theory cannot "serve as the last court of appeal . . . stand[ing] above the
contingent and variable world of fleeting morals," the theorist can only remind
herself and others, in the way of justification, "which particular community or
set of we-intentions" she identifies with.[20]

What is interesting about West's characterization of Marx as a radical
historicist is the role that political activism is made to play in West's narrative.
It is one of the causes of Marx's abandonment of the traditional conception of
philosophy's vocation as ahistorical court of appeal: as a political activist, Marx
came to appreciate the significance of social practices. This account is not
particularly helpful as an explanation of Marx's intellectual development,
especially since those Marx is being contrasted with, such as Engels, were
significant political activists in their own right. The remark is, however,
revealing in considering the differences between Rorty and West himself.

West has always been an activist. In the "critical inventory" of himself and
his "communities of struggle"[21] that West supplies in the published version of
his dissertation, he describes his activism and involvement in, among other
things, the Black Student Organization at Harvard and the takeover of the
president's office protesting Harvard's investments in apartheid. West's
activism was, as he describes in detail, all along in dialogue with Marxism,
whether expressed in the views of the Black Panthers, or in those of the
Trotskyists he met at Harvard. West's activism, and his continuing dialogue
with Marxism, are not for my purposes merely personal peculiarities, but must
be seen as closely connected to his standing as both postphilosopher *and*
African-American philosophical practitioner. West regards himself as a
"philosophically trained Christian," and just as a matter of philosophical
credentials, this is perhaps as close as one can get to a paradigm characterization
for a contributor to the African-American philosophical tradition. Mark the
examples of Alexander Crummell and Martin Luther King, Jr – not to mention
Frederick Douglass, who was a lay preacher before becoming an abolitionist
orator. This gets to the centrality not only of religious thought and rhetoric,
but also of activism and more generally social struggle in the tradition of
African-American (what is at least) social analysis and culture criticism. Let me
come back to this further on.

Returning to West's description of the historicist turn in philosophy, there

12 "she" referring to ironism
13

are broad parallels here to Rorty's narratives of the decline and disenchantment of the traditional philosophical vocation. It is the abandonment of a particular epistemologically oriented conception of philosophy as foundational and concerned with ahistorical justification of knowledge-claims that leads to a radical historicizing of the demands on philosophical theory. This, coupled with an identification of *philosophic* criteria as rooted in an ahistoric or transcendental notion of rationality or objectivity, leads to a rejection of philosophic activity as such. As West puts it, "Marx's radical historicist metaphilosophical vision enables him to stop doing philosophy," while Marxist theorists from Engels to Lukács fail because they "ultimately remain philosophers," trapped by a foundationalist view of philosophy.[22] West's radical historicist, on the model of Marx he constructs, shares two crucial features with Rorty's postphilosophical critic. She can appeal only to contingently shared "we-intentions" in justifying the moral principles and community solidarities her theoretical activity serves; because of this, she is able to stop doing philosophy. West's account differs from Rorty's in two important ways.

Emblematic of the first difference is that, while the pivot of Rorty's narrative is Hegel, West's story turns primarily about Karl Marx. The difference is in the way they treat the relation of philosophical practice to practices of power and its contestation, political practices. The difference is significant beyond their accounts of the hegemonic philosophical tradition; it is, obviously, a political as well as a theoretical difference. In a small way, the difference is symbolized by their attitude toward Marx. Rorty has become less and less sympathetic to Marx as his work has developed. While in *Philosophy and the Mirror of Nature* Marx received honorable mention along with Freud as "edifying philosophers,"[23] in *Contingency, Irony, and Solidarity* and more recently, the attitude toward Marx is cooler: Marxism has become primarily a moral stain on the twentieth century, an example of a metanarrative gone bad in a big way (recall the reference to "scientific socialism" in "Two cheers for the cultural left"). In a recent interview, Rorty is dismissive of Marx, admits to not having read him, and characterizes him as "third rate."[24] West, on the other hand, has been engaged with Marx and Marxism on a theoretical level all along. He wrote his doctoral dissertation on "ethical dimensions of Marxist thought" (admitting in the preface that his "interpretation of Marxist thought is influenced by the works of John Dewey, the early Sidney Hook, and Richard Rorty").[25] West's first book, in which he sets out to "launch the prospect of an Afro-American religious philosophy with a deep sense of political and cultural engagement," makes the case for a fusion of prophetic Afro-American Christianity and what he calls "progressive Marxism."[26]

13 What Marx represents in terms of the difference between Rorty and West is not only political activism and a particular attitude toward philosophy, but also a project of social analysis and critique. One of the things Marx attempted was to take a nineteenth-century German philosophical-literary genre, critique,

and turn it to practical use as a source of social-analytic categories and explanatory models. His working-up of the concepts of labor, capital, and class into an account of the dynamics of capitalist development is surely postphilosophical in relation to the Plato–Kant (or even the Plato–Heidegger) conception of the hegemonic philosophical mainstream, and has, until recently, been treated as such – that is, as "non-philosophical" – by the professionalized philosophic academy. Yet Marx's work does involve a dense articulation of many standard philosophic concepts – from "abstraction" to "world history" – in a project of social explanation that is historicist in just the sense West draws attention to. This last might be said of Hegel as well, but if we conceive of West as the Marx to Rorty's Hegel, it is because the practical-political intent of their practices – Marx's and Hegel's, I mean – would be decisive for the appropriateness of that parallel.

That brings me to a second difference between the Rorty and West accounts of the philosophical traditions. Rorty's account, while self-consciously redescriptive, leaves just as it was the mode of high-cultural practice as interpretive, turning only its literary-therapeutic form. West's account of the tradition, consciously social-analytic, makes possible a turn from high-cultural interpretation to transformative practice. In the case of Rorty, simply recall his list of postmodernist theses, cited at the beginning, especially the thesis that "there is no point in trying for grand totalizing theories of history." Rorty there takes pains to parenthetically mention the example of Marxist theory, using a description not of Marx's own making. Now Rorty does not himself avoid historical narratives, as we shall see in the next section; he is only ironic about them, treating them, as it were, with a grain of skeptical salt. His skepticism extends from "grand totalizing theory" to pretty much any theory at all: his narratives all have a literary, rather than an explanatory, intent. West's radical historicist is, by contrast, a full-fledged theorist. In commenting on Marx's eleventh thesis on Feuerbach, West writes:

> Marx's radical historicist viewpoint assumes that the heightened awareness of the limitations of traditional philosophy will soon render that philosophy barren . . . In its place will thrive a theory of history and society, able to account for its own appearance and status, aware of the paradoxes it cannot solve, grounded in ever changing personal needs and social interests, and beckoning for action in order to overcome certain conditions and realize new conditions . . . [T]he radical historicist viewpoint . . . is a recognition of a much-needed transformation of philosophy . . . For the philosophically inclined radical historicist who, like Wittgenstein, shies away from theoretic activity, this means to first and foremost change the dominant conception of philosophy . . . For a highly theoretically inclined radical historicist, like Marx, this means to leave the confines of philosophic discourse and reform of philosophy and plunge eagerly into full-fledged theory construction.[27]

Notice that there are at least two options, and that the choice depends as much on the personal needs as on the social interests of the historicist in question. In each case, however, there is a transformation of philosophy afoot. This transformation is not to be confused with the abandonment of philosophy by what West calls the "theoretically inclined" radical historicist, who may nonetheless conceive of philosophy as a particular kind of discourse, with a current agenda as well as a history marked by discontinuities and revolutions.[28] So the radical historicist turn effected by Marx leads both to a transformed conception and practice of philosophy, and to a new kind of theoretical practice, which can be described as critical social inquiry or perhaps social-explanatory cultural criticism.

West is not a Marxist, but he is professedly a radical historicist, and, theoretically minded, he has left "the confines of philosophic discourse." But that, notice, is not a disqualification for a postphilosopher, but is one of the trajectories a postphilosophical radical historicist might take. West has also not – so far – done much "full-fledged theory construction," at least not on the scale of his model radical historicist, Marx. This may in part be the result of West's more skeptical – because more postmodern – attitude toward theory. But West's reservations are far from those of Rorty. In a 1994 interview, West imagines the following exchange between Rorty and himself:

> Now it's true that Rorty, for example, says: "Cornel, you claim to be antifoundational, but when it comes to social theory, you fail. You become foundationalist. You invoke Marx and Weber and Lukacs and Simmel and Du Bois. You've got foundationalist claims being made, causal explanatory claims being made." And I say: "No, not at all." For me, the choice is never between foundationalism and some kind of empty anti-foundationalism. Mine is a historicism that is contextualist and revisionist, in the sense of recognizing that any causal explanatory claim is open to revision. But these claims are indispensable weapons in any serious struggle for radical democracy and freedom.[29]

Here the political intent of West's postphilosophic practice is evident. It is also clear from this that the narratives he constructs are explanatory, and rely heavily on borrowings from social theorists who are outside the philosophical canon. In this sense, then, West should be seen as a socialist – a "methodological" socialist, perhaps – as opposed to what I've called Rorty's libertarianism. Rorty's redescriptivism, by "shying away from" social-theoretic concepts, turns ironist postphilosophical practice into a kind of atheoretic literary activity aimed at the individual's self-image and sentiments. West's thick-descriptivist use of theory turns the radical historicist postphilosopher into an engaged social and cultural critic.[30] How this difference reappears in their views about the historic moment and what is to be done, we shall examine in the next section.

I mentioned, in discussing West's activism, that it betokened two things.

First, it is in contrast with Rorty, who, though a participant in some politically charged controversies on the campuses and a sometimes left-leaning commentator on political events in the commercial press, has always had a more conventional academic comportment. Second, it is not atypical of the tradition of African-American social and cultural critics and intellectual liberation fighters. A question that has attracted some attention is whether that tradition should be conceived as "philosophical" or given some other characterization. It would seem as if the two conflicting reflexes – to characterize, say, Douglass, as a philosopher, on the one hand, or not to do so, but "hold the line" to the place assigned it by the tradition – would stem from competing conceptions of the point and career of philosophical practice. And one might expect postphilosophers to be critical, at least, of the tendency to hold the line against revisions in the traditional canon. There seems to be a difference in this regard, however, between our two postphilosophers: Rorty is skeptical of an inclusive approach to the philosophical canon, while West seems more willing, even anxious, to count in those who have, until now, been counted out.

In an interview conducted in April 1993, Rorty seems to reject the usefulness of including Asian or African philosophy in the philosophy curriculum. In doing so he says this about "philosophy":

> [W]hat we in the West call "philosophy" is something that has evolved in the context of quite specific conflicts, between the Greeks and the Christians, the Newtonians and the Catholics, and the like. The philosophical problematic of Europe is a function of particular European quarrels . . . philosophy is a parochial European phenomenon.[31]

Here we have a conflation of philosophy with European philosophy which rests on a less explicit conflation of "the West" with Europe. The suggestion is that only those doing "European philosophy" are doing philosophy at all. This suggestion is accompanied by a disclaimer: philosophy does not matter all that much, Rorty adds, so that "it's crazy . . . to think that changing the philosophical curriculum will have a political impact."[32]

Is Rorty thinking here exclusively of the Plato–Kant tradition? Is American philosophy merely an extension of European? These – admittedly off-the-cuff – remarks by the erstwhile self-described pragmatist, would seem, if taken at face value, to suggest the futility of an "African-American philosophical tradition." But in this case the conflation of "Western" with European does as much work as that of European philosophy with "what we in the West call 'philosophy'." And it is here, in the Western hemisphere, if anywhere, that the conflation of Western with European should seem most problematic.

Rorty seems to want to use that distanced standard of classical philosophical practice in order to both *dismiss* as useless and irrelevant contemporary instances of such practice *and exclude* non-standard critical-literary practices from qualifying as "philosophy." Perhaps this is a matter of being true to the dictum that philosophy "leaves everything as it is." If that is so, not even philosophy's self-image can change at philosophy's hands, and it would indeed be "crazy" to imagine that anything would come of changing the philosophy curriculum. But Rorty has himself already done much to show that the dictum is wrong. It is also true that Rorty is using "Western" to refer to a philosophical tradition formed in the context of European struggles and constituting a canon of white European "fathers." But as he would admit, that tradition is a story of old that has been told; Rorty himself seemed to be telling a different story, and one that involved crucially American characters and heroes such as James, Dewey, and Quine. Perhaps all this is not so strange, however.

"American philosophy has never taken the Afro-American experience seriously."[33] This, the first claim made in West's first book, remains true of most post-Rortyan redescriptions of the American tradition. When West came to write his own account of American philosophy, he included W.E.B. Du Bois, described as an "organic" "pragmatic intellectual,"[34] in part because of Du Bois's formal philosophical apprenticeship with William James. But West's overall characterization of the American pragmatic tradition involves both "the evasion of epistemology-centered philosophy" and also "a conception of philosophy as a form of cultural criticism in which the meaning of America is put forward by intellectuals in response to distinct social and cultural crises."[35] This account can easily contain the many African-American intellectuals who have engaged in social criticism in the service of the freedom of their people. It is also in keeping with Leonard Harris's recent suggestion that an African-American philosophical tradition would be as much an invention – or redescription – as any tradition is.[36]

3

How the problem of the sociohistorical density of descriptions gets resolved is immediately apparent in the most pertinent of all descriptions – where we are at now, and where we are heading. This involves specifying a locus or site of engagement, a unit of solidarity or circle of interlocutors, a historical moment or conjuncture, and a vision of what is to be done. These points of description come together for our two writers, in the form of a narrative. Such narratives are likely to lead quickly to political conclusions; they do in the cases we are considering.

Rorty is straightforwardly modernist in the narrative he prefers to tell, which mostly involves the provincial celebration of the achievements of the "lucky, rich, literate democracies."[37] This narrative is one of "moral progress" made possible by "the contingencies which brought about the development of the moral and political vocabularies typical of the secularized democratic societies of the West."[38] It is a "historical narrative about the rise of liberal institutions and customs – the institutions and customs which were designed to diminish cruelty, make possible government by the consent of the governed, and permit as much domination-free communication as possible."[39] It is not a metanarrative in Lyotard's sense, not a philosophical version of a suprahistorical ground of history, because it is conjoined to the ironist insistence that "it *just happened* that rule in Europe passed into the hands of people who pitied the humiliated and dreamed of human equality."[40] These people are the liberals whose moral claims Rorty affirms, and whose distinguishing characteristic, Rorty says, borrowing from Judith Shklar, is that they are "more afraid of being cruel than of anything else."[41] They see "parliamentary democracy and the welfare state as very good things," but only "on the basis of invidious comparisons with suggested concrete alternatives, not on the basis of claims that these institutions are truer to human nature, or more rational, or in better accord with the universal moral law, than feudalism or totalitarianism."[42] That is, Rorty is concerned with ironist liberals who accept that they "cannot look back behind the processes of socialization which convinced . . . [them] of the validity" of these claims about cruelty and liberal capitalism.[43]

Rorty does not hesitate to embrace the term "ethnocentrism" in redescribing the form of solidarity that ironist liberalism advocates and issues in. Central to this redescription is his insistence on the "contingency of community," which involves the claim that there are no overarching, universally shared (non-biological) attributes which could constitute an identity for "humanity." But it is ultimately an estimate of the pragmatic (in the common sense) political possibilities for solidarity that leads to Rorty's affirmation of limited forms of identification:

> *We* have to start from where *we* are – that is part of the force of Sellars' claim that we are under no obligations other than the "we-intentions" of the communities with which we identify. What takes the curse off this ethnocentrism is not that the largest such group is "humanity" or "all rational beings" – no one, I have been claiming, *can* make *that* identification – but, rather, that it is the ethnocentrism of a "we" ("we liberals") which is dedicated to enlarging itself, to creating an ever larger and more variegated *ethnos*. It is the "we" of the people who have been brought up to distrust ethnocentrism.[44]

Notice that it is under cover of "ironism" – the "distrust" of ethnocentrism – that a sort of pseudo-universalism is brought back into the picture of this postphilosophical culture criticism. (It is not only "our ethnocentrism" that "we" are suspicious of, but ethnocentrism as such!) This pseudo-universalism is served also by ironism's disciplinary transgressiveness: while standard philosophical discourse, with its concern for foundations and justification, plays no edifying role, the energies of literary accounts of the lives of others, accounts which bring us into imaginative identification with "them," help to widen the circle of our sympathies, allowing an enhancement of "the range of 'us'." As it has turned out (contingently, of course) it is precisely the creators and beneficiaries of the liberal institutions of the Western democracies who are most likely to have developed the capacities that make possible the enlarged solidarities Rorty advocates, and who speak in the vocabularies of liberalism and ironism as well. This, I am tempted to add, is the same old story, which, "contingently" or not, we have been hearing for a very long time.

Ethnocentrism leads to provincialism: this does not seem to bother Rorty, who thinks provincialism can be countered with solidarity, aided by the ennobling description of how others live, suffer, and experience pain. But in the American context, a celebration of ethnocentrism might be troubling indeed for anyone familiar with the history of American "race relations." American society has, throughout its history, been segregated (to say the least), and little that has happened since the sixties has changed that significantly. But a society in which segregation on racial lines is a fact of life will tend to breed ethnocentrisms of a particular racialized kind. These ethnocentrisms, it should be said, will not be restricted to the uneducated masses who are the targets of the liberal ironist's enlightening tracts, according to Rorty. Indeed, these very (white) liberal ironist's may find themselves part of a distinct, segregated public:

> [I]n the United States you have a racially bifurcated society, not simply due to the legacy of segregation, going back to slavery, but also due to the fact that different publics are often unacknowledged or uninterrogated by different intellectuals . . . The kind of nostalgia that Russell Jacoby has for the "New York intellectuals" concerns only a really miniscule sector of our society. *Partisan Review* was read by 3,500 people . . . Du Bois' *The Crisis* had 100,000 subscribers, more readers, but Russell Jacoby has no nostalgia for Du Bois' public intellectual activity, because it's not part of his world, unfortunately. That's the segregated life of the mind in our society.[45]

Yet Rorty never even raises this question, of how ethnocentrisms are to be enlightened if those doing the enlightening are ethnocentric themselves. This problem, a version of the problem of who will "educate the educator," might have been identified and discussed by Rorty had he begun with a narrative more richly reflective of the social structures and problems of liberal democracies.

Rorty passes over these issues in silence, and, indeed, "shies away" from any specifically American examples in his account of ethnocentrism, save one:

> Consider . . . the attitude of contemporary American liberals to the unending hopelessness and misery of the lives of the young blacks in American cities. Do we say that these people must be helped because they are our fellow human beings? We may, but it is much more persuasive, morally as well as politically, to describe them as our fellow *Americans* – to insist that it is outrageous that an *American* should live without hope. The point . . . is that our sense of solidarity

is strongest when those with whom solidarity is expressed are thought of as "one of us," where "us" means something smaller and more local than the human race.[46]

Rorty is honest in describing the process of thought necessary for coming to think of one of "these people" as "one of us." Yet he completely fails to note the fundamental condition making such thought necessary – the overwhelming role in the formation of American culture of the social construction of "race." That this is so would surely not come as a surprise to Rorty; he might even say it "isn't exactly a deep theoretical insight."[47] This, it might be said, is also part of the point about the "contingency" that is "race": it *appears* to be a natural fact while constituting a symbolic marker in a system of oppression. And while Rorty writes as though "there are no races,"[48] one wonders whether this is because he is an eliminativist concerning "race," or because his libertarianism regarding social explanation leads him to dismiss the significance of "race" as a persisting social construction. This is a question of whether there is a connection, in some way that is accessible to social explanation, between the "race" of "these people" Rorty is referring to, and the "contingency" that they, as he puts it, live lives of unending hopelessness and misery. But it is also a matter of how "we" are going to help "these people" and what role postphilosophic practice might play in their helping themselves. Here Rorty's liberal ironism, providing as it does the alternatives of "top-down techno-bureaucratic initiatives" of liberal social engineering[49] and ironic self-redescription, seems equally unhelpful.

The strategy of self-redescription – which Rorty describes as a means to personal autonomy – ultimately involves creation of a vocabulary of one's own – what might be described as a private language[50] in the paradigm case of the strong poet whose literary activity Rorty takes as the model of postphilosophical practice. "Private language" is misleading, it might be claimed, suggesting as it does a pre-Wittgensteinian or pre-postphilosophical conception of language which Rorty explicitly eschews. But that strategy has a solipsistic orientation that seems independent of any semantic deflationism: for the problem is not one of meanings, but of how the social practices of talking (even to oneself) are conceived. For Rorty suggests that individual autonomy can be a personal achievement, an achievement in which the strategy of literary redescription as *private* act plays the major part. In the African-American tradition, the overcoming of racism has always, and necessarily, been a major part of any personal achievement. That is because white supremacy creates a condition of possibility of "estrangement from ever becoming a self that is not defined in the terms of the dominant group," as Howard McGary has recently put it. McGary goes on to argue that this condition precludes the possibility that "individual blacks acting alone can overcome racism. Individual blacks who succeed in this country do so because of the struggles and sacrifices of others, and these others always extend beyond family members and friends."[51]

McGary's article is on the concept of alienation and its relevance to the historical experience of African-Americans; he considers a particular conception of alienation that is constructed on the basis of that experience and discusses, among other things, the extent to which such alienation is inherent in the condition of "being an American of African descent." McGary's answer is that black folk in America have alway formed "supportive communities" through which "slaves and their descendants were able to maintain healthy self-concepts through acts of resistance and communal nourishment."[52] This argument, which weaves together a concept of paradigmatically European philosophical provenance, and literary-narrative, social-scientific, and historical accounts of the experience of black folk in America, is an example of the transdisciplinary, transgenre and transcultural hybridity of much African-American philosophical production. The tradition of such productions is, of course, an historically specific one, in the sense both of the social concerns which delimit its scope and of the cultural context in which it comes to be redescribed as a tradition. The writers who would have to be included in that tradition were all intellectuals who "spoke to those disenfranchised, stereotyped, stigmatized as parasites, raciated as inferiors, and immiserated," as Leonard Harris has recently put it.[53] These intellectuals came from communities that not only were supportive, but were "communities of struggle," to use West's phrase, and for that reason those intellectuals included in their descriptions of the world "the enslaved and the segregated as real agents – not phantoms whose rights would eventually be insured by . . . social experiments guided by the dialogue of a community from which they were excluded."[54]

In keeping with this, West's practice is aimed at addressing the misery and disempowerment of the oppressed and of finding ways to form publics and alliances directed against "the hegemony of capital." In this he begins with a far more social-theoretically and politically innovative account of where we are at historically. This more explicitly and radically politicized account is connected to West's critical claim that Rorty is not sufficiently historicist because "it is impossible to historicize philosophy without partly politicizing it."[55] Whereas Rorty merely repeats the old story about the history of liberal democracies and the virtues of liberal ironism, West produces a perspective in which "American civilization as we know it is simply running out of gas."[56]

For West, the sun has set on the "age of Europe," "an age that lasted from 1492 to 1945," in which "those nations between the Ural mountains and the Atlantic Ocean" were at the center of the historical stage.[57] Among the features given birth by the age of Europe has been a liberal democracy which has depended on "imperial conditions . . . Certain economic surpluses have been requisite for the social stability that has expanded liberal rights." The end of the age of Europe predated by mere decades the decline of American society, which West characterizes as the economic decline and cultural decay that none of us can deny: the debt, the stubborn incapacity of the nation to mobilize resources requisite to provide necessary and basic social goods, the short-term profiteering, the inability to provide education for a labor force, the inability to produce products of quality and quantity to compete with other countries, and most of all the cultural decay . . . the decomposition of civil society. We face shattered families, neighborhoods, civic associations . . . the social breakdown of nurturing systems for children, and hence deracinated individuals who have lost their existential moorings, who become easily caught within a subculture of violence.[58]

This description of the current situation in America is certainly less hopeful than the one Rorty's narrative suggests. West's most recent book, *Keeping Faith*, is a collection of his previously published essays. The preface, written partly in Addis Ababa, where he now has a home (he is married to an Ethiopian woman), is entitled "The difficulty of keeping faith." In describing his "urge to leave" America, West notes that "the extent to which race still so fundamentally matters in nearly every sphere of American life is – in the long run – depressing and debilitating."[59] West's version of postphilosophical practice, which he calls "prophetic criticism,"[60] is "based on a distinctly black tragic sense of life." It is the criticism of an organic intellectual, one who "attempts to be entrenched in and affiliated with organizations, associations, and, possibly, movements of grass-roots folk."[61]

Finally, West's prophetic criticism is a model of postphilosophic practice drawing directly from the tradition of African-American – or, as he puts it, New World African – philosophical activity. In self-consciously extending that tradition, West gives an account of the modernity of "a modern people beneath modernity"[62] which sums up his conception of that tradition and his own postphilosophic philosophic practice:

New World African modernity consists of degraded and exploited Africans in American circumstances using European languages and instruments to make sense of tragic predicaments – predicaments disproportionately shaped by white-supremacist bombardments on black beauty, intelligence, moral character and creativity. New World African modernity attempts to institutionalize critiques of white-supremacist authority and racist uses of power, to bestow dignity, grandeur and tragedy on the denigrated lives of ordinary black people, and to promote improvisational life-strategies of love and joy in black life-worlds of radical and brutish contingency. New World African modernity radically interrogates and creatively appropriates Euro-American modernity by examining how "race" and "Africa" – themselves modern European constructs – yield insights and blindness, springboards and roadblocks for our understanding of multivarious and multileveled modernities. Prophetic criticism rests on the best of New World African modernity by making explicit the personal and political aspects of existential democracy implicit in the visions, analyses and strategies of American African victims of Euro-American modernity.[63]

West here forgoes the language of "postmodernism" for that of "multivarious modernities." Yet the conception of prophetic criticism remains postphilosophical in the sense identified above. Here also West makes explicit the connection of such postphilosophical practice to the activities of "communities of struggle" within "New World African modernity."

The contrast I have drawn between Rorty's and West's versions of postphilosophic practice has focused on three related aspects – existential, theoretical or "metaphilosophical," and political. I have only roughly indicated the significant differences between these two writers: that between Rorty's ironism and West's emphasis on existential issues, that between Rorty's libertarianism and West's socialism with regard to the methods and aims of postphilosophy, and that between the politics of the narratives through which they position and situate themselves and their projects of cultural criticism. I have also tried to suggest some of the ways in which these differences involve issues about "race" and the historical differences between "Euro-American" and "New World African" experiences of modernity. I am not suggesting a simplistic racial reductionism of the differences between Rorty and West, but it is also more than coincidence – and more than a result of my strategy in writing – that the issues of race discussed show up such important differences between Rorty and West. I have tried to indicate that these sources of disagreement are not the product of some idiosyncrasy of West's by suggesting how other contemporary African-American philosophical practitioners view some of these issues. I have done this not to produce a "united front" for purposes of racial "solidarity," but to point out commonalities which show the significance to the African-American philosophical tradition as a source of materials for a viable conception of postphilosophic practice. African-American philosophers do not speak with one voice, and West's prophetic criticism is but one version of postphilosophical practice in black. But still, in the last years of the twentieth century, the color-line has not been breached, as this contrast of postphilosophical practices attests.

Notes

1 "Two cheers for the cultural left," *South Atlantic Quarterly*, vol. 89, no. 1, winter 1990, p. 232.

2 Most obviously, of course, in "Postmodernist bourgeois liberalism," in which, in specifying what he means by "us postmodern bourgeois liberals," he writes that "I use 'postmodernist' in a sense given to this term by Jean-François Lyotard, who says that the postmodern attitude is that of 'distrust of metanarratives,' narratives which describe or predict the activities of such entities as the noumenal self or the Absolute Spirit or the Proletariat." (*Journal of Philosophy*, vol. LXXX, no. 10, October 1983, p. 585).

3 Cornel West, *The Ethical Dimensions of Marxist Thought* (Monthly Review Press, New York, 1991), p. xx. This book will be cited hereafter as *EDMT*.

4 "The cultural politics of difference," reprinted in *Keeping Faith: Philosophy and Race in America* (Routledge, New York, 1993), p. 21. This book is hereafter cited as *KF*.

5 "American radicalism" (an interview with Cornel West conducted by Peter Osborne), *Radical Philosophy*, no. 71 (May/June, 1995), p. 27.

6 Adolph Reed, "What are the drums saying, Booker? The current crisis of the black intellectual," *Village Voice*, April 11, 1995, pp. 31–6; see also the response by Manning Marable, "Black intellectuals in conflict," *New Politics*, vol. 5, no. 3, (Summer 1995), pp. 35–40.

7 Richard Rorty, *Contingency, Irony, and Solidarity* (Cambridge University Press, Cambridge, 1989). Hereafter cited as *CIS*.

8 Ibid., p. 73.

9 Ibid., p. 75.

10 Ibid., pp. 53, pp. xv–xvi.

11 That is, of course, a piece of how Wittgenstein characterized the vocation of philosophy in the *Philosophical Investigations*, section 124. That work should, if any is, be regarded as central to the canon of postphilosophy.

12 *EDMT*, pp. xxvii–xxviii.

13 "American radicalism," p. 27.

14 W.E.B. Du Bois, in the *Souls of Black Folk*, cited by West in *The American Evasion of Philosophy* (University of Wisconsin Press, Madison, WI, 1989), p. 142. Hereafter cited as *AEP*.

15 See Laurence Thomas, "Next life, I'll be white," originally in the *New York Times* of August 13, 1991; reprinted in G. Lee Bowie, Meredith Michaels, and Robert G. Solomon (eds), *Twenty Questions: An Introduction to Philosophy*, 2nd edn (Harcourt Brace Jovanovich, New York, 1992), p. 471.

16 *CIS*, pp. 78–9.

17 In his essay on "Pragmatism and Philosophy," written as the introduction to *The Consequences of Pragmatism*, Rorty distinguishes between "philosophy" and capital-p "Philosophy", and goes on to suggest, after advocating the former and casting doubt on the fruitfulness of the latter, that in a "post-Philosophical culture" there would be philosophers, who would function as "culture critics," but no Philosophers. See "Pragmatism and philosophy," reprinted in Kenneth Baynes, James Bohman, and Thomas McCarthy, (eds), *After Philosophy* (MIT Press, Cambridge, MA, 1987), pp. 27–8 and 55–8.

18 *CIS*, p. 192.

19 *EDMT*, p. 14.

20 Ibid., p. 2.

21 The phrase is West's, from *EDMT*, p. xv. Such inventories can be found in Cornell West, *Prophecy Deliverance: An Afro-American Revolutionary Christianity* (Westminster Press, Philadelphia, PA, 1982); *AEP*, pp. 7–8; *EDMT*, pp. xv–xxxi; *Keeping Faith: Philosophy and Race In America* (Routledge, New York, 1992), pp. ix–xvii (hereafter *KF*).

22 *EDMT*, p. 190.

23 Richard Rorty, *Philosophy and the Mirror of Nature* (Princeton University Press,

Princeton, NJ 1979), pp. 249, 386. This book is hereafter cited as *PMN*.

24 Giovanna Borradori, *The American Philosopher: Conversations with Quine, Davidson, Putnam, Nozick, Danto, Rorty, Cavell, MacIntyre, and Kuhn* (University of Chicago Press, Chicago, IL, 1994), pp. 112, 116.

25 *EDMT*, p. xxi.

26 *PD*, p. 12.

27 *EDMT*, pp. 68–9.

28 Reminiscent of Rorty's conception of "revolutionary philosophy" developed in *PMN*, p. 6.

29 "American radicalism," p. 31.

30 How much in keeping with the tradition of African–American social criticism this sort of practice is, and how socially engaged and deeply social-explanatory that tradition is, can be seen in Bernard Boxill's consideration of the "Two traditions of African American political philosophy," in *African American Perspectives and Philosophical Traditions*, ed. John Pittman (*Philosophical Forum* Special Issue, vol. XXIV, nos 1–3, Fall–Spring, 1992–3), pp. 119–135.

31 "Stories of difference: a conversation with Richard Rorty," conducted by Gaurav Desai and published in the *Sapina Bulletin*, vol. V, no. 2/3 (July–December, 1993), pp. 23–45; see for this comment p. 43. (SAPINA is the Society for African Philosophy in North America; I am indebted to Emmanuel Eze for pointing out this journal, and interview, to me.)

32 Ibid., p. 45.

33 *PD*, p. 11.

34 *AEP*, p. 138.

35 Ibid., p. 5.

36 "The horror of tradition or how to burn Babylon and build Benin while reading 'A preface to a twenty-volume suicide note'," in *African-American Perspective and Philosophical Traditions*, pp. 94–118.

37 *CIS*, p. xv.

38 Ibid., p. 192.

39 Ibid., p. 68.

40 Ibid., p. 184.

41 Ibid., p. 192.

42 Rorty, "Cosmopolitanism without emancipation: a response to Jean-François Lyotard," in *Objectivism, Relativism, and Truth* (Cambridge University Press, Cambridge, 1991), p. 211.

43 *CIS*, p. 198.

44 Ibid.

45 "American radicalism," pp. 32–3.

46 *CIS*, p. 191.

47 "Stories of difference," p. 37.

48 Kwame Anthony Appiah, *In My Father's House: Africa in the Philosophy of Culture* (Oxford University Press, Oxford, 1992), p. 45.

49 Richard Rorty, "Love and Money," *Common Knowledge*, vol. 1, no. 1, Spring 1992, p. 15.

50 "Private" in the sense specified by Rorty in a recent interview as "what goes on when you talk to yourself about yourself"; see "Stories of difference," p. 24.

51   Howard McGary, "Alienation and the African-American experience," in *African-American Perspectives and Philosophical Traditions*, pp. 283, 294.

52   Ibid., p. 292.

53   "Horror of tradition," p. 112.

54   Ibid., p. 110.

55   *AEP*, p. 207.

56   "American radicalism," p. 38.

57   "Beyond Eurocentrism and multiculturalism," a presentation at the Chicago Humanities Institute Symposium, reprinted in *Modern Philology*, vol. 90, May 1993 (Supplementary Issue) p. S145.

58   Ibid, pp. S146–7.

59   *KF*, p. xv.

60   Ibid., p. xi. On the same page West characterizes himself as a "black philosopher."

61   *AEP*, p. 234.

62   "American radicalism," p. 27.

63   *KF*, p. xii.

13

African Philosophy and the Postcolonial: Some Misleading Abstractions about "Identity"

D. A. Masolo

For quite good reasons, one of the dominant themes of postcolonial theory is the issue of "identity," in most if not all its various forms – personal, class, race, ethnic, gender, cultural, formal, professional, and so on. Its justification lies in the very heart of the historical occurrence of colonialism and its political and cultural impact on those societies which persevered many centuries and decades under colonial domination, and in the perceived meaning and implications of the removal of this domination.

A number of factors make it difficult to define or assess what can or are to be the meaning and implications of a long period of domination of one society by another. Such factors can include the consideration of who it is that judges such meaning and implications. This in turn may require taking into consideration such other factors as the length, quality and intensity of the domination, as well as the experiences of the specific individuals and groups whose viewpoints such definitions of meaning and implications reflect. And there are always ways in and reasons for which different individuals and groups, all at once, experience historical episodes differently at different levels.

First, while a family of six members may live together under the tyranny of a dominant person of authority, parents in such a family could have an experience quite genuinely different from that of the children; then parents and children, as individuals of different gender, ages, and social roles performed under the tyranny of the same authority, could also have entirely different experiences from each other. And there is good reason to find among them several definitions of the meanings (in plural) and implications of such authority

– and this may be so regardless of whether or not they concur in calling the type of authority set up by the dominant person as tyranny. Then, at other times, individuals could also give different evaluations – meanings and implications – of historical episodes based on how they want to identify themselves at any given time. They could take a group stand for political and/ or moral reasons on a matter of which they themselves might never have had a direct experience or from which they might have in fact benefited; then at other times they could take a different stand, as individuals, on another matter out of the same general conditions of life and experience.

The definition of history, from the evidence provided by history itself, is more often than not a reflection of this kind of valuational ambivalence. Descartes, Hegel, Marx, Nietzsche, and most recently Heidegger, all reflect serious ambivalences in the valuational definition of history. And there is nothing wrong about it. Definitions of history as meaningful and implicative episodes are partly appropriations of traditions and other practices by the self, and projections of self in time. But while this is done, usually a line is drawn between perceptions (of meanings, implications and identities inferred by subjects) and facts of experience.

All such factors as I mention above affect and also demonstrate how persons, as individuals and as members of groups, dialectically identify themselves differently at different times in the face of historical episodes. Defining the "postcolonial" is no less difficult, as abundant recent literature has shown. Not all formerly colonized persons judge the colonial experience the same way; nor do all of them judge all aspects of colonization the same way. Irele, for example, says the following in his critique of Mudimbe:

> I do not see that any necessary ground for repudiating Western rationality has been provided. It is not enough to say that Africans need a kind of conceptual autonomy. What we really want to know is whether the Western system provides useful ideas, and I do not see Foucault [on whom Mudimbe depends for his deconstructive analysis of Western – that is, colonial – discourse on the idea of Africa] as having undermined that basic point.[1]

Irele's passage indicates several things. First, it clearly indicates two head-on views of the colonial period, quite similar to the post-Napoleonic German historiographies. Should this be a surprise? I do not think so. But should this very disagreement not have been sufficient to warrant the elimination of such rather pretentious occurrences in the passage as the shift from "I" to "We", or the phrase "What we really want to know . . . "? Second, the idea of *L'Odeur du père*, to which reference is also made in this critique, is that, despite the suggested patricide, the odor of the father continues to linger on because it is hard to get rid of. On the other hand, while it is impossible to get rid of the father completely due to his ineliminable odor, the goal is to eliminate him *in spite of himself.* It is in this paradoxical sense that, despite his murder of the father, a melancholy continues to hang over the liberated son, symbolized by the odor of the murdered father. So Foucault hangs over Mudimbe like the odor of the patriarchal figure whose imminent death he cunningly plans in the more recent works.

But above all, both Mudimbe's critique of the colonial archive and Irele's cautioning of the depth of such critique express the need for a stocktaking of the impact of colonialism. To both, the "post" in "postcolonialism" indicates the inseparability between the "colonial" as a period definable on the basis of certain characteristics, and another period after it which inherits but perhaps also modifies or reacts differently to such characteristics. In these senses, the postcolonial defines itself in the shadow of the colonial, from which it is inseparable. Remember, however, that saying that the postcolonial condition is determined by its preceding opposite is not the same as saying that that precedent condition was good. Nor does it mean that it could only have been bad. This is what I understand Irele to be saying. But Mudimbe also says this much. The difference, if it is at all, is that Mudimbe, like Edward Said, sees a combination of "poststructuralism, in the shape of Foucault, and Marxism" as a necessary tool for deconstructing and eventually overthrowing the dominance of Western discourse. If our understanding of Mudimbe is close, then he exemplifies the historical possibility envisaged by Fanon's outline of the role of the intellectual in the colonial and postcolonial situation: that he is able to assimilate and then reject the culture of the colonizer. He has the possibility of defying the odds of complete complicity with the colonizing bourgeois system.

Unfortunately, colonialism is not always seen only in this way, and rightly so. Frequently, colonialism is judged overwhelmingly for the political, social, and cultural ills associated with it. But while the overarching political view of postcoloniality as an emancipatory movement is completely justified, a problem arises with regard to its two-pronged assumption, prevalent in most influential postcolonial texts: first, that all formerly colonized persons ought to have one view of the impact of colonialism behind which they ought to unite to overthrow it; second, that the overthrow of colonialism be replaced with another, liberated and assumedly authentic identity. So strong is the pull toward the objectivity of this identity that most of those who speak of Africa from this emancipatory perspective think of it only as a solid rock which has withstood all the storms of history except colonialism. Because of the deeply political gist of the colonial/postcolonial discourse, we have come to think of our identities as natural rather than imagined and politically driven. The search for this identity and for what is *authentic* about it is the thread that runs through Odera Oruka's idea of "The four trends in African philosophy", and it reveals its own contradictions in the very search for a universal and homogeneous African difference. For, so long as the monolithism of the above assumptions remains suspect, the efforts of postcoloniality remain only, and validly so, a search for something that remains constantly illusive.

The philosophical analogy of this problem may be quite simple, and it goes back, in the history of philosophy, to the foundations of Berkeley's dictum *esse est percipi*. According to Berkeley, we know the things of the external world by way of how they appear to us, through the mediation of our senses on which the ways of the physical world play. Refusing to assign any definite meaning to the term *substratum*, Berkeley differed from Locke in refuting the absolute existence of the external world outside how we perceive and talk about it. Admittedly, almost all spoken human languages make the "mere ideas" of Berkeley look like they were *objects* independent of the language that fixes them as referents of speech and thought. Commenting on this Berkeleyan thesis, Quine says the following:

> For the trouble is that immediate experience simply will not, of itself, cohere as an autonomous domain. References to physical things are largely what hold [sense-datum language] together. These references are not just inessential vestiges of the initially intersubjective character of language, capable of being weeded out by devising an artificially subjective language for sense data. Rather they give us our main continuing access to past sense data themselves; for past sense data are mostly gone for good except as commemorated in physical posits. All we would have apart from posits and speculation are present sense data and present memories of past ones; and a memory trace of a past sense datum is too meager an affair to do much good. Actual memories mostly are traces not of past sensations but of past conceptualization or verbalization.
>
> There is [therefore] every reason to inquire into the sensory or stimulatory background of ordinary talk of physical things. The mistake comes only in seeking an implicit sub-basement of conceptualization, or of language. Conceptualization on any considerable scale is inseparable from language, and our ordinary language of physical things is about as basic as language gets.[2]

From another angle, Mudimbe has tried to show how the content of a trait of ordinary language in the West, understood as such even in its bizarre mythical representations of Africa, was gradually but steadily upheld, laced with political and racial qualifications, until it caused not only other and more widespread mythical referential posits, but also the subject matter of organized disciplines.[3] To Quine, "the proposition that external things are ultimately to be known only through their action on our bodies should be taken as one among various coordinate truths, in physics and elsewhere, about initially unquestioned physical things."[4] Analogously, given the contentional context in which it emerges, the issue of identity in the postcolonial condition continues to engage attention with varying degrees of intensity and articulation, and for that reason requires another look at its assumptions about the *realism* of identity.

Remember that questioning the *realist* sense of identity in the postcolonial condition and discourse is not a denial of the historical fact of colonialism or of the ills suffered by many of its subjects. The questioning is with reference to the gap or connection between postcolonial discourse as a historically inspired genre of language and the pretentions of objectivity in its implicit references. We can fairly commonly imagine, either by means of memories of direct experiences lived then, or by reasoning through the memories of others, that colonialism, in its social, cultural, and political gestures, is not and cannot have been good. But the details of this judgement, like those of ordinary language, are not supported by equally firm and objective references for all people who live in the postcolonial. The same argument applies to the other, colonial, side too. According to Quine, most of our ordinary language has that pull toward objectivity as its mechanism of survival. And this would seem more so for historico–ideologically inspired language as that which defines the colonial/postcolonial dichotomy.

> Words being social tools, objectivity counts towards their survival. When a word has considerable currency [and importance, especially of ideological nature] despite the subjective twist, it may be expected, like the pronouns "I" and "you", to have a valuable social function of some exceptional sort.[5]

But more than ordinary language, the pull toward objectivity is a characteristic of most rationalist theories of history and societies from Marx to Habermas. Indeed, Horkheimer and Adorno argue that classical Marxism had falsely imputed truly emancipatory potential to the proletariat, having failed to understand the social reality of the very people who were its object.[6] The question is whether we are not about to be heralded by a new crop of philosopher-soldiers into the cages of identity *Bewusstsein*.

In their view, Marx's theory may have been good and useful for understanding certain dynamics of social-political relations – those driven by economic interests. But Marxism has also been wrong in supposing that all people working under ideal oppressive systems identify themselves primarily as "proletariats." Not all individuals relate the same way to common historical events such as oppression; nor would all individuals who experience such events want to view themselves exclusively in those terms. The issue of identity thus puts into contrast the abstract metaphysical senses of interpretation and the "true nature" of experienced contexts. It defines the contrasts between "the external or rationalist critique and the immanent or critical variety."[7] Mudimbe's critique of Peter Rigby's Marxist reading of Maasai economic culture applies well here too.[8] According to John McCumber, "What this suggests is that critique has a problem with its knowledge not merely of its own standards, but also of the realities to which those standards (whether externally derived or 'immanent') are applied."[9] The same critique could well be applied to Henri Maurier's reading of African traditions.[10]

That the reading of history involves both the appropriation of tradition as past and the projection of self in time raises an interesting point about the nature of identities and about how individual and collective identities are constructed. At one level, the question of identity reproduces the old problem of the relation between concepts and things, names and referents or, in recent Quinean terms, between *word and object*, itself an excellent sifting – through Berkeley, as we have seen – of the old classical (Aristotelian) and medieval (Boethian) problem of metaphysical realism.

Juxtaposing these two points suggests the dialectical theory of identity, a position which argues that "identities which are formed in social movements, or which require social movements to be formed, are not only many-sided, but are also politically 'heteronomous'." Such heteronomy suggests that there is no group – a universal reference to persons under assumptions of commonly shared characteristics – with a given, monolithic, traditional identity, but rather only simple, unpredictable forces which compose and recompose themselves all the time in history. Could the defenders of the idea of monolithic identity tell who they have in mind as belonging "within" the boundaries of their identity circle, or who to them belong "without," and what they would do with those who belong "in-between" – those whom Homi Bhabha calls the "hybrids?" And what are or would be the criteria for such inclusions, exclusions, and undecidables?

1 Identity and the Question of the Subject

It can be said with a fair amount of security that the postcolonial, a term definable in the context of its political and historical significance, aims at the rectification of the power order established by the one-sidedness of the idea and use of power of colonialism. In this ideological sense, the postcolonial aims at (re)empowering and/or (re)subjectivizing the disenfranchised under the colonial order. But despite this statement, it has not been entirely clear what the objectives of (re)empowerment and (re)subjectivization are in African philosophy as a postcolonial discourse. In particular, there is still a persistence towards a restrictive *kind* of methodology regarded as "appropriate" to the "postcolonial," where the latter is used with the Ngugian connotations of "decolonization." Hence the pertinent questions: Is methodological separatism part of the idea of the post-colonial? Is there, and should there be, such a thing as "methodological separatism?" Can methodological separatism be tenable at the same time as preserving a disciplinary unity?

With its objective of resetting the scale of power, one of the key themes of the postcolonial concerns the reorganization of the industry of knowledge production, confection, distribution, and consumption. But there are also those scholars who claim, from the other side of external standards, and with good reasons too, that by focusing on the re-examination of the wider issues of method and social conditions under which knowledge is produced, much of the body of literature considered under African philosophy deals with issues in the sociology of knowledge rather than with the formal subject matter of the philosophical discipline. Made recently by Carole Pearce, this logocentric claim finds its predecessor in Franz Crahay's famous critique of ethnophilosophy.[11] In hindsight, it is now apparent that this criticism is not altogether a new one, since Foucault taught that there are no value or conceptual systems, abstract philosophical categories included, which are devoid of some influence from the social and historical environment of the subject.

According to Christa Bürger, this rationalist version is not really critique at all, for, she says, "Within the tradition, critics are in possession of some yardsticks which assure them superiority over the object of criticism."[12] The implicit Cartesian individual as a sovereign and unaffected *res cogitans* imposed by both Crahay and Pearce is a case in point. Thinking of subjectivity as an abstract and unaffectable entity is always such a facile assumption of rationalism. Put in another, corrected way, the ethnophilosophical theme of the social embeddedness of the subject is an examination of the claim, implicit in Crahay's and Pearce's critiques, but also the core of the rationalist foundationalism since Descartes, of the necessary relations between specific, historically conditioned social structures and the "abstract" nature of disciplines. Insisting that the order of *exercitatio* is different and separate from the (*quid*) *exercitatum*, ethnophilosophers tried to impose an alternative order of practice on the discipline of philosophy. In counterdefence, Crahay and Pearce have argued that the order of the discipline, as (*quid*) *exercitatum*, has no reality of its own apart from the practices, the *exercitatio*, which bring and define it into existence.

But while the critiques of the abstract and unaffectable subject do not necessarily demolish old beliefs, they have contributed to fresher, more useful, and more critical ways of looking at the subject and his or her capacities than was previously assumed and done. As a result, much of the latter part of the twentieth century has devoted considerable efforts to the analysis of the social conditions which influence the production of knowledge. One such condition is identifiable in the influence of the eighteenth- and nineteenth-century European epistemological heritage on the definition and location of the criteria of knowledge. In turn, it is also believed that, despite the success, influence, and subsequent predominance of such criteria, the idea of individuals as the sovereign cognitive, moral, and legal agents and goals all at once is almost always set against that which makes them, and from which they must always struggle to separate themselves. Individuality, writes David F. Grüber in his analysis of Foucault's critique of the liberal individual,

is no longer an opportunity that lags as the political reforms of liberalism take their time to become effective; it is an imposed, inescapable necessity, a forced and enforced requirement. Attaining individuality is not graduating to a subjectivity that would exercise autonomy and spontaneity; in the institutions, discourses, and practices of the human sciences, individuals are constituted as the particular objects that have a dynamic of subjectivity. They are built so that they must be constantly in search of themselves and, ironically enough, so that they perpetually fail the criteria set for them and thus need ceaseless effort and re-examination, re-immersion in that which forms them.[13]

Yet, the incumbency of ideology at the turn of the twentieth century prevented even the most avid of the analytic minds generated from positivism from adequately appreciating the differences between groups, and between groups and their constituting individual subjects. The idea of the nature of the subject as cognitively unaffectable by his or her conditions appeared to stand in contrast to the sociological view of individuals as products of their social environment – a view also issuing out of the West, but changing now due partly to the influence of such people as Pierre Bourdieu and Charles Taylor – except that they were united via the persistent notion of the unity and objectivity of the product – the Kantian transcendental *Unum in Pluribus*. In this framework, the self as a transcendentally unified cognitive and moral *Unum* represents a triumph over the organic *Pluribus* which only provides it with a field to be coordinated and unified. In Kant, the picture of the free man as self-directing, as an integrated mind with a continuous controlling reason, is made complete: a man tries to preserve himself and his own distinct nature as an individual, and to increase his own power and activity in relation to his environment. Regarded as a thinking being, his overriding interest is to preserve the coherence and continuity of his own thought against the flow of the multiple and unconnected ideas which are his perceptions, sensations, and imaginations.

Because the field is supposed to facilitate the emergence of the *Unum* as subject and as its contradiction, its characteristic is defined as loose and as dependent on specific and objective laws working in the interest of the subject. Thus the subject and the social field of its construction are in mutual and constant conflict, which alone produces knowledge. Subjectivity and knowledge are both equally diminished proportionately in relation to the strength of the field: the stronger and more unified the field, the weaker the subject and his or her attributes or products. In other words, the more the sequence of an individual's own ideas can be explained without reference to causes outside his or her own thinking, the more active and self-determining the individual is, regarded as a thinking being. The more active and self-determining the individual is, to that degree he or she can be more regarded as a distinctive thing, having an individuality that sets him or her apart from the particular environment. The more self-determining and active he or she is, and the more free, in this sense of "free", the more he or she can be regarded as a "real" individual, real as an individual thinking being.

The cohesion of African societies has given false impressions of a subjectless unity, suggesting to Western scholarship the unanimity and sameness of all Africans. Appiah has already argued strongly enough against these disabling universals.[14] *In My Father's House* invests its strength in the critique of racial realism. It would be futile to repeat or paraphrase him here. What I have tried to do in this brief paper so far, which is what Appiah has done differently and efficiently, is to take on the challenge that in the dispute between nominalism and realism the onus of proof lies with the nominalists – those who argue, as we have done for this particular case about the abstractions of identity, that universals have no real existence outside their conceptual and linguistic construction. Because we have argued that the universals do not *exist* beyond their conceptual and linguistic parameters despite "the objective pull," it might be interesting to also state that both nominalism and realism are based on relational analysis – that is, both the nominalist and realist status of an idea is affirmed or denied on the basis of the comparison of some attributes identified as belonging to it with another set of attributes taken as reference. The basis for this is that concepts are by their very nature abstract-classificative. Thus to say that *a* is "real" is to say that it shares certain generic attributes with others of its type. And the same applies to calling *a* "a mere nomen."

The assumptions that issued in the imagination of ethnophilosophy were in turn based on the assumed realism of a universal collectivism to which thought and other types of agency could be attributed – different from, but likened to, the rationalist subjectivism described above. The paradox is, however, that while the collective was regarded as "real" because some attributes could be asserted of it as is done of individual "reals," the quality and outcome of their attributes were in sharp contrast with each other. They are, for example, the contrasts drawn by Karl Popper and Robin Horton between the "closed" and "open" societies. According to Popper, such a condition engenders a sort of fetishism in the form of epistemological dogmatism and stagnation.[15] In addition to this, according to Horton, the condition engenders the personification of the idea of force in explanatory models of reality.[16] And all this happens, it seems to both Popper and Horton, due to the replacement, in tribal (Popper) or traditional (Horton) thought, of the real individuals with real collectives as cognitive agents.

In the above senses, the *ethnos* is translated as the unequal variant of the unencumbered, autonomous and free self rather than as its negation (Tempels). The point is not that there are or can be no generalizations about peoples of Africa, as Appiah says, "at a certain abstract level." Rather, contrary to how we define and understand generalizations, African *ethnos* has been treated as if it were a "real" and unified agent, only perverse. In what follows, I wish to argue that this generalization of an African identity, like most universals, is not real because it does not reflect the social experiences of single subjects; that it is not only misleading, but also part of the politics of re-presenting.

2 Ideas/Images and Social Facts

In its entire history, the discipline of philosophy has been deeply engaged in the quest to explain how representation occurs and what its relations are with the *repraesentatum*. Considered generally as a mental act, it is the process by which images of objects of sensation are impressed on the mind. The image may occur with varying degrees of clarity depending on how close it is to the object of sensation which it is the *image* of, as the empiricist British philosopher David Hume explicated. Images of particular objects are usually clearer and more detailed than their more general counterparts. But while the formation of mental images of objects of sensation is a psychological event or act, it has been at the center of epistemological debates for as long as we can remember.

Representation or, better, re-presentation is the unifying process that connects minds, ideas, and even objects in the correlation we refer to as knowledge. Ideas, we are told, are the mental pictures or non-material forms that objects take in our minds. But how faithfully does the mind re-present an object? Knowledge is constituted when a knowing subject is aware of this mental reproduction of an object in his or her own mind, or secondarily in the minds of others, and regards it as true: that is, as consistent with the *repraesentatum*. "True belief" has therefore been the primary starting point for most epistemological enquiries. Recognition of its inadequacies, however, led to questions seeking to discover what cognitive states of the subjects other than just perception are involved in knowing.

In the *Republic*, for instance, Plato presents us, in the "Analogy of the line", with a four-stage progress from unreflective beliefs about particular things or objects to a systematic and teleological understanding of the nature of things. Aristotle, in his turn, distinguishes five cognitive states in which the subject "possesses the truth in asserting or denying," and two further states in which the subject can be mistaken. These Classic concerns with mapping out and describing the various cognitive states a subject can be in is part of – or perhaps initiates – a different tradition of epistemological method from that which centers on justification. In this respect, they have more in common with what has come to be called "natural" or "naturalistic" epistemology, in which the epistemologist's enterprise is part of – and often also prior to – psychology and cognitive science. It is sometimes thought that a naturalistic epistemology cannot be normative: that its function is to describe rather than prescribe. For Plato and Aristotle, the interest is not merely in how one derives one's beliefs, but also in how one structures them. Perceptual knowledge is possible without any reflection about either the reliability of the senses or the nature of knowledge, or about justification. In other words, the problem of truth as consisting in the consistency between a mental representation and the *repraesentatum* is not part of the experience upon which it depends. To reach the higher cognitive states described by Plato and Aristotle, however, reflection is essential. One could not achieve *episteme* without realizing it. In providing a hierarchy of cognitive states, Plato and Aristotle were engaging precisely in normative epistemological enquiry, which has become the focus of the ongoing discourse on the politics of representation.

A great deal of recent literature has addressed the issue of representation with reference to its role in how we talk of other people and their cultures. In creative literature, anthropology, history, comparative political science, and other transcultural disciplines, much of the discussion has argued that the act of representing and interpreting others has essentially been associated with power, derived, as Karp says, "from the capacity of cultural institutions to classify and define peoples and societies . . . to reproduce structures of belief and experience through which cultural differences are understood."[17] This power defines the colonial domination of most non-Western societies and their cultures, as Edward Said and V.Y. Mudimbe have so strongly and influentially argued.[18] Their assumption is that the cognitive act of representing, even if individual, cannot be separated from the wider structures provided by historical and institutional foundations from which a subject emerges. Put in another way, the argument is that a crisis has descended upon epistemology precisely because, for a long time, epistemologists have assumed that the universals exist.

We learn at least three things from Said and Mudimbe, and from several others who share with them their perspective in postcolonial critique. First, the subject is after all not as abstract as assumed in post-Enlightenment epistemology. Second, there is still a great gulf between the tools of judgement and the real world of subjects as learners and vehicles of specific values, both cognitive and moral. Third, the beauty of reason – whether this is viewed in terms of its role in judgements, or its role in communication and promotion of understanding among humans, as seems to be the *agendum absconditum* of the prophets of universalism – is not synonymous with the real. Although produced specifically as part of anticolonial critique, Said's and Mudimbe's works add to Richard Rorty's critique of the modern European idea of knowledge as constituted of accurate mental re-presentation of reality. Rorty makes the point when he observes that "Wittgenstein, Heidegger and Dewey are in agreement that the notion of knowledge as accurate representation, made possible by special mental process, and intelligible through a general theory of representation, needs to be abandoned."[19] By means of a critical use of Foucault, both Said and Mudimbe accomplish very successful deconstructions of Western discourses to expose the falsities in their re-presentations of Others as ironically founded on their nineteenth-century epistemological assumptions, leading to their claim or argument that the West has constructed or invented cultural images of Others – such as in the idea of "Orientals" or "Africans" – which have no concrete correlates other than the West's own ideological intentions.

Postcolonial theory challenges the assumption that science is unaffected by the social contexts of its formulation and uses. It tries to locate the broader social projects of Western cultures that have appropriated the resources of the sciences, and to identify the features of the practice of the sciences in the West which have made them susceptible to appropriation for political agenda.

One of the effects of modern European epistemology was its postulation of the idea of individual unity as the primary and centerpiece of the idea of progress. Not only did this idea acquire a strategic privilege in the area of political and social action; it also led to the view that human societies were trapped in the inexorable march toward unity in units – that is, the idea of the state as a social and political substance, as epitomized in Hegel's idea of the state as the *Grand Être*, the perfect embodiment of the Absolute Spirit. Justified as a theoretical and historical imagination through Victorian anthropology, this idea of progress and of history underlies the disregard for difference and diversity of identities among the human societies that came to be placed under colonial tutelage. Their differences were, within the framework of "real and universal history," too minor to qualify them for separate classifications. But while some disciplines in cultural studies, particularly linguistics and languages, in conjunction with history, modified this overarching political generalization by showing that "natives" were diverse, they too reduced the extent and nature of such diversity by creating other categories of generalization and classification under the social ideas of "cradle" and "explosion."

Despite the attacks,[20] the "postcolonial" is still a useful category for understanding two diverse genres of academic discourse and practice in several areas of African studies. In its general goal – as a critique of the verisimilitude yet ideologically bloated Eurocentric representation of Others – the "postcolonial" is quite on track. Methodologically, however, there may still be some genuine cause for caution in regard to generalization as a discourse method. Postcolonial theory is criticized, for example, for making generalizations – such as when making statements about history – while it criticizes the same in colonial discourse.[21] By and large, this is a "sour grape" argument. Any historian worth the name need not look hard to notice that some generalizations can indeed be made, as Appiah has shown, without discarding diversity.[22]

Put simply, perhaps even simplistically, "postcolonial" theory only challenges what seem to be exaggerations of the foundationalist postulates for knowledge in both of its branches. It challenges rationalist foundationalism by questioning the assumption that the acceptance of the existence of universally evident principles of rational intuition equals or must necessarily lead to the applicability of such principles in equally universally evident cases. The fact that p is the negation of $-p$ is not a sufficient ground for inferring that all claims involving p can be resolved in one way at all times by everybody. In the realist posture of foundationalism, says Sosa, "Criteria for knowledge are proposed on the basis of necessary truths, sensory experiences, or objective surfaces – all of which enjoy their own character independently of what anyone may believe."[23] While the critics of foundationalism have faced some problems in successfully dismantling this realist assumption, the failure or difficulty to do so does not *in se* prove true the claim for the existence of an objective foundational reality. Foundationalism reproduces, by appealing, like Descartes, to special faculties of the subject, but it does not adequately respond to the old critiques of the correspondence theory of truth as self-referencing or begging the question. The question against this position is a simple one: do or can first-person psychological beliefs provide a sufficient foundation for knowledge?

In Descartes' project, the foundations include the conjunctives *cogito* and *sum* and all first-person reports about the way the world seems to be to the agent. Descartes took to be indubitable first-person reports about the contents of the agent's experience that do not comment on the way the world is outside the agent's mind. This position exposes problems at different levels. At one, it exposes the problem of the indubitability of first-person beliefs about the way things seem as the foundation of knowledge. To this, the following statement by Sosa could be a response:

> A subject may have an internally justified belief B that derives from fine faculties of perception, memory, introspection, and abduction, in an environment E generally favorable to such faculties, while yet in this particular instance the abductive and other rational support is essentially flawed by falsehood. Such a flaw must be precluded through a requirement of *objective* justification, something a belief needs – in addition to aptness and subjective justification – in order to constitute knowledge.[24]

At another level, quite related with the first, is the problem of the relation between the mental and the re-presented world outside the mind. It is not difficult to show that, for a very large class of our beliefs, there is a big difference between believing a proposition and that proposition's actually being true.

In matters of the identity of individuals and groups, the assumed universalism derived from the foundationalist project fares with much success. Appiah defines the nature of this incongruency well:

> To speak of an African identity in the nineteenth century – if an identity is a coalescence of mutually responsive (if sometimes conflicting) modes of conduct, habits of thought, and patterns of evaluations; in short, a coherent kind of human social psychology – would have been "to give to aery nothing a local habitation and a name."
>
> Yet there is no doubt that now, a century later, an African identity is coming into being. I have argued . . . that the bases through which so far it has largely been theorized – race, a common historical experience, a shared metaphysics – presuppose falsehoods too serious for us to ignore.[25]

The practice of postcolonial critique exposes the diversity and pluralism of African identities,[26] thus undermining the tenets of Pan-Africanist ideology and the culturalism of Western ethnology. The thesis in this approach is that the practice of philosophy is often culture-relative in many more ways than is readily accepted. Recent approaches in African philosophy which base philosophical analyses on traditional discourses have the value of placing face to face the universal and the particular of everyday idioms through which the linguistic and conceptual constructs of reality are displayed.[27]

While this practice suggests an alternative approach to the generalizations of ethnophilosophy, it also suggests ways in which cultural diversity is not seen as a hindrance to the possibility of a *tradition* of practice among African philosophers. Wiredu has suggested one way of understanding the semantic of the supranational idiom "African philosophy" in this sense. According to him, the idiom "African philosophy" can be used to refer to a body of practices without suggesting the existence of elements of sameness either in the practices or in the expressions of tradition which organize the different ethnic cultures they reflect on. He writes:

> In any society in which there is a developed tradition of written philosophy, any reference to the philosophy of that area is normally taken simply as a reference to that tradition. Thus, "British philosophy" means the tradition of written philosophy that has its head and spring in the (written) philosophies of ancient Greece and Rome. [It is made up of] the thought of the individual philosophers whose works constitute the British tradition of philosophy.[28]

But *tradition* can also be actively invented, as most of them are, not as an objective in itself, but as a result of interactive discourse. This is because, as Wiredu says:

> a tradition presupposes a certain minimum of organic relationships among (at least some of) its elements. If a tradition of modern philosophy is to develop and flourish in Africa, there will have to be philosophical interaction and cross-fertilization among contemporary African workers in philosophy.[29]

Mudimbe too has referred to the possibility of this interaction between diversely located discourses when he talks of "the geography of rationality."[30] In this sense it becomes possible and indeed enriching for Wiredu, an Akan, to debate Okot p'Bitek on Acholi concepts.[31]

This interaction takes its character not from the specific cultural traditions – the beliefs and practices – from which the individual philosophers emerge, but from the results of the specific cognitive processes in the mind of every knowing subject. In other words, judgements, discourse, communication, etc., are made possible on account of abstract ideas and language. But, as I have argued above, the abstracts are themselves not real. Rather, they are part of a system of culturally learned beliefs, values, and perceptual skills of a community – the community of philosophers. Whether they are philosophers or members of other formal organizations, the lives and identities of individuals are regulated by the range of their interactive relations. Their identities change – because focus on them changes – as the individuals constantly move back and forth between multiple congregational communities in which such individuals participate regularly.

One individual may attend congregations of three or more organizations – scholarly, ethnic, commercial, fun-club, or religious – within short periods of each other without confusing his or her distinctively different roles in each. In each of these, his or her identity is determined by the roles and encounters which define each congregation as a particular social setting or event. The dynamics which separate each of these settings from each other do not only reveal that the subjects who comprise them are heterogeneous. They also reveal, as Karp says, that

> [e]very society can be seen as a constantly changing mosaic of multiple communities and organizations . . . An individual can in the space of a short time move from emphasizing the part of his or her identity that comes from membership in an ethnic community to highlighting his or her participation in a formal organization such as a professional society and then back to being an ethnic-community member again. We experience these identities not as all-encompassing entities but through specific social events: encounters and social settings where identities are made relevant by the people participating in them.[32]

Yet, such – to use Benedict Anderson's now classic reference[33] – "imaginary communities," whether ethnic, national, supranational, or purely professional, are often referred to as if they were homogeneous entities with recognizable unity. The point here is that collective formations emerge out of specific social-historical settings and acquire a collective means of responding to needs and threats. Such communities can then be said to be definable by their common political and other interests beneficial to them. This is, at least partly, what explains such supranational categorizations as "Third World," "Group of Seventy-seven (G-77)," and "African, Caribbean, and Pacific Countries (ACP)." While the categorizations assume certain generalizable similarities between the nations comprised in the categories – one thinks, for example, of the political and economic predicaments faced by these nations as a result of their commonly shared histories of colonization – the net results of their similar predicaments in history are experienced differently by and within each nation.

Are such abstractions bad? Not necessarily. They allow us to generalize and to write history on the basis of "patterns." The problem arises when such "patterns," as rational abstractions, are taken for the indubitable real. For, says Quine, "a general term in good standing can still, like 'unicorn', be true of nothing." About them we can now say that as "ideas and images [they] are enacted within a power system [and used] to reproduce structures of belief and experience through which cultural differences are understood."[34] According to Quine:

> The uniformity that unites us in communication and belief is a uniformity of resultant patterns overlying a chaotic subjective diversity of connections between words and experience. Uniformity comes where [and when] it matters socially; hence rather in point of intersubjectively conspicuous circumstances of utterance than in point of privately conspicuous ones.[35]

With respect to all critics, it is pertinent to reiterate that asserting, first, the difference between the imaginaries and the real; and second, that the way identities have been defined reflects the imaginaries rather than the real does not in itself necessarily amount to an underestimation of how the political – power – often manipulates the imaginaries in order to effect *real* experiences of *real* individuals. In this sense, the critique of attribution of identities by means of the separation of the imaginaries from the real becomes a political critique which in itself closes the gap between itself and the positions which critique and decry the moral and political aberrations of those who victimize individuals and groups of people on the basis of erroneous senses of identity. This is what Appiah says so well and so strongly when he writes that "If an African identity is to empower us, so it seems to me, what is required is not so much that we throw out falsehood but that we acknowledge first of all that race and history and metaphysics do not enforce an identity."[36] Mudimbe alludes to it when he frequently refers to the Sartrean dictum: "I am what I am not, and I am not what I am." In other words, essentialist and imagined, determinate and dialectical identities suppose each other all the time:

> that essential identities will ultimately be required, by their own conceptual incoherence in the face of the unpredictable nature of experience, to maintain themselves by exercising force against the very individuals whose identities they constitute. Dialectical identities, on the other hand, are not subject to this particular incoherence, for while they are based on a set of experiences, and an internalization of what is common to those experiences, they do not exclude the possibility that future experiences will subvert present identities.[37]

Is this so hard to see? Perhaps, but hopefully not. A closure with a quote from Quine *contra* realists might be appropriate:

> Pressed, they may explain that abstract objects do not exist the way physical ones do. The difference is not, they say, just a difference in two sorts of objects, one in space-time and one not, but a difference in two senses of "there are"; so that, in the sense in which there are concrete objects, there are no abstract ones. But then there remain two difficulties, a little one and a big one. The little one is that

the philosopher who would repudiate abstract objects seems to be left saying that there are such after all, in the sense of "there are" appropriate to them. The big one is that the distinction between there being one sense of "there are" for concrete objects and another for abstract ones, and there being just one sense of "there are" for both, makes no sense.

Such philosophical double talk, which would repudiate an ontology while enjoying its benefits, thrives on vagaries of ordinary language.[38]

Notes

1   Abiola Irele, "Contemporary thought in French-speaking Africa," in Albert Mosley (ed.), *African Philosophy: Selected Readings* (Prentice Hall, Englewood Cliffs, NJ, 1995), pp. 263–96; quote from p. 296.

2   Willard V.O. Quine, *Word and Object* (MIT Press, Cambridge, MA, 1960), pp. 2–3.

3   V.Y. Mudimbe, *The Idea of Africa* (Indiana University Press, Bloomington, IN, 1994).

4   Quine, *Word and Object*, p. 4.

5   Ibid., p. 7.

6   Max Horkheimer and Theodor W. Adorno, *Dialectics of Enlightenment*, trans. John Cumming (Continuum, New York, 1975).

7   John McCumber, "Dialectical identity in a 'post-critical' era: a Hegelian reading," *South Atlantic Quarterly*, vol. 94, no. 4, 1995 (special issue on *Nations, Identities, Cultures*), pp. 1145–60.

8   V.Y. Mudimbe, *Parables and Fables: Exegesis, Textuality, and Politics in Central Africa* (University of Wisconsin Press, Madison, WI, 1991); Peter Rigby, *Persistent Pastoralists: Nomadic Socieities in Transition* (Zed, London, 1985).

9   McCumber, "Dialectical identity," p. 1147.

10 Henri Maurier, *Philosophie de l'Afrique noire* (Verlag St Augustin, Bonn, 1976, 2nd edn 1985).

11 Carole Pearce, "African philosophy and the sociological thesis," *Philosophy of the Social Sciences*, vol. 22, no. 4, 1992; Franz Cahay, "Le Décollage conceptual: conditions d'une philosophie bantoue," *Diogène*, no. 52, 1965.

12 Christa Bürger, "Modernity as Post-Modernity: Lyotard," in Scott Lash and Jonathan Friedman (eds), *Modernity and Identity* (Oxford University Press, Oxford, 1992).

13 David F. Grüber, "Foucault's critique of the liberal individual," *Journal of Philosophy*, vol. 86, 1989, p. 617.

14 Kwame A. Appiah, *In My Father's House: Africa in the Philosophy of Culture* (Oxford University Press, London and New York, 1992).

15 Karl Popper, *Conjectures and Refutations: The Growth of Scientific Knowledge* (Routledge and Kegan Paul, London, 1962).

16 Robin Horton, "African traditional religion and Western science," *Africa*, vol. 37, nos 1 and 2, 1967, pp. 50–71, 155–87; *Patterns of Thought in Africa and the West* (Cambridge University Press, Cambridge, 1994).

17 Ivan Karp, "Introduction: museums and communities: the politics of public culture," in Ivan Karp, Christine Mullen Kreamer, and Steven D. Levine (eds), *Museums and Communities: The Politics of Public Culture* (Smithsonian Institution Press, Washington, DC, 1992), pp. 1–2.

18 Edward Said, *Orientalism* (Pantheon, New York, 1978); Mudimbe, *Idea of Africa*.

19 Richard Rorty, *Philosophy and the Mirror of Nature* (Princeton University Press, Princeton, NJ, 1979), p. 6.

20 Russell Jacoby, "Marginal returns: the trouble with post-colonial theory," *Lingua Franca*, September/October 1995, pp. 30–7.

21 Ibid.

22 Appiah, *In My Father's House*, p. 74.

23 Ernest Sosa, *Knowledge in Perspective: Selected Essays in Epistemology* (Cambridge University Press, Cambridge, 1991).

24 Ibid., p. 11.

25 Appiah, *In My Father's House*, p. 174.

26 See, among others, Paulin J. Hountondji, *African Philosophy: Myth and Reality* (Indiana University Press, Bloomington, IN, 1983); Kwame Gyekye, *An Essay on African Philosophical Thought: The Akan Conceptual Scheme* (Cambridge University Press, Cambridge, 1987; 2nd edn Temple University Press, Philadelphia, PA, 1995); Appiah, *In My Father's House*.

27 Initiated by the late Oruka, and well used in Barry Hallen and J.O. Sodipo, *Knowledge, Belief and Witchcraft: Analytical Experiments in African Philosophy* (Ethnographica, London, 1986); Gyekye, *Essay on African Philosophical Thought*; Henry O. Oruka, *Sage Philosophy: Indigenous Thinkers and Modern Debate on African Philosophy* (E.J. Brill, Leiden and New York, 1990); and Appiah, *In My Father's House*.

28 Kwasi Wiredu, "On defining African philosophy," in Herta Nagl-Docekal and Franz M. Wimmer (eds), *Postkoloniales Philosophieren: Afrika* (R. Oldenbourg Verlag, Vienna and Munich, 1992), p. 51.

29 Ibid., p. 46.

30 V.Y. Mudimbe, *The Invention of Africa* (Indiana University Press, Bloomington, IN, 1988).

31 Kwasi Wiredu, "Formulating modern thought in African languages: some theoretical considerations," in V.Y. Mudimbe (ed.), *The Surreptitious Speech: Présence Africaine and the Politics of Otherness 1947–1987* (University of Chicago Press, Chicage, IL, 1992).

32 Karp, "Introduction," pp. 3–4.

33 Benedict Anderson, *Imagined Communities: Reflections on the Origin and Spread of Nationalism* (Verso, London, 1983).

34 Quine, *Word and Object*, p. 240.

35 Ibid., p. 8.

36 Appiah, *In My Father's House*, p. 176. On pp. 177–80, Appiah gives excellent illustrations of his point. Certainly, anyone could add a long line of examples to that list.

37 McCumber, "Dialectical identity," pp. 1157–8.

38 Quine, *Word and Object*, pp. 241–2.

PART V

Thoughts for a Postcolonial Future

14

Democracy and Consensus in African Traditional Politics: A Plea for a Non-party Polity

Kwasi Wiredu

It is often remarked that decision making in traditional African life and governance was, as a rule, by consensus. Like all generalizations about complex subjects, it may be legitimate to take this with a pinch of prudence. But there is considerable evidence that decision by consensus was often the order of the day in African deliberations, and on principle. So it was not just an exercise in hyperbole when Kaunda, (democratically) displaced President of Zambia, said "In our original societies we operated by consensus. An issue was talked out in solemn conclave until such time as agreement could be achieved,"[1] or when Nyerere, retired President of Tanzania, also said, "in African society the traditional method of conducting affairs is by free discussion" and quoted Guy Clutton-Brock with approval to the effect that "The elders sit under the big trees, and talk until they agree."[2]

Ironically, both pronouncements were made in the course of a defence of the one-party system. Of this I will have more to say below. But for now, let us note an important fact about the role of consensus in African life. It is that the reliance on consensus is not a peculiarly political phenomenon. Where consensus characterizes political decision making in Africa, it is manifestation of an immanent approach to social interaction. Generally, in interpersonal relations among adults, consensus as a basis of joint action was taken as axiomatic. This is not to say it was always attained. Nowhere was African society a realm of unbroken harmony. On the contrary, conflicts (including mortal ones) among lineages and ethnic groups and within them were not infrequent. The remarkable thing, however, is that if and when a resolution of the issues was negotiated, the point of it was seen in the attainment of reconciliation rather than the mere abstention from further recriminations or collisions. It is important to note that disputes can be settled without the achievement of reconciliation.

Reconciliation is, in fact, a form of consensus. It is a restoration of goodwill through a reappraisal of the significance of the initial bones of contention. It does not necessarily involve a complete identity of moral or cognitive opinions. It suffices that all parties are able to feel that adequate account has been taken of their points of view in any proposed scheme of future action or coexistence. Similarly, consensus does not in general entail total agreement. To begin with, consensus usually presupposes an original position of diversity. Because issues do not always polarize opinion on lines of strict contradictoriness, dialogue can function, by means, for example, of the smoothing of edges, to produce compromises that are agreeable to all or, at least, not obnoxious to any. Furthermore, where there is the will to consensus, dialogue can lead to a willing suspension of disagreement, making possible agreed actions without necessarily agreed notions. This is important because certain situations do, indeed, precipitate exhaustive disjunctions which no dialogic accommodations can mediate. For example, either we are to go to war or we are not. The problem then is how a group without unanimity may settle on one option rather than the other without alienating anyone. This is the severest challenge of consensus, and it can only be met by the willing suspension of disbelief in the prevailing option on the part of the residual minority. The feasibility of this depends not only on the patience and persuasiveness of the right people, but also on the fact that African traditional systems of the consensual type were not such as to place any one group of persons consistently in the position of a minority. Of this, too, more below.

But, first, let us see how faith in consensus worked in one concrete example of an African traditional system of politics. It may be well to note, as a preliminary, that African political systems of the past displayed considerable variety. There is a basic distinction between those systems with a centralized authority exercised through the machinery of government, and those without any such authority in which social life was not regulated at any level by the sort of machinery that might be called a government. Fortes and Evans-Pritchard classify the Zulu (of South Africa), the Ngwato (also of South Africa), the Bemba (of Zambia), the Banyankole (of Uganda), and the Kede (of northern Nigeria) under the first category, and the Logoli (of western Kenya), the Tallensi (of northern Ghana), and the Nuer (of southern Sudan) under the second.[3] It is, or should be, a matter of substantial interest to political thinkers that societies of the second description – that is, anarchistic societies – existed and functioned in an orderly manner, or at least not with any less order than the more centralized ones. It is also, perhaps, easier in the context of the less centralized social orders to appreciate the necessity of consensus. Where the exercise of authority (as, for example, in the settlement of disputes) rested purely on moral and, perhaps, metaphysical prestige, it is obvious that decision by the preponderance of numbers would be likely to be dysfunctional. But it is more interesting to observe that the habit of decision by consensus in politics was studiously cultivated in some of the most centralized and, if it comes to it, warlike, ethnic groups of Africa, such as the Zulu and the Ashantis. By a somewhat paradoxical contrast, the authorities in some of the comparatively less militaristic of the centralized societies, such as the Bemba or the Banyankole, seem to have manifested less enthusiasm for consensus in political decision making than the Ashantis or the Zulu.[4] In what immediately follows I propose to take advantage of the elaborate description and analysis of the Ashanti traditional system of politics in K.A. Busia's *The Position of the Chief in the Modern Political System of Ashanti*[5] and my own personal experience to trace the course of consensus in the Ashanti political example.

The lineage is the basic political unit among the Ashantis. Because they are a matrilineal group, this unit consists of all the people in a town or village having a common female ancestor, which, as a rule, is quite a considerable body of persons. Every such unit has a head, and every such head is automatically a member of the council which is the governing body of the town or village. The qualifications for lineage headship are seniority in age, wisdom, a sense of civic responsibility and logical persuasiveness. All these qualities are often united in the most senior, but non-senile, member of the lineage. In that case, election is almost routine. But where these qualities do not seem to converge in one person, election may entail prolonged and painstaking consultations and discussions aimed at consensus. There is never an act of formal voting. Indeed, there is no longstanding word for voting in the language of the Ashantis. The expression which is currently used for that process (*aba to*) is an obvious modern coinage for a modern cultural import or, shall we say, imposition.

The point, then, at which the head of a lineage is elected is the point at which consensus first makes itself felt in the Ashanti political process. This office, when conferred on a person, is for life unless moral, intellectual, or physical degeneration sets in. As the representative of the lineage in the governing council of a town, he or, in rare cases, she is in duty bound to hold consultations with the adult members of the lineage regarding municipal matters. In any matter of particular significance, consensus is always the watchword. It is also the watchword at the level of the municipal council, which, as indicated, consists of the lineage heads. That council is presided over by the "natural ruler" of the town, called a *chief*. This word, though tainted with colonial condescension, has remained in general use even in the postindependence era by dint of terminological inertia. The "natural" aspect of this position lies in its basic hereditary status: normally, a chief can only come from the royal lineage. But it is only basically hereditary, for a lineage being a quite substantial kinship group, there is at any one time a non-negligible number of qualified candidates. The choice, which is proposed by the "queen mother" (the mother or aunt or maternal sister or cousin of the chief), has to be approved by the council and endorsed by the populace through an organization called, in literal translation, "the young people's association" in order to become final.

Contrary to a deliberately fostered appearance, the personal word of the chief was not law. His official word, on the other hand, is the consensus of his council, and it is only in this capacity that it may be law; which is why the Akans have the saying that there are no bad kings, only bad councilors. Of course, an especially opinionated chief, if he also had the temerity, might try, sometimes with success, to impose his will upon a council. But a chief of such habits was as likely as not to be eventually deposed. In truth, as Abraham, also speaking of the Akans, points out in *The Mind of Africa*, "kingship was more a sacred office than a political one."[6] The office was "sacred" because a chief was supposed to be the link between the living population and their departed ancestors, who were supposed to supervise human interests from their postmortem vantage point. In so far as it was political, it bore substantial analogies to the status of a constitutional monarch. The chief was the symbol of the unity of his kingdom and, in the normal course of his duties, fulfilled a variety of ceremonial functions. But he was unlike a constitutional monarch in being a member (at least as a lineage personage) of the ruling council, and in being in a position to exercise legitimate influence on its deliberations by virtue, not of any supposed divine inspiration, but rather of whatever intrinsic persuasiveness his ideas may have had.

If these facts are borne in mind, it becomes apparent that the council was strongly representative with respect to both the nature of its composition and the content of its decisions. This representativeness was duplicated at all levels of authority in the Ashanti state. The town or city councils were the most basic theater of political authority. Representatives from these councils constituted divisional councils presided over by "paramount" chiefs. These latter units also sent representatives to the national council presided over by the "Asantehene," the king of the Ashantis, at the highest level of traditional government. It is at this stage, perhaps, needless to say that decision was by consensus at all these levels.

Now, this adherence to the principle of consensus was a premeditated option. It was based on the belief that *ultimately* the interests of all members of society are the same, although their immediate perceptions of those interests may be different. This thought is given expression in an art motif depicting a crocodile with one stomach and two heads locked in struggle over food. If they could but see that the food was, in any case, destined for the same stomach, the irrationality of the conflict would be manifest to them. But is there a chance of it? The Ashanti answer is "Yes, human beings have the ability eventually to cut through their differences to the rock bottom identity of interests." And, on this view, the means to that objective is simply rational discussion. Of the capabilities of this means the Ashantis are explicit. "There is," they say, "no problem of human relations that cannot be resolved by dialogue." Dialogue, of course, presupposes not just two parties (at least), but also two conflicting positions: "One head does not hold council." Nor was any suggestion that one voice might be entitled to be heard to the exclusion of others countenanced for one moment: "Two heads are better than one," says another maxim. Indeed, so much did the Ashantis (and the Akans in general) prize rational discussion as an avenue to consensus among adults that the capacity for elegant and persuasive discourse was made one of the most crucial qualifications for high office.

I would like to emphasize that the pursuit of consensus was a deliberate effort to go beyond decision by majority opinion. It is easier to secure majority agreement than to achieve consensus. And the fact was not lost upon the Ashantis. But they spurned that line of least resistance. To them, majority opinion is not in itself a good enough basis for decision making, for it deprives the minority of the right to have their will reflected in the given decision. Or, to put it in terms of the concept of representation, it deprives the minority of the right of representation in the decision in question. Two concepts of representation are involved in these considerations. There is the representation of a given constituency in council, and there is the representation of the will of a representative in the making of a given decision. Let us call the first formal and the second substantive representation. Then, it is obvious that you can have formal representation without its substantive correlate. Yet, the formal is for the sake of the substantive. On the Ashanti view, substantive representation is a matter of a fundamental human right. Each human being has the right to be represented not only in council, but also in counsel in any matter relevant to his or her interests or those of their groups. This is why consensus is so important.

Nor are pragmatic reasons lacking to the same purport. Formal representation without substance is apt to induce disaffection. If the system in use is such as to cause some groups periodically to be in substantively unrepresented minorities, then seasonal disaffection becomes institutionalized. The results are the well-known inclemencies of adversarial politics. From the Ashanti standpoint, consensus is the antidote. But, again, can consensus always be had? As already noted, the Ashantis seem to have thought that it could, at least in principle. But suppose this is not the case. Even so, it can always be aimed at, and the point is that any system of politics that is seriously dedicated to this aim must be institutionally different from a system based on the sway of the majority, however hedged around with "checks and balances."

What is the bearing of these considerations on democracy? Current forms of democracy are generally systems based on the majority principle. The party that wins the majority of seats or the greatest proportion of the votes, if the system in force is one of proportional representation, is invested with governmental power. Parties under this scheme of political things are organizations of people of similar tendencies and aspirations with the sole aim of gaining power for the implementation of their policies. Let us call such systems *majoritarian democracies*. Then, those based on consensus may be called *consensual democracies*. The Ashanti system was a consensual democracy. It was a democracy because government was by the consent, and subject to the control, of the people as expressed through their representatives. It was consensual because, at least as a rule, that consent was negotiated on the principle of consensus. (By contrast, the majoritarian system might be said to be, in principle, based on "consent" without consensus.)

The Ashanti system, furthermore, was not a *party* system in the sense of the word "party" noted in the last paragraph, which is basic to majoritarian democracy. But in a broad lexical sense there were parties. The lineages were parties to the project of good government. Moreover, in every Ashanti town the youth constituted themselves into an organized party under a recognized leader who was entitled to make representations directly (though not as a member) to the relevant council on all matters of public interest. The sense in which the system in question did not feature parties is that none of the groups mentioned organized themselves for the purpose of gaining power in a way which entailed others not being in power or, worse, being out of it. For all concerned, the system was set up for participation in power, not its appropriation, and the underlying philosophy was one of cooperation, not confrontation.

This is the aspect of the traditional system to which the advocates of the one-party system appealed in their attempts to prove its African ancestry and authenticity. The illusory analogy was this. In a one-party system there is no conflict of parties. No party loses because *the* party wins. The comparison is faulty for the following reason. In the traditional set-up, no party lost because all the parties were natural partners in power or, more strictly, because there were no parties. In the one-party situation, the reason why no party loses is because murdered parties do not compete. (If these last remarks should occasion any sense of inconsistency, a careful disambiguation of the term "party" in this context should dissipate it.) *Now Gone*

The disappearance of the one-party system from the African scene is, and should remain, unlamented. But my reason for mentioning that subject is not to flog a dead horse; it is, in fact, to point out the good parts of a bad case. One valid point which was made again and again by the one-party persuaders is that there is no necessary connection between democracy and the multiparty system. An associated insight was that indigenous African systems of politics, at least in some well-known instances, offered examples of democracy without a multiparty mechanism. But although the traditional systems in question avoided this mechanism, it should be constantly borne in mind that, as already noted, it had room for parties in the broad sense. This is important because these parties provided the centers of independent thought presupposed by the very idea of meaningful dialogue in the process of political decision making – those conditions of rational interaction that the one-party system was so efficient in destroying.

In the drive towards democracy that occurred in Africa in the past half decade or so, African dictators, civilian and military, were under sustained Western pressure to adopt the multiparty way of life. This proved politically fatal to some of them, though others eventually discovered tricks for surviving multiparty elections. There is no denying, of course, that some gains in freedom have accrued to the African populations. But how substantial have these been and to what extent have these developments built on the strengths of the indigenous institutions of politics in Africa? It is hard to be convinced that this question has yet attracted enough attention.

The cause of this relative neglect of the question may conceivably be connected with its difficulty. The conditions of traditional political life were surely less complicated than those of the present. The kinship networks that provided the mainstay of the consensual politics of traditional times are simply incapable of serving the same purpose in modern Africa. This is especially so in the urban areas, where industrialization, albeit paltry in many parts of Africa, has created conditions, such as sharp socioeconomic cleavages, which carry all or many of the ingredients of ideological politics. In these circumstances it may well seem a trifle too utopian to envisage the possibility of a non-party approach to politics.

It might seem, furthermore, that the account of traditional politics given above essentially involves exaggerations of harmony in traditional life. In fact, even if consensus prevailed in the politics of certain ethnic groups in Africa, historically, interethnic relations involving those same groups have, *by nature*, been marked, or more strictly, marred by frequent wars, the most extreme negations of consensus. The point is not just that there have been ethnic wars from time to time, as was conceded early on, but more seriously, that the ethnic orientation of the various groups, by their own inward fixations, has tended to generate conflict in their external relations. Of this the contemporary world has unspeakably tragic illustrations. It might seem, therefore, that neither in the past nor in the present nor in any foreseeable future can consensus be seen to have been, or to promise, a realistic basis for politics in any African state that is a composite of distinct ethnic units. On the contrary, so it might appear, the more pluralistic approach of a multiparty system, provided it incorporates reasonable safeguards against the tyranny of the majority, offers the more practical option.

The premises of both objections may be granted, quite readily in the first case and with a qualification in the second. But the conclusions in favor of the multiparty system in both cases are non sequiturs. As regards the premises, it is true that any suggestion that the kinship basis of traditional politics could be a model for contemporary African politics can be dismissed as an anachronistic nostalgia. But, in the matter of conflict among the ethnic groups, it should be noted that African history furnishes examples not only of conflict, but also of cooperation among them. Still, the history of interethnic conflict and the problem of its contemporary reverberations ought not to be minimized. Interestingly, exactly this is one of the reasons why the idea of a consensual non-party system ought to be taken especially seriously in Africa.

One of the most persistent causes of political instability in Africa derives from the fact that, in ever so many contemporary African states, certain ethnic groups have found themselves in the minority both numerically and politically. Under a system of majoritarian democracy this means that, even with all the safeguards, they will consistently find themselves outside the corridors of power. The frustrations and disaffections, with their disruptive consequences for the polity, should not have caught anybody by surprise.

Consider the non-party alternative. Imagine a dispensation under which governments are formed not by parties, but by the consensus of elected representatives. Government, in other words, becomes a kind of coalition – a coalition not, as in the common acceptation, of parties, but of citizens. There is no impediment whatsoever to the formation of political associations to propagate preferred ideologies. But in councils of state, affiliation with any such association does not necessarily determine the chances of selection for a position of responsibility. Two things can be expected. First, political associations will be avenues for channeling all desirable pluralisms, but they will be without the Hobbesian proclivities of political parties, as they are known under majoritarian politics. And second, without the constraints of membership in parties relentlessly dedicated to wrestling power or retaining it, representatives will be more likely to be actuated by the objective merits of given proposals than by ulterior considerations. In such an environment, willingness to compromise, and with it the prospects of consensus, will be enhanced.

Consensus is not just an optional bonus. As can be inferred from my earlier remarks, it is essential for securing substantive, or what might also be called decisional, representation for representatives and, through them, for the citizens at large. This is nothing short of a matter of fundamental human rights. Consensus as a political decision procedure requires, in principle, that each representative should be persuaded, if not of the optimality of each decision, at least of its practical necessity, all things considered. If discussion has been even moderately rational and the spirit has been one of respectful accommodation on all sides, surviving reservations on the part of a momentary minority will not prevent the recognition that, if the community is to go forward, a particular line of action must be taken. This should not be confused with decision making on the principle of the supreme right of the majority. In the case under discussion, the majority prevails not over, but upon, the minority – it prevails upon them to accept the proposal in question, not just to live with it, which latter is the basic plight of minorities under majoritarian democracy. In a consensus system, the voluntary acquiescence of the minority with respect to a given issue would normally be necessary for the adoption of a decision. In the rare case of an intractable division, a majority vote might be used to break the impasse. But the success of the system must be judged by the rarity of such predicaments in the workings of the decision-making bodies of the state. A less unwelcome use of majorities might occur in the election of representatives. Here choice may have to be determined by superior numbers in terms of votes. But even here the representatives will be under obligation to consult with all the tendencies of opinion in their constituencies and work out, as much as possible, a consensual basis of representation.

Further points of detail and even of principle remain to be spelled out, but these indications must make it plausible to suppose that, in the consensual non-party system, no one group, ethnic or ideological, will be afflicted with the sense of being permanent outsiders to state power. That alone should suffice to forestall some, at least, of the unhappy conflicts that have bedeviled African life on to our own times. Thus, far from the complexities of contemporary African life making the consensual, non-party precedents of traditional African politics now unusable, they make them indispensable. For this reason, if for no other, the exploration of that alternative to multiparty politics should commend itself to the urgent attention of contemporary African philosophers and political scientists. But there is nothing peculiarly African about the idea itself. If it is valid, especially with respect to its human rights dimension, it ought to be a concern for our whole species.

Notes

1 Gideon-Cyrus M. Mutiso and S.W. Rohio (eds), *Readings in African Political Thought* (Heinemann, London, 1975), p. 476.

2 Ibid., p. 478. K.A. Busia also comments on the same single-minded pursuit of consensus as it obtained among the traditional Akans of Ghana in his *Africa in Search of Democracy* (Routledge and Kegan Paul, London, 1967). The passage will bear extended quotation:

> When a council, each member of which was the representative of a lineage, met to discuss matters affecting the whole community, it had always to grapple with the problem of reconciling sectional and common interests. In order to do this, the members had to talk things over: they had to listen to all the different points of view. So strong was the value of solidarity that the chief aim of the councilors was to reach unanimity, and they talked till this was achieved. (p. 28)

3 M. Fortes and E.E. Evans-Pritchard (eds), *African Political Systems* (Oxford

University Press, Oxford, 1940), p. 5.

4   See, for example, Max Gluckman, "The Kingdom of the Zulu of South Africa",
I. Schapera, "The political organization of the Ngwato of Bechuanaland Protec-
torate" (present-day Botswana); and Audrey I. Richards, "The political system of
the Bemba tribe – north-eastern Rhodesia" (in present-day Zambia), all in Fortes
and Evans-Pritchard, *African Political Systems*.

5   K.A. Busia, *The Position of the Chief in the Modern Political System of Ashanti* (Frank
Cass, London, 1951). The Ashantis are a subgroup of the Akans. Other subgroups
are the Akims, Akuapims, Denkyiras, Fantes, Kwahus, Brongs, Wassas, and
Nzimas. The Akans, as a whole, constitute nearly half of the population of Ghana,
occupying parts of the middle and southern regions of the country. The Ivory Coast
is also home to some Akan groups. The account given of the Ashanti system is true,
in all essentials, of the Akans in general.

6   W.E. Abraham, *The Mind of Africa* (University of Chicago Press, Chicago, IL,
1962):

> [B]ecause the king was surrounded by councilors whose offices were
> political, and was himself only a representation of the unity of the people,
> it was quite possible to remove him from office; the catalogue of the possible
> grounds of removal was already held in advance. (p. 77)

Stance: Democracy & Consensus (Ashanti method) don't mix.

*Consensus method allowed for individuals, for the
most part, be heard & everyone gets something. Being
forced to have a one party system forces people to
think critically & fraternize w/ one another to resolve issues.
Having a multi-party mechanism creates too much
division. Having a one party system is better.*

15

Democracy or Consensus? A Response to Wiredu

Emmanuel Chukwudi Eze

Summary of Wiredu ⤵

In the preceding chapter, Kwasi Wiredu undertakes an important and necessary task: the search for a conceptual political paradigm that would end the chronic conflicts and destruction that plague numerous African societies – from Rwanda and Somalia to Sudan and Nigeria. Wiredu's particular angle on this problem, as he states it here, may be classified along with those African thinkers who *Answer* advocated a "return" to the "tradition"; or a "return to the source" as Amilcar Cabral would call it. It is an attempt to (re)discover in the African precolonial past resilient forms of social and political organization that, with proper reworking, would lead some African countries out of their current self-destructive patterns of political existence. In addition to Cabral's "return to the source," efforts similar to Wiredu's thought include the "African socialism" of Senghor, Nyerere's "Ujamaa," and, with strong qualifications, Ousmane Sembene's dialectical constructions of "the people" as the source of political salvation in his movies (*Xala*, for example). *The differences*

The "return to the source" model is quite different from the route taken today by many African countries that seek democratic ideals through movements whose historical examples are rooted in the modern European traditions. The most recent examples include the movement that led to the overthrow of Kenneth Kaunda's government through the ballot. The African demand for a Western-style democratic process is also evident in the varied forms of Moshood Abiola's campaign for "democracy" in Nigeria. When the military regime of Ibrahim Babangida arbitrarily suspended the 1993 elections and paved the way for Nigeria's current dictatorship, Abiola, as the front-runner in the quashed election, initiated his campaign against the military by flying out of the country to London, Paris, and then Washington, and by

Ex of "Adversarial Democracy"

[Handwritten margin notes, top:]

2. Understood by general public
3. Different approaches of democracy
4. Deriving ideas/styles from a broad and diverse range of sources

5. Combining different belief while blending schools of thought

[Handwritten left margin, vertical:]
1. Understood by a small amount of people

establishing in each place – with backing from the governments – effective pressure on Abacha to restore "democracy." So "democracy" here is understood and articulated in the multiparty language of the political traditions of the West, a democracy that the West also sometimes requires of African states as a precondition for economic and military aid.

If we label the first ("return to the source") search for African democracy as an esoteric movement, then we can call the second type exoteric. In Wiredu's formulation, and with reference to the Ashanti tradition, the first route would lead to an indigenously inspired African form of "consensual democracy." The second, however, would lead to a Western-style "adversarial democracy." I should point out that Wiredu's terminology is sometimes different from the one I would choose: for example, according to him, "consensual democracy" belongs to the African "traditional," precolonial past, while "adversarial" democracy is a Western import to "modern," postcolonial Africa. I do not favor the characterizations of one model as automatically "Western" and therefore "modern" and "postcolonial", while the other is automatically "African" and therefore "traditional" and "precolonial." (These are the sort of not-always-accurate conceptual dichotomies within which anthropologists love to reify African existence.) If we were to look at the way many "modern" African dictators have manipulated the traditional ideals of consensus politics to centralize power in their arbitrary hands, we would know that political practices in Africa today are a more flexible and often highly eclectic or syncretic melange of the African and the Western, the old and the new, the precolonial, colonial and postcolonial, and so forth.

However, these sorts of flexibility, eclecticism, and overlap between the workings of "modern" and "traditional" political formations in Africa do not obscure Wiredu's basic distinctions between the two forms of "democratic" impulse competing with each other on the continent. According to Wiredu:

> [In traditional Akan political system, for example,] there is never an act of formal voting. Indeed, there is no longstanding word for voting in the language of the Ashantis. The expression which is currently used for that process (*aba to*) is an obvious modern coinage for the modern cultural import or, shall we say, imposition.[1] *Traditional Thought*

Working within these distinctions, it is clear that – to stick with our Nigerian examples – Abiola's campaign derives from the exercise of a democratic political tradition which Wiredu, in the quote given, describes as a "modern cultural import," or "imposition." On the other hand, the African dictators I refer to above – such as Abacha – exploit the traditional resources of "consensual" democracy to build up national support for their regimes.

I do not wish to give the impression that there is something inherent in "consensual" politics that makes it any more susceptible to dictatorial abuse

[Handwritten bottom margin:]
6 & 7. Wiredu v Eze view

than any other form of political practice. A major strength of Wiredu's analysis of "consensual" democracy is precisely this: he exposes how the many dictatorial practices in Africa that flourish under the name of "national unity" or "consensus," one-party governments are indeed not democratic at all, and very repressive of opposition. For Wiredu, the disappearance of these "one-party" forms of government, even by means of the exoteric forms of democratic pressure, should be most welcome. The consensual democracy advocated by Wiredu is not that of one party exercising all the power and – to use Wiredu's word – "murdering" opponents; it is, rather, a framework for sharing with every party the exercise of governing power.

It is the context of political realities such as in Nigeria, the Sudan, Liberia, Rwanda, and Zaire that leads Wiredu, I think, to say that if "imported" or "imposed" forms of democracy succeed in saving Africans from political repression, all the better. But we know that African dictators have invented "tricks" to resist such external pressures: they put up mock multiparty elections that deceive the Western governments (who, we all know, need lots of convincing!) into continuing the supply of military weapons, while keeping intact and untransformed the mechanisms of autocratic, dictatorial, and terroristic exercise of state power. Hence, the need to explore other models of, or models for, African democracy. Wiredu sees the idea of "consensus," or consensual democracy, as "an alternative" to both one-party dictatorship and multiparty, winner-takes-all, adversarial political practices.

The appeal of Wiredu's conception of consensus politics lies primarily in the fact that it promises not just formal, but *substantive* representation. In a classical, multiparty democracy – in the USA or current South Africa, for example, where majority rule is the principle of governance – the issue is how to safeguard the rights of the minority parties who did not "win" elections. In a consensual democracy, however, there is no "winner" (and therefore no "loser"): every party is a government party, and the principle of governance is the reconciliation of competing social interests. Reconciliation, agreement, consensus – not the rule of the majority party – would make up the political axiom. Hence, Wiredu's statements: "consensus was . . . the order of the day in African [political] deliberations, and on principle"; "the elders sit under the big trees, and talk until they agree"; "majority opinion is not in itself a good enough basis for decision making, for it deprives the minority of the right to have their will reflected in the given decision"; and so forth.[2]

In what follows I will examine more critically and closely the quite appealing idea of "consensus" presented to us by Wiredu as a possible way forward. I have some remarks and questions, and will organize them into three, related, themes. First, I will examine Wiredu's presentation of the origins of Ashanti political authority. Second, I will raise some questions about Wiredu's (or the traditional Ashanti's) understanding of the nature of political interests. Finally, I will conclude by looking closely at the numerous meanings that the word "democracy" would have assumed (or shed) through Wiredu's reconstruction of the traditional Ashanti consensual political culture.

1. It is easy to notice that, in a number of places, Wiredu points out – although he does not develop, or scrutinize – the Akan conception of several possible sources of legitimate political power. We read, for example, that qualification for the political office of the head of an Ashanti lineage involves moral considerations: "moral degeneration" is an impediment for this office.[3] Wiredu does not, however, spell out to us what sorts of behavior or conditions qualify as "moral degeneration." (How widely acceptable would the ancient Ashanti moral codes be in today's African worlds?) Moreover, when he approvingly quotes Willy Abraham, Wiredu states that among the Akan "kingship was more a sacred office than a political one."[4] Wiredu's observation on this statement is as follows: "The office was 'sacred' because a chief was *supposed* to be the link between the living population and their departed ancestors, who were *supposed* to supervise human interests from their postmortem vantage point."[5]

The quote from Abraham and Wiredu's comments point directly to notions of "sacred" and "ancestral" sources of legitimation of political power and authority among the Akan. But Wiredu, in his continued commentary, is quick to assure us that, unlike the European monarchs of old, who ruled through "divine" right, the Akan chief exercised "legitimate" influence "by virtue, not of any supposed divine inspiration, but rather of whatever *intrinsic persuasiveness his ideas may have had*."[6]

Thus, of the several possible sources of legitimation of political authority presented here – the "divine" and the "sacred," the "ancestral," and the "virtue . . . of persuasive ideas," Wiredu leads us to believe that the Ashanti relied not on the *supposed* sacred, ancestral, or divine origins of authority, but solely on "the intrinsic persuasiveness [of the king's] ideas." However, Wiredu does not provide clarification of the relations – distinctions, similarities, and, especially, overlaps – that may exist or occur between the enunciated sources of moral legitimation and the normative justification of the exercise of political power. My hypothesis is as follows. First, it is rarely, and perhaps never, the case that one of the sources of legitimation of authority listed by Wiredu exists solely and cleanly independent of the others. Second, I do not understand why we should believe that not only the Akan leader but also his subjects – the distinction is important – thought or believed that the king's or a chief's only legitimate source of exercise of political influence was "the intrinsic persuasiveness of his ideas," and that the gods and the dead are merely *supposed* players in the game.

I think that Wiredu might need further evidence to make a successful case that the king and the chiefs actually ruled, and believed, along with their subjects, that authority could be legitimized only through the secular "virtue of persuasiveness of ideas" (rather than through religious – and sometimes clearly superstitious – appeal to the "sacred," "god," or "ancestors"); although such a case is yet to be made, I must however commend Wiredu's attempt to perform a careful incision between the Akan's beliefs about *supposed* sacred/divine/ancestral sources of power on the one hand, and, I presume, the Akan *actual* political practices on the basis of the virtue of good, rational, and convincing ideas on the other. This incision is needed because, if the aim of this exercise is to recover, re-establish, or simply inspire our current political · practices by means of some viable aspects of the ancient political systems, then it is important to identify what would or would not be workable in the now largely secular states and, certainly, religiously pluralistic African countries. But here is a problem: I wonder whether Wiredu does not – in his rationalistic position and method of separating the "divine," the "sacred," and the "ancestral" on the one hand, and the secular, intrinsically persuasive ideas on the other – undermine the very belief systems that made possible the "consensual" politics of the past – a political framework he now admires. Certainly, one easily notices that when he characterizes "consensus," Wiredu uses terms such as "faith," "belief," "reconciliation," "restoration of goodwill," "moral opinions," and so forth. To what extent, we should ask, do these ideas and notions make sense for the vast majority of African peoples without appeal to mythological, ancestral, and religious scaffoldings?

By treating such scaffolds as merely "supposed," and the "rational" ideas as alone having "real" or "actual" legitimate power and influence, Wiredu seems to suggest that consensual democracy was simply based upon Akan understanding that "human beings have the ability eventually to cut through their differences to the rock bottom identity of interest" through "rational discussion."[7] But which is the fundamental belief, one might ask: is it the belief in the power of reason that led the Ashantis to believe that "*ultimately* the interests of all members of society are the same," or is it the power of their belief in a shared and common past and future (carried forward in the myths of origins) that leads them to the employment of reason and rational discussion as a means of achieving and sustaining this shared life-form?

In this connection, we cannot fail to consider the following: what makes one political idea more persuasive than the other? Wiredu seems to suggest that it is the logical power of the ideas presented. Any observation of successful political formation or governance, however, will show that exercise of public power relies heavily on mythologies and symbols: the flag, the *patrie*, the Motherland, "the Party," "God," "freedom," "liberation," "progress," etc. Many of these notions invite, and often demand, allegiance and assent from those subjected to them. Yet most of them are simply well-formed ancestral, social, religious, or mythological fantasies that succeed in achieving their effects quite often with little or no "reason." These fantasies frequently enable and persuade peoples to participate, to collaborate, and to "see reason" with each other and act together. To conclude: if my suspicions here are correct, then what we need from Wiredu is a more adequate reconstruction of the origins and the basis of traditional consensual democracy. If the traditional mythologi-cal origins and justifications of consensual politics can no longer hold today (due to secularization and religious pluralisms, for example), and it is determined that what we need today is a form of consensual politics, then we may have to (re)invent usable – even as we discard unusable – mythologies. For, even – and especially – a secular political institution, if it renounces brute force as a mode of mobilization, needs some sort of mythology – Plato's "truthful lies," or various forms of utopia – in order to endure.[8]

2. It seems to me, then, that Wiredu would not just reconstruct an abstract normative basis for Ashanti political practices, but do so taking adequate account of *actually* existing social conditions and competing interests. Such a reconstruction would go hand in hand with a re-examination of Wiredu's controversial claim that "*ultimately* the interests of all members of society are the same, although their immediate perceptions of those interests may be different."[9] If we isolate the first part of this statement: "the interests of all members of society are the same," why would one accept it as true – even if we added the qualification "ultimately?" The interests of some members or a member of a society may be to dominate the rest, for the sheer morbid enjoyment of power. Now, how is such psychological "interest" of the dictator reconcilable with that of the dominated? Here is another example. Consider some "conflicts of interests" that might develop out of the nature of international capitalism. How do the *commercial* interests of a Texan oil company, or the Anglo-Dutch Shell oil company, in Nigeria simply to get oil out of the soil as quickly and as safely as possible, coincide with the political and survival interests of, comparatively speaking, a few thousand people called the Ogonis? Or yet another example: how do the interests of some 95 percent of Americans who share only as much wealth as another 1 percent of the same population coincide? How are the social and political interests of such groups in a society "ultimately" "the same" – unless the word "ultimate" here simply means in eternity (for example, "In heaven everyone will be equal")? Wiredu's answer – and he tells us it is also the traditional Akan's – is that it is ignorance that precludes these various groups (and us, I suppose) from seeing that these groups *at bottom* "really" desire or want the same things. According to Wiredu, it is "their [and our?] immediate *perceptions* of those interests [that] may be different."[10] So it is the *mis*perceptions of the actors that make them see and pursue divergent interests! Our "immediate perceptions" render them unaware that "ultimately" our own interests are the same as those of others. What I want to highlight here, in the second part of Wiredu's statement, is the suggestion that it is all about "perception." If only we would "see" better, "understand" better, "think" better, "know" better, or "reason" better – if only this, we will know how "irrational" it is to defend our sectarian, class, or ethnic interests in opposition to others. Furthermore, we will abandon

14. Immediate perception v. Good Knowledge — Purpose of good Knowledge, Why it's important.

A Response to Wiredu 319

this irrational behavior in favor of consensual and mutually beneficial actions upon attainment of such knowledge; hence the statement: "human beings have the [rational] ability eventually to cut through their differences to the rock bottom identity of interests."[11] The truth of this statement can easily be challenged.

Although Wiredu does not elaborate on the meaning of qualifying terms such as "eventually" or "ultimately" as they are deployed in these contexts, he nevertheless presents two main ideas in the statement: (1) there exists human "rock bottom identity of interests," and (2) good knowledge – long-term instead of "immediate" perceptions, to be precise – might be all we need to become convinced of the need to act harmoniously in function of the rock bottom identity of interests. In this second claim, one can easily notice the additional problem of conflation of right knowledge (or understanding or perception) and right action: if we "perceive" better, we will somehow act better morally (a classic problem of Plato's Socrates, too, in "knowledge is virtue"?)[12]

To remain with the logic of the Ashanti political tradition which Wiredu presents to us, however, we must follow the original and unique metaphors. Wiredu speaks of a two-headed crocodile. "If they [the two heads of the lone crocodile] could see that the food before them was, in any case, destined for the same stomach, the *irrationality* of the heads' fight [over who masticates the food] would be manifest to them." On the other hand, if they "saw" (i.e., perceived or understood) the common destination of the food, the heads would change their behavior from the "irrational" (conflictual) to the "rational" (consensual). This conclusion, drawn by Wiredu, however, assumes two pieces of information which were not given, or self-evident, in the art motif described. Wiredu's conclusion, it seems to me, assumes that there is no "rational" basis for each of the crocodile heads to fight for passage of food: the more food that passes through *my* mouth (teeth, jaws, tongue, etc.) rather than through yours, the better. In order to declare "irrational" such struggles and conflicts over the privilege of food passage through mouth A rather than B, one would have to rule out any possibility that, first, there may exist, *strictum dictu*, extranutritional reasons – such as aesthetic pleasure, the sheer joy of chewing food; in fact, the joy of eating! – which could accrue to one head independently of the other. Second, if there is *no* possibility of such head-specific primal masticatory enjoyment, then why would either of the heads *fight* to masticate the food – it would be irrational indeed to engage in such fight. If however, there are head-specific masticatory benefits of whatever sort that would make either or both of the heads *want* to chew food, then the only way to justifiably declare "irrational" the struggles and conflicts over food is to guarantee that, no matter what quantity of food each head chewed, both would *equally* (quantitatively and qualitatively) share the enjoyment. Now, what if the heads cannot *want*, individually, because the two-headed beast knows itself as one, instead of many? Well, then, of course, there would be no struggles or conflict about food, or

320   *Emmanuel Chukwudi Eze*

about power as we know it in politics. Thus, finally, the ultimate guarantee that would ensure the possibility of *identical* interests at "rock bottom" is that neither of the heads could develop an *individuated* structure of *desire* – the absolute guarantee against (inclination to, or suspicion of) greed and (infliction of, or fear of) domination.

Unless such absolute guarantee can be obtained, we may never *justly* prohibit or condemn a priori "struggles" or "conflicts" among the crocodile heads over resources for satisfaction of needs or privileges; nor could we declare such struggles and conflicts, following Wiredu, as behaviors whose "irrationality" is "manifest."[13] If the *human* condition, in principle, cannot guarantee, or is denied, the possibility of absolute justice, then struggles and conflicts – i.e., the agonistics of competitive (and, hopefully, democratic) politics – would always be manifestly rational. I will return to this point at the end.

There is not much self-evident truth in the assertion that, at "rock bottom," all interests of members of a given society are "identical."[14] This "rock bottom" level at which all "human" interests may be same, I would argue, could not possibly be a human bottom, or at least not in the ordinary human world, where humans experience themselves as individuals. I am also hard put to discover incontrovertible truth in Wiredu's suggestion that it is *mis*perception that prevents one from seeing the supposed "rock bottom identity of interests." What if it is this belief about a "rock bottom" identity of human interests that *is* a misperception? An illusion? What if, in addition, such illusions are cultivated – precisely by those who benefit most from specific social and political arrangements – as a way of convincing the rest that "we are all the same?"

Eze view of democracy—Final Thoughts

3.   Now let me indicate some of the characteristics which I believe that a "democracy," by whatever name, would have. When I spoke above about an impossible guarantee of conditions for absolute justice, I chose the word "absolute" in contradistinction to "perfect" justice. The former, as I use the term, should suggest an arguably conceivable condition of "justice" guaranteed by, or in, pre-"human," pre-social nature. The latter I use to mark off humanly socially achieved, achievable (or, as the case may be, unachieved or unachievable) justice. It seems obvious to me that a "democracy" is one of the several sorts of social framework that a people adopt in order to mediate the struggles and the conflicts that *necessarily* arise from the necessarily *competitive* nature of individuated identities and desires. A democracy's *raison d'être* is the legitimation – and "management" – of this always already competitive (i.e., inherently political) condition of relativized desires. In this sense, "consensus" or "unanimity" of substantive decisions cannot be the ultimate goal of democracy, but only one of its moments. Democracy, as a political institution, I think, has its own end within itself: it is a social compact that says, "We will agree or agree to disagree, and here are the established mechanisms or rules according to which

16. Disagree

we shall secure and maintain as long as necessary each of these possibilities." It seems to me that this is the spirit of democracy by any name, not the elevation of the moment of substantive "agreement," "reconciliation," or "consensus" to the axiomatic. A democratic process is defined not by achievement of ideological or practical/ pragmatic consensus on specific decisions (or decisional representation), but simply by the orderly securing of a *means* or a *framework* for initiating, cultivating, and sustaining disagreement and oppositional political activities which are nurtured and cherished for their sake and benefits as much as agreement and consensus are nurtured and cherished for their sake and benefits.

It seems to me that a society opts for this form or "frame" for political life for the reasons Wiredu tells us the Ashantis had: "Two heads are better than one," or, as the Igbos say, *Onwe gi onye bu Ọmada Ọmachara*: No one individual is Mother Wisdom. Political wisdom comes in many forms, and democracy becomes, in deed, a market place of *competing* – not just consenting or consensing – ideas. The only "consensus" primary to democracy – democracy's most privileged moment, if any – is the initial, formal, agreement to play by a set of rules that allows the institutions and respect of dissent as much as its opposite. Thus we cannot reduce democracy to one moment of its outcomes: decisional representation or consensus. The most distinguishing mark of it seems to me to be in the processes itself: in the debates, and the refrain from the use of force, not in a specific type or nature of outcome.

Should we find another name to describe what Wiredu tells us the ancient Ashantis did? Or should we question the veracity or accuracy of Wiredu's report? It seems to me that we could do either, or both. The ancient Akan political practices, if Wiredu's description is accurate, may not be democracy as it is practiced in the West. It may not also fit the description of democracy as I have it in mind and have stated it here. If this is the case, the question then becomes: which one is best suited for Africa? Democracy as a formal framework for agreement and disagreement (which does not, in principle, privilege "consensus" or decisional representation), or democracy, according to Wiredu, as the African past practiced it: a "democracy" that holds as axiomatic and elevates to the level of principle the moment of "consensus" and unanimity? If the appeal of the former is in the greater sense of freedom – the invitation to inventiveness without demand or requirement for decision of a specific nature, and the pluralism, inherent to competing (as well as cooperating) forces – the appeal of the latter is in its promise of greater political stability – a "stability" which, nevertheless, offers no guarantee that its bases are founded upon ideal pursuits of the public good. It seems to me that neither of these tendencies of "democracy" is intrinsically "Western" or "African," and that the best form of democracy is one that culturally reconciles both centripetal and centrifugal political forces of its constituents – while preserving each current in its most vital *élan*. In fact, only such a political culture may be called truly democratic.

Notes

1 Chapter 14, p. 305.
2 Wiredu continues: "Formal representation without substance is apt to induce disaffection. If the system in use is such as to cause some groups periodically to be in substantively underrepresented minorities, then seasonal disaffection becomes institutionalized. The results are well-known inclemencies of adversarial politics" (p. 307). This statement made me think of Lani Guinier's critique of the American political system: that in order for minorities in the United States to have substantive and not just formal representation in government, the current system may have to be redesigned. Interestingly, Wiredu says that "there is nothing peculiarly African about the idea [of consensual democracy] itself," and expresses the outlook that it could universally be adopted by any society (p. 311). (See Lani Guinier, *The Tyranny of Majority: Fundamental Fairness in Representative Democracy*, Free Press, New York, 1994).
3 Chapter 14, p. 305.
4 Ibid., p. 306.
5 Ibid., p. 306; my emphases.
6 Ibid.
7 Ibid.
8 There is a sense in which we might, quite generously, interpret Wiredu as indeed proposing the idea of "consensus" as precisely such a "truthful lie" or utopia. If this is the case, we may need to ask: why is *this* "lie" better than others? Why, for example, is "consensus" a better framework for achieving "unanimous" decisions or compromises than, say, more *laissez-faire* political ideals? A more important critique of the Ashanti "ideal" of "consensus," however, would be to ask to what extent it is not a cloak, a pretext, for all the formal and informal "cola-nut" systems of compromises, deal-makings, and favor-swapping which, when practiced on a massive scale, organize sociopolitical and economic activities around norms and expectations that have little or nothing to do with a genuine ideal of public or general good? (Houtondji, in an essay called "Everyday life in Black Africa" provides a vignette of the sort of stabilizing but, idealistically speaking, unpublic minded social and political environment I have in mind: "the whole gamut of worldly artfulness, the complete panoply of cat-and-mouse games, from the friendly slap on the back to angry scenes (real or mimed), while going through the visits to the house, the stuffed envelopes and other gratuities, the touching allusion to mutual friends, indeed, to some distant relative -- through the aunt-in-law of the uncle of the grandmother. This is also called a 'dialogue'" and, of course, "consensus." (See Hountondji, "Daily life in Black Africa," in V.Y. Mudimbe (ed.), *The Surreptitious Speech: Présence Africaine and the Politics of Otherness 1947–1987*, University of Chicago Press, Chicago, IL, 1992, pp. 344–64. The quote is from p. 358.)
9 Chapter 14, p. 306.
10 Ibid.
11 Ibid.

12 I am not convinced by Wiredu that what moves humans to act — or to not act — does not often transcend, or precede, the philosopher's idea of "reason" or "knowledge." After Nietzsche and Freud, how are we to believe that (1) our "rock bottom . . . interests" are largely accessible and discursively articulate to us through "rational discussion"; or that (2) our most elegant "rational" discussions directly mirror our deepest interests? Wiredu is correct to recognize that dialogue can make possible "agreed actions without . . . agreed notions"; in his systematics of consensual democracy, however, there is no recognition of the equal truth of the reverse: agreed notions do not necessarily produce agreed actions!

13 Chapter 14.

14 Ibid.

16

Of the Good Use of Tradition: Keeping the Critical Perspective in African Philosophy

Jean-Marie Makang

We consider the task of African philosophy in America to be basically the same as in Africa: namely, a reflection on our being in today's world and a call for action in the face of many challenges which confront people of African descent. Indeed, a great majority of people of African descent live in America, either as American-born or as foreign residents. African philosophy can, therefore, be seen to be at home in America in the same way as it is in Africa. What unites the African people of the continent with those of the Diaspora is not only the fact that they descend from people whose homeland is Africa, but also the fact that they share a same historical consciousness, and are linked by the same destiny and the same hope for a full realization of their humanity. In this regard, what happens to the Africans of the continent is not without bearing for those of the Diaspora, and vice versa. Historical consciousness, as Cheikh Anta Diop indicates, is, indeed, the most solid rampart for people's unity. As a consciousness of historical continuity with a common past, historical conscious-ness feeds the unity of people of African descent.[1]

I have chosen the issue of tradition as a typical case of the common heritage and a common concern for people of African descent – although to bring up such an issue in contemporary debate of African philosophy may sound awkward, for many seldom perceive the importance of tradition in this age of electronics, advanced information technology, and transnational corporations. But the perception of tradition as something out of place in our age is due to a type of discourse whereby "tradition" is used to designate a mode of thought and a praxis proper to a certain kind of society known as *tribe* or *clan*, and is conceived in opposition to modernity or progress. This use of tradition coins it narrowly as an unchanging or static corpus of representations, beliefs, ideas, values, rules, or customs that are handed over by the ancestors of the tribe to subsequent generations.

The approach that underlies this chapter, on the contrary, is one that views human traditions as processes and as "historical phenomena which occur everywhere"[2] and in all stages of societies' development. Traditions are not frozen in time, but are in continual development, adapting themselves to new historical circumstances. It is, therefore, unduly that the notion of tradition is set in opposition to those of modernity and progress.

My major purpose in choosing to revive the debate on the issue of tradition in African philosophy is to keep in the first place a critical perspective in African philosophy initiated and carried out by such people as Fabien Eboussi Boulaga, Paulin Hountondji, and Marcien Towa.[3] Because the works of these authors are written in French, and few of them have been translated into English, their perspective is either unknown or marginal to most anglophone readers. It is in order to help prevent the overshadowing of the perspective of these writers in African philosophy in America that I have chosen to revive the question of the good and bad use of tradition.

Although this discussion on African traditions includes different points of view, it is constructed around two main protagonists: Placide Tempels and Fabien Eboussi Boulaga. The reason for choosing these two authors is to confront two types of discourse on African traditions, one which *mystifies* tradition, and another that *demystifies* it.

1 The Problem of Historicity

The intellectual and philosophical discourse on African tradition has for very long been and still is dependent on data and the language of ethnology, especially from the writings of Western africanists. The dominant trend has consisted in emphasizing the particularity of the African people or their difference from the Western world as essential to the understanding of African mentality. Then, it is alleged that what characterizes the African people in the first place is an *ontology of participation*, meaning that the relation of the human being with nature is understood in terms of participation, insertion, communion, or harmony, instead of as a relation of domination and conquest over nature. The ontology of participation has moral and epistemological implications. On the one hand, it leads to the assertion that African people hold a deeply moral view of the world and the universe, and that solidarity is the key term in African moral attitude. On the other hand, African knowledge of the physical reality is spelled out as mystical knowledge, meaning that African people know things intuitively or in the mode of sympathy and communion with the thing known, and not in a conceptual and scientific way as do Western people. This philosophy, in which "the traditional African view of the world is one of extraordinary harmony,"[4] is summed up as the philosophy of *Ntu*. *Ntu*, the total reality of the universe as oneness, is a world in which harmony prevails and contradiction or dissent has no place, for each element of this monolithic universe is assigned a place once and for all. *Ntu* is a world which admits no dichotomy in terms of matter and spirit, good and evil, or life and death, for in this world interact sympathetically the living and the dead, and all the elements of the universe, meaning the humans, things, words, and modalities.[5]

Placide Tempels, a Belgian missionary in Congo, today Zaire, was an earlier exponent of this ontology of participation. In *Bantu Philosophy*, first published in 1945, Tempels describes the Bantu mentality as one which "is centered in a single value: vital force," where being is identical with force. In Bantu ontology, all realities in the universe are conceived as forces, and the order of the universe is one in which the interaction of forces follows a rigid hierarchy, according to the principle of primogeniture. In this hierarchical order, the elder forces stand higher than the younger ones, and the departed ancestors dominate over their living posterity. The only purpose pursued by the Bantu people is "to acquire life, strength or vital force, to live strongly," and to prevent the diminution of one's vital force, for "supreme happiness, the only kind of blessing, is, to the Bantu, to possess the greatest vital force; the worst misfortune and, in very truth, the only misfortune, is, he thinks the diminution of this power."[6]

But Tempels' dynamic Bantu ontology is unhistorical, for it does not admit the evolution in Bantu world-view, and is constantly regretting the disappearance of the past. In this ontology, the present is considered corrupted. The authentic Bantu tradition is one which had not departed from its source, and which had kept its original purity and innocence. In *Bantu Philosophy*, therefore, the emergence of the *évolué*, or the so-called modern Bantu, corresponds to the stage when Bantu ontology departed from its right original place, and had consequently lost the savage innocence of its origins.

"True" African tradition, in this perspective, is not subject to change and cannot be modified; its right observance consists in going further back to the past, to the point where it had not yet deviated from its source, either through contamination by Europe's materialist-dualist culture, or by espousing a rebelliousness towards "innate" superior forces. In Tempels' conception of Bantu mentality, as Eboussi puts it, "the source was pure, but waters are polluted" and "only the point of departure is valid, but it is out of the current stream of things."[7] The modern Bantu, who has been corrupted by his exposure to European materialism, is not an authentic Bantu any longer, but has become a *Europeanized* Bantu, who has lost the sense of the old, ageless wisdom of the ancestors, and of everything that was stable in Bantu tradition.[8] Those whom the Europeans called "savages" – that is, the people from the hinterland, the "bush people" (*les broussards*) – are for Tempels the only authentic Bantu, for they are unspoiled by European modernity. These are the ones who still represent the hope for the preservation of an authentic Bantu culture. However, the praise of the *broussard* as the only authentic Bantu philosopher is the praise of the past over and against the present, of archaism over and against progress, of the good soul over and against technical and material improvement.[9] Tradition as Tempels presents it, asserts itself as nostalgia for the past or for a lost paradise, and as avoidance of the present. But tradition as nostalgia for what ceased to be is not a living reality, but a dead tradition. Tempels' Bantu ontology illustrates best the worst in ethnological discourse on African tradition.

By reducing African traditions to a fixed past and to a nostalgia for an original state, the ethnological discourse strips African people of their historicity, and the universe on which tradition rests is mythical: that is, one which continues under the mode of its absence or its being passed over. But a mythical and nostalgic universe does not affect the ordering of things in the present; it is, therefore, incapable of helping present generations of Africans in their striving for control over their own destiny. By not taking into account the great upheavals, such as colonialism, which occurred in recent times in the African universe, tradition of the ethnological kind is condemned to marginalization.[10] The ethnological discourse – consciously or unconsciously – complies with the verdict passed by the Eurocentric discourse on the Africans: namely, that the latter had no place in the history of humanity apart from one assigned to them through their inclusion into the destiny of Europe.[11]

Is not this archaism of the ethnological discourse regarding African traditions the consequence of the projection of the writers' own views on African past? What Tempels saw as a degeneration of an African tradition – the members' abandonment of what is/was irrelevant to today's world, can instead be seen as a sign of vitality and a sense of historicity of members of the Bantu tradition, a tradition which Tempels tried unsuccessfully to freeze in the past. It is the capacity of adaptation of African traditions that accounts for their survival over time and space. As an illustration of this African sense of historicity, Melville Herskovits had noted that a great flexibility characterized the religious systems of the Congo Valley and West Africa, where most Africans transported in the Atlantic slave trade came from. While resisting the political domination of their invaders, African people could still adopt new deities from outside, even from their invaders. These new deities were integrated within their polytheistic systems or pantheons, and the adoption of new deities was perceived as an enrichment rather than a threat. This flexibility in African religious systems accounts for their survival, or for the retention of some African beliefs in America when African slaves were forced to convert to Christianity. African slaves in America could retain their traditions by reinterpreting them in the face of a new context, because such a possibility already was inherent to the African traditions. The survival of African religious systems generally took the form of syncretism as in the case of the *Vodûn* (or *Voodoo*), and the latter became a major factor of black resistance in America during slavery and was used by slave insurrectionists such as the Maroons.[12]

This example of the vitality of the religious systems of the Congo Valley and West Africa gives an idea of what a living tradition does. A tradition survives by adapting itself to new historical situations, and most of the time by learning from other traditions and assimilating from them elements which can contribute to its revitalization. This suggests that we hardly have access to an original culture, and that we can construct hypotheses about it only through its elements that have survived. Tradition survives by evolving, not by remaining the same. This perspective precludes an understanding of tradition as something fixed once and for all, or as self-sufficient and as essentially and absolutely different from other traditions. We are inclined to side with Janheinz Jahn on the position that "all human cultures resemble one another up to a point," that "different cultures only value their common elements differently in so far as one puts the accent here, another there," and consequently, that "one can voluntarily abandon or acquire a culture, that custom and capabilities, thoughts and judgments are not innate."[13]

Tempels attempted to freeze Bantu tradition to its past. Unfortunately, Eboussi argues, it is too late to go back to the innocent Bantu ontology, for that world has long passed away and cannot be retrieved, and the Bantu of Father Tempels is equally dead with the universe that supported his Bantu ontology. "It is in vain that ontology tries to arrest the course of time, to fix for ever the rules of the evolution."[14] The course of history cannot be arrested, and the majority of the Bantu have deserted or perhaps hardly totally subscribed to the mystical universe of Bantu ontology. The ancient world is deadly compromised by the intrusion of the Western world. The power of money decried by Tempels has revealed the fragility of the Bantu world. The new Bantu cannot continue to venerate a tradition that has been defeated and marginalized by the present world order.

2 The Problem of Generalization

Besides stripping African traditions of their historicity, the ethnological discourse is plagued with its ignorance of the diversity that characterizes African people and societies. This results in excessive generalization, whereby African people are considered as forming one single tradition, and Africa is perceived as one village where all the African people come from. What is observed in a limited point of space and time is quickly applied to all African people. Once again, this can be verified in the case of Bantu dynamic ontology, whereby a simple fact of language and a particular behavior which were observed in a specific ethnic group in Congo led to the construction of an ontology supposed to be valid for all the Bantu people, and by extension to all the African people.[15]

On the other hand, what is described as a peculiarity of the African world-view is sometimes too general and simply common to all humans to characterize the Africans, remarks Okolo Okonda.[16] This point is illustrated in Eboussi's critique of Tempels' assertion that dynamic ontology is peculiar to the Bantu. Eboussi objects that the frequent reference to being or existence as force or as dynamic is so frequent in the history of Western philosophy – he cites Aristotle's notions of *dunamis* and *energia* – and in daily speech that it loses its significance as specifically African.[17]

There is, in effect, no such a thing as *the* African tradition, according to arguments by Eboussi and Hountondji. In the origin, there were only particular tribal groups which inhabited the physical space later designated as Africa, with each tribe viewing itself as a totality and as the center of the world. Indeed, in the language of ethnology tradition is only synonymous with tribe, for the horizon of ethnology is the tribe, and rarely the nation or the region. The later designation of all these tribal entities as African did not result from a deliberate choice of people of African descent; on the contrary, it is a reality that was imposed often through institutionalized violence. The community of those called Africans has its origin in their common suffering, which comes from the violence inflicted upon them by European invaders. The unity of African people or their africanity, Eboussi would show, is negative in origin, it is the unity of a *Passion*. It is the violence inflicted upon African tribes from outside that united what, by itself, would have continued to coexist in mutual indifference or hostility. The negative unity of the Africans is their *colonizability*, indicating that it is their privation, common weaknesses, shortcomings, and vulnerability that primarily brought them together.[18] This colonizability has many names: technological backwardness, social fragmentation, etc.

In addition, in their need to affirm the particularity and difference of "the African" tradition, the ethnological apologists are led to bypass internal contradictions within today's African communities, including the generational gap, class differences, and intertribal conflicts. Indeed, in Africa as anywhere else, it is common knowledge, argues Hountondji, that the development of a common tradition or civilization proceeds by selection, and that the dominant tradition of a region or a community is but the tradition of the dominant group.[19] In reference to the history of Africa, there is not one tradition, not one mentality, but a plurality of traditions. An under-standing of African unity and tradition from the perspective of historicity, Eboussi insists, does not leave room for an "ontologized" and unquestionable African tradition in the way it is spelled out by the ethnological discourse.[20]

But while Hountondji does not admit any basis for unity or identity of African people other than that of having Africa as their common geographical homeland, Eboussi admits the possibility of a unity or identity of ideals among Africans, based on a common action, and which would result from the effort to transform necessity into a community of destiny.[21] Indeed, African identity or tradition, viewed in its relation to destiny, is more a construction than a *fatum*. Destiny, as notes Okolo Okonda W'Oleko, is the tension that allows a tradition to renew itself while it perpetuates itself.[22] In this regard, an ideology of identity in today's world based essentially on tribal or ethnic solidarity can be a mystification, for the tribal or ethnic group is rarely a community of destiny today, in the sense, for instance, that the oligarchies that rule Africa today are associations of members of different ethnic groups.

A living tradition is, therefore, one which is at the service of people instead of people being subjected to tradition. For those linked by a community of destiny, the past has a meaning only when it is provided with conditions of its influence in the present.

3 The Presumed African Particularity: Culturalism and its Diversion

The most pernicious feature of the ethnological discourse is its reduction of African traditions and identity to culture, whereby culture is synonymous with folklore, and designates only artistic productions and external manifestations of Negro-Africans' emotional life, primarily in music, dances, and rituals. This ethnological vice, termed *culturalism* by Paulin Hountondji, is responsible for setting African traditions as a marginalized domain of African life in present-day global society.

Culturalism is an ideology in the Marxian sense, and mystifying as such, for in giving priority to African cultural particularism, the ethnological apologists intend to divert the attention of African people from the most crucial problems which confront them today, and which are political and economic in nature.

The negritude movement, with Senghor as its leading representative, is frequently mentioned as a clear example of culturalism carried out by the Africans themselves. Also cited is the cultural nationalism branded by some African leaders at the dawn of their national independence. The clear case of this, which V.Y. Mudimbe characterizes as "a notorious mystification" of African tradition, is the ideology of *authenticity* developed in Zaire by the Popular Movement of Revolution (MPR) of President Mobutu Sese Seko.[23] The main characteristics of the ideologies of African cultural nationalism, also designated as the ideologies of identity, are their denunciation of European or Western racism, and their emphasis on African cultural difference from the West. Because of this emphasis on the difference from the West, Asian and Latin American traditions, for instance, are out of sight in our perspective of intercultural exchange.

The danger of culturalism during the colonial era was in overshadowing the demand for national liberation by putting forward the demand for cultural recognition, whereas in postcolonial time it is meant to cover the problem of political oppression and of economic injustice perpetrated by autocratic African regimes. Under the pretext of their common participation in a national culture, the African masses and revolutionary forces are diverted from gaining true social consciousness and from organizing themselves for effective class struggle against their indigenous and foreign oppressors. Regarding negritude, however, a distinction must be made between the revolutionary negritude of Aimé Césaire and the culturalism of Léopold S. Senghor. While the latter used cultural nationalism as an excuse to divert from the political problem of national liberation against French colonialism, the former subordinated cultural rehabilitation to the more fundamental problem of political liberation.[24]

Another example of culturalism and its mystifying character is the movement of *inculturation* led by theologians and leaders of the Roman Catholic Church in Africa since the end of the 1960s, when Pope Paul VI visited Kampala and announced that the Africans should become their own missionaries. But the movement of inculturation, which has occupied African theology in the three last decades and which is dependent on church hierarchy and on the financial support of European churches, is often used to oppose the more revolutionary movement of Liberation Theology, and to overshadow the crucial issues of social and international justice. Thus the inculturation of Christian faith in African reality which is favored by Church hierarchy is one that limits itself to African music, dances, rituals, and symbols in Church liturgy, but is not allowed to go deeper and to question Roman Catholic dogmas, the authoritarianism of Church leadership, Church ministry, and priesthood, and the hypocrisy of the Catholic moral doctrine, all of which are aimed not at serving evangelical purposes but at perpetuating European neocolonial supremacy and male domination in the Church.

Preferring generalization over attention to diversity of African patrimony, African cultural nationalism functions as a Pan-Negroism, which overlooks national realities. And being extracted from national realities and from people's daily life, the culture which is affirmed functions as a museum.

> Culture is becoming more and more cut off from the events of today. It finds its refuge beside a hearth that glows with passionate emotion, and from there makes its way by realistic paths which are the only means by which it may be made fruitful, homogeneous and consistent . . . In order to ensure his salvation and to escape from the supremacy of the white man's culture the native feels the need to turn backwards towards his unknown roots and to lose himself at whatever cost in his own barbarous people.[25]

When it is called to play a pernicious role in politics and society, tradition, understood as folkloric culture, becomes a means to put the African masses to sleep, instead of waking them up and stimulating their creative impulse.

African assertion of the cultural difference and particularity was in colonial time a way of legitimizing the demand for political equality and self-determination as well as a call for rehabilitation of the humanity of African people. In postcolonial time, it ought to be directed toward the latter purpose where political independence has been formally achieved. As for Western africanists, declared friends of the Africans, to recognize African particularity does not necessarily imply a readiness on their side to stand for equality for "primitive" Africans.

In the colonial era as in postcolonial time, calling upon the Africans to preserve their particularity – namely, their mystical and moral world-views – was often synonymous with diverting them from acquiring what they lacked and needed most in order to become equal to the West: that is, political self-determination and technical efficiency. Indeed, it looks as if the whole point of the ideology of difference as carried out by Western africanists was and still is to prevent African folk from becoming equal to Westerners or from competing with them. If the African people lack what allowed Westerners to conquer the world in modern time, mostly technical efficiency, they will be forced to remain under the control of the West. However, the reason for the superiority of the white man is his control over natural forces.

This dangerous role of the africanists towards African well-being and self-determination is noticeable in Tempels' *Bantu Philosophy*. While Tempels paid respect to the mystical tradition of the Luba-Shaba people in Congo, he never questioned Belgian colonial domination over these Bantu people. Instead, he subscribed to the colonial ideology by admitting as natural the domination of the Europeans over the Africans. His own attempt at reconstructing the Bantu ontology was to make it an instrument at the disposal of European colonialists and missionaries in order for them to gain a better control over the Bantu people. Bantu philosophy, in effect, had no truth in itself, its truth lay somewhere else, in both the judgment of the White man and the use the white man wanted to make of it. That is why Tempels advised that "all men of good will," meaning the colonialists and the missionaries, "must cooperate in it, to test what is valid in Bantu philosophy and what is false, in order that all that is of real value may be put to use at once in the education and civilization of these 'primitive' peoples."[26] Indeed, it is the European civilizer who was supposed to show the right direction and orientation to Bantu ontology, which, for Tempels, was supposedly deviating from its origins and was in the process of degenerating into magic. According to Tempels:

> We have the heavy responsibility of examining, assessing and judging this philosophy and not failing to discover that kernel of truth which must needs be found in so complete and universal a system, constituting the common possession of a host of primitive and semi-primitive peoples. We must proceed with the

Bantu towards its sources to the point of departure, help the Bantu to build their own Bantu civilization, a stable and noble one of their own.[27]

The respect for Bantu philosophy was thus advocated because it was not a threat to European hegemony and supremacy. The Bantu were encouraged to preserve their cultural identity, but never to seek their self-determination and their political identity away from the Europeans. Aimé Césaire and Fabien Eboussi rightly noted the complicity of Tempels' dynamic ontology of the Bantu with the colonial regime. Indeed, if there is anything Tempels was unwilling to question, it is white supremacy over the Africans. According to his interpretation of Bantu ontology, the latter offers all guarantees for a continued white domination: the white man is placed at the top of the Bantu hierarchy of forces according to the principle of primogeniture. Tempels writes:

> Let us observe that the Bantu have considered us whites, from our first contact with them, from the only point of view possible to them, that of their Bantu philosophy. They have included us within their order of forces, at an exalted level. They think that we must be powerful forces. Do we not seem to be masters of natural forces that they have never mastered ... The natural aspiration of the Bantu soul was therefore to be able to take some part in our superior force.[28]

Clearly, then, the call to the colonialists and Christian missionaries to study Bantu philosophy was not a call for conversion and equal communication with the Bantu; it was a call to adapt European civilizing power to new circumstances, a call to find a better strategy for subduing the Bantu. As Eboussi has commented, the discovery of the past mistakes in the method of colonization does not lead to renunciation of colonialism.[29] "Our system of education, our civilizing power, should learn to adapt themselves to this idea of vital force and fullness of life," Tempels insisted.[30] Indeed, Bantu ontology was meant to provide a key to the penetration of the thought of "the primitive man," to make the Bantu transparent to the white man: that is, to the colonialist and the missionary. Besides, *Bantu Philosophy*, as is clearly spelled out by the author, was not addressed to Bantu people, but "to colonials of *good will*." It was to their judgment, not to that of the Bantu themselves, that the Belgian missionary subjected his reflection on Bantu people.[31]

Even Franz Crahay, the so-called originator of the critical tradition in African philosophy, never questioned Placide Tempels' colonial purpose, which was to illuminate Belgian colonial and missionary enterprises in their domestication and control of the Congolese.[32] Crahay consented in the colonial enterprise. The only thing he really questioned in his critique of Tempels and of ethnophilosophy was the method. According to V.Y. Mudimbe, Crahay had no interest in opposing Tempels' double project of guiding colonizers towards an "African soul" and stimulating original ethnographic studies. He respected the project in its practicality and intent.[33]

Tempels himself noted that it was technical progress that gave whites their prestige and superiority over the Africans. "The technological skill of the white man impressed the Bantu. The white man seemed to be the master of great natural forces. It had, therefore, to be admitted that the white man was an elder, a superior human force, surpassing the vital force of all Africans."[34] It is because of their technical superiority that the Whites are situated higher in Tempels' Bantu ontology, and this may also explain partly why they are often deified in the supposed African mystical universe.

Yet, when the *évolués* or modern Bantu coveted this technique, they were reminded that it is not the technique or material success but the good soul that makes a great man. And while the *backward* Bantu are praised as the only authentic Bantu, the *évolués* are decried for losing their Bantu identity, for giving up their Bantu philosophy, and for adopting the European way of life. They are called misguided and "renegades from Bantu thought whom we shall have decked out elegantly, housed comfortably, fed rationally, but without our having been able to prevent their becoming *évolués* with empty and unsatisfied beings. We shall turn them into moral and intellectual tramps, capable only, despite themselves, of being elements of strife."[35]

But why is technique good for the whites and bad for the Bantu? Tempels did not tell. This inconsistency in the discourse of the Belgian priest can be explained only by having in mind that his ontology was designed to keep the Bantu "in their place": that is, at the margin of history. For, in his mind, the contribution of the African people to civilization is conceived neither in terms of scientific and technical efficiency, nor in terms of industry building or state building, but in terms of preserving a mystical and a moral view of the world. If we need to learn from our creative African traditions, we need to learn as well from the West and other non-African traditions the secret of their superiority over us in recent history. Obviously, technical know-how, efficient organization, discipline, unity, and effective domination over one's physical and social environment are the keys to that superiority. While Tempels' Africans are supposed to have a knowledge of forces, this knowledge does not give them power over their physical environment and over their human invaders. For, as Eboussi argues, if we are to believe Tempels, the Bantu do not exercise their force in the concrete, but instead dream or imagine it. Their vital force, as a mystical power, belongs to the imaginary world and has no impact upon physical reality. As compared with the technical knowledge of the white man which confers concrete power upon Europe, the force of the Bantu is powerlessness, because it is confined to the mystical order. Because the vital force of the Bantu does not belong to the order of technical efficiency, the Bantu are doomed to remain under the tutelage and control of white men, who alone possess the key for effective domination of the physical environment and over human society. By encouraging the Africans to go back to their mystical ideal of life and of communion with nature, European missionaries and ethnologists clearly revealed that African mysticism can be used, like the Christian religion, as a "spiritual aroma" or opium to perpetuate the domination of colonized and subjugated people.

What should take place is more than simply equipping ourselves with more efficient techniques; it is a matter of giving up what is claimed by Tempels to be the peculiarity of the African people. In our quest for realization of a better humanity, African people need to acquire this fundamental disposition according to which it is their essential mission as human beings to dominate and transform nature in order to acquire a maximum freedom from necessity and want, instead of perceiving themselves as people meant to live in communion with nature. This fundamental attitude or disposition toward physical nature is no more Japanese, Chinese, or Anglo-Saxon, than it is African or Latin American. The primary quality of the human being, as Marx shows, consists in transforming nature in order to impose one's seal upon it. Culture, understood as the construction of artifacts upon nature in order to create a human habitat, is an essential vocation for the human being. However, we must equally avoid the extreme of emergence, which Reinhold Niebuhr calls *anxiety*, which is the human tendency to seek infinity and to overcome or negate one's contingence.[36]

4 A Living Tradition as Ideology of Society

If the ethnological discourse was telling the whole truth about African traditions, then the only exit from archaism for those Africans who do not recognize themselves in this discourse would be a capitulation to mass culture, secreted by Western capitalism, and which is being imposed on the rest of the world. But there exist meaningful alternatives to both extremes, one of which views tradition as a process and not as a corpus of unalterable truths revealed once and for all. For this position, tradition has an important role to play in the conduct of our lives in present-day society, just as it did in the past. This importance of tradition is not peculiar to African people, but it is true of all human groups and communities, who rely on a common *ethos* as a common reference in the conduct of their common destiny.

There is, therefore, another type of discourse that pleads for a critical use of tradition to make it congruent with basic and major requirements of today's society. From a critical perspective of African philosophy, a living tradition will function as a "regulating *utopia*" in the words of Fabien Eboussi, or as an ideology of society, in the sense given to the notion of ideology by Kwame Nkrumah. An ideology of society, Nkrumah suggests, permeates all fields of knowledge and all institutions of society, and must thereby yield concrete effects in society.[37]

To envision an African tradition as an ideology of society for people of Africa and the African Diaspora implies pointing out common references in particular contexts in which Africans and African-descended peoples daily construct societies. By a common reference we mean a system of ideas, ideals, thought, opinions, values, beliefs, representations, aspirations, or attitudes which bind members of a group together in a common praxis which is geared toward a common purpose. An ideology makes a group of people a community of destiny, whereas a human group without a minimum of ideology is only a population.

The use of tradition as an ideology or a utopia, as Eboussi shows, "aims at a mode of historical intelligibility that leads to action," to collective creativity. A living tradition, therefore, is neither a repetition of practices and customs of the past, nor a dream of "the origin" or of a "lost paradise," but is meant to provide a utopian model of action, a mobilizing ideal. Such an approach is ethical in perspective. Indeed, as an ideology meant to be a mobilizing discourse that indicates what an individual must be ready to sacrifice for a good cause, tradition cannot be value-free. "In the presence of an alienated society, tradition would provide norms and models of organization of a community more human and of a superior rationality."[38]

As such, tradition in this sense does not leave any domain of life untouched. It would allow for a radical critique and transformation of prevailing relationships in all sectors of life in present African societies, including politics, economic management and productivity. It should lead to a critique of unproductivity and deficient management, of squandering of common patrimony and national resources, a critique of injustice, oppression, and exploitation, a critique of irrational choices which are detrimental to the well-being and emancipation of African people and which condemn them to perpetual subordination and dependency. Tradition must also allow and encourage critique of the bad distribution of political power, including its personalization and confiscation within a few hands. The critique of the mismanagement of political power should result in alternative models of authority.[39]

Tradition as an ideology of society or as a utopia aims at enlightening African people in their striving for adaptation to new material conditions of the present world, with their self-determination and a better quality of their humanity as their common purpose. By appealing to the praxis and wisdom of our African foreparents, we do not mean to repeat them, but we mean to make use of this praxis and wisdom as interpretative tools to enlighten present generations of Africans.

Notes

1   Cheikh Anta Diop, *Civilization ou Barbarie, Anthropologie sans complaisance* (Présence Africaine, Paris, 1981), pp. 272–3.

2   Jan Vansina, *Paths in the Rainforests: Toward a History of Political Tradition in Equatorial Africa* (University of Wiscosin Press, Madison, WI, 1990), p. 257. A lengthy development of the understanding of tradition as a process is given in chapter 9, "On history and tradition."

3   The major philosophical works of these three writers are as follows: Fabien Eboussi Boulaga, "Le Bantou Problématique," *Présence Africaine*, no. 66, 1968, pp. 3–40; *La Crise du Muntu: Authenticity africaine et philosophie* (Présence Africaine, Paris, 1977); "La suite de Cheikh Anta Diop," *Terroirs: Revue africaine de sciences sociales*, no. 001, May 1992; Paulin Hountondji, *Sur la "philosophie africain": critique de l'ethnophilosophie* (Clé, Yaoundé, Cameroon, 1980); Marcien Towa, *Léopold Sédor Senghor, négritude ou servitude* (Clé, Yaoundé, 1971); *Essai sur la problématique philosophique dans l'Afrique actuelle*, 2nd edn (Clé, Yaoundé, 1979); *L'idée d'une philosophie négro-africaine* (Clé, Yaoundé, 1979).

4   Janheinz Jahn, *Muntu: African Culture and the Western World* (Grove, Weidenfeld, New York, 1961), p. 96.

5   Different African ontologies, especially the theories of harmony and non-contradiction of the African universe are summed up in chapter 4, 5, and 6 of Jahn's *Muntu*, while Alassane Ndaw gives an exposition of the Negro-African ontology, particularly as developed by Placide Tempels and Alexis Kagamé, in his *La pensée africaine: Recherches sur les fondements de la pensée négro-africaine* (Les Nouvelles Editions Africaines, Dakar, 1983), chapter 6.

6   Placide Tempels, *Bantu Philosophy* (Présence Africaine, Paris, 1959), pp. 30, 32, 35.

7   Eboussi Boulaga, "Le Bantou Problématique," p. 27.

8   Tempels, *Bantu Philosophy*, p. 118.

9   Ibid.

10 Eboussi Boulaga, "Le Bantou Problématique," p. 27; Towa, *Essai sur la problématique philosophique*, p. 11.

11 W.E.B. Du Bois, *Black Folk, Then and Now: An Essay in the History and Sociology of the Negro Race* (Kraus-Thomson, Millwood, NY, 1975; 1st edn 1939), pp. 228–9. Du Bois shows how European colonialism transformed Africa into an appendix of Europe which he designated as "Black Europe in Africa." For an analysis of the Eurocentric view on Africa by European philosophers, such as Hume, Kant, Hegel, and Heidegger, see Towa, *Essai sur la problématique philosophique*, pp. 12–22; Cornel West, *Prophesy Deliverance! An Afro–American Revolutionary Christianity* (Westminster Press, Philadelphia, PA, 1982), chapter 2, "A genealogy of modern racism;" and Okolo Okonda W'Oleko, *Pour une Philosophie de la culture et du développement: Recherches d'herméneutique et de praxis africaines*, (Presses Universitaires du Zaïre, Kinshasa, 1986), p. 92.

12 Melville J. Herskovits, *The Myth of the Negro Past* (Beacon, Boston, MA, 1958), pp. 52, 72.

13 Jahn, *Muntu*, p. 19.

14 Eboussi Boulaga, "Le Bantou Problématique," p. 34.

15 For a critique of this excessive generalization of Tempels' Bantu ontology, see Eboussi Boulaga, "Le Bantou Problématique," pp. 6–7, 11; V.Y. Mudimbe, *The Invention of Africa: Gnosis, Philosophy, and the Order of Knowledge* (Indiana University Press, Bloomington, IN, and James Curry, London, 1988), pp. 139–46;

D.A. Masolo, *African Philosophy in Search of Identity*, (Indiana University Press, Bloomington, IN, and Edinburgh University Press, 1994), pp. 57–9.

16 Okolo Okonda W'Oleko, "Pour une Philosophie de la culture et du développement," pp. 89–90.

17 Eboussi Boulaga, "Le Bantou Problématique," pp. 7–9, 17–18.

18 Eboussi Boulaga, *La Crise du Muntu*, pp. 144–7.

19 Hountondji, *Sur la "philosophie africaine,"* p. 228.

20 Eboussi Boulaga, *La Crise du Muntu*, p. 157.

21 Hountondji, *Sur la "philosophie africaine,"* p. 227; Eboussi Boulaga, *La Crise du Muntu*, p. 146.

22 Okolo Okonda W'Oleko, "Pour une Philosophie de la culture et du développement," p. 92.

23 Mudimbe, *Invention of Africa*, p. 153; Hountondji, *Sur la "philosophie africaine,"* p. 229.

24 Paulin Hountondji, *Sur la "philosophie africaine,"* pp. 225–9. A critique of L.S. Senghor's negritude is especially developed by Marcien Towa in *Léopold Sédar Senghor* and *Essai sur la problématique philosophique*, p. 24.

25 Frantz Fanon, *The Wretched of the Earth* (Grove, New York, 1961), p. 175.

26 Tempels, *Bantu Philosophy*, p. 112.

27 Ibid., p. 113.

28 Ibid., p. 116.

29 Eboussi Boulaga, "Le Bantou Problématique," pp. 21–4.

30 Tempels, *Bantu Philosophy*, p. 117.

31 Ibid., pp. 119, 120.

32 Franz Crahay, "Le *decollage* conceptuel: conditions d'une Philosophie Bantoue," in A.J. Smet (ed.), *Philosophie Africaine, Textes choisis II* (Presses Universitaires du Zaïre, Kinshasha, 1975), pp. 327–47.

33 Mudimbe, *Invention of Africa*, p. 155.

34 Tempels, *Bantu Philosophy*, p. 44.

35 Ibid., p. 117.

36 This idea is developed in Reinhold Niebuhr's *The Nature and Destiny of Man*.

37 Eboussi Boulaga, *La Crise du Muntu*, pp. 151, 158; Kwame Nkrumah, *Consciencism: Philosophy and Ideology for De-colonization*, revised edn (Monthly Review Press, New York, 1970), pp. 56–70.

38 Eboussi Boulaga, *La Crise du Muntu*, pp. 155, 158.

39 Ibid., pp. 149–50.

17

Toward a Critical Theory of Postcolonial African Identities

Emmanuel Chukwudi Eze

> When we inquire about the Other . . . this question implies inquiring about one's own self, for whom others are "other."
> Löwith, *Das Individuum in der Rolle des Mitmenschen*[1]

What I set out to do here is really to continue a train of thought of a little known Congolese social philosopher, Mabika Kalanda. I am especially referring to a work by Kalanda that has remained untranslated into English: *La Rémise en question: Base de la décolonisation mentale*. Obviously, I am reading this work from the perspective of someone who comes of philosophical age in the 1990s, about thirty years after *La Rémise en question* was first published. I am also reading the work bearing in mind the intervening years, in which Africa and the territories usually referred to as the "Third World" have witnessed the collapse of the colonial and Cold War imperial structures. These were structures that immensely influenced, beyond the merely political, our sense of ourselves and of others – "la mentalité coloniale" of which Kalanda speaks. Furthermore, from the specific standpoint of intellectual developments, we have also witnessed in the intervening years the publication of Ngugi wa Thiong'o's *Decolonizing the Mind*, and Chinweizu, Jemie, and Madubuike's *Toward the Decolonization of African Literature*, as well as V.Y. Mudimbe's *The Invention of Africa*.[2] These more recent works, in different and various ways, are all preoccupied, like *La Rémise en question*, with the question of "mental" colonization and decolonization. So what is new in an old, little-known book written in French?

Mabika Kalanda was born in 1923 in the Belgian-occupied Congo, where he also had formal education. At a very young age he joined the civil service and quickly climbed the ranks, first in the districts, and then at the national level, and, at one point, served as the Foreign Minister. The book we are looking at was published when he was thirty-four, and had had extensive experience of colonial and postcolonial developments in the Congo and in other parts of Africa, both as actor with policy-making power and as observer. In the first chapter of the book, thinking through what he called "cinq années d'une liberté nominale" in Congo – or "five years of nominal freedom" – Kalanda states:

> We have fallen into the habit of accusing the imperialists and the communists [of our every failing]. Is this a purely harmless self-serving propaganda? Should we not recognize and affirm the portion of responsibility that falls on the politicians and the [African] people?[3]

We cannot miss the sardonic and prescient characterization of the Congolese situation: "five years of *nominal* freedom." My remarks, however, are focused on two other elements of Kalanda's questions: (1) "Is this a purely *harmless* propaganda?" and (2) what about "the portion of responsibility" that falls on the African politicians and peoples? In fact, I am more interested in the first question than in second, although the questions are connected.

"We have fallen into the habit of accusing the imperialists and the communists [of our every failing]," Kalanda says, and then quickly asks the perplexing question: "Is this a *harmless* propaganda?" Propaganda: "the spreading of ideas, information, or rumor for the purpose of helping or injuring an institution, a cause, or a person," says a dictionary; "ideas, facts, or allegations spread deliberately to further one's cause or to damage an opposing cause;" etc. The idea that there could be elements of propaganda in our relationship to the West, and in the West's relationship to us, is not news. What is news is this: a propaganda propagated by us (supposedly, or even definitely, against the West) but also damaging *to us*? Does propaganda, like the proverbial medicine – pharmakon – have also deadly effects: at once medicine and poison? Kalanda, as far as I know, is one of the few in the sixties to raise this sort of question in this specific form: namely, the need to examine our "intellectual" and rhetorical schematizations of "the West," because these schematizations could be injurious to our very own health. This form of questioning, Kalanda states, is characterized by "la rémise en question des certains principes et prejugés recus d' héritage, soit de nos ancêtres soit de la colonisation." As we know, critics of ethnophilosophy became unusually very vocal about the first aspect of this critical task (the critique of the inheritance of ancestral wisdom/principles and prejudices), but are often not as vocal or enthusiastic about the second (critique of the wisdom/principles and the prejudices of the colonizing culture and philosophy).

Let me, however, be more specific about what is at stake here. Usually we cast the issues of our modern and contemporary experience of the West in terms of how the Occidental conceptions of itself and the rest of us have damaged and constrained, distorted and inferiorized "the African mind." We denounce – and rightly so – anthropologists and philosophers such as Lévy-Bruhl and Crahay who deform and misrepresent our sense of ourselves. Even sympathetic "outsiders," such as Pierre Bourdieu, could agree that "the racist contempt" that permeates the "false solicitude of primitivism" in Western anthropology, "through the self-contempt it induces in its victims," works "to deny them [i.e., us, the victims] knowledge and recognition of [ourselves] and [of our] traditions."[4]

Kalanda recognizes this phenomenon. But his questions – particularly the question I have isolated for examination – is also primarily in pursuit of something related, but quite different: namely, how does *our* sense of the West distort *our* sense of ourselves and of *our* traditions? Is this not what Kalanda means when he warns of the pitfalls and the dangers of – in his words – "verbeuse phraseologie anti-colonialiste?" Kalanda's question, in other words, is a matter of how seriously we are willing to take Karl Löwith's epigrammatic statement: "When we inquire about the Other . . . this question implies inquiring about one's own self, for whom others are 'other.'" This is another way, I believe, of extending, and deepening, our critique of Eurocentrism, while at the same time elucidating our situation, faced with the project of "la réconstruction mentale."

Aware that alerting us to this crucial autocritical and introspective examination of African anticolonial projects could easily be misunderstood from both sides, Kalanda repeatedly warns the reader that the question "n' a pas pour but de flatter les colonialists." To avoid confusion let me specify the presuppositions – the preconditions, if you will – that, in these times when we speak of the "(post)colonial," nevertheless, call for, and justify, this sort of self-reflection and autocritique.

I refer to the "(post)colonial" with the "post" in brackets. The brackets are to be opened, but only as far as the lived actuality of the peoples and the lands formerly occupied by European imperial powers can suggest, or confirm, in some meaningful ways, the sense of that word, the "post" of the (post)colonial. Thirty years ago Kalanda spoke of "five years of *nominal* freedom" in Congo. Can we not ourselves, today, with some sense of both failure and bafflement, speak of Africa's "thirty years of *nominal* independences;" of Africa's nominal and abstract freedoms – "abstract" understood in the Hegelian sense of the unactualized, the only potentially possible?

Whether one operates out of the classical Fanonian and the traditional conceptions of the colonizer and the colonized (or the neocolonizer and the neocolonized) as a situation of Manichean entanglement and struggles,[5] or from the perspective of poststructuralist and postmodern affirmation and exploration of the interstices of the colonial and (post)colonial experiences theorized through the prism of Lacan or the Derridan notion of *différance*,[6] both perspectives recognize – even when they unevenly represent – the reality of contemporary cultural, political, and economic *hegemony* that Europe and the West exercises upon the rest of the world (including the "post" colonial territories). Gramsci and Said, Sachs and Mudimbe, have all written important works to be consulted for incisive descriptions of this European hegemony. Sachs, for example, writes (in *La Découverte du tiers monde*) that Eurocentrism "dominates our thought, and given its projection on the world scale by the expansion of capitalism and the colonial phenomenon, it marks contemporary culture imposing itself as strongly conditioning model for some, and forced deculturation for others."[7] Colonialism, then, is safe and sound and prospering in its *neo*-varieties, and in many places. Very recently, at the height of the Somalia crisis, many popular letters published in major United States newspapers recommended European occupation of parts of the continent.[8]

Yet, if we recognize that the "post" in (post)colonial is not completely "post" because of some pervasive and continued European and American dominations of our mind, culture, and economy, we must also be willing to recognize, as alive, the "verbeuse phraseologie anti-colonialiste" which Kalanda's questions pointed to, and to which I must now add our "verbeuse phraseologie *post*colonialiste." Accordingly, in addition to the critique of Eurocentrism, we ought to raise questions about possible "verbeuse phraseologie anti- and postcolonialiste" in our intellectual schematizations of the West. By "verbeuse phraseologie," I understand the "inflamed" rhetoric of, and about, the "Other," and therefore of, and about, ourselves and our self-descriptions or self-representations.

I use the word *inflamed* in the sense of: (1) the painful, and (2) the dramatic. Painful because it is an irritable (i.e., a pathological) condition. Pain, precisely, is what such conditions induce, for example, in the contradictions we experience in our ardent yearnings for freedom and at the same time our paralysis for action (a situation similar to the will to live of someone who does not want it). It is a debilitating – as opposed to productive – contradiction, manifest in the gap between our thought and action, word and deed. When such a gap is not utopic-revolutionary in any sense, then, it is merely a dream-state, a nightmare.

And nightmares share with the fantastic the character of the dramatic and the theatrical. Contradictions lived in these circumstances become unhinged from critical objectivity *vis-à-vis* the world; and tortured yearnings (re)locate to the level of the *ir*real, endured psychotically in the contexts of the brutality and the misery of concrete history. The social contortions and the pain we suffer under these conditions are usually equally verbally represented in psychological terms. For example, very recently a friend who runs a prominent bank in Lagos called to let me know – in case I had not heard – that Nigeria's economy is in "deep depression." The farming, the manufacturing, the banking and the rest of the industries, he says, are in "distress." And recently Wole Soyinka, forced into exile in London, warned, with that sense of drama typical to tragedy, that Nigeria is "blowing apart."

In depression and distress and always on the verge of the tragic, our engagement with the West becomes susceptible, and in fact readily transposes itself, to the realm of the radically mythical: the West is against us, yet the West is our savior. In this role the West becomes not just the (objective) West, but the Absolute West – which repels and fascinates us all at once. The Absolute West in our social imaginary enjoys the categorical status of Rudolph Otto's *Mysterium fascinans et tremendum*. It becomes what Kä Mana refers to as "le mythe de l' O'ccident ... constitué par l' image d'enchantement et de désenchantement." The way we live our (post)colonial contradictions is to transpose, project, and elevate our schematizations of the West to the level of the mythical and the fantasmagoric, and it is in this context, I believe, that Kalanda's question acquires its meaning and contemporary pertinence.

The transpositions of the actuality of our tortured and contorted existence and humanity to the plane of mythical enchantment and disenchantment, the *fascinans et tremendum*, the Absolute West, *the West in us*, and the phantasms of our "verbeuse phraseologie anti- and postcolonialiste," inevitably lead down a certain path. As Mana eloquently puts it: "the phantasmagory of the West in us consists in dramatizing the myth to the point of making it the key to all our world, the total explanation of whatever happens to us;" and with such totalistic and totalizing explanation, "we then swim along in mythology and in representations that have nothing to do with putting into question the structures of our conscience."[9] This is not surprising in the least because both the pain and the drama of our self-representations and misrepresentations have this quality in common (a quality that, perhaps, explains their durability): they are dangerous as they are seductive.

So, if you ask me what characterizes the propaganda condition that Kalanda described as seductive yet harmful – the "verbeuse phraseologie anti- and postcolonialiste" – I would say that it is this: the "inflammation of the social imaginary." I speak of the "social imaginary" in the senses that Castoriadis, Habermas, and Kä Mana have, directly or indirectly, employed the phrase.[10] The notion of the "social imaginary" nearly coincides, in form and function, with that of "world-view." It is the prethematic plane that makes possible (i.e., enables, structures, and constrains) actual social and cultural practices and knowledges. It is part and parcel of the horizon of the life-world, in and through which reality occurs to us as objects of value and/or of knowledge. It is a zone charged with the energy of myth and utopia. But between the truths that myths in their fictional energy impose at the very depths of our being, and the more objective truths provided by reflective and critical analysis, it is the field of the imaginary representations that carries the heaviest weight in the determination of conduct and collective orientation. Thus, when this "zone" – the zone of the social imaginary – is "distorted" or "diseased" and "inflamed," our actions and "knowledge" become *systematically* distorted as well. Are we surprised, therefore, that our will to freedom is riddled with inconsistencies that have rendered us enigma – even to ourselves?

Notes

1　Karl Löwith, *Das Individuum in der Rolle des Mitmenschen* (Wissenschaftliche Buchgesellschaft, Darmstadt, 1969), p. 1.
2　Ngugi wa Thiong'o, *Decolonizing the Mind* (Heinemann, Portsmouth, NH, 1986); Chinweizu, Onwu-Chekwa Jemie, and Ihechukwu Madubuike, *Toward the Decolonization of African Literature: African Fiction and Poetry and Their Critics* (KPI, London, 1985); V.Y. Mudimbe, *The Invention of Africa* (Indiana University Press, Bloomington, IN, 1988).
3　Mabika Kalanda, *La Rémise en question: Base de la décolonisation mentale* (Paris, 1967), pp. 9 and 10. Specifically on p. 9: "On a pris l'habitude d'accuser les impérialistes et les communistes. Pure propagande suggérée et intéresée? Ne faudrait-il pas reconnaître et affirmer la part de responsabilité qui revient aux hommes politiques et au peuple congolais lui-même?"
4　*The Logic of Practice* (Stanford University Press, Stanford, CA, 1990), p. 3.
5　For example, as in Abdul R. JanMohamed's *Manichean Aesthetics: The Politics of Literature in Colonial Africa* (University of Massachusetts Press, Amherst, MA, 1983), and, with qualifications, Aijaz Ahmad, *In Theory* (Verso, London, 1992).
6　For example, as in Homi Bhabha's *The Location of Culture* (Routledge, London, 1992). Anthony's Appiah's *In My Father's House*, in its arguments and substantive positions, may also be situated here – although it lacks the explicit poststructuralist psychoanalytic theorizings that characterize *The Location of Culture*.
7　Quoted and translated by V.Y. Mudimbe, in Mudimbe: *The Invention of Africa*, p. 4.
8　We should understand "recommend" here in its two senses of *(re)commend* (i.e., re-congratulate) those who brought and maintained "order" among the "savages" until the years of independence; and of a *proposition* for future, old-style, colonization efforts.
9　"la phantasmagorie de l'Occident en nous consiste a dramatiser le mythe au point d'en faire la clé de tout notre univers, l'explication totale de ce que nous est arrivé et de ce que nous concerne aujourd'hui". This and other references to Mana are from chapter 2, "Les Mythes fondamentaux," in *L'Afrique va-t-elle mourir* (Paris, 1991). Translations are mine.
10　Cornelius Castoriadis, *The Imaginary Institution of Society* (MIT Press, Boston, MA, 1987); Jürgen Habermas, *The Theory of Communicative Action*, trans. Thomas McCarthy (Beacon Press, Boston, MA, 1983), especially vol. 1; Kä Mana, *L'Afrique va-t-elle mourir?* (Les Editions du Cerf, Paris, 1991).

Select Bibliography

Abraham, W.E., *The Mind of Africa*, University of Chicago Press, Chicago, IL, 1962.

Achebe, Chinua, *Things Fall Apart*, Fawcett Cress/Ballentine, New York, 1959.

Adas, Michael, *Machines as the Measure of Man*, Cornell University Press, Ithaca, NY, 1989.

Ahmad, Aijaz, *In Theory*, Verso, London, 1992.

"The politics of literary postcoloniality," *Race and Class*, vol. 36, no. 3, January–March 1995.

Alfred, *Ecological Imperialism: The Biological Expansion of Europe*, Cambridge University Press, Cambridge, 1987.

Amin, Samir, *Eurocentrism*, Monthly Review Press, New York, 1989.

Anderson, Benedict, *Imagined Communitites: Reflections on the Origin and Spread of Nationalism*, Verso, London, 1983.

Appiah, Kwame Anthony, *In My Father's House*, Oxford University Press, New York, 1992.

Arendt, Hannah, *The Human Condition*, University of Chicago Press, Chicago, IL, 1958.
The Origins of Totalitarianism, Harcourt, Brace, Jovanovich, New York, 1979.
Lectures on Kant's Political Philosophy, ed. R. Beiner, University of Chicago Press, Chicago, IL, 1982.

Arens, W. and Ivan Karp (eds), *Creativity of Power: Cosmology and Action in African Societies*, Smithsonian Institution Press, Washington, DC, 1989.

Aristotle, *The Basic Works of Aristotle*, ed. Richard McKeon, Random House, New York, 1941.

Bhabha, Homi, *The Location of Culture*, Routledge, London, 1992.

Berman, Morris, *The Reenchantment of the World*, Cornell University Press, Ithaca, NY, 1981.

Bernasconi, Robert, "Who is my neighbor? Who is the Other? Questioning 'the generosity of Western thought,'" *Ethics and Responsibility in the Phenomenological Tradition*, The Ninth Annual Symposium of the Simon Silverman Phenomenology Center, Pittsburgh: Duquesne University, 1992.
"On deconstructing nostalgia for community within the West: the debate between Nancy and Blanchot," *Research in Phenomenology*, vol. 23, 1993.
"Sartre's gaze returned: the transformation of the phenomenology of racism," *Graduate Faculty Philosophy Journal*, vol. 18, no. 2, 1995.

Bloor, David, *Knowledge and Social Imagery*, Routledge and Kegan Paul, London, 1977.

Bourdieu, Pierre, *The Logic of Practice*, Stanford University Press, Stanford, CA, 1992.

Braudel, Fernand, *Civilization and Capitalism, 15th–18th Century, Vol. 1: The Structures of Everyday Life*, trans. Sian Reynolds, Harper and Row, New York, 1989.

Brown, Joshua, Patrick Manning, Karin Shapiro, Jon Wiener, Bolinda Bozzoli, and Peter Delius, *History from South Africa: Alternative Visions and Practices*. Temple University Press, Philadelphia, PA, 1991.

Busia, K.A., *The Position of the Chief in the Modern Political System of Ashanti*, Frank Cass, London, 1951.

Africa in Search of Democracy, Kegan Paul, London, 1967.

Cabral, Amilcar, *Return to the Source: Selected Speeches*, Monthly Review Press, New York, 1979.

Callari, Antonio, Stephen Cullenberg, and Carole Biewener, *Marxism in the Postmodern Age: Confronting the New World Order*, Guilford Press, New York and London, 1995.

Carter, Gwendolen M. and Patrick O'Meara (eds), *African Independence: The First Twenty-Five Years*, Indiana University Press, Bloomington, IN, 1985.

Castoriadis, Cornelius, *The Imaginary Institution of Society*, MIT Press, Boston, MA, 1987.

Philosophy, Politics, Autonomy, Oxford University Press, New York, 1991.

Chinweizu, Onwu–Chekwa Jemie, and Mechukwu Madubuike, *Toward the Decolonization of African Literature: African Fiction and Poetry and Their Critics*, KPI, London, 1985.

Clark, Leone E. (ed.), *Through African Eyes, Vol. IV The Colonial Experience: An Inside View*, Praeger, New York, 1973.

Conrad, Joseph, *Heart of Darkness*, Pocket Books, New York, 1972.

Cornell, Drucilla, Michel Rosenfeld, and David Gray Carlson (eds), *Deconstruction and the Possibility of Justice*, Routledge, New York, 1992.

Crossman, Richard (ed.), *The God That Failed*, Harper and Row, New York, 1965.

Czerniawski, Adam, *The Presence of Myth*, University of Chicago Press, Chicago, IL, 1989.

Davis, David Brian, *The Problem of Slavery in Western Culture*, Cornell University Press, Ithaca, NY, 1966.

Debrunner, Hans Werner, *Presence and Prestige: Africans in Europe*, Basler Afrika Bibliographien, Basel, 1979.

Derrida, Jacques, *Margins of Philosophy*, trans. Alan Bass, University of Chicago Press, Chicago, IL, 1982.

Glas, trans. John P. Leavey, Jr, and Richard Rand, University of Nebraska Press, Lincoln, NB, 1986.

Descartes, René, *Discourse on Method and Meditations*, trans. Laurence J. Lafleur, Bobbs–Merrill, Indianapolis, IN, 1960.

Diop, Cheikh Anta, *Nations Nègres et Culture*, Présence Africaine, Paris, 1955.

L'Unité culturelle de l'Afrique noire, Présence Africaine, Paris, 1959.

Civilization or Barbarism, trans. Yaa–Lengi Meema Ngemi, Lawrence Hill, New York, 1991.

Du Bois, W.E.B, *Black Folk, Then and Now: An Essay in the History and Sociology of the Negro Race*, Kraus–Thomson, Millwood, NY, 1975.

Souls of Black Folk, Fawcett, Greenwich, NY, 1961.

Eboussi Boulaga, Fabien, "Le Bantou Problématique," *Présence Africaine*, no. 66, 1968.

La Crise du Muntu: Authenticité africaine et philosophie, Présence Africaine, Paris, 1977.

Eliot, T.S. (ed.), *A Choice of Kipling's Verse*, Anchor, New York, 1962.

Elphick, Richard and Herman Giliomee (eds), *The Shaping of South African Society 1652–1840*, Wesleyan University Press, Middletown, CT, 1988.

Evans–Pritchard, E.E., *Theories of Primitive Religion*, Oxford University Press, Oxford, 1965.

Eze, Emmanuel Chukwudi (ed.), *Race and the Enlightenment: A Reader*, Blackwell, Oxford, 1996.

(ed.), *Africana Philosophy: An Anthology*, Blackwell, Oxford, 1996.

Fanon, Frantz, *The Wretched of the Earth*, trans. Constance Farrington, Grove New York, 1963.

Black Skin, White Masks, trans. Charles Lam Markmann, Grove Weidenfeld, New York, 1967.

Faull, Katherine (ed.), *Anthropology and the German Enlightenment*, *Bucknell Review*, vol. 38, no. 2, Associated University Press, Lewisburg and London, 1994.

Feyerabend, Paul, *Against Method*, New Left Books, London, 1975.

Floistad, Guttorm (ed.), *Contemporary Philosophy, Vol. 5, African Philosophy*, Martinus Nijhoff, The Hague, 1987.

Fortes, M. and E.E. Evans–Pritchard (eds), *African Political Systems*, Oxford University Press, Oxford, 1940.

Foucault, Michel, *Discipline and Punish*, Pantheon, New York, 1977.

Power/Knowledge: Selected Interviews and Other Writings 1972–1977, Pantheon, New York, 1980.

Gates, Henry Louis, Jr (ed.), *"Race," Writing and Difference*, University of Chicago, Press, Chicago, IL., 1986.

Gessen, Boris, *The Social and Economic Roots of Newton's "Principia"*, Howard Fertig, New York, 1970.

Gilman, Sander L., *On Blackness without Blacks*, G.K. Hall, Boston, MA.

Goonatilake, Susantha, *Aborted Discovery: Science and Creativity in the Third World*, Zed, London, 1984.

"The Voyages of Discovery and the loss and rediscovery of the 'Other's' Knowledge," *Impact of Science on Society*, no. 167, 1992.

Gordon, Lewis, *Fanon and the Crisis of European Man: An Essay on Philosophy and the Human Sciences*, Routledge, New York, 1995.

Gould, S.J., *Ontogeny and Phylogeny*, MIT Press, Cambridge, MA, 1977.

The Mismeasure of Man, Norton, New York, 1981.

Grene, David and Richmond Lattimore (eds), *Sophocles 1: "Oedipus the King," "Oedipus at Colonus," and "Antigone"*, trans., respectively, David Grene, Robert Fitzgerald, and Elizabeth Wykoff, University of Chicago Press, Chicago, IL, and London, 1954.

Gyekye, Kwame, *An Essay on African Philosophical Thought*, revised edn, Temple University Press, Philadelphia, PA, 1995.

Habermas, Jürgen, *The Theory of Communicative Action*, 2 vols, trans. Thomas McCarthy, Beacon Press, Boston, MA, 1983.

Hallen, Barry and J.O. Sodipo, *Knowledge, Belief and Witchcraft: Analytical Experiments in African Philosophy*, Ethnographica, London, 1986.

Haraway, Donna, *Primate Visions: Gender, Race and Nature in the World of Modern Science*, Routledge, New York, 1989.

Harding, Sandra (ed.), *Can Theories Be Refuted? Essays on the Durkhem–Quine Thesis*, Reidel, Dordrecht, 1976.

The Science Question in Feminism, Cornell University Press, Ithaca, NY, 1986.

Whose Science? Whose Knowledge?, Cornell University Press, Ithaca, NY, 1991.

"After the neutrality ideal: science, politics and 'strong objectivity,'" *Social Research*, vol. 59, 1992, pp. 567–87.

(ed.), *The "Racial" Economy of Science: Toward a Democratic Future*, Indiana University Press, Bloomington, IN.

"Is science multicultural? Challenges, resources, opportunities, uncertainties," *Configurations*, vol. 2, no. 2, and in David Theo Goldberg (ed.), *Multiculturalism: A Reader*, Blackwell, London, 1994.

Harris, Leonard, *Philosophy Born of Struggle*, Kendall/Hunt Publishing, Dubuque, IA, 1993.

Harris, Marvin, *The Rise of Anthropological Theory*, Crowell, New York, 1968.

Hegel, G.W., *The Introduction to Hegel's Philosophy of Fine Art*, trans. Bernard Bosanquet, K. Paul, Trench and Co., London, 1886.

Philosophy of Fine Art, trans. F.P.B. Somaston, 4 vols, G. Bell and Sons, London, 1920.

Lectures on the Philosophy of World History, trans. H.B. Nisbett, Cambridge University Press, Cambridge, 1975.

Vorlesungen über die Geschichte der Philosophie. Einleitung, ed. Walter Jaeschke, Felix Meaner, Hamburg, 1993.

Heidegger, Martin, *Being and Time*, Harper and Row, New York, 1962.

What is called Thinking?, trans. F.D. Wieck and J. Glenn Gray, Harper and Row, New York, 1968.

Herskovits, Melville J., *The Myth of the Negro Past*, Beacon Press, Boston, MA, 1958.

Hesse, Mary, *Models and Analogies in Science*, University of Notre Dame Press, Notre Dame, IN, 1966.

Hill, Melvyn (ed.), *Hannah Arendt: The Recovery of the Public World*, St Martin's Press, New York, 1979.

Hobbes, Thomas, *Leviathan*, ed. Michael Oakeshott, Collier Macmillan, New York, 1962.

Hollis, Martin and Steven Lukes (eds), *Rationality and Relativism*, MIT Press, Cambridge, MA, 1992.

Honour, Hugh, *The Image of the Black in Western Art*, Harvard University Press, Cambridge, MA, 1989.

Horkheimer, Max and Theodor W. Adorno, *Dialectics of Enlightenment*, trans. John Cumming, Continuum, New York, 1975.

Horton, Robin, *Patterns of Thought in Africa and the West*, Cambridge University Press, Cambridge, 1994.

Hountondji, Paulin J., *African Philosophy: Myth and Reality*, Indiana University Press, Bloomington, IN, 1983.

Howells, Christina (ed.), *The Cambridge Companion to Sartre*, Cambridge University Press, Cambridge, 1992.

Huberman, Leo, *Man's Worldly Goods*, Monthly Review Press, New York, 1968.

Hume, David, *Inquiries Concerning Human Understanding and Concerning the Principles of Morals*, reprinted from the 1777 edition with Introduction and Analytical Index by L.A Selby–Bigge, 3rd edn with text revised and noted by P.H. Nidditch, Clarendon Press, Oxford, 1985.

Essays Moral, Political and Literary, Liberty Classics, Indianapolis, IN, 1985.

Jahn, Janheinz, *Muntu: African Culture and the Western World*, Grove Weidenfeld, New York, 1961.

Jones, W.T., *A History of Western Philosophy*, vol. III, 2nd revised edn, Harcourt, Brace, Jovanovich, New York, 1975.

Joseph, George Gheverghese, *The Crest of the Peacock: NonEuropean Roots of Mathematics*, I.B. Tauris, New York, 1991.

July, Robert W., *An African Voice: The Role of the Humanities in African Independence*, Duke University Press, Durham, NC, 1987.

Kane, Cheikh Hamidou, *Ambiguous Adventure*, Heinemann Educational, Portsmouth, NH, 1989.

Kant, Immanuel, *Gesammelte Schriften*, 24 vols, Reimer, Berlin, 1900–66.

Observations on the Feeling of the Beautiful and Sublime, trans. John T. Goldthwait, University of California Press, Berkeley, CA, 1960.

Kant on History, Bobbs–Merrill, Indianapolis, IN, 1963.

Critique of Pure Reason, trans. Norman Kemp Smith, St Martin's Press, New York, 1965.

Prolegomena to any Future Metaphysics, trans. Paul Carus, Hackett, Indianapolis, IN, 1977.

Kant: Political Writings, ed. Hans Reiss, 2nd edn, Cambridge University Press, Cambridge, 1991.

Kaptchuk, Ted J., *The Web That Has No Weaver: Understanding Chinese Medicine*, Congdon and Weed, New York, 1983.

Karp, Ivan, Christine Mullen Kreamer, and Steven D. Levine (eds), *Museums and Communities: The Politics of Public Culture*, Smithsonian Institute, Washington, DC, 1992.

Kateb, George, *Hannah Arendt: Politics, Conscience, Evil*, Rowman and Allanheld, Totowa, NJ, 1984.

Kaunda, Kenneth, *A Humanist in Africa*, Longman, London, 1966.

Keller, Evelyn Fox, *Reflections on Gender and Science*, Yale University Press, New Haven, CT, 1984.

Secrets of Life, Secrets of Death: Essays on Language, Gender and Science, Routledge, New York, 1992.

Kierkegaard, Søren, *Fear and Trembling*, trans. and ed. Howard V. Hong and Edna H. Hong, Princeton University Press, Princeton, NJ, 1983.

Ki–Zerbo, Joseph (ed.), *La natte des autres. Pour un développement endogène en Afrique*, Codesria, Dakar, 1992.

Kochhar, R.K., "Science in British India," parts I and II, *Current Science*, vol. 63, no. 11, vol. 64, no. 1, 1992–3 (India).

Kohler, Lotte and Hans Saner, *Hannah Arendt and Karl Jaspers Correspondence 1926–1969*, Harcourt, Brace, Jovanovich, New York, 1992.

Kuhn, Thomas S., *The Structure of Scientific Revolutions*, 2nd edn, University of Chicago Press, Chicago, IL, 1970.

Laing, E., *Science and Society in Ghana*, The J.B. Danquah Memorial Lectures, Ghana Academy of Arts and Sciences, 1990.

Lakatos, Imre and Alan Musgrave, *Criticism and the Growth of Knowledge*, Cambridge University Press, Cambridge, 1970.

Langness, L.L., *The Study of Culture*, revised edn, Chandler and Sharp, CA, 1987.

Lash, Scott and Jonathan Friedman (eds), *Modernity and Identity*, Oxford University Press, Oxford, 1992.

Latour, Bruno, *Science in Action*, Harvard University Press, Cambridge, MA, 1987.

The Pasteurization of France, Harvard University Press, Cambridge, MA, 1988.

and Steve Woolgar, *Laboratory Life: The Social Construction of Scientific Facts*, Sage, Beverly Hills, CA, 1979.

Levinas, Emmanuel, "Transcendance et Hauteur," *Bulletin de la Société française de Philosophie*, vol. 54., 1962.

Levine, George (ed.), *Realism and Representation*, University of Wisconsin Press, Madison, WI, 1993.

Li, C.P., "Chinese herbal medicine: recent experimental studies, clinical applications and pharmacognosy of certain herbs," in *Revolutionary Health Committee of Hunan Province: A Barefoot Doctor's Manual*, revised edn, Madrona, Seattle, WA, 1977.

Löwith, Karl, *Das Individuum in der Rolle des Mitmenschen*, Wissenchaftliche Buchgesellschaft, Darmstadt, 1969.

Lyotard, Jean François, *Peregrinations*, Columbia University Press, New York, 1988.

The Postmodern Condition, University of Minnesota Press, Minneapolis, MN, 1989.

The Postmodern Explained, University of Minnesota Press, Minneapolis, MN, 1992.

Mabila-Kalanda, P., *La Rémise en question: Base de la colonisation mentale*, Remarque Africaine, Brussels, 1967.

MacPherson, James, *The Political Theory of Possessive Individualism*, Oxford University Press, New York, 1964.

Macrae, R., R. Robinson, and M. Sadler (eds), *Encyclopedia of Food Science, Food Technology and Nutrition*, Academy Press, New York, 1993.

Mana, Kä, *L'Afrique va-t-elle mourir?*, Les Editions du Cerf, Paris, 1991.

Marx, Karl and Frederick Engels, *The Communist Manifesto*, International Publishers, New York, 1983.

Masolo, D.A., *You and Your Society*, book 2, Longman Kenya, Nairobi, 1988.

African Philosophy in Search of Identity, Indiana University Press, Bloomington, IN, 1994.

May, Larry and Robert A. Strinkwerda (eds), *Thinking Masculinity*, Rowman and Littlefield, New York, 1992.

Mazrui, Ali, *The Africans: A Triple Heritage*, Little, Brown and Co., Boston, MA, 1986.

Mbiti, John S., *African Religions and Philosophy*, Doubleday, New York, 1970.

McCarthy, Thomas, *Ideals and Illusions*, MIT Press, Cambridge, MA, 1991.

McEvedy, Colin, *The Penguin Atlas of African History*, Penguin, New York, 1987.

Mehta, J.L., *Martin Heidegger: The Way and the Vision*, University Press of Hawaii, 1976.

Merchant, Carolyn, *The Death of Nature: Women, Ecology and the Scientific Revolution*, Harper and Row, New York, 1980.

Mezu, S. Okechukwu, *The Poetry of L. S. Senghor*, Heinemann, London, 1973.

Mies, Maria, *Patriarchy and Accumulation on a World Scale: Women in the International Division of Labor*, Zed, Atlantic Highlands, NJ, 1986.

Moraze, Charles (ed.), *Science and the Factors of Inequality*, UNESCO, Paris, 1979.

Mudimbe, V.Y. *The Invention of Africa*, Indiana University Press, Bloomington, IN, 1988.

Parables and Fables: Exegesis, Textuality, and Politics in Central Africa, University of Wisconsin Press, Madison, WI, 1991.

(ed.), *The Surreptitious Speech*, University of Chicago Press, Chicago, IL, 1992.

The Idea of Africa, Indiana University Press, Bloomington, IN, 1994.

Murfin, Ross C., *Joseph Conrad Heart of Darkness: A Case Study in Contemporary Criticism*, St Martin's Press, New York, 1989.

Mutiso, Gideon–Cyrus M. and Rohio, S.W. (eds), *Readings in African Political Thought*, Heinemann, London, 1975.

Nandy, Ashis (ed.), *Science, Hegemony and Violence: A Requiem for Modernity*, Oxford, Delhi, 1990.

Ndaw, Alassane, *La Pensée africaine: Recherches sur les fondements de la pensée négro africaine*, Les Nouvelles Editions Africaines, Dakar, 1983.

Needham, Joseph, *The Grand Titration: Science and Society in East and West*, University of Toronto Press, Toronto, 1969.

Nizan, Paul, *The Watchdogs*, Monthly Review Press, New York, 1971.

Nkrumah, Kwame, *Consciencism: Philosophy and Ideology for Decolonization*, revised edn, Monthly Review Press, New York, 1970.

Obenga, Theophile, *Ancient Egypt and Black Africa*, Karnak House, London, 1992.

O'Connell, Robert, *Plato on the Human Paradox*, Fordham University Press, New York, 1987.

Okere, Theophilus, *African Philosophy: A Historico-hermeneutical Investigation of the Conditions of its Possibility*, University Press of America, Lanharn, MD, 1983.

Okolo Okonda W'Oleko, *Pour une Philosophie de la culture et du développement: Recherches d'hermeneutique et de praxis africaines*, Presses Universitaires du Zaïre, Kinshasa 1986.

O'Neill, John, *The Poverty of Postmodernism*, Routledge, New York and London.

Oruka, H. Odera (ed.), *Sage Philosophy*, African Centre for Technology Studies, Nairobi, 1991.

Osabutey–Aguedze, D., *Principles Underlying African Religion and Philosophy*, MBillu, Nairobi, 1990.

Outlaw, Lucius, "African Philosophy: Deconstructive and Reconstructive Challenges," in *Sage Philosophy: Indigenous Thinker and Modern Debate on African Philosophy*, E.J. Brill, Leiden, 1990.

"African, African–American, Africana Philosophy," *Philosophical Forum*, vol. 24, nos 1–3, Fall–Spring 1992–3, pp. 63–93.

Pacey, Arnold, *The Culture of Technology*, Blackwell, Oxford, 1983.

Parrinder, G., *African Traditional Religion*, Harper and Row, New York, 1962.

Patterson, Orlando, *Slavery and Social Death*, Harvard University Press, Boston, MA, 1982.

p'Bitek, Okot, *Song of Lawino and Song of Ocol*, Heinemann, London, 1984.

Peperzak, Adriaan (ed.), *Ethics as First Philosophy*, Routledge, New York, 1995.

Petitjean, Patrick, *Studies About Scientific Development and European Expansion*, Kluwer, Dordrecht, 1992.

Pickering, Andrew, *Constructing Quarks*, University of Chicago Press, Chicago, IL, 1984.

(ed.), *Science as Practice and Culture*, University of Chicago Press, Chicago, IL, 1992.

Pittman, John (ed.), "African–American perspectives and philosophical traditions," *Philosophical Forum*, vol. XXIV, nos 1–3, 1992–3.

Plato, *The Collected Dialogues*, ed. Edith Hamilton and Huntington Cairns, Princeton University Press, Princeton, NJ, 1987.

Popper, Karl, *Conjectures and Refutations*, Harper, New York, 1962.

Proctor, Robert, *Cancer Wars: How Politics Shapes What We Know and Don't Know About Cancer*, Basic Books, Boston, MA, 1995.

Quine, W.V.O., *From a Logical Point of View*, Harvard University Press, Harvard, MA, 1953.

Word and Object, MIT Press, Cambridge, MA, 1960.

Rabasa, Jose, *Inventing America*, University of Oklahoma Press, Norman, OK, and London, 1993.

Rabinow, Paul (ed.), *The Foucault Reader*, Pantheon, New York, 1984.

Rigby, Peter, *Persistent Pastoralists: Nomadic Societies in Transition*, Zed, London, 1985.

Robinson, Cedric, *Black Marxism: The Making of the Black Radical Tradition*, Zed, London, 1983.

Rodney, Walter, *How Europe Underdeveloped Africa*, Howard University Press, Washington, DC, 1982.

Rorty, Richard, *Philosophy and the Mirror of Nature*, Princeton University Press, Princeton, NJ, 1979.

Rouse, Joseph, *Knowledge and Power: Toward a Political Philosophy of Science*, Cornell University Press, Ithaca, NY, 1987.

Said, Edward, *Orientalism*, Pantheon, New York, 1978.

The Question of Palestine, Vintage, New York, 1980.

The Pen and the Sword, Common Courage Press, Monroe, ME, 1994.

Sardar, Ziauddin (ed.), *The Revenge of Athena: Science, Exploitation and the Third World*, Mansell, London, 1988.

Sartre, J.-P., *Search for a Method*, trans. Hazel Barnes, Vintage, New York, 1968.

Schopenhauer, Arthur, *The World as Will and Idea*, vol. III, 7th edn, trans. R.B. Haldane and J. Kemp, Kegan Paul, Trench, Trubner and Co., London, 1883.

Sefa-Dede, S. and R. Orraca-Tetteh (eds), *Harnessing Traditional Food Technology for Development*, Department of Nutrition and Food Science, University of Ghana, Legon.

Serequeberhan, Tsenay, "The idea of colonialism in Hegel's *Philosophy of Right*," *International Philosophical Quarterly*, vol. 29, no. 3, issue no. 115, September 1989.

"Karl Marx and African emancipatory thought: a critique of Marx's Eurocentric metaphysics," *Praxis International*, vol. 10, nos 1/2, April and July 1990.

African Philosophy: The Essential Readings, Paragon, New York, 1991.

The Hermeneutics of African Philosophy: Horizon and Discourse, Routledge, New York, 1994.

Shapin, Steven and Simon Schaffer, *Leviathan and the Air Pump*, Princeton University Press, Princeton, NJ, 1985.

Shiva, Vandana, *Staying Alive: Women, Ecology and Development*, Zed, London, 1989.

Silvio, A. Bedini (ed.), *The Christopher Columbus Encyclopedia*, vol. 1, Simon and Schuster, New York, 1991.

Simons, H.J. and R.E., *Class and Colour in South Africa 1850–1950*, Penguin, Baltimore, MD, 1969.

Smet, A.J., *Philosophie Africaine, Textes Choisis II*, Presses Universitaires du Zäire, Kinshasa, 1975.

Smith, Dorothy E., *The Conceptual Practices of Power: A Feminist Sociology of Knowledge*, Northeastern University Press, Boston, MA, 1990.

Spivak, Gayatri, *The Postcolonial Critic*, Routledge, New York, 1990.

Outside the Teaching Machine, Routledge, New York, 1993.

Sohn–Rethel, Alfred, *Intellectual and Manual Labor*, Macmillan, London, 1978.

Stannard, David E., *American Holocaust: Columbus and the Conquest of the New World*, Oxford University Press, New York, 1992.

Taplin, Oliver, *Greek Tragedy in Action*, Routledge, London, 1993.

Tempels, Placide, *Bantu Philosophy*, Présence Africaine, Paris, 1959.

Third World Network, *Modern Science in Crisis: A Third World Response*, Penang, Malaysia, 1988.

Towa, Marcien, *Essai sur la problematique philosophique dans l'Afrique actuelle*, Clé, Yaoundé, 1968.

Léopold Sédar Senghor, Négritude ou Servitude, Clé, Yaoundé, 1971.

L'idée d'une philosophie Négro–africaine, Clé, Yaoundé, 1979.

Traweek, Sharon, *Beamtimes and Life Times*, MIT Press, Cambridge, MA, 1988.

Todd, Lord, *Problems of the Technological Society*, The Aggrey Fraser–Guggisberg Memorial Lectures, published for the University of Ghana by the Ghana Publishing Corporation, Accra, 1973.

Todorov, Tzvetan, *The Conquest of America: The Question of the Other*, trans. Richard Howard, New York: Harper and Row, New York, 1984.

Vansina, Jan, *Paths in the Rainforests: Toward a History of Political Tradition in Equatorial Africa*, University of Wisconsin Press, Madison, WI, 1990.

wa Thiong'o, Ngugi, *Decolonizing the Mind*, Heinemann, Portsmouth, NH, 1986.

Wauthier, Claude, *The Literature and Thought of Modern Africa*, Heinemann, London, 1978.

West, Cornel, *Prophesy Deliverance: An Afro–American Revolutionary Christianity*, Westminster Press, Philadelphia, PA, 1982.

The American Evasion of Philosophy, University of Wisconsin Press, Madison, WI, 1989.

The Ethical Dimensions of Marxist Thought, Monthly Review, Press, New York, 1991.

Keeping Faith: Philosophy and Race in America, Routledge, New York, 1992.

Whellwright, Philip, *The Presocratics*, Bobbs–Merrill, Indianapolis, IN, 1975.

White, Lynn, *Medieval Religion and Technology: Collected Essays*, University of California Press, Berkeley, CA, 1978.

Whitehead, Alfred North, *Science and the Modern World*, Macmillan, New York, 1966.

Wiredu, Kwasi, *Philosophy and an African Culture: The Case of the Akan*, Cambridge University Press, Cambridge, 1980.

Wiredu, Kwasi and Kwame Gyekye (eds), *Person and Community: Ghanaian Philosophical Studies*, Council for Research in Values and Philosophy, Washington, DC, 1992.

Wright, Richard, *Native Son*, Harper and Row, New York, 1966.

Young, Robert, *White Mythologies: Writing History and the West*, Routledge, New York, 1990.

Young–Breuhl, Elizabeth, *Hannah Arendt: For Love of the World*, Yale University Press, New Haven, CT, 1982.

Zilsel, Edgar, "The sociological roots of science," *American Journal of Sociology*, vol. 47, 1942.

Index

Abacha, Sanni, 314
Abiola, Moshood, campaign for
   democracy in Nigeria, 313–14
aborigines, of Australia, 63
Abraham, Willy, 306, 316
absolutism, as model for European
   philosophy of nature, 52
Achebe, Chinua, 19n, 20n, 175, 248
acupuncture, 61, 62
Adorno, Theodor, 287
aesthetic consciousness, as reflective, 211
Africa,
   European colonialism in, 4–6, 7–10,
     15, 144–5, 165–7, 168–9
   excluded from history in Western
     rhetoric, 8, 185
   Greek philosophy in, 82–3
   negation of in rhetoric of European
     modernity, 13, 73–5
   not monolithic, 203–6, 296, 328–30
   as "Other" to the West, 14, 87, 226
   postcolonial political situation of,
     14–15, 21n, 25, 206, 308–11,
     313–15
   role of consensus in traditional politics
     of, 303–8
   see also African(s); African philosophy;
     individual countries and *ethnic groups*
African(s)
   and art, 31, 176
   attitudes of toward European heritage,
     205–6
   auto-critique in the postcolonial, 341
   Boers compared to, 167–70, 174–5
   cultural élite among, 246–7, 248, 257
   and cultural nationalism, 330–2

   in ethnological discourse, 328–35
   humanist ethics of, 42, 43
   iconic tradition of, 211, 214–15
   identity of in the postcolonial, 164–5,
     285–6, 291, 295–6, 298
   mythology of the West in the
     postcolonial social imaginary of,
     343–4
   as "Other" to Europeans, 185, 205,
     206, 226, 231, 293
   participatory ontology of, 325–6
   religiousness of, 27, 28–9, 36, 204–5,
     317, 327–8
   and science, 26, 26–32
   shift in European characterizations of,
     6
   as slaves, 8, 9, 116, 117, 168–9, 170,
     174–5, 327–8
   as subhuman in Western discourse,
     6–7, 9, 121, 122, 172–4, 176
   as uncivilized, 145, 332–3
   as unphilosophical, 76
   use of technology, 26, 32–6, 42
   Westernized, 155–6, 242, 248
   work ethic of, 167–9
   see also Africa; African philosophy;
     individual ethnic groups; Negroes
African-American philosophy
   interdisciplinary nature of, 277
   possibility of, 272
   and prophetic criticism, 278, 279
   C. West as paradigmatic of, 268
African-Americans
   and alienation, 276–7
   Christianity of, 269
   and forgiveness, 207

CPSIA information can be obtained
at www.ICGtesting.com
Printed in the USA
FSHW012326101118
53710FS